The Global Anti-Corruption Regime

This book tackles the challenging topic of corruption. It explores the evolution of a global prohibition regime against corrupt activity (the global anti-corruption regime). It analyses the structure of the transnational legal framework against corruption, evaluating the impact of global anti-corruption efforts at a national level. The book focuses on the United Nations Convention against Corruption (UNCAC) as the primary tool of the global anti-corruption regime. It provides new and engaging material gathered in the field, including first-hand accounts from actors at international, regional, and domestic levels. By documenting the experiences of diverse actors, the book makes a substantial contribution to literature on corruption and anti-corruption efforts. Synthesising empirical research with an exploration of theoretical literature on corruption and regime evolution results in novel suggestions for improvement of the global anti-corruption regime and its legal tools.

The *Global Anti-Corruption Regime* is a well-rounded text with a wealth of new information that will be valuable to both academic and policy audiences. It clarifies the factors that prevent current anti-corruption efforts from successfully eliminating corrupt activity and applies the five-stage model of global prohibition regime evolution to the global anti-corruption regime. It will be of interest to researchers, academics, policymakers, and students interested in anti-corruption law, comparative law, transnational criminal law, international law, international relations, politics, economics, and trade.

Dr Hannah Harris is a legal academic, freelance data scientist and Research Fellow at the Centre for Law Markets and Regulation, University of New South Wales. Her research area is transnational law and the implementation and enforcement of regulatory regimes, focusing on financial crime, bribery, and corruption.

The Law of Financial Crime
Series Editor: Nicholas Ryder

Available titles in this series include:

Fighting Financial Crime in the Global Economic Crisis
Nicholas Ryder, Umut Turksen and Sabine Hassler

The Financial War on Terror
A Review of Counter-Terrorist Financing Strategies Since 2001
Nicholas Ryder

The Financial Crisis and White Collar Crime- Legislative and Policy Responses
A Critical Assessment
Edited by Nicholas Ryder, Jon Tucker and Umut Turksen

Countering Economic Crime
A Comparative Analysis
Axel Palmer

The Global Anti-Corruption Regime
The Case of Papua New Guinea
Hannah Harris

Financial Crime and Corporate Misconduct
A Critical Evaluation of Fraud Legislation
Edited by Chris Monaghan and Nicola Monaghan

For more information about this series, please visit: www.routledge.com/The-Law-of-Financial-Crime/book-series/FINCRIME

The Global Anti-Corruption Regime

The Case of Papua New Guinea

Hannah Harris

Routledge
Taylor & Francis Group
LONDON AND NEW YORK

First published 2019
by Routledge
2 Park Square, Milton Park, Abingdon, Oxon OX14 4RN

and by Routledge
52 Vanderbilt Avenue, New York, NY 10017, USA

First issued in paperback 2020

Routledge is an imprint of the Taylor & Francis Group, an informa business

British Library Cataloguing-in-Publication Data
A catalogue record for this book is available from the British Library

Library of Congress Cataloging-in-Publication Data
A catalog record for this title has been requested

ISBN 13: 978-0-367-58683-6 (pbk)
ISBN 13: 978-1-138-29892-7 (hbk)

Typeset in Galliard
by Swales & Willis Ltd, Exeter, Devon, UK

This book is dedicated to my husband, Drew. Without you, there would be no book. Thank you for being my best friend, my partner in love and adventure, my constant support, and my inspiration.

Contents

Acknowledgements

The process of creating this book has been a fascinating and fulfilling experience. I am happily indebted to the extensive network of individuals who supported me throughout the journey.

I am supremely grateful to each interview participant who took part in this research. Thank you for your generosity in speaking with me, for your honesty and openness, and for teaching me and inspiring me through your incredible commitment to making the world a better place.

I would like to thank Professor Sarah Williams and Professor Michael Grewcock, for their far-reaching support and guidance throughout this process.

I am also grateful for the continuing research opportunity provided to me by the Centre for Law Markets and Regulation at the University of New South Wales, Sydney.

Thank you to my family. Mum, you laid the foundation that makes it possible for me to achieve anything I dream. Dad, you taught me to follow my heart and that kindness is the greatest gift. I love you both and am the luckiest woman in the world to have you as my parents. Auntie Sue and Uncle Tony, thanks for giving two kids a second home when we were starting out on this adventure! The security you provided us helped to make this all possible.

To my husband Drew, you are my everything. Thank you. I love you. I win!

Abbreviations

ADB	Asian Development Bank
COI	Commission of Inquiry
DFAT	Department of Foreign Affairs and Trade
FATF	Financial Action Task Force
FIFA	International Federation of Football Association
NGO	Non-Government Organisation
OECD	Organisation for Economic Co-operation and Development
PNG	Papua New Guinea
SABLs	Special Agricultural Business Leases
SIDS	Small Island Developing States
TCL	Transnational Criminal Law
TI	Transparency International
TI CPI	Corruption Perceptions Index
UN	United Nations
UNCAC	United Nations Convention against Corruption
UNDP	United Nations Development Program
UNODC	United Nations Office on Drugs and Crime
US	United States of America

Introduction

In 1990, a report was published on corruption in the forestry sector in Papua New Guinea (PNG). This report, referred to as the Barnett Report, was titled 'A summary of the report of the Commission of Inquiry into Aspects of the Timber Industry in Papua New Guinea'.[1] In the report, foreign logging companies operating in PNG were referred to as 'robber barons . . . bribing politicians and leaders, creating social disharmony and ignoring laws in order to gain access to, rip out and export the last remnants of the province's valuable timber'.[2] More than two decades later, corruption remains a pressing challenge for PNG, within the forestry sector and elsewhere.

In 2011, a Commission of Inquiry (COI) began into the granting of Special Agricultural Business Leases (SABLs) in PNG. SABLs were set up to promote economic empowerment and support customary landowners, allowing them to lease their land to the government.[3] It was intended that the government could then lease this land to commercial entities for small scale agricultural projects.[4] The scheme was abused. Under the scheme, 11% of the total land-mass of PNG was leased to corporations for large scale logging and commercial exploitation.

The Commission of Inquiry found that 66 of the 75 SABLs issued were illegal[5] and had been provided to logging companies in order that they could appropriate more land from traditional land owners and exploit this land for profit.[6] The final report of the COI found no direct evidence of corruption. However, it made very strong statements suggesting corruption was a central issue to the SABLs:

> [T]he C.O.I. noted very strong inferential evidence during the Inquiry into individual SABLs throughout the Provinces that extrinsic matters affected the processing of SABLs including conflicts of interest, compromising conducts and possible frauds involving landowners, developers, Provincial officials, DLPP officials, Forestry officials and DEC officials. These extrinsic matters in the C.O.I.'s view are part of the more universal problem of graft and corruption in PNG.[7]

Despite the Commission's findings, the licences continue to operate. In 2012, logs worth an estimated PGK172 million were exported from areas covered by the illegal SABLs,[8] the equivalent of AUD84 million. '[T]he government has not taken any decisive action to cancel deceptive land deals, stop illegal logging, or return land to traditional owners'.[9] In March 2017, the Prime Minister stated that he and the National Executive Council 'cancelled all the licences' and further emphasised that 'all the SABL licenses are illegal in this country'.[10] The Prime Minister blamed various government departments for allowing the continued operation of SABLs and urged customary land holders to act against companies still logging on their land.[11] However, at the time of writing, no legal action has been taken to abolish these licences. The issue remains unresolved and customary land is still under threat from foreign corporate interests.

Establishment of a dedicated anti-corruption body in PNG did not overcome the challenge of corruption. In June 2014, Task Force Sweep (the primary anti-corruption body in PNG at the time) issued an arrest warrant for Prime Minister O'Neill.[12] In response, the Prime Minister stated that the warrant was politically motivated and promptly disbanded the Task Force, terminating the employment of the Deputy Police Commissioner of Operations who allegedly signed the warrant. Prime Minister O'Neill stated:

> We cannot continue to have police men and women who are government employees, running around trying to undermine government decisions . . . we are going to continue to terminate everybody who is going to undermine the work of the government.[13]

On 27 July 2014, the National Court issued a permanent stay on the decision by the Prime Minister to disband the Task Force.[14] However, a subsequent court ruling established that the Prime Minister's disbandment of the Task Force was legitimate, as the Task Force was created by the executive branch of government without true independence. This spelled the end for Task Force Sweep. An Independent Commission Against Corruption (ICAC) was supposed to replace the Task Force, however, the process continues to be delayed and the ICAC is not yet operational.

The above examples illustrate the extent of corruption in PNG, as well as the challenges that emerge when attempting to tackle corruption domestically. These challenges are not restricted to PNG, they are relevant to all states, regardless of political, economic, social, and cultural variation. An internet search combining 'corruption' with the name of almost any state, turns up a long list of examples.[15] The International Federation of Football Association (FIFA) corruption scandal that began in May 2015 is a recent high-profile case.[16] Even in countries that rank highly on anti-corruption indexes, such as Australia and New Zealand,[17] examples of corruption and concern regarding corrupt activity remain substantial. A recent report by Chartered Accountants Australia and New Zealand warns that corruption is a growing problem in both countries.[18]

Corruption occurs everywhere and is not a new phenomenon. It has been acknowledged as a challenge to social, political, and economic systems for millennia. As an example, Farrales points to the Arthashastra, an approximately 2400-year-old Indian text, in which the inevitability of corruption and the need to restrain it is openly discussed.[19] Historically, anti-corruption efforts have been domestically focused. This focus began to shift in the latter half of the 20th

Century. Since 1990, no fewer than nine multilateral legal instruments targeting corrupt activity have entered into force.[20] The United Nations Convention against Corruption (UNCAC) is the most widely ratified of these legal instruments. However, despite the upsurge in transnational anti-corruption efforts, corruption remains a substantial problem globally. Between 2002 and 2005 (the three years preceding UNCAC entry into force), 39.5% of countries ranked below three out of ten on the Transparency International Corruption Perceptions Index (TI CPI). From 2006 through 2009 (the three years following UNCAC entry into force), 42% of countries ranked below three out of ten on the same index.[21] One interpretation of these statistics suggests that corruption is worsening around the world, rather than abating.

The goal of this book is to increase understanding of the factors that are preventing current anti-corruption efforts from successfully eliminating corrupt activity. A multidisciplinary approach is adopted, applying Nadelmann and Andreas' five-stage model of global prohibition regime evolution (the model) to the global anti-corruption regime.[22] The model assists in understanding the evolution of the global anti-corruption regime, its nature, and the challenges facing the regime in seeking to substantially reduce corruption levels. The model is further developed using the work of other transnational legal theorists, to deepen understanding of the complex actors, organisations, values, and interests that have shaped the evolution of the global anti-corruption regime and influence the operation of the regime through its legal tools.

The United Nations Convention against Corruption is presented as the primary legal tool of the global anti-corruption regime. Domestic implementation and enforcement of this Convention is essential, if the regime is to achieve its goal of reducing corruption levels globally. On this basis, the model is developed into a broad theoretical framework, which is applied to analysis of UNCAC and the case study of Papua New Guinea (PNG). Exploration of UNCAC and its implementation and enforcement in PNG combines analysis of existing research material with fresh insights from fieldwork and semi-structured interviews.

The structure of the book is as follows: Chapter 1 introduces the theoretical framework, building on the five-stage model of global prohibition regime evolution. The book seeks to understand why large scale ratification of UNCAC and participation in the implementation and review process has not substantially reduced global corruption levels. Chapter 1 introduces four research questions, answered throughout the book.

1 How has UNCAC evolved within the emergent global anti-corruption regime?
2 What impact has UNCAC had on PNG's approach to combatting corruption?
3 Does PNG's experience with implementation and enforcement of UNCAC support the existing theoretical and practical criticisms of UNCAC and the emergent global anti-corruption regime more generally?
4 What insights does the PNG case study provide in terms of potential improvements to UNCAC and its implementation and enforcement, with the goal of securing the final stage of evolution for the global anti-corruption regime?

Chapter 2 discusses UNCAC in detail. It explores the process of negotiation and the areas of conflict and contestation that were resolved in the final text of the Convention. The answer to the first research question is provided at the end of this chapter. Chapter 3 provides an overview of the regional context of the South Pacific, addressing both unique and generalisable elements of this regional sphere. This chapter also explores the dynamic relationships at play between diverse actors, values, and interests in the region. Chapter 4 introduces the case study of Papua New Guinea and the unique qualities of this case study. Chapter 5 documents the findings from fieldwork, including the experiences and insights provided by interviews conducted with key actors involved in anti-corruption efforts at the domestic, regional, and international levels. Chapter 6 analyses the research findings in detail, synthesising them with the theoretical framework and presenting answers to the second and third research questions. This analysis prepares the reader for the concluding discussion in Chapter 7.

In the final chapter, UNCAC's limitations are summarised. Discussion focuses on the impact of public perceptions, international reputation, and the complex interaction between domestic and external actors. These factors may limit the effectiveness of UNCAC and the global anti-corruption regime. However, findings also suggest that criticisms of UNCAC may overstate the coercive power and influence of the Convention. On this basis, a range of possibilities emerge for overcoming the key risks and challenges facing UNCAC and the global anti-corruption regime.

Possibilities for improvement centre on increasing levels of engagement with UNCAC, especially between domestic state and non-state actors. Enhanced engagement requires education of relevant actors regarding the substance of the Convention and must account for inherent power imbalances between actors. Adaptability of UNCAC and the global anti-corruption regime should be facilitated through engagement with the Implementation Review Mechanism of the Convention. Rather than engagement being one way (from the international to the domestic), engagement should support feedback loops that enhance the relevance of UNCAC to the unique contexts where it must operate. Increased education, engagement, and adaptability, may neutralise the most significant risk factors and challenges documented by the research, subsequently supporting evolution of the regime to the final stage.

Notes

1 Papua New Guinea, Barnett TE, Asia–Pacific Action Group, The Barnett Report: A summary of the report of the commission of inquiry into aspects of the timber industry in Papua New Guinea (1990) ('The Barnett Report, 1990')

2 PNG Exposed, *Foreign logging companies still firmly in control in PNG*, 3 March 2014, available at https://pngexposed.wordpress.com/2014/03/03/foreign-logging-companies-still-firmly-in-control-in-png (last visited 10 March 2018)

3 Greenpeace, *Briefing: Special-purpose agricultural and business leases in Papua New Guinea* (October, 2011) available at http://www.greenpeace.org/australia/Global/australia/11-076%20PNG%20Press%20Briefing_smaller_F-1.pdf (last visited 10 March 2018)

4 Garrett J, *PNG's land scandal inquiry names and Australian-led Company*, 2014, available at http://www.abc.net.au/news/2014-02-12/an-png-land-scandal-inquiry-names-an-australian-led-company/5255528?section=australianetworknews (last visited 10 March 2018)
5 ABC News, *PNG land inquiry boss calls for leases to be revoked*, 3 February 2014, available at http://www.abc.net.au/news/2014-02-03/an-png-land-inquiry-boss-calls-for-leases- to-be-revoked/5235792 (last visited 10 March 2018)
6 above n3
7 Papua New Guinea, Mirou, Commission of Inquiry into Special Agriculture and Business Leases (SABL): Report (June, 2013) at 185
8 above n2
9 Mousseau F, 'The Great Timber Heist: The logging industry in Papua New Guinea', *Oakland Institute* (2016) at 8
10 Act Now! PNG (14 March 2017), 'All SABLs Unlawful', available at: http://actnow-png.org/blog/all-sabls-unlawful (last visited 2018.
11 Tlozek E (2 August 2017), 'Papua New Guinea 'illegal logging exports continue', despite Peter O'Neill's promise to stop it', *ABC News*, available at: http://www.abc.net.au/news/2017-08-03/ pngs-illegal-logging-exports-continue/8770756 (last visited 10 March 2018)
12 ABC News, Cochrain and team, *PNG Prime Minister Peter O'Neill says political motivation behind arrest warrant from anti-corruption body*, 17 June 2014, available at: http://www.abc.net.au/news/2014-06-16/arrest-warrant-for-papua-new-guinea-prime-minis ter2c-peter-/5526748?section=australianetworknews (last visited 10 March 2018)
13 ABC News, Cochrain, *Papua New Guinea Prime Minister Peter O'Neill axes anti-corruption Taskforce Sweep*, 19 June 2014, available at: http://www.abc.net.au/news/2014-06-18/an-png-pm-axes-anti-corruption-task-force-sweep/5533400 (last visited 10 March 2018)
14 PNG Today, *Task Force Sweep permanently stayed*, 28 July 2014, available at: http://news.pngfacts.com/2014/07/task-force-sweep-permanently-stayed.html (last visited 10 March 2018)
15 Searches conducted on 17 September 2015 for Australia, USA, New Zealand, Papua New Guinea, Sweden and the UK each returned millions of results (from 2.27 and 99.7 million per search)
16 For an overview see: BBC News, *FIFA corruption crisis: Key questions answered* (25 September 2015) available at: http://www.bbc.com/news/world-europe-32897066 (last visited 10 March 2018)
17 Australia has ranked between 11th and 7th on the Transparency International Corruption Perception Index (TI CPI) from 2010 to 2014, New Zealand has been first in all but one of those years, slipping to second in 2014.
18 ABC News, *Chartered Accountants say Australia and New Zealand need to do more to tackle corruption* (17 September 2015) available at: http://www.abc.net.au/news/2015-09-17/chartered-accountants-say-australia-and-new/6783610 (last visited 10 March 2018)
19 Farrales M, 'What is Corruption? A history of corruption studies and the great definitions debate', *University of San Diego Working Paper Series* [2005] available at: http://papers.ssrn.com/sol3/papers.cfm?abstract_id=1739962 (last visited 10 March 2018)
20 A complete list of all multilateral legal instruments targeting corruption is provided in Annex A of this book
21 TI Corruption Perceptions Index, available at: https://www.transparency.org/research/cpi/overview (last visited 10 March 2018)
22 Nadelmann EA, 'Global Prohibition Regimes: The evolution of norms in international society' 44(4) *International Organization* (22 May 1990) 479; Nadelmann EA and Andreas P, *Policing the Globe: Criminalization and crime control in international relations* (Oxford University Press, 1st Edition, 2006)

References

ABC News, *Chartered Accountants say Australia and New Zealand need to do more to tackle corruption*, (17 September 2015) available at: http://www.abc.net.au/news/2015-09-17/chartered-accountants-say-australia-and-new/6783610 (last visited 1 March 2018).

ABC News, Cochrain and team, *PNG Prime Minister Peter O'Neill says political motivation behind arrest warrant from anti-corruption body* (17 June 2014) available at: http://www.abc.net.au/news/2014-06-16/arrest-warrant-for-papua-new-guinea-prime-minister2c-peter-/5526748?section=australianetworknews (last visited 1 March 2018).

ABC News, Cochrain, *Papua New Guinea Prime Minister Peter O'Neill axes anti-corruption Taskforce Sweep* (19 June 2014) available at: http://www.abc.net.au/news/2014-06-18/an-png-pm-axes-anti-corruption-task-force-sweep/5533400 (last visited 1 March 2018).

ABC News, Garrett J, *PNG's land scandal inquiry names and Australian-led Company* (12 Febuary 2014) available at: http://www.abc.net.au/news/2014-02-12/an-png-land-scandal-inquiry-names-an-australian-led-company/5255528?section=australianetwork news (last visited 1 March 2018).

ABC News, *PNG land inquiry boss calls for leases to be revoked* (3 February 2014), available at: http://www.abc.net.au/news/2014-02-03/an-png-land-inquiry-boss-calls-for-leases-to-be-revoked/5235792 (last visited 1 March 2018).

ABC News, Tlozek E, *Papua New Guinea 'illegal logging exports continue', despite Peter O'Neill's promise to stop it* (3 August 2017) available at: http://www.abc.net.au/news/2017-08-03/pngs-illegal-logging-exports-continue/8770756 (last visited 1 March 2018).

Act Now! PNG, 'All SABLs Unlawful'(14 March 2017) available at: http://actnowpng.org/blog/all-sabls-unlawful (last visited 1 March 2018).

BBC News, *FIFA corruption crisis: Key questions answered* (25 September 2015) available at: http://www.bbc.com/news/world-europe-32897066 (last visited 1 March 2018).

Farrales M, 'What is Corruption? A history of corruption studies and the great definitions debate', *University of San Diego Working Paper Series* [2005] available at: http://papers.ssrn.com/sol3/papers.cfm?abstract_id=1739962 (last visited 1 March 2018).

Greenpeace Australia, *Briefing: Special-purpose agricultural and business leases in Papua New Guinea* (October 2011) available at: http://www.greenpeace.org/australia/Global/australia/11-076%20PNG%20Press%20Briefing_smaller_F-1.pdf (last visited 1 March 2018).

Mousseau F, 'The Great Timber Heist: The logging industry in Papua New Guinea', *Oakland Institute* (2016).

Nadelmann E and Andreas P, *Policing the Globe: Criminalization and Crime Control in International Relations* (Oxford University Press, 1st Edition, 2006).

Nadelmann EA, 'Global prohibition regimes: The evolution of norms in international society' 44(4) *International Organization* (22 May 1990) 479.

Papua New Guinea, Barnett TE, Asia-Pacific Action Group, *The Barnett Report: A summary of the report of the Commission of Inquiry into Aspects of the Timber Industry in Papua New Guinea* (1990).

Papua New Guinea, Mirou, *Commission of Inquiry into Special Agriculture and Business Leases (SABL): Report* (June, 2013) ('SABL Report 2013').

PNG Exposed, *Foreign logging companies still firmly in control in PNG* (3 March 2014) available at: https://pngexposed.wordpress.com/2014/03/03/foreign-logging-companies-still-firmly-in-control-in-png (last visited 1 March 2018).

PNG Today, *Task Force Sweep permanently stayed* (28 July 2014) available at: http://news.pngfacts.com/2014/07/task-force-sweep-permanently-stayed.html (last visited 1 March 2018).

TI, *Corruption Perceptions Index*, available at: https://www.transparency.org/research/cpi/overview (last visited 1 March 2018).

1 Setting the stage – corruption and the global anti-corruption regime

This chapter introduces the term corruption, the concept of global prohibition regimes, and the evolutionary pattern of these regimes. The emergence of a dominant approach to the universal criminalisation, prevention and punishment of corruption has failed to substantially reduce corruption levels globally. The reasons for this failure are the topic of this book. After introducing the term corruption and providing some initial context, this chapter sets out the five-stage model of global prohibition regime evolution first developed by Nadelmann,[1] and expanded upon by Nadelmann and Andreas.[2] This model provides the foundation that informs the analysis throughout this book, with the goal of understanding why the emergent global anti-corruption regime has failed to successfully reduce corruption levels globally.

Additional theoretical insights are introduced to supplement the model, emphasising the importance of diverse values and interests at the international, regional, and domestic levels. These values and interests demonstrate the transnational nature of modern prohibition regimes, illustrating the overlap between local, national, regional, and international spheres. Diverse values and interests shape not only regime evolution, but also the implementation and enforcement of these regimes and their ultimate success or failure.

Corruption: in search of a definition

The concept of corruption and its related harms is as old as civilisation. Many authors also cite the ubiquitous and trans-temporal nature of both corruption and the criminal activities which often accompany it.[3] From ancient Greece[4] to modern Papua New Guinea (PNG),[5] examples of corruption are bountiful. However, the trans-temporal nature of corruption has not resulted in a clear understanding of the term or the various activities contained within the umbrella term. A clear definition of corruption remains elusive, as does consensus regarding the harms that result from corrupt activity. Although the emergent global anti-corruption regime presents corruption as a universal ill, the only thing most scholars seem to be able to agree upon is the complexity and variability of the term.

Conflict and contestation surrounding the definition and nature of corruption intensified during the mid-20th Century. Decolonisation, the end of the Cold War, the emergence of globalisation discourses, and increased interest in international regulation of previously domestic issues all contributed to heightened debate.[6] An increased interest in international criminalisation of corruption fueled the desire to establish a consistent definition and conceptual clarity. However, such consistency and clarity proved difficult to realise. Continuing uncertainty regarding a precise definition of corruption is noted by many as a significant limitation on current efforts to combat corruption consistently.

One of the earliest points of conflict in the intensified anti-corruption debate was that between moralists and revisionists, who disagreed on the effects of corruption on society and economy.[7] Moralists universally condemned corruption as harmful to society, while revisionists argued for a more pragmatic approach where corruption was seen as 'an inevitable and necessary part of the adjustment process'.[8] The adjustment referred to by revisionists was adjustment to the modern, western liberal model of democracy and free market economics. As this debate continued, the power of international organisations to shape developing economies became more evident.[9] Through the efforts of organisations such as the World Bank and the International Monetary Fund (IMF), the moralist understanding of corruption as inherently 'bad' overpowered revisionist arguments. The view that corruption could be a productive path to development and a way of levelling the international playing field was delegitimised.

With this focus on the inherently 'bad' nature of corruption, the harms associated with corrupt behaviour were increasingly emphasised. In 1996, World Bank president Wolfensohn famously referred to corruption as a 'cancer' and noted that it prohibited equitable development and the alleviation of poverty.[10] The harms associated with corruption provided justification for attempting to establish a unified and universal approach to combatting corruption. However, despite this victory for moralist arguments, a variety of perspectives remained regarding the elements of corruption that should be the focus of further analysis and criminalisation efforts.

Farrales highlights three conflicting views: 'Public Office' centred approaches relating to the misuse of public office or authority for private gain; a 'Market' or 'Economic' centred approach focusing solely on profit maximisation; and a 'Public Interest' centred view that emphasises the pursuit of private interest *at the expense* of the public interest.[11] There is also conflict between public opinion and legalistic understandings of corruption. The public opinion approach argues for the 'necessity of . . . incorporating norms into our definition of corruption'[12] acknowledging that different societies will perceive corruption differently and that the definition of corruption will remain fluid over time. A legalistic view, however, argues for a focus on *illegality*, thus limiting the study of corruption to the confines of legally defined acts established as corrupt within a given jurisdiction.

Modern debates on corruption incorporate elements of public interest and legalistic definitions. The approach promoted through international law and the policies of international organisations centres on the application of an expansive legal regime.[13] This regime defines key activities as crimes of corruption and promotes universal adoption of these crimes into domestic law. However, although the goal of this regime is to secure a universally consistent approach to criminalising corruption, existing multilateral legal instruments acknowledge domestic variation in legal approaches and systems.[14] In this way, elements of a public opinion approach remain part of the regime, allowing for domestic law to reflect domestic norms, albeit within an internationally negotiated framework.

In academic literature, arguments regarding the best way to define corruption, the fundamental elements of the definition, and the exact causes and nature of corrupt activity, remain largely unresolved. Most authors, however, seem to acknowledge the complexity of the term and its variant nature across a broad range of societies, cultures, and geographies. It is largely because of this complexity that the most commonly cited definition of corruption is one that is both broad and simplistic. Farrales argues that the dominant 'Public Office' approach is 'the least common denominator'.[15] This definition, simply put, relates to the misuse of public office for private gain. It avoids the limitations of a purely monetary approach to gain – as in the 'Economic' approach – while also acknowledging the contextual variation of the concept and the issues which arise from a view that includes, but fails to define, 'the public interest', as in the 'Public Interest' approach. Furthermore, Farrales notes that this simplistic definition avoids contestation surrounding legalistic versus public opinion approaches as 'the entire dispute revolves around how to operationalise "abuse" or "misuse" of public office'.[16]

The 'Public Office' definition is perhaps the most widely referenced in academia, the media, and the discourse of the international community. However, in many respects this definition is tantamount to no definition at all. Such a broad definition allows corruption-based rhetoric to be co-opted for the promotion of political agendas. The co-optation of prohibition regime rhetoric is an issue that many critical authors engage with. Beare argues that approaches to combatting a specific activity are driven by perceptions of that activity as harmful. A real threat may be distorted and expanded upon by those charged with combatting it.[17] Beare argues that corruption rhetoric 'may too easily become a political platform for ranking and evaluating nations'.[18] Similar concerns have been raised by many critics in relation to the rhetoric of organised crime and the prohibition of drugs.[19] In addition to co-optation, 'unintentional' side effects may result from poorly designed policies against corruption. If the concept of corruption is not clearly defined and its causes are not well understood, policies aimed at suppressing associated harms may cause other harmful side effects, or even exacerbate existing problems.[20] Poorly constructed policies may also make the targeted activity more difficult to uncover, as it changes and adapts to attempts to control it.

In sum, corruption as a term is difficult to define. A general definition has emerged that is extremely broad and open to interpretation. This definition, specifically 'the misuse of public office for private gain' has become popular in international discourse on corruption, especially amongst organisations and institutions that promote a universal criminal law approach to combatting corruption. This dominant approach emphasises a view of corruption as inherently harmful to all societies. This position justifies the need to control the harms related to 'corrupt' activities, with a consistent approach to criminalisation and law enforcement cooperation, combined with institutional change, seen as the best tools to do so. However, while the use of the general 'Public Office' definition allows for flexibility of interpretation, which may be beneficial in order to reflect unique domestic contexts, it also poses challenges regarding potential manipulation, misuse, and co-optation. These challenges have significant implications for the success of the global anti-corruption regime.

The global anti-corruption regime

Despite substantial controversy regarding the definition of corruption, a transnational approach to combatting corrupt activity has emerged in the latter half of the 20th Century. This approach is based on consistent and universal criminalisation of corrupt acts and has all of the salient features of a global prohibition regime. This global anti-corruption regime (the regime), will be the focus of this book. The regime draws on combined moralist and legalist approaches and is supported by dominant actors at the international level including the United Nations (UN), World Bank, and Transparency International (TI). The global anti-corruption regime utilises and is reflected in multilateral legal instruments, including the United Nations Convention against Corruption (UNCAC), which represents the primary legal tool of the regime. UNCAC will become the central focus of this book from Chapter 2 onward. However, before exploring the legal dimensions of the regime, the role of non-legal dynamics must be understood. These dynamics have shaped and continue to shape the context in which the global anti-corruption regime and its legal tools have developed.

The emergence of the global anti-corruption regime has involved extensive interaction between national, regional, and international actors and a variety of rationalist interests and normative values. The five-stage evolutionary model first established by Nadelmann[21] and expanded upon by Nadelmann and Andreas[22] provides a useful starting point for examining the dynamic process of the regime's evolution, and the role of UNCAC as the primary legal tool of this regime.[23] The model also supports analysis of the challenges that the regime faces in implementing and enforcing legal tools such as UNCAC within unique domestic contexts. The theory of Nadelmann and Andreas can be situated within broader regime theory, as defined by Stephen Krasner. From this perspective, regimes are defined as: '. . . sets of implicit or explicit principles, norms, rules, and decision-making procedures around which actors' expectations converge in a given area of international relations'.[24]

The author continues to expand and explain this definition by stating:

> Principles are beliefs of fact, causation, and rectitude. Norms are standards of behaviour defined in terms of rights and obligations. Rules are specific prescriptions or proscriptions for action. Decision-making procedures are prevailing practices for making and implementing collective choice.[25]

Throughout this book, the importance of principles, norms, rules and procedures are repeatedly emphasised. These factors impact the evolution, nature, and effectiveness of the global anti-corruption regime. If regimes are understood to have some level of influence on the behaviour of actors, Krasner notes the importance of understanding 'the conditions that lead to regime creation, persistence, and dissipation'.[26] In this regard, Krasner emphasises the importance of self-interest, power, and values. Each of these factors plays a role in the evolution of the global anti-corruption regime and its implementation and enforcement.

Building on the foundation of regime theory noted above, Nadelmann and Andreas' five-stage model provides substantial analytical value for the exploration of the global anti-corruption regime, its evolution, and impact. The particularities of this five-stage model are introduced below. This introduction is followed by an analysis of the global anti-corruption regime, illustrating its evolution following the five-stage model. It is argued that the regime is currently in the fourth stage of evolution. The existence of the regime is illustrated by the substantial number of multilateral legal instruments that target corruption. The entry into force of UNCAC in 2005,[27] and its subsequent ratification by a total of 183 states, has solidified the regime in the fourth stage.[28] The initiation of the Implementation Review Mechanism for UNCAC, developed in 2009, has acted to strengthen the regime further. However, despite the existence of this global anti-corruption regime, the final stage of evolution remains elusive. Corruption remains a substantial global challenge.

Before introducing the five-stage model of Nadelmann and Andreas, it is important to also mention the additional theoretical insights that will be used to supplement the model. Nadelmann and Andreas argue that 'only an analytically eclectic approach, selectively combining elements of different perspectives, can effectively make sense of the internationalisation of crime control'.[29] This book supplements the model with contributions from other transnational theorists. These authors support and expand on the five-stage model of Nadelmann and Andreas emphasising the importance of domestic context and diverse actors, values, and interests. These transnational features influence the nature, diffusion, implementation, and enforcement of any global prohibition regime. Enhancing the model in this way supports analysis of the impact that a regime can have on domestic law and policy. This is an essential component of this book, which documents the impact of UNCAC on PNG.

The concept of 'criminogenic asymmetries' is particularly useful as it provides an analytical tool for understanding the causes of criminal activity, including corruption, and the role of global dynamics in contributing to such criminal activity. Passas defines 'criminogenic asymmetries' as 'structural disjunctions, mismatches and inequalities in the sphere of politics, culture, the economy and law'.[30] These mismatches produce opportunities for criminal activity by strengthening demand for illegal goods and services, generating incentives for actors to participate in illegal transactions and reducing the ability of authorities to control illegal activities.[31] Passas illustrates that corruption is both the result of asymmetries, and 'a conservative force that maintains or increases asymmetries'.[32] On the one hand, the author notes:

> [E]conomic asymmetries foster attitudes justifying corruption as functional to local economies and as a way of redistributing wealth . . . Moreover,

> legal asymmetries provide a shield against the discovery or sanctioning of corruption.[33]

On the other hand, corruption also undermines economic development, thereby contributing to misallocation of resources, increased distrust of government, and facilitation of criminal enterprise.[34] Thus, corruption is both consequence and cause of criminogenic asymmetries.

Furthermore, Passas argues convincingly that globalisation 'multiplies, intensifies or activates asymmetries' and therefore significantly increases criminogenesis.[35] The author defines globalisation as 'a transformation of the world order through the multiplication and intensification of linkages and interconnectedness'.[36] Passas argues that:

> Globalization processes produce a number of asymmetries with complex criminogenic effects . . . We can identify cultural, economic, political, technological, legal and other asymmetries . . . however, most of them are interlinked with or simultaneously constitute power asymmetries.[37]

Globalisation 'reinforces inequalities of power and wealth both within nation states and among them'.[38] As awareness of pre-existing economic asymmetries is increased, the criminogenic potential is activated. Additionally, 'the independence, sovereignty and autonomy of nation states are systematically undermined by external actors and supranational bodies'.[39] Finally, the increasingly free movement of people, goods, and services across borders hampers state-based crime prevention measures:

> To the extent that transactions cross jurisdictions with differing legal traditions and cultures, both compliance and control become highly problematic . . . legal cacophonies are accompanied by jurisdictional conflicts, nightmares in collaboration, cultural conflicts and power differentials among both actors and regulators.[40]

Despite the challenges to state control posed by globalisation, Passas emphasises that states maintain ultimate power over the nature and extent of asymmetries. The author stresses that 'it is through policies decided on and carried out at the national level that asymmetries materialize their criminogenic potential'.[41] Domestic economic policies result in diverse outcomes within and between states; protectionism and contradictory foreign policies of powerful states perpetuate asymmetric development and promote internal and international conflict; domestic prohibition creates illegal opportunities; and criminal justice methods provide incentives for more sophisticated crime and increased corruption.[42] The power of the state as emphasised by Passas reflects and supports the argument of Andreas that 'states are not simply being pushed aside by the globalization of illicit markets but are essential to their creation and perpetuation'.[43]

The dynamics that contribute to criminogenic asymmetries highlight the role of domestic actors, power imbalances, and diverse values and interests, in shaping the nature of transnational criminal activity and the impact and effectiveness of responses to this activity. The work of Passas is drawn on throughout analysis in this book, and insights from additional authors are discussed in this chapter, following the introduction of the regime framework. In addition to an eclectic theoretical framework, this book acknowledges the challenges faced by global prohibition regimes, as well as specific critiques of UNCAC and the global anti-corruption regime. These specific criticisms are distilled into four key regime risk factors that provide possible explanations for why extensive ratification of UNCAC and commitment to implement and enforce the global anti-corruption regime have failed to substantially reduce instances of corrupt activity.

Introducing the five-stage model: the theory of Nadelmann and Andreas

Nadelmann and Andreas explore the way that legal norms develop within the international sphere through analysis of the dynamics that contribute to the evolution of 'global prohibition regimes'.[44] The authors suggest that 'most global prohibition regimes . . . evidence a common evolutionary pattern, one roughly divisible into four, and in some cases five, stages'.[45] This five-stage model highlights the various non-legal dynamics involved in the formation of regulatory regimes, including the global anti-corruption regime. Global prohibition regimes represent the way in which criminal norms are enforced and institutionalised.[46] While the regime itself consists of legal instruments – for example UNCAC in the case of the global anti-corruption regime – the process of development, institutionalisation, and enforcement of the regime involves a range of non-legal dynamics. These dynamics include rationalist interests and normative values within international, regional, and national spheres.

Nadelmann suggests that the evolution of global prohibition regimes is a complex process involving economic interests, security interests and moral dynamics:

> . . . the actions of states must be understood as the culmination of both external pressures and domestic political struggles, in which national and transnational organisations and movements shape the actions of states as well as the actions and opinions of diverse societies, and in which the norms of dominant societies, notably those of Europe and the United States, are not only internationalized but also internalized by diverse societies throughout the world.[47]

The process of regime evolution can be divided into five stages. Each stage illustrates the unique interaction of interests and values that contribute to the ultimate creation of a regime. Some notable regimes include those against piracy, slavery, and the trafficking of people, drugs, and small arms. The regimes against slavery and piracy have been largely successful in reducing instances of these activities globally, although piracy has recently re-emerged as a substantial challenge for criminal law and enforcement in some parts of the world.[48] The argument has also been made that slavery, in the form of human trafficking and forced labour, continues to be a substantial challenge.[49] However, modern forms of slavery differ from the acts condoned by most of the western world between the 14th and 19th Centuries. It was this 'traditional' form of slavery, 'characterized by the complete ownership of human beings',[50] that was the subject of a global prohibition regime. The successes of regimes against piracy and slavery have not emerged for regimes against trafficking in drugs, small arms, or human beings. These more recent regimes have encountered substantial challenges, with instances of each of these activities continuing largely unabated.[51]

For Nadelmann and Andreas, a substantial global reduction in the target activity globally is the ultimate goal of a global prohibition regime and is defined as the fifth and final stage of regime evolution.[52] This stage is seldom achieved. Regimes face challenges that, if not overcome, will result in continued or even increased instances of the target activity. Nadelmann and Andreas describe four preliminary stages that occur before this fifth stage can eventuate. The preliminary stages will be referred to in this book as 'initial', 'delegitimation', 'dissemination', and 'criminalisation', respectively.

In the initial stage, the activity is regarded as legitimate by most societies under certain conditions and with regard to certain actors.[53] In the delegitimation stage, 'the activity is redefined as problem and as evil'.[54] This stage is usually achieved through the efforts of 'moral entrepreneurs' and results in the 'delegitimation of explicit government involvement in the activity'.[55] The dissemination stage involves 'moral entrepreneurs' and hegemonic states agitating for the suppression and criminalisation of the activity by all states and the formation of international conventions. In the criminalisation stage, 'the activity becomes the subject of criminal laws and police action throughout much of the world',[56] and 'international institutions and conventions emerge to play a coordinating role'.[57]

Nadelmann and Andreas argue that it is only once the criminalisation stage is achieved that a global prohibition regime has fully come into existence.[58] The regime will then be required to overcome a range of challenges, in order to achieve the fifth and final stage. As noted above, many regimes do not achieve this final stage. Even those regimes that appear to have done so at one point in history, such as the anti-piracy regime, may face renewed challenges as the target activity evolves and develops.

It is essential to understand the centrality of state action in the suppression of activities targeted by global prohibition regimes. Nadelmann and Andreas hold that no global prohibition regime could attain the final stage of evolution until the 19th Century because of the existence of vacuums of sovereign authority in which regime dissenters could maintain freedom and sanctuary.[59] However, in the past two centuries, the power of states to enforce their criminal laws both within and outside their territory, and to cooperate amongst themselves in such efforts, has increased substantially. This has allowed for the possibility of achieving the fifth stage of regime evolution, resulting in successful global prohibition of a specific target activity.

The challenges that must be overcome, for a regime to achieve the final stage of evolution, fall into three categories. The first category is that of dissident and deviant actors. A global prohibition regime must contend with those states that are unwilling to support or comply with the regime, as well as those individuals and criminal organisations that continue to engage in the target activity with no regard for the regime or its legal tools.[60] The second category of challenges relates to non-compliant states. The regime is not only challenged by dissident or deviant states, organisations, and individuals, but also by states that formally support the regime but are unable or unwilling to take the necessary measures to implement and enforce the regime domestically.[61] This category of challenges is especially relevant in the case of the global anti-corruption regime and is a recurring theme in the case study of PNG covered in Chapters 4 to 6.

The final category of challenges revolves around the susceptibility of the target activity to criminal law and enforcement measures. Nadelmann and Andreas focus on five features that impact the success of criminal law and enforcement measures:

1 Resources
2 Expertise
3 Concealment
4 Reporting
5 Demand

They argue that:

> Criminal laws and international prohibition regimes are particularly ineffective in suppressing criminal activities that require limited and readily available resources and no particular expertise to commit, those that are easily concealed, those that are unlikely to be reported to authorities, and those for which the consumer demand is substantial, resilient, and not readily substituted for by alternative activities or products.[62]

On this basis, Nadelmann and Andreas suggest that the global drug prohibition regime will never achieve success in the final stage of evolution.[63] The nature of drug trafficking is such that the challenges faced by the regime appear insurmountable. The UNODC 'World Drug Report' notes that the extent of drug use and 'problem' drug use remains stable globally.[64] Many commentators have criticised attempts to combat drug trafficking through transnational criminal law and enforcement measures, arguing that such efforts have resulted in more harm than good.[65] Similar criticisms have been levelled at UNCAC and the global anti-corruption regime. These criticisms are explored further, later in this chapter.

To summarise, the five-stage model of regime evolution developed by Nadelmann and Andreas consists of four preliminary stages: an initial stage where the target activity is deemed legitimate, a delegitimation stage, a dissemination stage, and a criminalisation stage. Then, if the challenges of deviant actors, non-compliant states, and susceptibility to criminal law and enforcement measures are successfully overcome, a final stage can be achieved, resulting in a substantial global reduction in the target activity.

The global anti-corruption regime was in the early stages of evolution when this model was established. However, the model applies as well to the anti-corruption regime as it does to those regimes regulating piracy and slavery. Writing shortly after UNCAC entered into force, Nadelmann and Andreas noted that the evolution of a 'global prohibition regime against corruption' was in the third stage of regime development.[66] The regime has continued to develop and is not in the fourth stage of evolution. This evolutionary process is documented in the following sections of this chapter, with a focus on the process leading up to negotiation of UNCAC. The details of UNCAC and the negotiation of this multilateral legal instrument and tool of the global anti-corruption regime will be the subject of extensive analysis in Chapter 2.

Applying the five-stage model to the global anti-corruption regime

In the initial stage of any regime's evolution, the activity that will become the subject of the regime is generally regarded by society and state as legitimate, at least in certain contexts or when conducted by specific actors.[67] This was certainly true for corruption. Before the initial push towards global prohibition, corruption was often considered an unavoidable reality and, in some cases, a necessity.[68,69] Justification of corrupt behaviour was especially prevalent in the case of bribery of public officials by foreign corporations. It is important to note that domestic corruption, in the form of giving and receiving bribes for example, has a long history of criminalisation in most states, although the exact nature of the crimes covered and related legislation varies substantially. Despite these domestic laws, many corporations paid bribes to domestic government representatives as a matter of course. In certain cases, these corporations were even enabled by their own domestic legal systems to claim bribes as tax deductible expenses.[70]

For a global anti-corruption regime to develop, corrupt activity had to be redefined as a problem and as harmful to societies.[71] The role of 'moral entrepreneurs' is fundamental to this process. Nadelmann suggests that such 'moral entrepreneurs' include 'international legal scholars, religious groups' and others.[72] These actors are often concerned with elevating the importance of the target activity beyond national borders.[73] Nadelmann and Andreas note that 'efforts are often directed towards persuading foreign audiences . . . that a particular prohibition regime reflects a widely shared or even universal moral sense, rather than the peculiar moral code of one society'.[74] In the case of corruption, TI is perhaps the most notable moral entrepreneur. Multinational corporations, especially those domiciled in the United States (US), also acted as moral entrepreneurs in the evolution of the anti-corruption regime.[75] In fact, these corporations have strong links to TI.[76] The World Bank is another actor that supported the reclassification of corruption as a harmful transnational threat, as was noted earlier during the discussion of the moralist and revisionist definitions of corruption. The role of moral entrepreneurs in shaping the global anti-corruption regime is expanded upon later in this chapter, illustrating the important impact diverse values and interests have on the nature of the regime.

The initial stage of the global anti-corruption regime existed prior to 1970. The delegitimation stage developed between 1970 and 1980. The dissemination stage spanned two decades, beginning in the 1980s with catalysing events in the USA. The dissemination stage involved the complex interaction of diverse actors with unique and varied motivations who worked together to re-shape understandings of corrupt behaviour and promote global regulation of corrupt acts. During this stage, the US can be understood as a 'hegemonic state' agitating along with moral entrepreneurs for consistent criminalisation of the target activity around the world.

The success of the dissemination stage substantially strengthens the regime, allowing for a transition to the fourth stage.[77] During this criminalisation stage, consistent criminal laws and enforcement measures are established across much of the world and, most significantly, multilateral legal instruments and related international institutions are developed and utilised to regulate the target activity.[78] For the global anti-corruption regime, 'near universal membership' of UNCAC, combined with the development and operation of an Implementation Review Mechanism, suggest that the fourth stage of evolution has been achieved. The regime must now contend with the three categories of challenges introduced earlier in this chapter, if it is to achieve the fifth and final stage of evolution.

> [R]egime proponents must contend with the challenges of deviant states . . . weak states . . . and dissident individuals and criminal organisations that elude enforcement efforts and continue to engage in the proscribed activity.[79]

In addition to dissident and deviant actors, and non-compliant states, the target activity's susceptibility to criminal law and enforcement measures is also a challenge. Issues of resources, expertise, concealment, reporting, and demand will all be relevant to regime success.

Corruption requires resources in the form of capital for payments, but those in positions of power may have a readily available supply of both money and influence. As an example, transnational corporations have substantial financial resources and government officials are in a strong position to provide beneficial contracts or regulatory changes in exchange for financial benefit. Expertise is not a prerequisite for corruption, which is an activity that has existed for millennia. However as criminal law and enforcement efforts increase, the expertise required to continue to engage in corrupt activity without detection will increase. The profits of corrupt acts may be increasingly difficult to conceal, although the positions of power often held by the actors involved in corrupt activities may reduce this challenge.

Corruption is an activity that is unlikely to be reported. It involves both a supply and demand side with benefits to both parties. Victims of corruption are often not immediately involved in or aware of the corrupt activity. Furthermore, criminalisation of both supply and demand side activities makes it unlikely an involved party will report the activity. Once again, the powerful positions often held by those actors involved may limit the likelihood of reporting. This is in part due to these actors being able to conceal their actions, but also because of the risks posed to whistle-blowers based on the powerful positions of the perpetrators.

Consumer demand is also an important factor for the success of criminal law and enforcement efforts. The longstanding history of corrupt activity suggests demand is substantial. However, many commentators have suggested that this is an area that could be targeted to support anti-corruption efforts. Substitutions for corruption may include streamlined government processes, clear legislations, and increased wages for civil servants. The best way to curb demand for corruption will depend on the reasons for the corrupt activity, which will vary in different contexts. It is certainly difficult to imagine a scenario in which pure greed could be eliminated as a driving force for corruption, and this motivation is not easily substituted.

Corruption remains a substantial challenge in most countries. Understanding the challenges that face anti-corruption efforts is essential to overcoming them and securing regime success. If the complexities and challenges of implementing and enforcing UNCAC can be understood, solutions to these challenges will support effective implementation and enforcement. If these solutions can be successfully applied across diverse contexts, the result may be a substantial reduction in corrupt activity globally. This outcome would allow for evolution of the global anti-corruption regime to the final stage, securing the ultimate success of the regime.

Nadelmann notes that:

> International prohibition regimes are intended to minimize or eliminate the potential havens from which certain crimes can be committed and to which criminals can flee to escape prosecution and punishment. They provide an element of standardization to cooperation among governments that have few other law enforcement concerns in common. And they create an expectation of cooperation that governments challenge only at the cost of some international embarrassment.[80]

The concept of 'international embarrassment', combined with the role of 'moral entrepreneurs', illustrates the central importance of perceptions in developing and sustaining a global prohibition regime. Moral arguments are only successful in a context where the targeted actors are concerned with how they are perceived. In the international sphere, states are constantly interacting and seeking support from other states, profitable relations with corporates, and beneficial partnerships with multilateral lenders. Perceptions are essential to the success or failure of a partnership and may impact other regional and domestic interactions and outcomes. The impact of perceptions and the complexity of transnational partnerships are documented in Chapters 3 and 4.

Economic and political interests, as well as normative values, shape international interactions. These values and interests are subsequently employed in the development of global prohibition regimes. Such regimes are justified based on economic and political interests, especially those of dominant actors in international society, as well as on moral arguments based on the risks and harms associated with the target activity.[81] This reality reflects the views of Abbott and Snidal, who highlight the importance and interaction of both rationalist interest and normative value arguments in the creation, development, and operation of legal regimes.[82]

The work of Abbott and Snidal merges normative and constructivist views of international law, with rationalist theories. The authors suggest that 'law both reflects (and shapes) the values and serves (and shapes) the interests of those it governs'.[83] Therefore, a normative and constructivist focus on values is incomplete without acknowledgement of the role played by rationalist interests. Equally, the rationalist focus on interests (even broadly construed) is limited if it fails to acknowledge the unique qualities of value-based motives and reasoning. This understanding is usefully applied to the exploration of the global anti-corruption regime. Utilising such a multifaceted approach, combined with recognition of the criminogenic asymmetries that result from and stimulate corruption, lends insight into the complex interactions that have influenced the development of the global anti-corruption regime. This multifaceted approach provides a well-rounded contextual setting from which to analyse and evaluate negotiation of UNCAC, implementation and enforcement of this multilateral legal instrument, the continued evolution of the global anti-corruption regime, and the regime's potential for achieving the fifth and final stage of development.

Theoretical expansion: emphasising values and interests in the evolution of the global anti-corruption regime

Abbott and Snidal illustrate the importance of values and interests through the example of the Organisation for Economic Cooperation and Development Anti-Bribery Convention (OECD Convention).[84] Emphasis is placed on the various turning points during negotiation, to illustrate the complex interaction between normative values and rationalist interests in the development of multilateral legal instruments. The OECD Convention was the first binding multilateral legal instrument to regulate corrupt activity beyond the region of the Americas.[85] Because of this, the work of Abbott and Snidal is a useful contribution to understanding the evolution of the global anti-corruption regime. In the ten years following the adoption of the OECD Convention there have been no fewer than seven binding regional and multilateral instruments adopted to regulate corrupt acts, bringing the total number to nine.[86] The adoption of the OECD Convention was a watershed for the global anti-corruption regime, accelerating the regime toward the fourth stage of evolution that culminated with the entry into force of UNCAC in 2005.

Mirroring the first stage of regime evolution, Abbott and Snidal note that historically 'the dominant view was that some forms of corruption are necessary, even beneficial, aspects of development'.[87] Existing domestic criminal law frameworks to combat bribery and corrupt acts have been applied with varying degrees of consistency for centuries. However, these laws did not have jurisdiction over transnational acts of corruption and enforcement, even in purely domestic contexts, was inconsistent. Furthermore, domestic law often reflects differing social or cultural views on appropriate conduct. Therefore, there was substantial variation in the approaches taken by different domestic anti-corruption laws. It took extensive efforts on behalf of certain hegemonic nation states, moral entrepreneurs, and other interested actors, to reinvent and problematise corruption as an inherently harmful activity requiring global regulatory action. The domestic political context in the US, during the 1970s, was a key catalyst for the problematisation of corruption and the development of the global anti-corruption regime.

Two events in the US in the mid to late 1970s initiated a move towards a global anti-corruption regime. In 1977, the Securities and Exchange Commission (SEC) reported that US corporations had spent in excess of USD300 million bribing foreign officials.[88] This report, combined with an 'upsurge in values around the Watergate Scandal',[89] allowed the US government to enact strong legislation prohibiting transnational bribery. This legislation, in the form of the United States Foreign Corrupt Practices Act (the FCPA),[90] was 'the first move against transnational bribery'.[91] Such legislation proved to be 'sticky' and impossible to repeal, despite the interest-based motivations of US corporates, who were now at a disadvantage when operating transnationally.[92]

The FCPA is a domestic legal instrument that deals with the issue of corporate/government corruption, focusing on the criminalisation of a specific activity (bribery), rather than the criminalisation of 'corruption' per se. The focus is on 'active bribery', meaning bribery by the person who promises or gives the bribe. The law has no power over the foreign officials who are 'passively' engaged in bribery, either by accepting or soliciting bribes. This is in part because, due to its transnational nature, the FCPA could not risk impinging on the sovereignty of other nations. The FCPA has no authority to criminalise the actions of foreign state representatives. However, the FCPA did 'establish broad criminal prohibitions in spite of the uncertainty these created for US firms and executives'.[93] It illustrates the power of strong moral and normative views, triggered by unique political events, which drove legal action. These normative views continued to influence the anti-corruption debate as it emerged on the international agenda.

The FCPA's value-based dimension, in terms of its moral and normative justifications, helps to explain its 'stickiness' domestically.[94] The FCPA aligned with the political and ideological sentiments in the US at that time, developed in response to specific domestic events. This allowed the law to be localised and internalised with relative ease. However, the imposition of this normative position outside of the US proved difficult. Such difficulty can be related in part to the differing contexts which existed outside of the US, where political and ideological sentiments of the public and dominant political actors did not align with those that had motivated the FCPA domestically. As an example, Abbott and Snidal note that early US efforts to open OECD negotiations on an anti-corruption convention were unsuccessful, not least because 'European interests benefited from the status quo'.[95]

The International Chamber of Commerce drafted a non-binding regulatory code to combat extortion and bribery in 1977. However, it was not until 1996 that the first binding multilateral legal instrument against corruption was adopted. This instrument was the Organisation of American States Inter-American Convention against Corruption (the OAS Convention),[96] which was followed a year later by the OECD Convention.[97] The enactment of the OECD Convention represented the internationalisation of the FCPA and the creation of the first binding multilateral legal instrument to regulate corrupt activity beyond the region of the Americas. Since then, seven additional instruments have entered into force, including UNCAC in 2005.

The internationalisation of the FCPA required extended and intensive agitation by government, corporate, and non-state actors. This mirrors the transition from the delegitimation stage to the dissemination stage of regime evolution. This transition clearly illustrates the complex interaction of values and interests introduced by Abbott and Snidal. In the years preceding the adoption of the OECD Convention, business interests in the US (negatively impacted by the unilateral nature of the FCPA) joined forces with NGO actors such as TI. Together, these actors promoted a normative argument regarding the negative impacts and fundamental 'wrongness' of corruption. This moral argument made it increasingly difficult for European nations to argue against the anti-corruption agenda, despite interest-based incentives to maintain the status quo.[98] Aggregation of normative and value-based arguments proved persuasive, pushing the global anti-corruption regime towards the third, dissemination, stage of the evolutionary model. The normative discourse of actors from the US, as well as certain international actors and institutions such as the World Bank and the UN Crime Prevention and Criminal Justice Branch, were especially successful when combined with other contextual factors. For example, widespread media attention regarding corruption within Europe and increasing interest in and exposure of domestic corruption scandals acted to mobilise public sentiment against corruption, bringing Europe onside and supporting the push for global regulation of corrupt activities.[99] These events reflect the assertion of Passas that 'scandal is an opportunity for reform'.[100] The author notes that 'the role of embarrassment should not be under-estimated as an attempt to partially redress power asymmetries'.[101] The catalysing role of transparency, scandal, and public perceptions is explored further, later in this book. These factors may motivate domestic action in situations of limited political will.

Using the example of the OECD Convention, Abbott and Snidal draw several conclusions regarding the complex interaction between values and interests that shape the creation of multilateral legal instruments. First, values 'provide an important backdrop against which value activists and interest entrepreneurs interact'.[102] Second, in developing multilateral legal instruments 'interests provide a constant pressure'[103] and value activists must behave strategically to establish their goals. Third, the process of developing multilateral legal instruments is dynamic – 'over time, interests generate values'[104] and interest actors may adopt value-based arguments to secure their agendas. Finally, values 'impart a "stickiness" to legal arrangements that hinders backsliding even when powerful interests are involved'.[105]

Abbott and Snidal show that the dynamic conflict and alignment of value-based and interest-based agendas have a range of specific effects on the evolution of multilateral legal instruments. These values and interests shape the development and evolution of prohibition regimes.

The work of theorists including Koh, Twining, and Zumbansen, further enhance analysis of regime evolution. These theorists emphasise the importance of domestic context and diverse values and interests, which not only shape the development of transnational legal instruments, but also impact their domestic application. This perspective is especially useful for the analysis of UNCAC and its implementation and enforcement domestically in PNG. Successful domestic application is essential to overcoming the challenges facing regime evolution from the criminalisation stage to the final stage of the model.

Similar to Abbott and Snidal, Koh emphasises the importance of rationalist interest and normative values. However, Koh is particularly interested in what he terms 'transnational legal process', that is:

> [T]he theory and practice of how public and private actors – nation states, international organisations, multinational enterprises, non-governmental organisations, and private individuals – interact in a variety of public and private, domestic and international fora to make, interpret, enforce, and ultimately, internalize rules of transnational law.[106]

For Koh, global prohibition regimes are essentially transnational. To succeed, they must be internalised and entrenched in domestic legal and political process 'through a complex process of rational self-interest and norm internalization'.[107]

Koh highlights three distinctive features of transnational legal process, which is said to be non-traditional, dynamic, and normative. Transnational legal process is non-traditional in that the dichotomies between domestic and international, public and private are broken down. Both state and non-state actors are involved in the diffusion and internalisation of a transnational regulatory regime and interaction occurs within and between states.[108] This is essentially why the term 'transnational' is used, rather than international, global, domestic, or regional. Transnational legal process is dynamic in that 'transnational law transforms, mutates, and percolates up and down, from the public to the private from the domestic to the international level and back down again'.[109] Therefore, just as a transnational regulatory regime shapes domestic legal processes, domestic processes, both legal and non-legal, have the capacity to re-shape transnational regulatory regimes. Finally, transnational legal process is normative, as the outcome of such a process is the solidification of new laws which are in turn 'interpreted, internalized, and enforced'.[110]

The three distinctive features of transnational legal process established by Koh are reflected by the work of Twining, who discusses the concept of 'global legal pluralism'[111] and 'diffusion of law'.[112,113] Twining is critical of the term 'global legal pluralism' but suggests that utilising elements from social fact legal pluralism in an exploration of law beyond the state may be useful in order to highlight four important points.[114] First, in the analysis of transnational regulatory regimes there is a need to include normative orders beyond the state. Second, law is rarely introduced into a vacuum and thus must interact with existing legal and normative processes and institutions. Third, it is essential to acknowledge the concept of 'interlegality'; that is, the interaction between multiple legal and non-legal (normative) orders, which will influence the application of transnational regulatory regimes in unique domestic contexts. Fourth, even when focusing on the implementation and enforcement of transnational regulatory regimes, it is essential that the relationship between the state and diverse communities and beliefs is acknowledged. This domestic relationship will shape, facilitate, and limit the application of transnational regulatory regimes.

Zumbansen also emphasises the importance of domestic experiences when seeking to understand the implementation and enforcement of transnational regulatory regimes. Zumbansen warns that research into transnational regulatory regimes is often conducted without interest or acknowledgement of national pasts.[115] Drawing on the historical insights of legal pluralism, 'domestic experience with law are crucial points of orientation'[116] when conducting transnational analysis. Many of the challenges faced by transnational regulatory regimes may be understood as unique illustrations of old socio-legal challenges relating to the tension between law and non-law, legality and legitimacy, law and justice, and society or other.[117]

Ultimately, in exploring the development and dissemination of any legal regime, it is important to account for the role of both values and interests. These two forces interact in complex and dynamic ways to shape the potential for, and nature of, global prohibition regimes and their legal tools. Furthermore, diverse values and interests can also shape the implementation and enforcement of multilateral legal tools operating in unique domestic contexts. This influence may affect the nature and relative success of both the legal tool and the regime. A transnational lens is valuable when exploring regime evolution because it acknowledges the importance of values, interests, and actors, that transcend standard divisions between domestic, regional, and international spheres.

As was noted earlier in this chapter, the OECD Convention catalysed the negotiation and entry into force of an additional seven regional and multilateral instruments, each targeting various forms of corrupt activity.[118] This illustrates the momentum gained between the third and fourth stages of regime evolution. Once the target activity is established as a substantial and universal challenge with harmful consequences across diverse contexts, arguments in support of the activity are increasingly difficult to make and justification for a consistent and universal criminal law approach is enhanced.[119]

UNCAC is the most recent multilateral legal instrument for the regulation of corruption. It is also the most widely ratified anti-corruption convention with signatories from diverse geographic, socio-political, economic, and cultural backgrounds. UNCAC represents the culmination of almost 30 years of transnational discourse and interaction regarding universal control of corruption. UNCAC incorporates key values and interests established in preceding legal instruments and represents the solidification of the global anti-corruption regime within the fourth stage of regime evolution. UNCAC is thus the primary multilateral legal instrument explored in this book. A preliminary introduction to this tool of the global anti-corruption regime is presented below.

Introducing the United Nations Convention against Corruption: a transnational criminal law tool of the global anti-corruption regime

Chapter 2 explores UNCAC in detail, analysing its development and the complex interaction of values and interests that contributed to its final form. The introduction presented here provides some necessary background and emphasises the importance of the UNCAC as the primary legal tool of the global anti-corruption regime. This builds the foundation for exploring the limitations and challenges faced by the global anti-corruption regime and implementation and enforcement of UNCAC. These limitations include the challenges presented by Nadelmann and Andreas and discussed above, as well as additional challenges, risks, and limitations that are introuduced below. These challenges and limitations emphasise the problems that arise when attempting to implement and enforce multilateral legal instruments in unique domestic contexts. Implementation and enforcement challenges reflect the dynamics discussed by Abbott and Snidal, Koh, Twining, and Zumbansen. These challenges are often presented as an explanation for the failure of both UNCAC and the anti-corruption regime more generally to achieve substantial reductions in corruption levels globally. To understand what has prevented the regime from achieving the fifth stage of norm evolution, it is necessary to understand these challenges and limitations fully. It will then be possible to suggest options for the future of the regime, including tools and methods for overcoming the most pressing challenges.

UNCAC should be understood first and foremost as a multilateral treaty. Beyond its nature as a treaty, UNCAC seeks the criminalisation of certain acts of corruption and can therefore also be understood as an example of Transnational Criminal Law (TCL), as established by Boister.[120] TCL refers to those multilateral instruments that constitute their own unique area of law, separate from, but at the same time attenuating the distinction between, international law *stricto sensu* and the municipal law of the state.[121] This definition is useful because it emphasises the importance of regional and domestic dynamics in securing implementation and enforcement of TCL and also illustrates the rationale for establishing such laws. This definition is also aligned with the transnational legal theory discussed earlier in this chapter.

Boister draws on Jessup's use of the term transnational law, encompassing 'all law that regulates actions or events that transcend national frontiers',[122] to establish a definition of TCL as 'the indirect suppression by international law through domestic penal law of criminal activities that have actual or potential trans-boundary effects'.[123] Boister's approach is one which carves out a new sphere of law and legal scholarship. This approach illustrates the unique dimensions of, and challenges faced by, UNCAC as a tool of the global anti-corruption regime. The TCL perspective provides the basis for some insightful critiques of the risks and limitations of multilateral legal instruments such as UNCAC. These critiques are relevant to understanding why the global anti-corruption regime has not achieved the fifth and final stage of evolution.

Transnational criminal law is distinguished from international criminal law in at least four, strongly interrelated, ways. First, it is indirect rather than direct. Transnational criminal law relies on domestic penal law for implementation and enforcement compared with international criminal law that establishes institutions beyond the state to regulate and enforce its rules. There are still limitations to the exercise of jurisdiction by international criminal courts, not least the challenge of enforcement, which is dependent on state cooperation.[124] However, in the case of TCL, there is no international court with automatic jurisdiction to hear complaints or adjudicate breaches. Because of this, the central importance of domestic criminal law, domestic courts, domestic enforcement, and transnational cooperation, are enhanced.

Second, TCL can be understood as extra-territorial rather than universal in jurisdiction. While in international criminal law 'the jurisdictional connection is said to be in the interests of international society as a whole',[125] TCL limits its jurisdiction, as defined within the treaty itself, and usually related to some substantive threat or injury, or at least connection, to the state seeking jurisdiction.

Third, the nature of the threat varies between transnational and international criminal law. In the case of TCL, the threat is somewhat more limited than in the case of international criminal law. TCL may be triggered either by 'a factual or phenomenological transnational element'[126] to the crime itself, or a 'normative transnational element'.[127] Nadelmann and Andreas note that 'only those crimes that evidence a strong transnational dimension are likely to become the subject of international prohibitions regimes'.[128] However, such a transnational element is unlikely to meet the threshold of an international crime, which is generally agreed to be a threat to international order and international values.[129]

The fourth distinguishing element between transnational and international criminal law relates to the way international society is constructed, based on the perceived threat of the criminal activity. Boister draws on Abi-Saab,[130] suggesting that 'international society has a variable nature that depends upon the problem faced'.[131] Transnational criminal law presupposes a community interest, but 'sovereignty remains the key restrictive factor'.[132] This contrasts with a Kantian approach suggesting universal solidarity and, to a certain degree, the erosion of sovereignty for the benefit of the global good, as with international criminal law. Nadelmann too acknowledges the importance of the concept of 'international society' in the evolution of global prohibition regimes. He states that:

> Underlying the emergence of most global prohibition regimes and the emergence of much international cooperation in criminal matters has been the evolution of what British scholars have termed 'a universal international

society' grounded in the gradual homogenization and globalization of norms developed initially among the European states.[133]

For Boister, it is important to understand that this international society is more constrained by sovereignty concerns when constructing transnational criminal law, compared to the development of international criminal law. The distinctions made by Boister are somewhat simplified. Even international law *stricto sensu* requires extensive engagement by nation states in terms of domestic legislation and cooperation on issues including investigation, jurisdiction, and extradition. It could be argued that all multilateral instruments should be considered transnationally. However, Boister's definition of transnational criminal law emphasises the unique dynamics likely to impact the operation of multilateral legal instruments (including UNCAC), that operate transnationally. Such dynamics include the importance of national law and the often highly political interaction between international, regional, and domestic spheres which shape the context of implementation and enforcement. In this context, the balance between domestic implementation and enforcement, and the protection of state sovereignty, is a pressing challenge.

Transnational criminal law: concerns and critique

Boister points to several concerns unique to TCL that are reflected in the dominant criticisms of the global anti-corruption regime and its legal tools. Boister argues that 'TCL is probably the most significant existing mechanism for the globalization of substantive criminal norms'.[134] However, he also points out significant deficiencies in the TCL system relating 'to the development of the international components of TCL, the suppression conventions, and . . . the impact of these conventions on the national components of TCL, the crimes themselves'.[135]

With respect to the development of TCL, Boister raises issues regarding democracy deficits in the process of transnational criminalisation, in particular 'the social construction of transnational threats and the appropriateness of transnational penal responses'.[136] In addition to the democracy deficit, only limited attention is paid to human rights concerns within the criminalisation framework. Furthermore, there is extensive potential for co-optation and coercion in the control and diffusion of the TCL system. Relating to national components of the TCL system, Boister notes doctrinal weakness due to a reliance on domestic law for implementation and enforcement. Transnational Criminal Law tends to assume 'the existence of fully developed domestic penal systems',[137] where often none exist. Additional concerns include overlap and influence from other related legislation, and limited enforcement power beyond diplomacy and political influence are also concerns. Domestic overlap and conflict between domestic law and transnational law reflect the perspective of other transnational authors, including Twining and Zumbansen. In general, many of the concerns raised regarding the limits of TCL reflect criticisms of the global anti-corruption regime and UNCAC. These specific criticisms are introduced below.

Criticisms of UNCAC and the global anti-corruption regime

As noted by John Lea, 'crime has no ontological reality. Criminalisation is one of the many ways of constructing social reality'.[138] Accepting this view, promoting corruption as a transnational crime and a threat that must be dealt with through coordinated law and transnational law enforcement, constructs this social reality, which in turn has its own set of consequences. This perspective aligns with Nadelmann and Andreas' assertion that movement between the first and second stage of regime evolution requires a redefinition of the target activity. This redefining process involves construction of the activity as having transnational effects that are harmful to states or groups of actors within states. This threat construction is usually reactionary, responding to specific events or sentiments, and therefore may not be based on sound reasoning and research regarding the potential side effects or consequences of transnational criminalisation or criminal law and enforcement measures.[139] As Harfield warns, often 'the very mechanisms of regulation and control create the potential illicit markets for criminals to exploit'.[140] This is aligned with the idea of regulatory asymmetries discussed by Passas. These asymmetries can themselves create criminal opportunities, even if they are the result of criminalisation efforts.[141]

The transnational approach to corruption justifies criminalisation on the basis of harm and related threats to economic and social development, the rule of law, and even national security. The multilateral legal instruments developed to combat corruption use common language when they condemn corrupt activity, taking a largely moralist approach to the issue. Several regional and international treaties cite the relationship between corruption and other criminal activity as further justification for its criminalisation.[142] However, some critics argue that this approach is an oversimplification. Without establishing a clear definition of corruption, there is a risk that the justification for action may pre-empt the harm or criminality that it purports to prevent and punish. Critiques of the global anti-corruption regime, and global prohibition regimes generally, are plentiful. Many criticisms raise important points about the nature and impact of such regimes.

Beare warns that 'corruption (or a focus on corruption), may be the means towards very diverse ends and each may have a different impact on the society'.[143] This illustrates that the nature of the crime and motivation for criminal behaviour will impact the effectiveness of prohibition activities. Furthermore, the nature of the suggested cure may say more about the goals of the proponents than the nature of the target activity. There may even be situations where the proscribed cure is designed to have a different impact than the one publically promoted by the proponents.

Reed argues that more attention must be paid to the 'unintentional side effects' of policies designed to tackle corruption.[144] This is a view supported by Tusikov who argues that risk analysis related to transnational organised crime threats should take into account collateral damage of counter-measures, as well as harm directly resulting from the crime.[145] One report notes: 'anti-corruption interventions that are misapplied, misunderstood or mismatched have the potential of hardening and shifting corrupt practices to less detectable, more robust forms'.[146] The same report points to the possibility that, in the case of water resources, anti-corruption efforts may in fact harm the poor, cutting off their access to water in the short term.[147] Shah and Schacter put forward several examples of 'failed' anti-corruption efforts. One example is the decentralisation efforts in the Philippines during the 1990s. The authors suggest that 'decentralization may multiply, rather than limit, opportunities for corruption if implemented under the wrong circumstances.'[148] In such cases, the goal of regulatory change may in fact have been decentralisation. Anti-corruption programmes can be used by proponents as a smoke screen for this alternative, political, agenda. This possible duplicity complicates analysis of anti-corruption policies and may impact regime success.

Reed argues that the reason for harmful side effects relates to 'a tendency to be reacting to a crisis rather than tackling underlying causes'.[149] Such a view is supported by Nadelmann and Andreas who note the prominence of a catalysing event that promotes a redefining of the target activity.[150] This reactionary approach often fails to base its strategies on proper research and analysis concerning the underlying causes of the crisis and thus the best method for addressing them. The result is a legislative and law enforcement focus that is unlikely to consider the relevant contextual factors of society, culture, history, geography, and politics. These factors influence the nature and extent of corruption and thus the most effective means for its prevention and suppression. Reed further argues:

> Nowhere is the ineffectiveness of the criminal law enforcement approach more clear than in efforts to tackle the illegal production, trafficking, and distribution of drugs . . . In practice, the effect of the 'War on Drugs' does not appear to have been to reduce consumption . . . many argue that the war has effectively created failed and failing states by encouraging systemic corruption and/or violence as the means for organised narco-criminals to maintain their operations, as well as having other negative side-effects.[151]

This view reflects Nadelmann and Andreas' perspective on the impossibility of an effective drug prohibition regime. The authors argue that it is the third category of challenges, related to the nature of the target activity, that prevent the drug prohibition regime from succeeding.

> [P]rohibition laws, like prohibition laws directed at prostitution, gambling and other vices, can powerfully affect the nature of the activity and the market, but they cannot effectively deter or suppress most of those determined to participate in the activity.[152]

When combined with the fact that no substantial expertise or resources are required to produce drugs, they are easily concealed by all involved parties, and victims do not have an interest in notifying criminal justice authorities, the enforcement challenge is further expanded. This last factor, relating to reporting incentives, is the direct result of the criminal law enforcement approach that has been adopted in response to the target activity. It illustrates how the approach can shape the nature of the activity and the environment in which it operates, but may not always support an actual decrease in instances of the activity.

The global drug prohibition regime was a product of US and European dominance in the international sphere. Nadelmann argues that it was reactionary, in the manner suggested by Reed. Efforts by the US, both domestically and internationally, to suppress drug use and trafficking in drugs, have been driven by fear, moralistic abhorrence, a sense of righteousness, and the compulsion to proselytise.[153] This driving force has resulted in a particularly strict prohibition regime, despite the fact that other states and regions may have adopted a more flexible regime, reflecting unique aspects of their societies and cultures.[154] Again, the importance of culture and context become apparent. Furthermore, as societal norms change, regimes may need to adapt. This may be a further challenge for the rigid criminal law and enforcement approach.[155]

Reed's assertion, that the prohibition regime against drug trafficking has contributed to systemic corruption, warrants further exploration. It suggests that the interaction between corruption and other forms of criminality may not be based upon the nature of the crimes, but may result from incentives established through the mechanisms of criminalisation. This reflects Passas, who notes that when states resort to criminal justice methods they often 'provide incentives for more sophisticated organization of crime and raise the price of corruption'.[156] Extending this concept significantly, McCulloch suggests that the apparent failure of law enforcement and legislative approaches to transnational criminal threats like organised crime and corruption illustrate a success, if viewed in a different light.[157] The author argues that 'criminal justice concerns are being used increasingly as a tool of foreign policy'.[158] Thus, instead of viewing side effects of current crime and corruption policies as unintentional, McCulloch suggests that the side effects of such policies are in fact well understood. Referring to the dominant policy approach to transnational criminal threats as the 'war on' model, the author argues that this approach almost always results in failure of the publically promoted goal of reducing the relevant crime.[159] However, such policies are often 'successful' in fulfilling their unpublicised political purposes, namely the maintenance of the Military Industrial Complex and the 'expansion, consolidation, and intensification of neoliberal globalization'.[160]

McCulloch argues that national security interests have eclipsed social security concerns. The international fora thus become a location for 'policy laundering', where political state-centric agendas are transformed into what appear to be rational global norms.[161] Some parallels can be drawn between this critical view and the assertions of Nadelmann and Andreas regarding the centrality of hegemonic state actors in the early stages of regime development.[162] Certainly, as will be seen in Chapter 2, states involved in the negotiation of UNCAC were concerned with protecting their sovereignty. This concern shaped the outcome of negotiations. Furthermore, negotiation of an Implementation Review Mechanism was challenging, as many states 'were concerned that the process could be misused for political ends'.[163] This suggests that states are acutely aware of the policy laundering potential of global prohibition regimes and their legal tools. The risks of policy laundering are substantial and noteworthy. However, McCulloch avoids taking a stance on any specific 'crime' and does not offer much in the way of alternative models or suggested improvements. Her arguments act more as a warning of the dangers of the status quo, rather than presenting any substantial suggestions for alteration or development.

Carr also warns of the dangers and side effects of the current approach to combatting corruption. He argues that, in an attempt to criminalise corruption, issues of due process have been disregarded, threatening the fundamental underpinnings of the rule of law and impinging on individual rights (especially in regards to 'illicit enrichment' as an act of corruption).[164] This view aligns with the earlier criticisms of TCL raised by Boister, regarding democracy deficits in regime construction. Carr does not challenge the underlying harms of corruption, but warns against the dominant approach focused on criminalisation and law enforcement. He suggests that a process of 're-socialization' is also necessary.[165] This process involves 'making people aware of the long term effects of corruption',[166] building awareness and educating people who may not realise how corruption impacts them and their lives, societies, and economies. 'Re-socialisation' is something that dominant actors such as the UN and the World Bank have promoted discursively in their anti-corruption efforts. The concept has even been alluded to in conventions like UNCAC, which supports participation of Civil Society in anti-corruption efforts and various preventive measures.[167] The Implementation Review Mechanism for UNCAC encourages involvement by non-state actors and promotes dialogue between and within *States Parties* about best practices and unique experiences with application of UNCAC domestically.

These methods of engagement are limited, as they do not question the moralistic underpinnings of the existing approach and opportunities for reshaping the regime appear limited. Opportunities to engage in the dynamic potential of transnational legal process, discussed by Koh, seem to be one-dimensional in the context of the global anti-corruption regime. Anti-corruption norms and methods move from the international to the domestic sphere and then horizontally between states. Without genuine opportunities to reshape the regime at the international level, the possibility of altering and improving the underlying approach is limited. Thus, critiques of the dominant approach are likely to remain relevant. Corva, with special reference to the war on drugs, notes that criminalisation, as a means to target a specific activity, can act to isolate and exclude. The threat is depoliticised and ignores relevant contextual factors including class, gender, race, and international power dynamics.[168]

The failure of the global anti-corruption regime to acknowledge relevant contextual factors is perhaps its most far-reaching criticism. Some authors, such as Bridenthal, argue for a more rationalist approach to understanding corruption, acknowledging that corruption in early modern Europe was often mobilised for political change. Bridenthal suggests a link between the emergence of globally intensified dynamics of corruption and globalisation relating to labour, production, and international finance.[169] Other authors emphasise the importance of context in shaping both the nature of the target activity and the motivation to combat it. Henshaw argues that current efforts to combat corruption and crime in the South Pacific region are abstract and do not focus on specific difficulties experienced by Pacific Island countries.[170] The possibility of policy laundering is raised again in this context.

> Development of a regional response to transnational crime has not arisen from strong evidence of actual damage caused to Forum Island Countries by transnational crime. Rather, it has been motivated largely by powerful partners' concerns about the threats to themselves posed by weak legal regimes and law enforcement in the island countries, accompanied by a fairly generic argument about potential harm to Forum Island Countries.[171]

Henshaw argues that, in order to be effective, any anti-corruption or transnational crime policy in the South Pacific 'must show respect and sensitivity to the limited resources and relative priorities facing the Pacific Island Countries'.[172]

The importance of context is further emphasised by Reed, noting the relationship between corruption, the state, and organised crime. Reed states that the following factors all play a role in the nature of organised criminal activity:

> . . . geographical size, geographical location, the degree of consolidation of state authority or power, the aims of the political/administrative elite, political and administrative structure, ethnic structure and relations, the structure of the licit and illicit economy, and levels and distribution of income.[173]

Reed provides examples where legislative and law enforcement strategies that fail to acknowledge these factors have failed to achieve their anti-crime and corruption goals and have contributed to increase levels of one or both undesirable activity. These examples include efforts to eradicate opium production in Afghanistan, as well as the failures of anti-organised crime policies in Central and South America, particularly the case of Columbian Coca production.[174] Reed's discussion reflects Nadelmann and Andreas' model of regime evolution and the challenges that must be overcome to achieve the fifth and final stage of evolution. Nadelmann and Andreas cite maintained political will as essential for regime success and emphasise the impact of vacuums of sovereignty, preventing successful enforcement.[175] These vacuums can be related to geographic factors, where the physical presence of the state is difficult to maintain.[176] Furthermore, the target activity's susceptibility to criminal law and enforcement measures relates to the structure of both licit and illicit economies, in particular the demand for the target activity and the potential for licit substitutes.[177]

Schutte uses the Indonesian Corruption Eradication Commission (KPK) as an illustration of a relatively successful anti-corruption initiative that was 'home grown' and thus based on a more holistic understanding of contextual factors relevant to the programme's success.[178] This suggests that while a failure to acknowledge context will limit success, policies and programmes designed with context in mind may be able to reduce the target activity, despite encountering substantial challenges. It should be noted that Schutte's KPK example is technical rather than holistic in its analysis. The author notes that, between 2005 and 2009, only 51% of defendants indicted by the Attorney-General's Office were found guilty, but until October 2011 100% of KPK defendants were found guilty.[179] This suggests extremely high effectiveness with respect to the KPK. However, the author goes on to point out that the KPK only took on 3% of the overall number of corruption cases between 2004 and 2009 and that a peculiarity of the KPK requires all cases to be brought to court. This makes the KPK 'extra cautious in the selection of cases it brings to the investigation stage'[180] and may account for the high conviction rate, high quality of evidence and low number of cases compared to other agencies. This example illustrates the difficulties with effectively evaluating policies and programmes designed to target complex behaviours like corruption.

In addition to the challenges of measurement and evaluation, Windybank points to the role of societal, economic and political factors in influencing the success of anti-corruption policies and programmes.[181] The author argues that 'better governance and law enforcement are only possible with improvements in economic, social, and political conditions'.[182]

> Corruption cannot be addressed if there is no economy outside resources and aid. Only the demands of citizens can improve governance, and demands are more likely to arise with jobs, rising incomes, and better living standards. The South Pacific is a rare case where strategic and humanitarian interests converge.[183]

From all corners of the critical arena, there is a call for greater breadth of analysis when exploring the causes of corruption and the appropriate means for preventing and suppressing corrupt activities and their associated harms. It is essential to account for variation in the nature and effects of corruption based on unique social, economic, political or cultural, and legal dynamics. A moralistic approach that suggests a set of overarching and universal harms related to corruption and ignoring contextual factors, may be a dangerous tool for policy laundering, having harmful side effects when applied in diverse contexts, and is also likely to fail in achieving its stated goals.

The critical literature introduced above raises valuable points regarding the limitations and dangers of the existing approach of the global anti-corruption regime. However, there is limited research exploring the validity of such criticism in practice, based on a case study methodology.[184] This book undertakes such a case study, analysing the interaction between transnational anti-corruption law (specifically UNCAC) and the social, political cultural, economic, and legal contexts that affect its implementation and enforcement.

Four primary risk factors

The analysis in this book pays careful attention to four regime risk factors. These regime risk factors stem from the criticisms of UNCAC and the global anti-corruption regime that were introduced above. Each of these four factors aligns with and supplements the challenges presented by Nadelmann and Andreas in their five-stage model.

Risk factor one: diversity and definition

The first regime risk factor relates to the diversity, complexity, and controversy surrounding attempts to measure and manage corruption. The challenges of measurement and management in part stem from pre-existing definitional challenges which in turn result from the ubiquitous nature of corruption, combined with the diversity and secretive character of corrupt activities.[185] Despite the continuing disagreement surrounding the nature, definition, and dangers of corruption, the global anti-corruption regime has evolved to use a criminalisation and law enforcement approach in an attempt to deal with the perceived harms of corrupt activity. The regime utilises regional and transnational legal instruments that attempt to enlist the cooperation of all states regardless of economic, social, cultural, or geographic variation.

Most of these multilateral legal instruments deal with the contested nature and diversity of the perceived corruption threat by avoiding any definition at all.[186] Not even UNCAC, the most widely ratified anti-corruption treaty, provides guidance on this issue. This lack of definition may allow for abuse of regime tools and potentially contribute to the continuation or even creation of harms, rather than their mitigation. As noted by Beare, corruption rhetoric may be used as a political tool with contextual dimensions often being disregarded.[187] Harmful side effects of this form of policy laundering include stigmatisation of nations struggling with corruption. These states may be unwilling or unable to adopt the standardised approach to anti- corruption supported by the global anti-corruption regime. If states are stigmatised or ostracised by the international community, the result may be continued or intensified instances of the target activity in that jurisdiction, or creation of new asymmetries that contribute to other forms of undesirable activity. Furthermore, if the regime was established through uneven participation and a failure to acknowledge the diversity of contexts in which corruption occurs, the resulting legal tools may be ineffective when implemented and enforced domestically, draining resources and worsening rather than elevating an already fragile situation. Without a clear definition of the target activity, there is a danger that implementing states, especially those already steeped in corruption, may interpret UNCAC to appear compliant, while allowing for the continuation of corrupt activities.[188]

Risk factor two: corruption as facilitation – the organised crime link

The second regime risk factor relates to the relationship between corruption and the 'war on' organised crime. Academic authors and international organisations have argued that corruption and transnational organised crime are intrinsically linked. In combination with other risks, the perceived link between corruption and organised crime may contribute to ineffective and potentially harmful anti-corruption policies. A 2010 report by the Center for the Study of Democracy asserts that 'political corruption is organised crime's most powerful tool'.[189] This view of corruption as a tool of organised crime enhances its potential harm and threat to global society. The speech of the UN Secretary General at the adoption of UNCAC demonstrates that this link is supported by actors at the international level. In the speech, the Secretary General notes that 'Corruption is an insidious plague that has a wide range of corrosive effects on societies . . . and allows organised crime, terrorism and other threats to human security to flourish'.[190] The preamble to UNCAC links corruption 'and other forms of crime, in particular organised crime and economic crime, including money-laundering'.[191] Based on these links, the preamble goes on to state that 'corruption is no longer a local matter but a transnational phenomenon that affects all societies and economies, making international cooperation to prevent and control it essential'.[192] It is also noteworthy that the negotiation of UNCAC followed the development of the UN Convention against Transnational Organised Crime (UNTOC) and introductory materials to UNCAC emphasise that the new convention compliments this existing framework.[193]

The National Institute of Justice Panel Discussion on Organised Crime discusses links between organised criminal activity and corruption, noting the role of facilitators and complicit as well as unknowing actors who operate in legitimate markets but aid illicit networks.[194] Some authors who are critical of the global anti-corruption regime note the links between transnational organised crime and corruption. Harfield argues that 'the illicit-legitimate nexus (the corruption necessary to sustain large-scale organised crime) poses as great if not a greater threat to society in general than does the crime-terror nexus'.[195] Reed argues that corruption can be understood as '. . . one of the primary enabling activities of organised crime, it makes possible and/or facilitates the conduct of these types of criminal activities'.[196]

The relationship between corruption and transnational organised crime appears to be generally accepted.[197] However, the link raises concerns for many commentators, especially regarding the negative side effects and additional harms caused by laws and policies designed to target both issues together. Concern is focused on the effects of these policies on each other, and on the societies in which they are enforced. McCulloch warns of countermeasures that 'work as proxies for (future) crimes, in effect creating the crime they are countering'.[198] Policy laundering is also a substantial concern in this context.[199] Thus, it could be argued that when an already loosely defined threat, such as corruption, is linked to the highly politicised and often sensationalised threat of transnational organised crime, the potential for negative side effects is increased.

Even if both threats are substantial and regime efforts are legitimate, the existing approach to transnational organised crime and corruption has been largely ineffectual. Reed notes several cases where attempts to deal with the transnational organised crime threat have led to increased levels of social harm and corruption.[200] Examples of failure illustrate the dangers of under-researched and reactionary policies aimed at targeting transnational organised crime and corruption issues. Reed defines the impact of these failures as 'squeezing the balloon'.[201] This occurs when well-intentioned policies result in unintentional side effects that shift and in some cases magnify, rather than reduce the problem and harms related to criminal activity.[202] This danger is linked, not only to the relationship between transnational organised crime and corruption policies, but to the nature of those policies. In the author's words, 'there is a pressing need to correct the current bias towards criminal law enforcement solutions'.[203]

Risk factor three: the criminal law enforcement method

Keeping in mind the risks already mentioned – both the loose definition of corruption and the links between transnational organised crime and anti-corruption policy – the focus of the global anti-corruption regime on criminalisation and criminal law enforcement measures is concerning. Snider and Kidane note that:

> [T]he most important substantive measures that the FCPA, the IACAC, the UNCAC, and the AU Corruption Convention all adopt in order to combat corrupt practices in transnational commercial relations is the *criminalisation* of certain conduct and omissions.[204]

This focus on criminalisation may be problematic, especially when the challenge of corruption is understood within the context of diverse social, cultural, and political environments that influence the nature, extent, and effects of corruption and anti-corruption policy in practice.

The modern 21st Century approach to corruption is a complex hybrid of moralist and revisionist views.[205] The global anti-corruption regime emphasises the moral repugnance and societal harms of corruption, but international instruments are careful to defend state sovereignty and acknowledge variation in legal and social norms. Despite this hybrid approach, the distinction remains important for understanding the challenges and limitations of anti-corruption law today. The revisionist view stemmed partially from a political preoccupation with communism, where corruption could be seen as the lesser of two evils.[206] However, the revisionist approach also recognises the contextual elements of diverse societies which contributed to the nature of politics and economics, shaping the relationships between government and other actors, and influencing perceptions of corruption. Moving beyond a simplistic view that it is culturally acceptable to act in a corrupt manner in some societies, the revisionist approach recognises that 'before we seek to understand how or why corruption works, we must first be familiar with the context in which it occurs'.[207] This contrasts with a traditional moralist approach, where all corrupt activity is deemed to be harmful and consistent universal action to eliminate corrupt activity is the only viable solution. Beare warns that in countries where political and economic instability are rife, the temptation is to blame corruption and promote anti-corruption law and law enforcement as the solution. However, it is important to acknowledge that 'corruption may not be to blame for this chaos, but in fact may be reflective of it'.[208] Bridenthal supports this view, noting that historically corruption has often been a means for groups to mobilise for political change or secure social outcomes otherwise restricted by formal structures.[209] This emphasis on context reflects the theories of Koh, Twining and Zumbansen, who focus on the importance of context in enabling successful implementation and enforcement efforts domestically.[210]

The dominant criminal law enforcement approach to corruption, promoted through the global anti-corruption regime, is limited in its ability to acknowledge the diversity of political, cultural, and economic structures within states where the laws and policies must be implemented. The risk is that such laws and policies will be wholly ineffective and potentially harmful. If the underlying causes of corruption in a given context are not acknowledged, Reed's concept of squeezing the balloon – simply shifting the problem to other realms of society – will again become relevant. Furthermore, as illustrated by Henshaw, if law does not recognise the specific challenges that exist in a given context and the potential harms that may develop as a result of the laws and policies themselves, the situation may worsen, or at best stagnate.[211]Beare notes that 'just as new government arrangements and new political alignments create new opportunities for corrupt officials, so do new regulations and new laws'.[212] Building on this assertion and adding in the dimension of organised crime, Harfield states that 'the very mechanisms of regulation and control create the potential illicit markets for criminals to exploit'.[213] To combat this risk, a more holistic approach may be necessary going beyond criminalisation and law enforcement and targeting root causes, which in turn may vary across different contexts.

Risk factor four: the limits of a singular solution

This brings us to the final risk factor, the potential inapplicability of a universal anti-corruption approach to the myriad of unique domestic contexts that exist globally. This risk factor is reflected in all three of the factors already discussed above. It is the most general and most substantial risk faced by the global anti-corruption regime. In seeking a universal and consistent approach to combatting corruption, the regime and its legal tools risk ignoring important contextual elements that may affect the nature of corruption in a given state, the causes of that corruption, and the best approach for combatting it.

These four factors – the diversity and complexity of corruption as a concept, the perceived links between corruption and organised crime, the dominant focus on criminal and enforcement measures, and the general risk of inapplicability inherent to a universal approach – must be taken into account when exploring the implementation and enforcement of the global anti-corruption regime through multilateral legal instruments such as UNCAC. These factors stand out as the most obvious points of weakness for the global anti-corruption regime. All four factors individually, and especially when taken together, have the potential to limit the effectiveness of anti-corruption laws and policies that seek to reduce and mitigate harms associated with corrupt activity. Furthermore, these risk factors raise the possibility that transnational anti-corruption laws, when implemented, may create additional harms or even contribute to the social and economic instability that has been used to justify action in the first place.

The criticisms and regime risk factors discussed above point to some limitations of the global anti-corruption regime. The challenges are substantial when seeking to apply regime legal tools such as UNCAC across diverse geographic, socio-political, economic, and cultural contexts. The critiques of the global anti-corruption regime align with the risks and challenges introduced by Nadelmann and Andreas, regarding transition from the fourth to the final stage of regime evolution. However, specific criticisms of UNCAC and the global anti-corruption regime are based primarily on theoretical assumptions and abstract observation. This book is the first to evaluate such criticisms through empirical research and a case study of UNCAC's implementation and enforcement in PNG. The reader's understanding of UNCAC and the global anti-corruption regime will be enhanced by this case study approach to critical analysis.

Summary and research agenda: four key research questions

UNCAC is the main focus of the research, as the primary multilateral legal tool of the global anti-corruption regime. Analysing its evolution, implementation, and enforcement using the case study of PNG will provide vital insight into the challenges faced by the regime and possible improvements that may support continued evolution and ultimate success of the global anti-corruption regime.

In the chapters that follow, four key research questions are answered:

1. How has UNCAC evolved within the emergent global anti-corruption regime?
2. What impact has UNCAC had on PNG's approach to combatting corruption?
3. Does PNG's experience with implementation and enforcement of UNCAC support existing theoretical and practical criticisms of UNCAC and the emergent global anti-corruption regime more generally?
4. What insights does the PNG case study provide in terms of potential improvements to UNCAC and to engagement with, implementation, and enforcement of, the Convention; with the goal of securing the final stage of evolution for the global anti-corruption regime?

Chapter 2 explores the negotiation of UNCAC and its place within the global anti-corruption regime. A preliminary answer to the first research question is provided at the end of that chapter.

Chapter 3 lays the foundation for the domestic case study; exploring the regional dynamics in the South Pacific and the unique actors, values, and interests that have shaped corruption and anti-corruption efforts in this region. Chapter 4 details the history, society, culture, economy, and politics of PNG as they are relevant to corruption in the country and existing efforts to combat corruption domestically.

Chapter 5 documents the fieldwork process and interview findings conducted by the author. Key insights gained from semi-structured interviews with diverse actors from government, multilateral organisations, intergovernmental bodies, NGOs, and Civil Society groups are presented here. The qualitative research conducted for this book is well suited to exploring the complex interaction between actors from international, regional, and domestic spheres. 'Interviews can reveal ideas and deliver insights no other method can provide'.[214] The analysis in Chapters 5 and 6 emphasise the unique perceptions and experiences of participants, in relation to corruption and the role of UNCAC in combatting corrupt activity.

All interview insights are analysed within the theoretical framework of diverse actors, interests, and values that interact across geographical, socio-political, legal, economic, and cultural contexts. Interview responses enhance understanding of the nature of the global anti-corruption regime in practice, and assist in the evaluation of criticisms levelled at UNCAC and the global anti-corruption regime. Interviews provide insight into the experiences of actors engaged with, affected by, or excluded from, the development and functioning of the regime and its legal tools.

Chapter 6 answers the second and third research questions for this book. Findings from the empirical research are resituated within the broader geopolitical, social, legal, economic, and cultural context of the global anti-corruption regime and the negotiation, implementation, and enforcement of UNCAC.

Ultimately, Chapter 6 summarises the evolution of UNCAC and its role as a tool of the global anti-corruption regime, presenting findings on the impact of UNCAC in the PNG context and suggesting what this means for criticisms of this legal tool, and the global anti-corruption regime more generally. The primary challenges faced by UNCAC in PNG are discussed, focusing on the future of UNCAC and the regime as a whole.

Chapter 7 answers the final research question and suggests possible actions to enhance the potential success of the global anti-corruption regime. Success of the regime is understood as achievement of the final stage of evolution: the substantial reduction of corruption levels globally. Chapter 7 also presents a continuing research agenda, emphasiing the need for sustained analysis of regime operation in various contexts, focusing on the experiences of diverse actors and the factors that motivate behaviour. The chapter presents opportunities for enhancing the regime and its legal tools through facilitation of feedback loops, adaptability, and cross sector engagement.

Notes

1 Nadelmann EA, 'Global prohibition regimes: The evolution of norms in international society' 44(4) *International Organization* (22 May 1990) 479
2 Nadelmann EA and Andreas P, *Policing the Globe: Criminalization and crime control in international relations* (Oxford University Press, 1st Edition, 2006) at 20

3 Farrales M, 'What is Corruption? A history of corruption studies and the great definitions debate', *University of San Diego Working Paper Series* [2005] available at: http://papers.ssrn.com/sol3/papers.cfm?abstract_id=1739962 (last visited 1 March 2018); Schloenhardt A, 'Fighting Organised Crime in the Asia Pacific Region: New weapons, lost wars' 2 *Asian Journal of International Law* (2012) 137; McCulloch J, 'Transnational Crime as Productive Fiction' 24(2) *Social Justice* (2007) 19
4 Koven SG, *Responsible Governance: A case study approach* (ME Sharpe, 1st Edition, 2008) at 44
5 ABC News, Cochrain and team, *PNG Anti-corruption Taskforce Broke after Making Allegations against Prime Minister Peter O'Neill* (5 February 2015) available at: http://www.abc.net.au/news/2015-02-04/png-anti-corruption-taskforce-starved-of-funding/6070170 (last visited 1 March 2018)
6 Farrales, above n3
7 ibid.
8 ibid. at 7. The revisionist position reflects the first stage of regime evolution following the model of Nadelmann and Andreas, above n2
9 Farrales, above n3 at 10
10 World Bank, 'People and Development: Annual Meeting Address by James D Wolfenshon' (1 October 1996) No. 99712.
11 ibid. at 10
12 ibid.
13 These organisations include: the World Bank, IMF, Transparency International (TI), Organisation for Economic Cooperation and Development (OECD), and United Nations (UN)
14 See *Convention on Combating Bribery of Foreign Public Officials in International Business Transactions*, signed 17 December 1997, 37 ILM 1 (entered into force 15 February 1999) ('OECD Convention'). The Commentaries included in the text of this convention (at 14(2)), note 'This Convention seeks to assure a functional equivalence among the measures taken by the Parties to sanction bribery of foreign public officials, without requiring uniformity or changes in fundamental principles of a party's legal system'. See also the *United Nations Convention against Corruption*, opened for signature 9 December 2003, 2349 UNTS 41 (entered into force 14 December 2005) ('UNCAC'), which makes consistent references to the phrase 'where appropriate and in accordance with the fundamental principles of its legal system'
15 Farrales, above n3 at 32
16 ibid. at 25
17 Beare ME, 'Corruption and Organised Crime: Lessons from History' 28 *Crime, Law and Social Change* (1997) 155
18 ibid.
19 ibid.; see also: Corva D, 'Neoliberal Globalization and the War on Drugs: Transnationalizing illiberal governance in the Americas' 27 *Political Geography* (2008) 176; McCulloch J, 'Transnational Crime as Productive Fiction' 24(2) *Social Justice* (2007) 19; Wonders N, 'Globalization, Border Reconstruction Projects, and Transnational Crime' 34(2) *Social Justice* (2007) 33
20 See Harfield C, 'The organization of "organized crime policing" and its international context' 8 *Criminology and Criminal Justice* (2008) 483; Picarelli JT, 'Responding to Transnational Organized Crime — Supporting research, improving practice' 268 *NIJ Journal* (2011) 4; Reed Q, 'Squeezing a Balloon? Challenging the nexus between organised crime and corruption' (7) *CMI U4 Issue* (2009); Sandgren C, 'Combating Corruption: The Misunderstood Role of Law' 39 *International Law* (2005) 717
21 above n1
22 above n2

23 Throughout this book, 'the model' or 'the five-stage model' refers to Nadelmann and Andreas' five-stage model, unless otherwise stated.
24 Krasner SD, 'Structural causes and regime consequences: regimes as intervening variables' 36(2) *International Organizations* (1982) 186
25 ibid. at 187
26 ibid. at 195
27 *United Nations Convention against Corruption*, opened for signature 9 December 2003, 2349 UNTS 41 (entered into force 14 December 2005) ('*UNCAC*')
28 Ratification status as of October 2017: https://www.unodc.org/unodc/en/corruption/ratification- status.html (last visited 1 March 2018)
29 above n2 at 7
30 Passas N, 'Globalization and Transnational Crime: Effects of criminogenic asymmetries', in Williams P and Vlassis D (Eds), *Combatting Transnational Crime: Concepts, Activities and Responses* (Frank Cass, 2013) 22 at 23
31 ibid.
32 ibid. 26–27
33 ibid. 27–28
34 ibid. at 26–27
35 ibid. at 28
36 ibid.
37 ibid. at 33
38 Passas N, 'Globalization, Criminogenic Asymmetries and Economic Crime' 1(4) *European Journal of Law Reform* (1999) 399 at 406
39 above n30 at 29
40 above n38 at 414
41 above n30 at 28
42 ibid. at 40
43 Andreas P, 'Illicit Globalization: Myths, misconceptions, and historical lessons' 126 *Political Science Quarterly* 3 (2011) 403, at 423
44 above n1
45 above n2 at 20
46 above n1
47 above n1 at 480
48 above n2. See also Murphy MN, *Small Boats, Weak States, Dirty Money: Piracy and maritime terrorism in the modern world* (ME Sharpe, 1st Edition, 2008)
49 Weissbrodt D, 'Slavery', *Max Planck Encyclopedia of Public International Law* (March 2014) available at: http://opil.ouplaw.com.wwwproxy0.library.unsw.edu.au/view/10.1093/law:epil/ 9780199231690/law-9780199231690-e874?rskey=4vfgfh&result=1&prd=OPIL (last visited 1 March 2018)
50 above n2
51 ibid.
52 ibid.
53 ibid.
54 ibid. at 21
55 ibid.
56 ibid.
57 ibid.
58 above n2. Nadelmann (above n1 at 485) also notes that the exact point at which a regime comes into existence is flexible and up for debate.
59 above n2 at 21
60 ibid.
61 ibid.
62 ibid.

63 ibid.
64 UNODC, *World Drug Report* (2014) No. E.14.XI.7
65 See Andreas (above n43), who provides an insightful exploration of the limitations of a criminal law enforcement approach to trafficking and transnational crime
66 above n2 at 56
67 above n1 at 484. The author uses several examples to illustrate this point including with regard to Piracy which was 'widely sanctioned in much of the world' (486). Slavery is another example of an activity once seen to be legitimate which has since become the subject of an extensive and extremely successful global prohibition regime (491)
68 Carr I, 'Corruption, legal solution and limits of law' 3(3) *International Journal of Law in Context* (2007) 227
69 Abbott KW and Snidal D, 'Values and Interests: International legalization in the fight against corruption' 31 *Journal of Legal Studies* (2002) 141
70 Elliot KA, *Corruption and the Global Economy* (Institute for International Economics, 1997) at 157
71 above n1
72 ibid.
73 ibid. at 482
74 above n2 at 19
75 above n69
76 The founders of TI were executives from General Electric. TI continues to be sponsored by corporates, in addition to government agencies, the list includes Shell and Ernst & Young, with members of TI's Business Principles Steering Committee including BP, Rio Tinto, Shell, HSBC, Corona, PricewaterhouseCoopers, and Tata and Sons
77 above n1
78 ibid.
79 ibid. at 485
80 ibid. at 481
81 ibid. at 480
82 above n69 at 144
83 ibid. at 142
84 *Convention on Combating Bribery of Foreign Public Officials in International Business Transactions*, opened for signature 17 December 1997, 37 ILM 1 (entered into force 15 February 1999) ('OECD Convention')
85 *Inter-American Convention against Corruption*, opened for signature 29 March 1996, 35 ILM 724 (entered into force 6 March 1997) ('OAS Convention'). This convention was adopted before the OECD Convention. However, the OAS Convention was the result of regional agreement between States of the Americas and therefore does not reflect a transnational perspective and approach to the same extent as the OECD Convention
86 above n68. In this text Carr notes that there are a total of nine regional and multilateral legal instruments against corruption, including the OAS Convention and the OECD Convention.
87 above n69 at 158
88 Feld K, 'Controlling the Prosecution of Bribery: Applying corporate law principles to define a "Foreign Official" in the Foreign Corrupt Practices Act' 88(1) *Washington Law Review* (2013) 245, quoting HR Report No 95–640 (1997) at 4–6
89 above n69
90 Foreign Corrupt Practices Act (1997) 15 USC §§ 78dd–1 (FCPA)
91 above n69
92 ibid.
93 ibid. at 162

94 ibid.
95 ibid.
96 OAS Convention
97 OECD Convention
98 above n69 at 168
99 ibid.
100 above n30 at 51
101 ibid.
102 above n69 at 176
103 ibid.
104 ibid.
105 ibid.
106 Koh HH, 'Transnational Legal Process' 75 *Neb. L. Rev.* (1996) 181
107 ibid. at 199
108 ibid.
109 ibid. at 184
110 ibid.
111 Twining W, 'Normative and Legal Pluralism' 20 *Duke Journal of Comparative & International Law* (2010) 473
112 Twining W, 'Diffusion of Law: A global perspective' 49 *Journal of Legal Pluralism* (2004) 1
113 Twining W, 'Diffusion and Globalization Discourse' 47(2) *Harvard International Law Journal* (2006) 507
114 above n111 at 516–517
115 Zumbansen P, 'Defining the Space of Transnational Law: Legal theory, global governance, and legal pluralism' 21 *Transnational Law & Contemporary Problems* (2011) 305 at 344
116 ibid. at 323
117 ibid. at 324
118 above n68
119 above n69
120 Boister N, 'Transnational Criminal Law?' 14(5) *EJIL* (2003) 953
121 ibid.
122 ibid. at 954
123 ibid. at 955
124 Ooserveld V, Perry M, and McManus J, 'The Cooperation of States with the International Criminal Court' 25(3) *Fordham International Law Journal* (2001) 767
125 above n120 at 936
126 ibid.
127 ibid. at 967
128 above n2 at 18
129 above n120 at 966
130 Abi-Saab G, 'Wither the International Community?' 9 *EJIL* (1998) 248
131 above n120 at 971
132 ibid. at 972
133 above n1 at 483
134 above n120 at 956
135 ibid.
136 ibid.
137 ibid.
138 Bridenthal R, 'Special Issue: The hidden history of crime, corruption, and states' 45(3) *Journal of Social History* (2012) 575, at 579
139 Reed Q, 'Squeezing a Balloon? Challenging the nexus between organised crime and corruption' (7) *CMI U4 Issue* (2009)

140 Harfield C, 'The organization of "organized crime policing" and its international context' 8 *Criminology and Criminal Justice* (2008) 483 at 484
141 above n30 at 25
142 see the OECD convention and the OAS convention, and the preamble to UNCAC
143 above n17 at 155
144 above n139 at 31
145 Tusikov N, 'Measuring organised crime-related harms: Exploring five policing methods' 57 *Crime Law and Social Change* (2012) 99
146 Swedish Water House (2007) *Report 22: Making Anti-Corruption Approaches Work for the Poor*, at 5
147 ibid. at 21
148 Shah A and Schacter M, 'Combating Corruption: Look Before You Leap' 4 *Finance and Development* (2004) at 41
149 above n139 at 26
150 above n2
151 above n139 at 26–27
152 ibid. at 46
153 above n1 at 508
154 above n2 at 45
155 Note Sanchez GJG, 'A New International Legal Regime for a New Reality in the War Against Drugs' 58 *HILJ Online* (2017) 39. The author explores how shifts in the US approach to drugs, in particular legalisation of marijuana, are now incongruous with the Mexican 'war on' model that was driven by previous US interests in suppressing all supply from Mexico to the USA
156 Above n30 at 40
157 McCulloch J, 'Transnational Crime as Productive Fiction' 24(2) *Social Justice* (2007) 19
158 ibid. at 20
159 above n157 at 19
160 ibid. at 26
161 ibid. at 27
162 above n2
163 Joutsen M, 'The United Nations Convention Against Corruption' Chapter 16 in Graycar A and Smith R (Eds), *Handbook of Global Research and Practice in Corruption* (Edward Elgar Publishing, 2011) 303–318, at 312
164 above n68
165 ibid. at 241
166 iIbid. at 228
167 UNCAC, Article 13
168 Corva D, 'Neoliberal Globalization and the War on Drugs: Transnationalizing illiberal governance in the Americas' 27 *Political Geography* (2008) 176
169 above n138
170 Henshaw C, 'Strengthening the Rule of Law in the Pacific through International Crime Cooperation' 15 *Australian International Law Journal* (2008) 109
171 ibid. at 121
172 ibid.
173 above n149 at 13–14
174 ibid.
175 above n2
176 ibid.
177 ibid.
178 Schutte SA, 'Against the Odds: Anti-corruption reform in Indonesia' 32 *Public Admin. Dev.* (2012) 38
179 ibid. at 44

180 ibid. at 45
181 Windybank S, 'The Illegal Pacific, Part 1: Organised crime' 24(1) *Policy* (2008) 32
182 ibid.
183 ibid. at 38
184 Larmour has undertaken some interesting research on corruption and anti-corruption in the South Pacific. See Larmour P, 'International Action against Corruption in the Pacific Islands: Policy transfer, coercion and effectiveness' 15(1) *Asian Journal of Political Science* (2007) 1; Larmour P, *ANU Policy and Governance Discussion Paper: Culture and corruption in the Pacific Islands — Some conceptual issues and findings from studies of national integrity systems* (2006). However, there is room for a more complete analysis drawing on both the social and legal context of a specific state, the way this has developed, and how it has influenced the effectiveness and integrity of anti-corruption law and policy
185 above n68; above n3; above n139; above n178; Schloenhardt A, 'Fighting Organised Crime in the Asia Pacific Region: New weapons, lost wars' 2 *Asian Journal of International Law* (2012) 137
186 above n68
187 Williams JW and Beare ME, 'The Business of Bribery: Globalization, economic liberalization, and the 'problem' of corruption', in Beare ME (Ed), *Critical Reflections on Transnational Organized Crime, Money Laundering, and Corruption* (University of Toronto Press, 2003) 88
188 Chapters Four to Six discuss the challenge of limited political will in more detail relating to its role in preventing meaningful implementation and enforcement of UNCAC
189 CSD, *Examining the Links between Organised Crime and Corruption* (2010) at 14
190 Secretary-General, *Statement on the Adoption by the General Assembly of the United Nations Convention against Corruption*, 31 October 2003, available at: https://www.unodc.org/unodc/en/treaties/CAC/background/secretary-general-speech.html (last visited 1 March 2018)
191 UNCAC, preamble, para 2
192 UNCAC, preamble, para 4
193 UNCAC, foreword, para 4. See also *United Nations Convention against Transnational Organised Crime*, open for signature 12 December 2000, 2225 UNTS 209 (entered into force 29 September 2003) ('*UNTOC*') Art 8, which covers the criminalisation of corruption
194 Picarelli JT, National Institute of Justice, *Expert Working Group Report on International Organized Crime* (June 2010)
195 above n140 at 500
196 above n139 at 8
197 See Beare ME, 'North America: A perspective on the globalisation of organised crime' 6(1) *Journal of Financial Crime* (1993) 81. Despite a critical view of the dominant anti-corruption approach, the author argues that a real issue exists with relation to 'the overlap and intermingling of markets facilitated by corruption and shades of corruption' at 82. See also Windybank (2008), with special reference to the Pacific, and Wonders (2007) noting Dandurand and Chin (2000)
198 above n157 at 24
199 ibid. at 27
200 Above n139, examples include attempts to eradicate opium production in Afghanistan as well as failures in South and Central America with regard to coca production chains
201 ibid.
202 ibid.
203 ibid. at 8
204 Snider KR and Kidane W, 'Combating Corruption Through International Law in Africa: A comparative analysis' 40 *Cornell Int'l L.J.* (2007) 691, at 719, emphasis added

205 Ala'I P, 'The Legacy of Geographical Morality and Colonialism: A historical assessment of the current crusade against corruption' 33 *Vand. J. Transnat'l L.* (2000) 877
206 ibid., at 901 noting Joseph Nye (1967), further at 903
207 Farrales, above n3 at 33
208 above n17 at 163
209 above n138 at 578
210 above n106; above n112; above n113; above n115
211 above n170
212 above n17 at 166
213 above n140 at 484
214 Diefenbach T, 'Are case studies more than sophisticated storytelling?' 43 *Qual Quant* (2009) 875, at 882

References

Abbott KW and Snidal D, 'Values and Interests: International legalization in the fight against corruption' 31 *Journal of Legal Studies* (2002) 141.

ABC News, Cochrain and team, *PNG Anti-corruption Taskforce Broke after Making Allegations against Prime Minister Peter O'Neill* (5 February 2015) available at: http://www.abc.net.au/news/2015-02-04/png-anti-corruption-taskforce-starved-of-funding/6070170 (last visited 1 March 2018).

Abi-Saab G, 'Wither the International Community?' 9 *EJIL* (1998) 248.

Ala'I P, 'The Legacy of Geographical Morality and Colonialism: A historical assessment of the current crusade against corruption' 33 *Vanderbilt Journal of Transnational Law* (2000) 877.

Andreas P, 'Illicit Globalization: Myths, misconceptions, and historical lessons' 126 *Political Science Quarterly* 3 (2011) 403.

Beare ME, 'North America: A perspective on the globalisation of organised crime' 6(1) *Journal of Financial Crime* (1993) 81.

Beare ME, 'Corruption and Organised Crime: Lessons from History' 28 *Crime, Law and Social Change* (1997) 155.

Boister N, 'Transnational Criminal Law?' 14(5) *EJIL* (2003) 953.

Bridenthal R, 'Special Issue: The hidden history of crime, corruption, and states' 45(3) *Journal of Social History* (2012) 575.

Carr I, 'Corruption, legal solution and limits of law' 3(3) *International Journal of Law in Context* (2007) 227.

Convention on Combating Bribery of Foreign Public Officials in International Business Transactions, opened for signature 17 December 1997, 37 ILM 1 (entered into force 15 February 1999) ('OECD Convention').

Convention on Combating Bribery of Foreign Public Officials in International Business Transactions, opened for signature 17 December 1997, 37 ILM 1 (entered into force 15 February 1999) ('OECD Convention').

Corva D, 'Neoliberal Globalization and the War on Drugs: Transnationalizing illiberal governance in the Americas' 27 *Political Geography* (2008) 176.

CSD, *Examining the Links between Organised Crime and Corruption* (Report Commissioned by the European Commission, 2010).

Dandurand Y and Chin V, 'Women and Transnational Organized Crime.' Paper presented at the Workshop on Women in the Criminal Justice System, Tenth U.N. Congress on the Prevention of Crime and Treatment of Offenders, Vienna (10–17 April 2000).

Diefenbach T, 'Are case studies more than sophisticated storytelling?' 43 *Quality & Quantity* (2009) 875.

Elliot KA, *Corruption and the Global Economy* (Institute for International Economics, 1997).

Farrales M, 'What is Corruption? A history of corruption studies and the great definitions debate' *University of San Diego Working Paper Series* [2005] available at: http://papers.ssrn.com/sol3/papers.cfm?abstract_id=1739962 (last visited 1 March 2018).

Feld K, 'Controlling the Prosecution of Bribery: Applying corporate law principles to define a "Foreign Official" in the Foreign Corrupt Practices Act' 88(1) *Washington Law Review* (2013) 245.

Foreign Corrupt Practices Act 1977 15 USC §§ 78dd-1 ('FCPA')

Harfield C, 'The organization of "organized crime policing" and its international context' 8 *Criminology and Criminal Justice* (2008) 483.

Henshaw C, 'Strengthening the Rule of Law in the Pacific through International Crime Cooperation' 15 *Australian International Law Journal* (2008) 109.

Inter-American Convention against Corruption, opened for signature 29 March 1996, 35 ILM 724 (entered into force 6 March 1997) ('OAS Convention').

Joutsen M, 'The United Nations Convention Against Corruption', in Graycar A and Smith R (Eds), *Handbook of Global Research and Practice in Corruption* (Edward Elgar, 2011) 303.

Koh HH, 'Transnational Legal Process' 75 *Neb. L. Rev.* (1996) 181.

Koven SG, *Responsible Governance: A case study approach* (ME Sharpe, 1st Edition, 2008)

Krasner SD, 'Structural causes and regime consequences: regimes as intervening variables' 36(2) *International Organizations* (1982).

Larmour P, *ANU Policy and Governance Discussion Paper: Culture and corruption in the Pacific Islands — Some conceptual issues and findings from studies of national integrity systems* (2006).

Larmour P, 'International Action against Corruption in the Pacific Islands: Policy transfer, coercion and effectiveness' 15(1) *Asian Journal of Political Science* (2007) 1.

McCulloch J, 'Transnational Crime as Productive Fiction' 24(2) *Social Justice* (2007) 19.

Murphy MN, *Small Boats, Weak States, Dirty Money: Piracy and maritime terrorism in the modern world* (ME Sharpe, 1st Edition, 2008).

Nadelmann EA, 'Global prohibition regimes: The evolution of norms in international society' 44(4) *International Organization* (1990) 479.

Nadelmann EA and Andreas P, *Policing the Globe: Criminalization and crime control in international relations* (Oxford University Press, 1st Edition, 2006).

Ooserveld V, Perry M, and McManus J, 'The Cooperation of States with the International Criminal Court' 25(3) *Fordham International Law Journal* (2001) 767.

Passas N 'Globalization, Criminogenic Asymmetries and Economic Crime' 1(4) *European Journal of Law Reform* (1999) 399.

Passas N, 'Globalization and Transnational Crime: Effects of criminogenic asymmetries', in Williams P and Vlassis D (Eds), *Combatting Transnational Crime: Concepts, Activities and Responses* (Frank Cass Publishers, 2013) 22.

Picarelli JT, *Expert Working Group Report on International Organized Crime* (National Institute of Justice, June 2010).

Picarelli JT, 'Responding to Transnational Organized Crime — Supporting research, improving practice' 268 *NIJ Journal* (2011) 4.

Reed Q, 'Squeezing a Balloon? Challenging the nexus between organised crime and corruption' 7 *CMI U4 Issue* (2009).

Sanchez GJG, 'A New International Legal Regime for a New Reality in the War Against Drugs' *HILJ Online 58* (2017) 39.

Sandgren C, 'Combating Corruption: The Misunderstood Role of Law' 39 *International Law* (2005) 717.

Schloenhardt A, 'Fighting Organised Crime in the Asia Pacific Region: New weapons, lost wars' 2 *Asian Journal of International Law* (2012) 137.

Schutte SA, 'Against the Odds: Anti-corruption reform in Indonesia' 32 *Public Admin. Dev.* (2012) 38.

Secretary-General, *Statement on the Adoption by the General Assembly of the United Nations Convention against Corruption* (31 October 2003) available at: https://www.unodc.org/unodc/en/treaties/CAC/background/secretary-general-speech.html (last visited 1 March 2018).

Shah A and Schacter M, '*Combating Corruption: Look Before You Leap*' 41(4) *Finance and Development* (2004) 40.

Snider KR and Kidane W, 'Combating Corruption Through International Law in Africa: A comparative analysis' 40 *Cornell Int'l L.J.* (2007) 691.

Swedish Water House, *Report 22: Making Anti-Corruption Approaches Work for the Poor* (Stockholm International Water Institute, 2007).

Tusikov N, 'Measuring organised crime-related harms: Exploring five policing methods' 57 *Crime Law and Social Change* (2012) 99.

Twining W, 'Diffusion of Law: A global perspective' 49 *Journal of Legal Pluralism* (2004) 1.

Twining W, 'Diffusion and Globalization Discourse' 47(2) *Harvard International Law Journal* (2006) 507.

Twining W, 'Normative and Legal Pluralism' 20 *Duke Journal of Comparative & International Law* (2010) 473.

United Nations Convention against Corruption, opened for signature 9 December 2003, 2349 UNTS 41 (entered into force 14 December 2005) ('UNCAC').

United Nations Convention against Transnational Organised Crime, open for signature 12 December 2000, 2225 UNTS 209 (entered into force 29 September 2003) ('UNTOC').

UNODC, *World Drug Report* (2014) No. E.14.XI.7.

Weissbrodt D, 'Slavery' (at March 2014) in Oxford University Press, *Max Planck Encyclopedia of Public International Law*.

Williams JW and Beare ME, 'The Business of Bribery: Globalization, economic liberalization, and the 'problem' of corruption', in Beare ME (Ed), *Critical Reflections on Transnational Organized Crime, Money Laundering, and Corruption* (University of Toronto Press, 2003) 8.

Windybank S, 'The Illegal Pacific, Part 1: Organised crime' 24(1) *Policy* (2008) 32.

Wonders N, 'Globalization, Border Reconstruction Projects, and Transnational Crime' 34(2) *Social Justice* (2007) 33.

World Bank, 'People and Development: Annual Meeting Address by James D Wolfenshon' (1 October 1996) No. 99712.

Zumbansen P, 'Defining the Space of Transnational Law: Legal theory, global governance, and legal pluralism' 21 *Transnational Law & Contemporary Problems* (2011) 305.

2 The United Nations Convention against Corruption – the primary tool of the global anti-corruption regime

Introduction

This chapter provides answers to the following question:

1 How has UNCAC evolved within the emergent global anti-corruption regime?

The chapter explores the development of the United Nations Convention against Corruption (UNCAC). This exploration makes use of the theoretical framework established in Chapter 1 and emphasises the context from which UNCAC emerged, its structure, and the implementation review mechanism that accompanies it.

UNCAC is a primary tool of the global anti-corruption regime. Its entry into force in 2005, near universal ratification, and extensive participation in the implementation review mechanism have catalysed evolution of the global anti-corruption regime to the fourth stage.

Analysis in this chapter emphasises the points of conflict and contestation that arose during the negotiations process for UNCAC and how these were resolved in the final text of this multilateral legal instrument. The extent to which UNCAC reflects the regime risk factors and criticisms discussed in Chapter 1, and the likelihood that UNCAC can overcome the challenges noted by Nadelmann and Andreas regarding evolution of global prohibition regimes, are important issues.

Initially, building on the discussion in Chapter 1, UNCAC is situated within the emergent global anti-corruption regime. Following this, the debate and negotiation that led to the design and adoption of UNCAC in its final form are analysed. Key points of consensus and contestation within the international sphere are illustrated through this analysis. The chapter continues by exploring the text of UNCAC and the articles of this multilateral legal instrument. Textual analysis illustrates the manner in which conflict and contestation that emerged during negotiation were ultimately resolved. This background provides necessary perspective for addressing the implementation and enforcement challenges facing UNCAC and the global anti-corruption regime at regional and domestic levels.

Points of interest are highlighted throughout this chapter based on their potential to influence implementation and enforcement of UNCAC and the ultimate success of the global anti-corruption regime. One point relates to the under-representation of the South Pacific region in the negotiations of UNCAC. This is a relevant point for consideration based on the risk of inapplicability noted by critics in Chapter 1. Another point of interest is the consensus that emerged from the UNCAC negotiation, around corruption as a transnational threat requiring consistent and collective action. This position was justified based on the perceived links between corruption and other forms of transnational criminality. This is noteworthy in the context of criticisms introduced in Chapter 1, which emphasised the risk of adopting such a position. This justification for collective and consistent action may result in disregard for contextual variation and over reliance on criminal law and enforcement measures.

Additional points of interest include the wide range of preventive measures put forward during the UNCAC negotiation, many of which have been incorporated into the final instrument. These measures may help to overcome the risks associate with an extensive criminal law and enforcement focus discussed in Chapter 1. The manner in which definitional uncertainty around corruption is dealt with is also important. UNCAC uses a 'corrupt act' approach. This approach, and the combination of mandatory and non-mandatory criminalisation measures, may address the concerns of critics regarding the risk factor of definitional uncertainty on the one hand, and criminal law and enforcement focus on the other. Finally, the emphasis of UNCAC on the rights of state sovereignty and the need for domestic implementation and enforcement illustrate the importance of a case study approach and highlight the relevance of the non-compliant state challenge noted by Nadelmann and Andreas.[1]

Following analysis of UNCAC's negotiation and the nature of its provisions, the chapter provides a brief overview of the implementation review mechanism for UNCAC. This mechanism was developed following the adoption of UNCAC and illustrates the consensus reached by *States Parties* regarding domestic implementation of this multilateral legal instrument. The chapter concludes by presenting the key findings, summarising the nature of UNCAC and its evolution within the global anti-corruption regime, and presenting some hypotheses on how UNCAC may interact with anti-corruption efforts at the regional and domestic level. This prepares the reader for further exploration of UNCAC's interaction with the South Pacific region and implementation and enforcement of UNCAC in Papua New Guinea (PNG), undertaken from Chapter 3 onward.

Developing UNCAC: background and context

UNCAC is one of the most recent, influential, and widely ratified multilateral legal instruments targeting corruption.[2] The United Nations General Assembly adopted UNCAC by Resolution 58/4 on 31 October 2003.[3] The Convention opened for signature at the High-level Political Signing Conference in Merida,

Mexico, from 9 to 11 December 2003. During this conference, UNCAC received 95 signatures and one ratification (Kenya). Pursuant to Article 67 (1), UNCAC entered into force on 14 December 2005. As of October 2017, UNCAC has 183 *States Parties.*

UNCAC establishes the transnational nature of corruption as an 'insidious plague that has a wide range of corrosive effects on societies'.[4] This moralist understanding of corruption justifies the importance of a multilateral legal instrument dedicated to the prevention and punishment of corrupt acts.

The Secretary-General's foreword to UNCAC states that 'it took systemic efforts, first at the technical, and then gradually at the political, level to put the fight against corruption on the global agenda'.[5] This is an acknowledgement that the threat of corruption was not always recognised as a global issue. The shift required action by 'moral entrepreneurs', to re-define corruption and justify collective action. This reflects the processes of global prohibition regime evolution discussed in Chapter 1.[6]

To recap, the five-stage model of global prohibition regime evolution involves an initial stage, a delegitimation stage, a dissemination stage, a criminalisation stage, and a final stage where the target activity is substantially reduced across all jurisdictions. If the challenges of dissident and deviant actors, non-compliant states, and susceptibility of the target activity to criminal law enforcement measures are not overcome, the final stage cannot be achieved.[7] In the case of corruption, the first stage existed in the period before the 1970s. Between 1970 and 1989 the second stage of regime evolution was set in motion and the processes of delegitimisation took place. The establishment of early multilateral legal instruments against corruption represents a transition from the second to the third stage of evolution. The development of these instruments was justified based on the transnational harms associated with corruption and links to other forms of transnational criminal activity, including trafficking crimes, transnational organised crime, and terrorism. Discussion of corruption continued at the international level following the negotiation of these multilateral instruments. Ultimately, it was decided that a single multilateral legal instrument focused on corruption needed to be established, reflecting a unified approach to combatting corruption in all states. This led to the negotiation of UNCAC. With UNCAC's entry into force in 2005, near universal ratification, participation by 156 of 183 *States Parties* in the implementation review mechanism, and the extensive level of criminalisation in *States Parties*, the global anti-corruption regime has reached the fourth stage of evolution.

The regime must still overcome the challenges of dissident and deviant actors, non-compliant states and susceptibility of corruption to criminal law and enforcement measures; as well as the risks noted by critics relating to inapplicability of the regime across diverse contexts, excessive criminal law and enforcement focus, links to other forms of criminality, and a lack of definitional clarity regarding the term corruption. Each of these challenges and risk factors will influence the implementation and enforcement of UNCAC and the possibility of the global anti-corruption regime achieving the fifth stage of evolution, something that has not yet occurred.

With this context in mind, the next section of this chapter explores the key events and documents produced through the United Nations (UN), that led to the negotiation of UNCAC. This exploration summarises the state of the global anti-corruption regime at the time when the UNCAC negotiation began and foreshadows some of the focal points for analysis later in this chapter.

Early transnational discussion

Corruption emerged as a transnational challenge in the latter half of the 20th Century. The need to address corruption has been on the agenda of the UN since August 1970, when reference was made to the negative impacts of corruption at the 4th United Nations Congress on Crime Prevention and Criminal Justice (UN Crime Congress).

Corruption had been discussed as an emergent and threatening form of economic crime at every United Nations Crime Congress since 1970. However, the first mention of corruption in a UN instrument was not until 1979, in the Code of Conduct for Law Enforcement Officials, Article 7, adopted by General Assembly resolution 34/169.[8] This article states that 'law enforcement officials shall not commit any act of corruption. They shall also rigorously oppose and combat all such acts'.[9] This code of conduct attempts to provide a broad definition of corruption. The commentary of Article 7 of resolution 34/169 states:

> While the definition of corruption must be subject to national law, it should be understood to encompass the commission or omission of an act in the performance of or in connexion with one's duties, in response to gifts, promises or incentives demanded or accepted, or the wrongful receipt of these once the act has been committed or omitted.[10]

This was the first time such an attempt was made by the UN. This definition is one of the only general definitions that has been provided in a multilateral legal instrument.

Despite continued attention in the international arena, the potential for an independent multilateral legal instrument dealing with corruption was not addressed until 1989, during the Interregional Seminar on Corruption in Government held at The Hague between 11 and 15 December 1989.[11] Delegates explored varying forms of corruption in government and their causes and consequences. The relationship between corruption and organised crime was noted, and an assessment of existing measures against corruption was undertaken. The important role of international cooperation was highlighted at this seminar, as well as the need for greater information, expertise and facilitation of technical assistance and cooperation.[12]

The 8th Crime Congress held in Havana from 27 August to 7 September 1990 produced recommendations regarding corruption via resolution 7 'Corruption in Government'.[13] In this resolution, the report of the Interregional Seminar on Corruption was acknowledged and the Congress emphasised the importance of tackling corruption at the national, regional, and international levels.[14] 'The essential role that the UN should play in assisting states in eliminating the scourge of corruption'[15] was highlighted. Corruption was constructed as a universal problem having 'particularly deleterious effects on nations with vulnerable economies'.[16] Corruption was also recognised as a hindrance to development and was associated with 'other forms of economic crime, organised crime and illicit drug trafficking, including money laundering'.[17] The evolution of international discourse on corruption shows a shift in perspective. Corruption was initially viewed as a sub-category of economic and white collar crime. As debate intensified, corruption was reframed as a transnational threat related to other organised and insidious forms of criminal activity that negatively impact economic development and require concerted action across international, regional, and domestic spheres.

Associating corruption with other transnational crimes

The establishment of the UN crime prevention and criminal justice programme via General Assembly resolution 46/152[18] ensured that the topic of corruption remained high on the international agenda. The link between corruption and other forms of organised criminal activity, including trafficking in drugs and laundering of money, continued to strengthen within international debate, culminating in the inclusion of corruption within the United Nations Convention on Transnational Organised Crime (UNTOC).[19] The UN Commission on Human Rights also acknowledged the negative and transnational impact of corruption, particularly as it related to the trafficking of drugs and arms.[20] At the 1994 World Ministerial Conference on Organised Transnational Crime:

> corruption was linked to the systemic impact of organised transnational crime on development efforts, in that scarce resources had to be diverted from other projects in response to criminal activities. In addition, corruption had been found to weaken the commitment of the citizenry to the sacrifices demanded by development policies and impair the rational decision-making process required by public administration.[21]

This statement further emphasises the link between corruption and other forms of criminality, highlighting the threat posed by corruption to the stability of societies and their economic, social, and political development. The suggestion that development policies require sacrifices on the part of citizens, and corruption may reduce the likelihood that these sacrifices are made, brings up the possibility of policy laundering. This statement suggests that anti-corruption policies would facilitate 'development' policies, making anti-corruption a tool for achieving the development agenda. However, the link between anti-corruption and development requires some scrutiny. Questions should be asked about the nature of development policies that require 'sacrifices' on behalf of the citizens being 'developed'. Are such development policies reasonable? Are they likely to be effective? Should they be implemented by external actors under the auspices of the anti-corruption agenda?

It is important to note that the threat posed by corruption is constructed in terms of individual states, rather than the collective whole. All states are seen to struggle with corruption and in this way collective action is justified, but the threat itself, and therefore the jurisdiction of relevant legal measures, is limited. This limited threat and jurisdiction reflects Boister's distinction between international law *stricto sensu*, and transnational criminal law, discussed in Chapter 1.[22] Understanding the nature of the corruption threat also helps to explain the approach taken to combatting corruption through multilateral legal instruments. These instruments require state implementation and enforcement to achieve their goals and the broader goals of the global anti-corruption regime.

Continued discussion and early transnational legal action against corruption

Several multilateral legal instruments for the prohibition of corruption were adopted in the 1990s, including the Inter-American Convention against Corruption,[23] the OECD Convention,[24] and the Council of Europe (CoE) Civil Law and Criminal Law Conventions on Corruption.[25][26] It is not within the purview of this book to discuss any of these instruments at length. However, the sudden increase in the number of regional and multilateral anti-corruption instruments illustrates the continued evolution of the global anti-corruption regime towards stage four.

The push for multilateral legal instruments to combat corruption intensified as the perspective on corruption as a transnational challenge solidified, and the need for transnational criminalisation became widely supported by key actors (including the UN, World Bank, Transparency International, US and Europe). Entry into force of such legal instruments catalysed progression of the global anti-corruption regime towards the fourth stage of evolution.

Alongside the adoption of these instruments, discussion of corruption continued within the UN. In March 1997, the expert group meeting on corruption was held in Buenos Aires. The purpose of this meeting was to 'consider ways and means of strengthening international cooperation to promote the implementation of General Assembly resolutions 51/59 and 51/191'.[27] The conclusions and recommendations of this meeting were presented at the sixth session of the Commission on Crime Prevention and Criminal Justice, from 28 April to 9 May 1997. During the meeting, it was established that: '[T]he commission on crime prevention and criminal justice should elaborate an international convention against corruption and bribery in international commercial transactions'.[28]

The expert group further asserted that, as a result of globalisation and trade liberalisation, 'the phenomenon of corruption and bribery had become transnational in nature' and 'it was no longer possible to deal with it effectively through national action alone'.[29] Following the expert meeting on corruption, two regional ministerial workshops were held: one in Dakar in July 1997 and one in

Manila in March 1998. At both workshops ministers supported the possibility of developing an independent international convention to target corruption.[30]

Momentum for a separate, corruption specific, convention continued to build in the late 1990s. The justification was that corruption was a transnational, rather than purely domestic or regional challenge. The Expert Group Meeting on Corruption and its Financial Channels (held in Paris from 30 March to 1 April 1999) suggested that an international instrument should be based on existing best practices compiled by the Financial Action Task Force (FATF) on Money Laundering, the Basel Committee on Banking Supervisions, International Organisation of Securities Commissions (IOSC) and TI. This meeting was convened by the Economic and Social Council on the recommendation of the Commission on Crime Prevention and Criminal Justice.[31] It was suggested that a new international anti-corruption instrument should build on existing instruments, including those of the Council of Europe, EU and OECD and OAS; as well as drafting of UNTOC. This emphasis on consistency demonstrated consensus between various international organisations on the best approach to combatting corruption transnationally, and the importance placed on a coordinated approach. The focus also illuminates key actors who shaped the transnational approach, including the FTAF, financial regulatory bodies, and multilateral organisations dominated by western states.

Both UNTOC and UNCAC developed in an environment concerned about the negative impact of organised crime and corruption on development and international security. The possibility of including the crime of corruption as a protocol to UNTOC, rather than developing an independent convention, was discussed extensively in UNTOC negotiations. However, 'the view that prevailed was that corruption was too complex and broad an issue to be covered exhaustively by a convention dealing with transnational organised crime'.[32] This rationale ultimately led to the development of UNCAC as an independent instrument to combat corruption.

Agreement on the need for an independent anti-corruption convention

In resolution 55/61, the General Assembly recognised the need for an effective international legal instrument against corruption, independent of UNTOC.[33] In this resolution, the request was made to establish an ad hoc committee for the negotiation of such an instrument.[34]

To ensure that the new convention was developed to complement rather than contrast or contradict existing transnational legal tools, the UN Secretary-General was asked to report on existing international legal instruments and other documents on corruption. This report was to be used in the negotiation and development process for UNCAC. The report, entitled 'Existing International Legal Instruments, Recommendations and other Documents Addressing Corruption', was published on 2 April 2001 and presented at the Commission on Crime Prevention and Criminal Justice in its 10th Session from 8 to 17 May 2001.[35]

In the Secretary-General's report, eight key international legal instruments were highlighted and various other documents were discussed.[36] Other documents included UN General Assembly resolutions 51/59 (The International Code of Conduct for Public Officials), and 51/191 (Declaration against Corruption and Bribery in International Commercial Transactions). The Conclusions and Recommendations of the Expert Group Meeting on Corruption and its Financial Channels (E/CN.15/1999/20) were also mentioned, as were a range of recommendation documents from the Council of Europe and the EU.[37]

What came before? Influential ideas and existing multilateral legal instruments that pre-date UNCAC

Before exploring the negotiation of UNCAC in detail, it is useful to reflect on the pre-UNCAC context. Of particular interest are the key factors that drove negotiation of UNCAC, based on the approach of pre-existing legal instruments addressed in the Secretary-General's report. Three factors are discussed below, as they overlap with the criticisms raised by scholars regarding UNCAC and the global anti-corruption regime. This analysis also illustrates points of agreement and divergence between states. Differing positions of states involved in developing UNCAC influenced debate throughout the negotiation process and ultimately shaped the outcomes of this process. The key factors discussed below are: collective action, criminalisation, and prevention.

Collective action

Collective action is a key theme in all relevant multilateral legal instruments that pre-date UNCAC. The importance of collective action is based in large part on the nature of the perceived corruption threat and its links with other forms of transnational criminal activity. The preamble to the OAS Convention states that:

> [C]orruption undermines the legitimacy of public institutions and strike at society, moral order and justice, as well as at the comprehensive development of peoples . . . corruption is often a tool used by organised crime for the accomplishment of its purposes . . . corruption has international dimensions, which requires coordinated action by states to fight it effectively.[38]

The two protocols to the EU Convention on the Protection of the European Communities' Financial Interests call on the international nature of corrupt activity as a reason to engage consistent action across member states.[39] The second protocol links corruption to money laundering, which is often carried out across borders and is enabled by increasingly transnational flows of capital.[40]

UNTOC focuses on other forms of transnational criminal activity, but provides for the criminalisation of corruption under Article 9. UNTOC has the broadest membership of all pre-UNCAC instruments. Most other multilateral legal instruments targeting corruption are regional rather than international in nature. Corrupt activities, and all other forms of transnational organised crime under UNTOC, are seen to pose a significant threat to economic and social interests across the world and thus present an 'urgent need to strengthen cooperation to prevent and combat such activities'.[41] Urgency is further enhanced when newly established links between corruption, terrorism, and other transnational criminal behaviours are raised.[42]

This emphasis on the link between corrupt acts and other forms of transnational criminal activity reflects the second of the four key risk factors discussed in Chapter 1: Risk factor two: corruption as facilitation – the organised crime link.[43] In addition to this risk factor, critics also note the risk inherent to overemphasising criminal law and enforcement methods for combatting corruption.[44] Most multilateral instruments that were negotiated before UNCAC have just such an emphasis.

Criminalisation

Except for the Council of Europe Civil Law Convention on Corruption, every pre-UNCAC has focused on criminal law and enforcement measures as the solution to the corruption threat.[45] This approach is supported regardless of whether a definition of corruption is provided within the text of the instrument itself.

Article VII of the OAS Convention requires all members to criminalise the acts of corruption described in Article VI(1).[46] The first protocol of the EU Convention on the Protection of European Communities' Financial Interests defines active and passive corruption in Articles 2(1) and 3(1). In Articles 2(2) and 3(2), the protocol states that the 'Member State shall take the necessary measures to ensure that conduct of the type referred to in paragraph 1 is made a criminal offence'.[47] The EU Convention against Corruption adopts a similar approach, as does the Second Protocol of the EU Convention on the Protection of European Communities' Financial Interests, which focuses on criminalisation of money laundering linked to corruption and the negative effects of this activity on the financial interest of Europe.[48]

The purpose of the Council of Europe Criminal Law Convention on Corruption is precisely to establish 'a common *criminal* policy aimed at the protection of society against corruption' and the OECD Convention also clearly illustrates its focus on criminalisation. The OECD Convention states:

> Each Party shall take such measures as may be necessary to establish that it is a criminal offence under its law for any person internationally to offer promise or give any undue pecuniary or other advantage, whether directly or through intermediaries, to a foreign public official, for that official or for a third party, in order that the official act or refrain from acting in relation to the performance of official duties, in order to obtain or retain business or other improper advantage in the conduct of international business.[49]

The OECD Convention also requires that complicity in, or authorisation of, an act of bribery of a foreign public official be established as a criminal offence, along with attempt and conspiracy to bribe.

Reflecting on these pre-UNCAC instruments, the justification for collective action based on association with other forms of criminality clearly supports a criminalisation approach to combatting corruption. This book pays close attention to the influence this criminalisation approach has had on UNCAC. The extent to which UNCAC reflects this pre-existing emphasis on corruption's links to other crimes and the criminal law enforcement approach is likely to impact the success of UNCAC in practice. As noted by critics, excessive focus on a criminal law and enforcement approach may result in unintended side effects or negative outcomes when UNCAC is implemented in unique domestic contexts such as PNG.

Variation in approaches to prevention

Pre-UNCAC instruments converge in their framing of corruption as a threat requiring coordinated criminal law and enforcement actions. However, these instruments diverge in their approaches to prevention.

The *EU Joint Action on Corruption in the Private Sector* states expressly that 'prevention is no less important than repression in an integrated approach to corruption in the private sector'.[50] The joint action does not, however, reference the approach which should be taken in terms of such preventive measures. The *Council of Europe Criminal Law Convention on Corruption* mentions prevention only once, in the preamble, where it states that there is a need to pursue 'the adoption of appropriate legislation *and* preventive measures'.[51] The EU *Convention on the Fight against Corruption* does not cover any preventive measures, except to state in Article 5 that penalties shall be 'proportionate and dissuasive'.[52] The same language is used in the EU protocols 1 and 2 of the *Convention on European Financial Interests,* under Articles 5 and 4 respectively.

UNTOC focuses more expressly on prevention. Article 9 is devoted to the prevention of corruption, stating that there is a need to promote integrity and ensure that the relevant authorities, imbued with power to counteract corruption, are provided with 'adequate independence to deter the exertion of inappropriate influence on their actions'.[53] The OAS Convention also discusses a range of possible preventive measures, including strengthening participation by Civil Society.[54] Article III of the OAS Convention covers preventive measures, including standards of conduct for government officials, accounting standards for those persons who perform public functions, denying favourable tax treatment for payment of bribes, protection of whistle blowers. The OAS Convention calls for study of additional preventive measures 'that take into account the relationship between equitable compensation and probity in public service'.[55]

The OECD Convention recommends awareness-raising initiatives as a preventive measure against foreign bribery, and also recommends adequate accounting requirements, corporate financial disclosure and internal controls, ethics and compliance programmes. The Convention provides, in Annex II, a guide to good practice regarding these internal control measures where detection also features highly on the agenda.[56] Finally, the *CoE Civil Law*

Convention suggests audits under Article 10, 'with a view to preventing acts of corruption'.[57]

Ultimately, while pre-UNCAC instruments illustrate a consistent focus on criminalisation and emphasis on the links between corruption and other forms of transnational crime, the approach to preventive measures varies. This variation allowed for further evolution during negotiation of UNCAC, with an entire chapter dedicated to prevention within the text of the convention.

Before UNCAC: summarising the historical context

The Secretary-General's report on existing international legal instruments, documents, and recommendations on corruption provides a useful summary of the international community's pre-UNCAC position on corrupt activity. The report also explores the future of international legal developments to combat corruption.

> [C]orruption is multifaceted and affects every society regardless of its level of development . . . while the underlying causes may range from the societal to the institutional, one clear conclusion is that corruption exacerbates other problems and derails development efforts, while it wreaks havoc on efforts to build, consolidate and further develop democratic institutions.[58]

This quote provides another illustration of the link between corruption and the compromise of 'development' policies. The report further asserts that corruption is becoming increasingly complex and thus increased international efforts to stem its deleterious influence are warranted.[59] It suggests that points of consistency between pre-UNCAC instruments illustrate potential for further consolidation.[60] In order to justify the development of an 'independent international convention against corruption',[61] the report points out that all existing instruments (other than the OECD Convention) focus on the regional sphere.[62] Thus, there is room for experiences and attempts at regional control, which often overlap regarding certain key methods for criminalisation and prevention, to be expanded to the global sphere. Even the OECD Convention, which has a more international scope, is perceived to be limited in that 'it tackles solely a specific part of the global problem of corruption, the so-called "supply" side of the bribery of foreign public officials'.[63]

The report raises the important point of participation, to further justify the creation of an independent anti-corruption convention. It argues that, based on the lack of involvement by less developed countries in the negotiation of pre-UNCAC instruments, 'it is debatable whether the specific problems and concerns of many countries are fully reflected in the instruments'.[64] This is an important development, considering the risk of inapplicability noted by critics as a potential limit on the success of the global anti-corruption regime.[65] The acknowledgement that unique domestic context may not have been adequately addressed by previous anti-corruption instruments suggests a desire to address this issue in the negotiation of a new international anti-corruption convention.

The report concludes that the mandate set out in General Assembly Resolution 55/61, building on expertise developed thus far, 'represents a unique opportunity to develop a global legal instrument against corruption that can fully address the concerns of the international community as a whole'.[66] This reflects the perspective of Passas who stresses that, in developing stronger international criminal law, 'care must be taken to give a voice to all constituents, including less powerful developing countries'.[67] Passas mirrors the concern of critics regarding incompatibility of transnational legal instruments with unique domestic context when he notes:

> The risk in forging agreements under the influence of powerful states on the basis of some particular case of 'bad guys' is that future interpretations will vary reflecting the underlying and unaddressed cultural, legal, and other asymmetries.[68]

Early support for inclusive negotiation of an international convention against corruption is thus cause for optimism regarding the long term success of UNCAC and its applicability and effectiveness across unique domestic contexts. The extent to which negotiation was conducted in an inclusive manner, and the extent to which diverse perspectives were incorporated within the text of UNCAC, is the subject of further evaluation below.

Draft terms of reference for UNCAC: meetings of the expert group

Building on the Secretary-General's report, and following the adoption of UNTOC and its protocols, negotiation began on UNCAC with the meeting of the Inter-Governmental Open Ended Expert Group on the Negotiation of the Future Legal Instrument against Corruption (held from 30 July to 3 August 2001 in Vienna).[69] Following this meeting, the Ad Hoc Committee on the Negotiation of a United Nations Convention against Corruption began its work at the Informal Preparatory Meeting from 4 to 7 December 2001. Negotiations continued over seven sessions, beginning on 21 January 2002 and ending with approval of the final draft on 1 October 2003.[70] The work of the Ad Hoc Committee is explored in this chapter, following a review of consensus reached, and key issues raised, at the Expert Group meeting.

The mandate of the Expert Group meeting was the production of draft terms of reference to aid the Ad Hoc Committee in negotiating the new international instrument on corruption, which became known as UNCAC. The Expert Group achieved this goal at its fifth and final meeting on 3 August 2001. The draft terms of reference were adopted by General Assembly Resolution 56/260 on 21 January 2002. The finalised draft terms of reference note that corruption 'may endanger the stability and security of societies, undermine the values of democracy and morality and jeopardize social, economic and political development'.[71] The terms of reference support the preparation of 'a broad an effective international legal instrument against corruption'.[72]

In developing UNCAC, the draft terms of reference suggested 'a comprehensive and multidisciplinary approach'.[73] Fifteen key elements were set out by the draft terms of reference as needing to be addressed. It was further requested that all existing international legal instruments against corruption 'and, whenever relevant, the United Nations Convention against Transnational Organised Crime'[74] be taken into consideration. The draft terms of reference asserted that the Ad Hoc Committee should elect its own bureau consisting of two representatives from each of the five regional groups. It urged states 'to be fully involved in the negotiation of the convention'.[75] The involvement of NGOs and Civil Society groups was also supported.[76]

Missing voices: under-representation of the South Pacific region in negotiation of UNCAC

Pursuant to the call for inclusive negotiations of UNCAC, 98 states participated in the Expert Group meetings. Of those 98 participants, Australia was the only participant from the South Pacific region, defined to include Australia, New Zealand and the other 14 member states of the Pacific Islands Forum. Limited participation by states from the South Pacific region continued during the Ad Hoc Committee negotiations. Australia participated in every meeting and New Zealand participated in six of the seven meetings. PNG was the only other state from the South Pacific region to participate. PNG attended the Ad Hoc Committee negotiations once only, during the Second Session.[77]

The limited participation by South Pacific states in the negotiation of UNCAC heightens the relevance of criticisms regarding the inapplicability of the global anti-corruption regime to the diverse contexts in which it must operate. If the perspectives of countries and even entire regions were not considered during the negotiation process, concerns regarding the inapplicability of the global anti-corruption regime and its tools are heightened.[78] Lack of representation may result in a failure to address unique regional and domestic dynamics that affect application of UNCAC. This in turn may have a negative effect on the possibility of achieving the fifth stage of regime evolution, which requires a substantial reduction in the target activity across all states.[79] The relevance and applicability of UNCAC to the unique context of the South Pacific and Papua New Guinea is the subject of extensive analysis in Chapters 3 and 4.

Early points of conflict and contestation

The Draft Terms of Reference represent the consensus reached by states at the Expert Group meeting. However, interesting insight into aspects of conflict and controversy can be gained by exploring the report of the Expert Group. The comments from representatives of the five regional delegations present at the meeting are especially useful in this regard.

Before opening the meeting for discussion and debate the Executive Director of the United Nations Office for Drug Control and Crime Prevention spoke about the phenomenon of corruption. He highlighted the universal threat of corruption and the global consensus on the need to suppress corruption and develop effective mechanisms for its prevention and punishment.[80] Following this, the representatives of Egypt, Uruguay, Belgium, Morocco, and Jordan each spoke. Representatives from these five countries were speaking on behalf of the Group of 77 and China, the Group of Latin American and Caribbean States, the European Union and associated European States, the Group of African States, and the Group of Asian and Pacific States, respectively.

Controversial issues raised by various delegations included: the breadth of the convention's coverage and types of corruption to be included in the instrument; mechanisms for review; reversal of the burden of proof and bank secrecy; respect for sovereignty, territorial integrity, and non-interference; and the nature of preventive measures to supplement criminalisation.

> '[S]ome delegations were of the view that the new convention should be a broad-based instrument encompassing all forms of corruption . . . other delegations advised caution, because attempting to broaden the approach excessively was fraught with many conceptual, legal and policy-related difficulties'.[81]

The delegate for the Group of 77 and China supported a comprehensive approach, including a broad definition covering 'all aspects relating to public and private corruption'.[82] This view was mirrored by the delegate of Morocco, speaking on behalf of the Group of African States.[83] The Group of Asian and Pacific States, represented by the delegate from Jordan, endorsed the statements made on behalf of the group of 77 and China but were more reserved on the issue of definition and scope. The delegate stated that a clear definition of corruption in both public and private sectors should be established and 'particular care should be taken that the integrity of domestic legal systems was not compromised'.[84] There was no certainty around the definition of corruption during the early stages of UNCAC negotiation, a challenge that persisted throughout the negotiation process. Attempts to establish the extent of UNCAC's scope raised concerns of domestic sovereignty and compatibility of the multilateral legal instrument with domestic legal systems. Concerns for integrity of domestic legal systems and state sovereignty were also raised on the topic of review mechanisms.

The delegates of Egypt and Uruguay, speaking on behalf of their regional groups, strongly supported an international or, at the very least, multilateral mechanism for review and monitoring. However, the expert report notes: 'Other delegations expressed concern regarding the appropriateness of regional and multilateral mechanisms, as they had a bearing on sovereignty matters, and preferred national monitoring mechanisms.'[85]

It is noteworthy that many delegations used technical, rather than political, language throughout the discussion and negotiation of UNCAC. As an example, the representative for the EU delegation did not expressly support or disagree with the possibility of a multilateral review mechanism. Instead, the delegate stated that the establishment of a monitoring mechanism 'should be based on the equality of obligations and be effective and flexible'.[86]

Reversal of the burden of proof and bank secrecy were also topics of debate that raised issues of sovereignty, territorial integrity, and non-interference. There was some support for the benefits of reversal of the burden of proof and bank secrecy, most clearly from the delegation for the Group of 77 and China. However, there were also concerns that such measures 'would run contrary to constitutional principles or international obligations and would thus be difficult to envisage'.[87] This cautious view can be taken from the subtle language of the EU delegation, which noted further that 'criminalisation and sanction models should respect human rights and fundamental freedoms'.[88]

Extensive opportunities for prevention and points of consensus

In contrast to the above controversies, the debate concerning preventive measures illustrates a diversity of opinion, rather than any substantial conflict. Some delegations suggested the above-mentioned removal of bank secrecy laws as one preventive measure. The representative of Uruguay, on behalf of the Group of Latin American and Caribbean States, suggested the involvement of Civil Society, protection of 'whistleblowers' and establishment of anti-corruption bodies as potential preventive measures.[89] Similarly, the EU delegation supported a multi-disciplinary approach where preventive measures 'should be based on fundamental principles, such as good governance, integrity and transparency'.[90] The delegate of Morocco, who spoke on behalf of the Group of African States, suggested that 'prevention and law enforcement were equally crucial' and that 'penal sanctions should be supplemented by disciplinary, administrative and civil law sanctions'.[91] Many delegations also highlighted the importance of addressing social and economic factors in preventive measures, supporting the views expressed by NGOs. These views reflect a more inclusive and context specific approach compared to the strong concern for sovereignty that dominated discussion of the definitional issues and criminalisation.

It was widely agreed that all existing instruments and documents related to corruption should be utilised in drafting the new convention. There was consistent support for referring to UNTOC wherever possible, as this instrument encompassed a range of relevant solutions and 'represented significant achievements, reached by consensus'.[92] Other points of agreement included the importance of addressing the transfer of funds or assets of illicit origin derived from acts of corruption and insuring maximum levels of participation in the Ad Hoc Committee negotiations.

Ultimately, the Expert Group dialogue illustrates a constant tension between state sovereignty concerns and the desire to achieve a broadly inclusive and contextually relevant anti-corruption instrument. The next section of this chapter explores the text of UNCAC in detail, noting the relevant details from Ad Hoc Committee negotiations and paying special attention to the way contested issues were discussed and ultimately incorporated or excluded from the final text of UNCAC. This analysis provides a foundation for more extensive exploration of UNCAC's implementation and enforcement in both regional and domestic context, covered in Chapters 3 to 7. The complexities of UNCAC are demonstrated in the following sections, addressing the likelihood that this multilateral legal instrument can overcome the risks and challenges that stand between the global anti-corruption regime and its final stage of evolution.

Finalising the convention: resolving conflict and establishing structure for UNCAC

The text of UNCAC is divided into eight chapters, comprising 71 articles. UNCAC also contains a preamble and a foreword from the Secretary-General. Chapter I of UNCAC covers 'General provisions' and Chapter II documents 'Preventive measures'. Chapter III, 'Criminalisation and law enforcement', is the most extensive chapter, consisting of Articles 15–42. It covers many of the more actively discussed and consistently controversial elements of UNCAC. Chapter IV covers 'International cooperation'; Chapter V 'Asset recovery'; Chapter VI 'Technical assistance and information exchange'; Chapter VII 'Mechanisms for implementation'; and Chapter VIII 'Final provisions'.

The preamble of UNCAC complements Article 1, presenting the justification for UNCAC and the consensus of the international community regarding the threat of corruption. The preamble cites threats 'to stability and security of societies, undermining the intuitions and values of democracy, ethical values and justice and jeopardizing sustainable development and the rule of law'.[93] It also highlights the links between corruption, organised crime, and economic crimes including money laundering. The preamble presents corruption as 'a transnational phenomenon that affects all societies and economies, making international cooperation . . . essential'.[94] The work of other national and regional organisations, including UNTOC, and the importance of existing multilateral instruments are acknowledged. The preamble supports a 'multidisciplinary' approach to tackling corruption, drawing on language from the Draft Terms of Reference;[95] however no guidance is given regarding the meaning of the term 'multidisciplinary'. The importance of due process, engagement with non-state actors, and the need for inter-state cooperation are all emphasised.

The UN Office on Drugs and Crime (UNODC) Legislative Guide to UNCAC includes a useful overview of the specific provisions of UNCAC.[96] The Legislative Guide subdivides UNCAC into five key areas covering general provisions, criminalisation, prevention, international cooperation, and asset recovery. Provisions within UNCAC can be divided into mandatory provisions, measures that must be considered by states, and measures that are optional.[97] Each of these levels of obligation can be related to the perceived importance of the provision and the level of agreement and support that provision received during the negotiation process.

Articles of interest: resolving conflict and contestation

The remainder of this chapter is dedicated to analysis of the key provisions of UNCAC. Special attention is paid to specific provisions that were controversial or subject to extensive debate, during Expert Group meetings and during Ad Hoc Committee negotiations. Analysis illustrates how issues were discussed and ultimately resolved in the final text of UNCAC. To recap, issues include disagreement surrounding the breadth of UNCAC's coverage, protection of sovereignty and territorial integrity, reversal of the burden of proof and bank secrecy laws, and the nature of preventive measures. The resolution of these issues in the text of UNCAC has implications for the implementation and enforcement of this multilateral legal instrument and tool of the global anti-corruption regime. The approach taken to implementation and enforcement of UNCAC will in turn affect the success of the global anti-corruption regime in achieving the fifth and final stage of evolution.

General provisions

Chapter I of the UNCAC is entitled 'General provisions' and covers Articles 1 to 4. The legislative guide to UNCAC also includes Article 65 (Chapter VIII) 'Implementation of the Convention' and Article 30 'Prosecution, adjudication and sanctions' from Chapter III within the category of general provisions.

Article 65 holds that: 'Each State party shall take the necessary measures . . . in accordance with fundamental principles of its domestic law, to ensure implementation of its obligations under this convention'.[98]

States may also adopt 'more strict and severe measures' once they meet the threshold required under the Convention.[99] Article 65 aims to ensure that 'national legislators act to implement the provisions of the convention in conformity with the fundamental principles of their legal system'.[100] This highlights the importance of domestic implementation to the success of UNCAC. As noted by Joutsen and Graycar:

> [T]he impact of UNCAC is potentially weakened by the fact that it is not self-executing. Each state party has to take domestic action (legislation, policy formulation, allocation of resources) in order to implement the provisions of UNCAC, both mandatory and nonmandatory.[101]

Paragraph 9 of Article 30 from Chapter III holds that:

> Nothing contained in this Convention shall affect the principle that the description of the offences established in accordance with this Convention and of the applicable legal defences or other legal principles controlling the lawfulness of conduct is reserved to the domestic law of a State Party and that such offences shall be prosecuted and punished in accordance with that law.[102]

This paragraph reiterates that the description of offences is reserved for the domestic law of *States Parties*. Along similar lines, Passas holds that: '[B]oth regulatory and criminal law enforcement functions are stubbornly in the hands of national bodies that pursue objectives and employ methods that are inconsistent with each other'.[103]

UNCAC's recognition that states hold ultimate power to implement and enforce the rules UNCAC creates, re-enforces the need to explore domestic efforts through a case study approach. Despite the risks of weakening the international framework and allowing for legislative asymmetries between states, acknowledgement of the ultimate power of *States Parties* suggests a flexibility that may reduce the pitfalls of inapplicability noted by critics in Chapter 1.

Article 65 and Article 30 emphasise the importance of states establishing their own domestic legislation to implement UNCAC, as a means to secure compliance and protect state sovereignty. The balancing of sovereignty concerns with the need for international action, assistance, and coordinate law, is present throughout the Convention. This reflects the unwillingness of states to sacrifice their sovereignty for international objectives, unless 'diverse national interests converge'.[104]

Sovereignty is expressly addressed in Article 4 of UNCAC. This article is 'the primary vehicle for protection of national sovereignty in carrying out the terms of the convention'.[105] The phrase 'in accordance with the fundamental principles of its legal system' can be understood as a safeguard against UNCAC's potential encroachment on state sovereignty. This phrase is used 56 times through the text of UNCAC.

Concerns for sovereignty influenced negotiation of Article 1 and Article 2 of UNCAC, covering the purpose and scope of the Convention. The *Travaux Preparatoires* discuss the Ad Hoc Committee negotiations of both articles in some detail. Regarding Article 1, there was some disagreement over the inclusion of integrity and good governance in the objectives of UNCAC. It was felt that dealing with these subjects 'would allow for intervention in the affairs of States and non-respect for national sovereignty'.[106] Despite reservations, the finally accepted text of Article 1(c) includes the purpose 'to promote integrity, accountability and the proper management of public affairs and public property'.[107] As noted earlier in this chapter, the preamble to UNCAC also highlights the need to safeguard integrity.

The term 'good governance' is not included in the text of UNCAC. This term was removed from the draft of Article 1, following discussion at the Ad Hoc Committee's 6th session. The exclusion of this term illustrates a triumph for states seeking to limit UNCAC's use as a policy laundering tool.[108] As discussed by Passas, the realities of power politics mean that the transfer of power from states to transnational institutions is unlikely to occur unless the act 'can be used as a legitimating tool for controversial or self-serving policies'.[109] The unwillingness of states to include vague terms such as 'good governance' in UNCAC suggests awareness of this political reality. Avoidance of such broad terms in UNCAC may reduce opportunities for political cooperation: restricting the breadth of interpretation available to states and other actors when they interact on the basis of UNCAC or seek to draw on obligations under UNCAC within diplomatic contexts.

In addition to state sovereignty, defining corruption proved controversial during UNCAC negotiation. Article 2 of UNCAC was also the subject of extensive debate, due to its definitional subject matter. The term 'corruption' is notably absent in the final version of the article. Defining corruption was so controversial that, to move forward with negotiations, it was necessary to exclude the term entirely from Article 2.

Four options for defining corruption were presented over the course of the Ad Hoc Committee negotiations. These options were put forward based on the proposals of Peru, the Philippines, and Pakistan, and by the Vice-Chairman of the Ad Hoc Committee, in consultation with Azerbaijan, China, Slovenia, and the Ukraine.[110]

As part of the first session Colombia suggested:

> If a sufficiently broad definition could not be agreed upon, the convention should not include a definition . . . Instead, the convention should identify and criminalise acts of corruption in the chapter on criminalisation.[111]

It was this model (which mirrors other anti-corruption laws including the OAS Convention and the OECD Convention) which was adopted by UNCAC. However, not all states supported this approach.[112]

At the third session of the Ad Hoc Committee, the Vice-Chairman established it would be necessary to hold an open-ended informal consultation, during the 4th session, in order to seek a resolution to the challenge of defining corruption.[113] Two distinct approaches to defining corruption emerged from this consultation. One approach sought to provide a general definition of corruption. The other, more restrictive, approach sought to refer to corruption only as a term to be used in the text of UNCAC.[114] The more restrictive view reflects the legalistic approach to corruption noted in Chapter 1.

Option one appealed to those states that supported a general approach and was worded as follows:

> 'Corruption' shall mean engaging in acts that constitute improper performance of duty [or abuse of a position of authority], including acts of omission, in expectation of an advantage or to obtain an advantage, directly or indirectly promised, offered or requested, or following acceptance of an advantage directly or indirectly given, whether for oneself or on behalf of another.[115]

Option two appealed to states that favoured a more restrictive approach. Some states that were against any inclusion of a definition in Article 2 stated that they would consider inclusion based on the restrictive approach in option two. The wording presented for option two was as follows:

> Notwithstanding the acts of corruption generally recognized in various legal jurisdictions, the use of the term 'corruption' in this Convention shall include such acts as are provided in this Convention and are criminalised

> pursuant to chapter III, whether attributed to a public or private official, and any other acts that the State Party may have criminalised or defined as acts of corruption under its domestic law or may so criminalise or define in future. Nothing herein shall limit the future criminalisation of further acts of corruption or the adoption of measure to combat such acts.[116]

At the 5th Session of the Ad Hoc Committee, option one was deleted and 'most delegations expressed their preference for the deletion of [option two]'.[117] At the 6th Session of the Ad Hoc Committee, the second option was also removed.

The decision to remove option two was based on the fact that deliberations of the open-ended working group had come to a close and discussion 'was associated with certain core issues representing a sharp division for which the group had no mandate'.[118] The Chairman proposed that further consultation be conducted on the inclusion of the phrase:

> [T]he use of the term 'corruption' in this Convention shall refer to acts criminalised in chapter III, as well as to such acts as *States Parties* may criminalise of have already criminalised.[119]

This consultation was never conducted. As a result, Article 2 of UNCAC includes no definition of the term corruption or any reference to such a definition, legalistic or otherwise.

The avoidance of a clear definition of corruption reflects the contested nature of the term, as noted by critics in Chapter 1 of this thesis.[120] Failure to agree on a definition of the target activity and the sharp division of opinion illustrated in discussion of this issue raise concerns regarding the feasibility of a criminal law and enforcement approach to combatting corruption. The risk factor of definitional controversy discussed in Chapter 1 appears relevant in the context of UNCAC. However, failure to settle on a definition does not necessarily undermine the Convention in its entirety, as is discussed below.

Criminalisation

The final text of UNCAC takes a 'corrupt act' approach to criminalisation. This approach may provide a pragmatic legal solution to the definitional controversy discussed above and is aligned with several of the multilateral legal instruments that predate UNCAC. Passas notes that 'harmonization can be attempted even with respect to crimes that are hard to define, such as corruption'.[121] The author suggests that the benefit of a 'corrupt act' approach is that it is 'sensitive to issues of sovereignty and respect for different traditions'.[122] The 'corrupt act' approach, involving provisions that criminalise specific activities associated with corruption, does not provide a perfect solution. The possibility of extensive legal asymmetries, resulting from diverse approaches to domestic criminalisation, is substantial. However, the corrupt act approach allowed for agreement by most states involved in UNCAC negotiation and may in turn reduce the risks and harms associated with homogenous application of a legal concept that does not suit all domestic contexts.

The 'corrupt act' approach applies a flexible model of criminalisation. Some acts, described in Articles 15–17, 23, 25 and 27, must be criminalised. Other acts are to be considered, but criminalisation is not mandatory. This allows states to diverge in the level of criminalisation they adopt, depending on prevailing societal, cultural, legal, or political views in that jurisdiction. By making criminalisation of certain acts mandatory, some consistency of national legislation is achieved. Additionally, controversy regarding the nature of corruption is accommodated by a flexible approach to the criminalisation of other 'corrupt acts'.

Below is a table (Table 2.1) of the Articles that are mandatory and the acts they criminalise. Most of these articles were uncontroversial; the following paragraphs will focus on the few articles that were contested. Relevant extracts from UNCAC, including from those articles below, are included in Annex B.

Article 15 of UNCAC, 'Bribery of National Public Officials', was not the subject of extensive controversy, especially when compared to negotiation of Article 16. Debate centred on the definition of 'public official', the ultimate exclusion of the word 'national' in the title of the article and the use of the term 'bribery' as opposed to 'corruption'. The final version of Article 15 was agreed upon at the 7th session of the Ad Hoc Committee.

Article 16 requires criminalisation of bribery of a foreign public official. This article was more controversial than Article 15. Debate reflects states' concerns about jurisdiction, legal overlap, and the protection of sovereignty. '[S]everal delegations drew attention to potential difficulties . . . in relation to jurisdictional matters and conflict with other international legal instruments concerning privileges and immunities'.[123] The possibility of passive corruption of foreign public

Table 2.1 Mandatory Criminalisation under UNCAC

Mandatory Criminalisation under UNCAC	
Article	*Offence*
Article 15a	Active bribery of national public officials
Article 15b	Passive bribery of national public officials
Article 16 (1)	Active bribery of foreign public officials and officials of public international organisations
Article 17	Embezzlement, misappropriation or other diversion of property by a public official
Article 23	Money laundering (conversion and transfer; concealment and disguise; acquisition, possession or use of proceeds of crime; participation in, association with or conspiracy to commit, attempts to commit and aiding, abetting, facilitating and counselling the commission of any of the foregoing offences)
Article 25	Obstruction of justice
Article 27(1)	Participation

officials was also debated. Mexico was particularly concerned that the article should not be understood or interpreted to permit extraterritorial jurisdiction.[124]

Ultimately, it was agreed that Article 16 would cover both active and passive bribery of foreign public officials and that the article would be understood in relation to other articles on jurisdiction (specifically Article 42 and Article 30(2)). Article 42 covers basic jurisdictional issues. Article 30(2) tackles a more specific issue, stating that each state party shall establish 'an appropriate balance between any immunities or jurisdictional privileges . . . and the possibility . . . of effectively investigating, prosecuting and adjudicating offences established in accordance with this Convention'.[125]

On the topic of jurisdiction, Article 42 of UNCAC mandates *States Parties* to establish jurisdiction according to the 'territoriality principle', as well as if the alleged offender is present in the territory but will not be extradited on the basis of nationality.[126] Additionally, states *may* establish, but are not required to establish, jurisdiction based on the 'active or passive personality principle' and the 'protection principle'. A state may claim jurisdiction over offences committed by or against nationals of that state, as well as offences committed against the state itself.[127] UNCAC suggests that a state may want to establish jurisdiction in regard to participation or attempted money-laundering (Article 23(1)(b)(ii)) where the act itself was committed abroad but the view was to commit the primary act (under Article 23(1)(a) or 23(1)(b)(i)) in the territory of the state claiming jurisdiction.[128] It is important to note these jurisdictional elements of UNCAC, because they are essential to the functioning of the Convention as a whole. As noted in the Technical Guide to UNCAC:

> A central goal of the Convention is to promote international cooperation in the fight against corruption . . . Extradition, mutual legal assistance and asset recovery are forms of international cooperation in which the States Parties involved assist each other in supporting investigation, domestic prosecution or other judicial proceedings, but presuppose that domestic legislation has dealt with jurisdictional issues in an appropriate and functional manner.[129]

Interestingly, the technical guide also reflects that each of these various rationales for jurisdiction may be interpreted differently by different states. There may be cases where diverse claims to jurisdiction are made over the crimes set out in UNCAC, further enhancing the importance of international cooperation and mutual legal assistance. These two topics are discussed further below.

Returning to criminalisation of bribery, a distinction is made between active and passive bribery of foreign public officials and officials of public international organisations. Active bribery of these actors must be criminalised. However, passive bribery of such actors is not mandatory.[130] The optional nature of passive bribery in paragraph 2 of Article 16 does not reflect a willingness to tolerate passive bribery by a foreign public official. Instead, it reflects a more technical rationale.

> The difference in degree of obligation between the two paragraphs is due to the fact that the core conduct addressed by paragraph 2 is already covered by article 15, which requires that *States parties* criminalise the solicitation and acceptance of bribes by their own officials.[131]

This statement illustrates the importance of the language used in UNCAC and the need to understand the intent behind specific wording.

Negotiation of Articles 23, 25 and 27 was reasonably uncontroversial. Article 23 requires criminalisation of the laundering of proceeds of crimes established pursuant to UNCAC. Debate over this article related to the extent of the predicate offences to be included:

> [S]ome delegations expressed concern about the broad range of predicate offences . . . those delegations held the view that only serious predicate offences should be covered . . . other delegations expressed their preference for a broad range of predicate offences.[132]

In the final text, the broad approach was taken, tempered by the clause 'in accordance with fundamental principles of its domestic law'.[133]

Negotiation of Articles 25 and 27 was conducted with relative ease. These articles criminalise 'Obstruction of Justice' relating to other crimes established pursuant to UNCAC and 'Participation and Attempt'. The key issue was ensuring that the final text was compatible with all legal systems where implementation must take place. This issue further illustrates the importance of domestic implementation and enforcement for the success of UNCAC.

The non-mandatory articles included in Chapter III of UNCAC were some of the most controversial. In fact, this controversy helps to explain the categorisation of these articles as non-mandatory. With regard to Article 18, 'Trading in Influence':

> Some delegations expressed serious misgivings about the inclusion of this article. Still others expressed their preference for not including such a provision, but indicated that if there was consensus for inclusion, care should be taken to avoid inadvertent interference with legitimate political activity.[134]

As the debate continued, 'a number of delegations expressed the view that a mandatory formulation would be preferable',[135] however other delegations held that a non-mandatory approach should be taken in order to achieve consensus.[136] During the 6th Session of the Ad Hoc Committee the non-mandatory approach was adopted.[137]

Article 20 on 'Illicit Enrichment' is one of the most controversial articles in UNCAC. Originally drafted as a mandatory article, 'many delegations indicated that they faced serious difficulties, often of a constitutional nature, with the inclusion of the concept of the reversal of the burden of proof'.[138]

Illicit enrichment has a controversial history in anti-corruption law. The OAS Convention was the first corruption convention to criminalise illicit enrichment.

Under Article IX of the OAS Convention, the offence of illicit enrichment is established by 'a significant increase in the assets of a government official that he cannot reasonably explain in relation to his lawful earnings during the performance of his functions.'[139] This offence has been criticised for the extent to which it expands the law in relation to corrupt acts, arguably placing the onus on the accused.[140] Many multilateral legal instruments against corruption that preceded the OAS Convention, including the CoE Convention and SADC Protocol, avoid defining or criminalising illicit enrichment.

The dangers of the extension of law represented by the offence of illicit enrichment have been addressed by Schloenhardt[141] and Symeonidou-Kastanidou.[142] It is noted that, with reference to Transnational Organized Crime legislation:

> special offences to penalize associations with criminal organizations marks a significant extension to criminal liability. The limits of this extension are often unclear and the various organized crime laws can lack sufficient safeguards to prevent their misuse.[143]

Negotiation of illicit enrichment in UNCAC reflects these concerns. While some delegations supported an optional and preventive approach to illicit enrichment, others favoured the efficiency of a criminal approach. Some states suggested that the concept 'actually referred to the rules on evaluation of evidence and not necessarily to the shifting of the burden of proof'.[144]

At the first session of the Ad Hoc Committee, Pakistan proposed that the criminalisation of illicit enrichment be made optional, 'thus providing a way out for *States Parties* that would consider its provisions to be in contradiction with their domestic law'.[145] However, this was not sufficient to remove the reservations of several delegations, including the Russian Federation and the Member States of the EU.

After extensive negotiation and the deletion and re-wording of many paragraphs, consensus was finally achieved at the 6th Session of the Ad Hoc Committee. Article 20 consists of a single non-mandatory paragraph:

> Subject to its constitution and the fundamental principles of its legal system, each State Party shall consider adopting such legislative and other measures as may be necessary to establish as a criminal offence, when committed intentionally, illicit enrichment, that is, a significant increase in the assets of a public official that he or she cannot reasonably explain in relation to his or her lawful income.[146]

Debate surrounding this article, and the other controversial articles discussed above, illustrates the central concerns of states for their sovereignty and the compatibility of UNCAC with domestic law.

The sheer number of articles in Chapter III demonstrates the emphasis placed on consistent criminalisation as a primary method for combatting corruption. One concern raised by this extensive criminalisation approach is that states may not have the necessary resources or capacity to effectively implement and enforce relevant provisions. Because of resource and capacity limitations, legal asymmetries may continue, despite the harmonisation efforts of UNCAC. Political will is also an essential component for success of UNCAC. Criminalisation measures are particularly dependent on political will, as the institutions of the state are essential to implementation and enforcement of such measures. This contrasts with preventive measures, that can draw on engagement of non-state actors.

Considering the risks of an extensive criminalisation focus, it is promising to note that extensive criminalisation under UNCAC does not overshadow preventive measures covered by Chapter II. International cooperation is also a central focus of UNCAC, covered by Chapter IV. The extensive coverage of preventive measures in Chapter II reflects agreement between *States Parties* on the importance of preventive actions and the diversity of possible methods for prevention of corruption, reflecting unique domestic contexts and experiences. Analysis of these chapters suggests that UNCAC goes beyond a pure criminalisation model. This may reduce the Convention's susceptibility to the risks of inapplicability and related harmful side effects resulting from implementation and enforcement efforts.

Preventive measures

Article 5 of UNCAC is the primary article on prevention. It highlights the importance of developing, implementing, and maintaining 'effective, coordinated anti-corruption policies that promote the participation of society and reflect the principles of the rule of law, proper management of public affairs and public property, integrity, transparency and accountability'.[147] Article 5 does not introduce specific legislative requirements. Rather, it 'mandates the commitment of *States Parties* to develop and maintain a host of measures and policies preventive of corruption, in accordance with the fundamental principles of their legal system'.[148]

UNCAC contains a range of other optional provisions for the prevention of corruption. These provisions cover almost all the suggestions put forward during the Intergovernmental Expert Group Meeting. UNCAC's preventive chapter (Chapter II), is the most comprehensive of all international or regional instruments on corruption. UNCAC contains articles on establishment of anti-corruption bodies (Article 6); as well as measures to strengthen public sector systems against corruption through the promotion of equitable pay and specialised training (Article 7). Article 8 suggests the promotion of codes of conduct for public officials based on principles of 'integrity, honesty and responsibility'.[149] Furthermore, public procurement and finances, as well as transparency in public administration, are covered by Articles 9 and 10 respectively. Article 11 concerns the judiciary and prosecution services, illustrating the importance of the judiciary in combatting corruption and highlighting that articles must be relevant to states from a variety of legal and administrative backgrounds.

UNCAC requires *States Parties* 'to promote the active participation of individuals and groups *outside the public sector*, such as Civil Society, non-governmental organizations and community-based organizations, in the prevention and fight against corruption'.[150] This involvement of non-state actors in an international legal instrument such as UNCAC is novel and the mandatory language gives it additional strength. NGO and Civil Society involvement is gaining increasing influence in international law, particularly on issues such as human rights and the core crimes under the Rome Statute.[151] However, such involvement in the case of transnational criminal law is less common. Non-state actor involvement is not considered in the trafficking or terrorism conventions. Involvement of non-state actors in the case of UNCAC reflects a consensus that such actors have a vital role to play in overcoming corruption at all levels. If utilised effectively, such involvement could help to ensure UNCAC does not fall victim to the challenge of non-compliant states or the risk of inapplicability, both of which were discussed in Chapter 1.

The final article of interest in UNCAC's preventive chapter is Article 14: 'Measures to Prevent Money-Laundering'. This article covers regulatory and supervisory regimes for banks and non-bank financial institutions. It is suggested that states establish financial intelligence units and ensure multi-lateral cooperation to track funds of illicit origin. 'Global, regional, sub regional and bilateral cooperation among judicial, law enforcement and financial regulatory authorities'[152] is to be fostered to combat money-laundering. Similar methods for multi-lateral cooperation are promoted regarding all preventive measures established by Chapter II of UNCAC.

Chapter II reflects an extensive range of measures, beyond criminalisation, that are supported by states with the aim of combatting corruption. Such measures emphasise the role of non-state actors, reflect the importance of domestic context in choosing a relevant approach, and highlight the role of cooperation between states, regional groups and multilateral organisations. By utilising these elements of UNCAC, it may be possible to address the challenges facing the global anti-corruption regime and its evolution to stage five of Nadelmann and Andreas' model. Regarding non-compliant states, cooperation between diverse actors may assist in overcoming resource, capacity, and knowledge limitations and asymmetries, enabling more extensive and equal compliance amongst member states. Dissident and deviant actors may also be targeted through cooperative action amongst the diverse actors who support UNCAC. Furthermore, if preventive measures address the underlying causes of corruption in unique domestic contexts, instances of corrupt activity may be reduced, even in cases where activity is not susceptible to criminal law and enforcement measures.

Preventive measures may reduce asymmetries that contribute to corrupt opportunities, thus reducing the profitability of corrupt activity and the related incentives to engage in corrupt acts. The breadth of preventive measures within UNCAC may be utilised positively to balance the criminalisation focus of Chapter III. These measures could assist in overcoming the challenges facing the global anti-corruption regime, as introduced in Chapter 1. This potential is limited by the extent to which states are willing to utilise the preventive framework set out in UNCAC. Concerns for sovereignty, including in relation to international cooperation, may continue to limit the power of preventive efforts.

International cooperation

Chapter IV covers 'International cooperation', which is also one of the primary principles of the Convention. Negotiation of the articles in Chapter IV illustrates the continuing concern of states for their sovereignty, the persistent link between corruption and other forms of transnational crime, the desire to ensure harmonisation of the anti-corruption framework with existing multilateral legal instruments, and the coordinating role played by multilateral institutions in securing implementation and enforcement of multilateral legal instruments such as UNCAC.

Article 43 was originally proposed by Cameroon, Mexico, the Netherlands, and Thailand,[153] to include a measure that removed bank secrecy as a rationale for refusing assistance. This proposal was highly contested and ultimately removed from the final article, allowing for the continued use of bank secrecy as a rationale for refusing assistance. In its final form, Article 43 requires states to cooperate in criminal matters and 'where appropriate and consistent with their domestic legal system . . . consider assisting each other in investigations of and proceedings in civil and administrative matters relating to corruption'.[154] Article 43 also addresses the issue of dual criminality. This principle has traditionally formed the basis of international cooperation, particularly regarding extradition.

> According to that principle, States Parties are required to extradite fugitives or provide assistance in relation to offences committed outside their jurisdiction on the condition that those acts are criminalized by their own legislation.[155]

Article 43(2) of UNCAC sets a broad basis for establishing whether this principle is satisfied. The article holds:

> In matters of international cooperation, whenever dual criminality is considered a requirement, it shall be deemed fulfilled irrespective of whether the laws of the requested State Party place the offence within the same category of offence or denominate the offence by the same terminology as the requesting State Party, if the conduct underlying the offence for which assistance is sought is a criminal offence under the laws of both States Parties.[156]

This provision of UNCAC

> explicitly minimizes the significance of the particular legislative language used to penalize certain conduct and encourages a more pragmatic focus on whether the underlying factual conduct is punishable by both contracting States, even if under differently named statutory categories.[157]

The broad interpretation of dual criminality under UNCAC illustrates the Convention's goal of facilitating and enhancing international cooperation in the prevention and punishment of corruption. To achieve this goal, UNCAC must navigate the challenges that arise when attempting to coordinate between diverse legal systems, interpretations, and procedures.

Bank secrecy was also an issue during negotiation of Article 46, 'Mutual Legal Assistance'. This article follows the framework established by UNTOC, with an explanatory note allowing bank secrecy as an exception to using information or evidence for exculpatory purposes without prior approval of the requested state.[158] Following Passas, the bank secrecy exception shows how states are responsible for creating and maintaining criminogenic asymmetries. If states are unwilling to compromise or adapt their domestic legislation to support the goals of the global anti-corruption regime, opportunities to engage in corrupt behaviour will continue to exist and may become more profitable as legal asymmetries spring up between member states.

Other interesting and controversial articles within Chapter IV include 'Transfer of Criminal Proceedings' (Article 47) and 'Special Investigative Techniques' (Article 50). The former article raised sovereignty concerns. Algeria noted that such a provision 'might imply abandonment of the principle of jurisdictional sovereignty'.[159] Other delegations held that the form of this article was non-binding and that the concept was not intended 'as a threat to the sovereignty of States, but as a formula to ensure the efficient administration of justice'.[160] Ultimately, the article was included in UNCAC and no interpretive notes were added.

Article 50 draws on UNTOC and requires that states, subject to the basic principles of their domestic legal system:

> take such measures as may be necessary, within its means, to allow for the appropriate use by its competent authorities of controlled delivery and, where it deems appropriate, other special investigative techniques, such as electronic or other forms of surveillance and undercover operations, within its territory, and to allow for the admissibility in court of evidence derived therefrom.[161]

Some states questioned the relevance of controlled delivery in the context of corruption. Despite many states recognising this concern, the concept was retained, reflecting the perceived links between corruption and other forms of transnational criminality. Controlled delivery illustrates how the link between corruption and other forms of crime can impact the techniques used for prevention and punishment. Controlled delivery is a method common in anti-drug trafficking efforts. This method is not necessarily appropriate for targeting corruption, even if corruption and trafficking crimes are linked in some contexts.

Articles 60, 61 and 62 emphasise the importance of international cooperation (in the form of technical assistance) in training regulatory and law enforcement bodies; exchanging information on successful anti-corruption measures; and interacting with experts can suggest further prevention methods based on successful anti-corruption measures. These articles demonstrate the value UNCAC places on cooperation between states, non-state actors, and multilateral institutions. International cooperation as a preventive measure also illustrates the important coordinating role played by multilateral institutions in the fourth stage of regime evolution, as discussed by Nadelmann and Andreas.[162] Multilateral institutions emerge in the fourth stage of evolution to play a coordinating role in securing consistent legislative and enforcement measures across jurisdictions.[163] In the context of the global anti-corruption regime, UNCAC and its measures on international cooperation facilitate this role, especially for the UN. Information sharing and cooperation measures appear to be positive elements of UNCAC. However, it is possible that the provision of 'technical assistance' could be used as a means for political co-optation and may limit the domestic relevance and applicability of UNCAC. The manner in which actors cooperate under these articles, and the nature and extent of power asymmetries between actors, will shape the outcomes of this cooperation in terms of implementation and enforcement of UNCAC. If cooperation is undertaken in a context sensitive way, it may support effective implementation and enforcement. However, if cooperation fails to account for variation in corrupt activities and contexts, or is used as a smoke screen for the promotion of political agendas, the goals of UNCAC will be undermined, limiting the success of the global anti-corruption regime.

Asset recovery

Principles of international cooperation are of the upmost importance in Chapter V on 'Asset recovery', reflecting the general cooperative trend throughout UNCAC. The articles in this chapter illustrate the view that:

> The exportation of assets derived from corruption or other illicit sources has serious or even devastating consequences for the State of origin. It undermines foreign aid, drains currency reserves, reduces the tax base, increases poverty levels, harms competition and undercuts free trade . . . Consequently, any effective and deterrent response must be global and address the issue of asset return to victimized States or other parties.[164]

Chapter V thus acts as a deterrent to corrupt activity, and as an incentive to participate in implementation and enforcement of UNCAC, in order to secure the return of stolen assets transferred to foreign jurisdictions.

In negotiation of Article 51, issues of sovereignty and territorial integrity were again relevant. Subparagraph 1(d) of the draft article held:

> *States Parties* shall afford one another mutual technical assistance in the revision of their respective financial laws with a view to eliminating any regulatory gaps that might permit the uncontrolled transfer of assets, including funds, of illicit origin derived from acts of corruption.[165]

Many delegations stressed the need to specify that such technical assistance would be provided only upon request by a state party, so as not to encroach on domestic sovereignty and integrity.[166] Such concerns, combined with the desire to avoid overlap with other articles, led to a simplified Article 51:

> The return of assets pursuant to this chapter is a fundamental principle of this Convention, and *States Parties* shall afford one another the widest measure of cooperation and assistance in this regard.[167]

Articles 52–59 cover a variety of measures to combat the illicit transfer of assets and return such assets to their country of origin. Principles of international cooperation are of upmost importance in these articles. A controversial issue that arose during negotiation of these articles was the threshold for which public officials and certain accounts would be subject to enhanced scrutiny or administrative requirements (Article 52). Ultimately, a broad and subjective approach was taken and the term 'appropriate public officials' was used, along with non-mandatory language. This provides another example of non-binding form being used as a mechanism to secure consensus.

The negotiation of the Asset recovery chapter illustrates the trend towards broad and interpretive language within UNCAC, especially in cases where state sovereignty concerns arose and were not easily resolved. Articles in this chapter may incentivise implementation of UNCAC and cooperation between states parties. However, the effectiveness of these measures, and the Convention more generally, maybe limited by its broad language and concerns for the protection of state sovereignty.

Application and adaption: Chapter VII and the implementation review mechanism for UNCAC

This section explores the implementation and review mechanism for UNCAC. The adoption of the implementation review mechanism, and subsequent participation of 177 *States Parties* in this mechanism, has substantially strengthened the global prohibition regime against corruption and the position of UNCAC as the primary legal tool of this regime. This progress illustrates near universal agreement by states on the need to cooperate and combat corruption in a consistent and transnational manner.

Chapter VII of UNCAC is entitled 'Mechanisms for implementation'. In this chapter, Article 63 establishes a Conference of States Parties (CoSP) 'to improve the capacity of and cooperation between *States Parties* to achieve the objectives set forth in this Convention and to promote and review its implementation'.[168] This CoSP is charged with a range of facilitative activities to support implementation of UNCAC. These include: exchange of information between states; cooperation with international, regional, and non-government organisations; utilising information produced by other regional and international organisations on corruption and its prevention; reviewing implementation of UNCAC; making recommendations for technical assistance and for improvements to UNCAC and its implementation.[169] Considering these objectives, Article 63(5) notes the importance of acquiring knowledge regarding state efforts to implement UNCAC and the difficulties encountered.[170] Article 63(7) then formally states that 'the Conference of the *States Parties* shall establish, if it deems it necessary, any appropriate mechanism or body to assist in the effective implementation of the convention'.[171]

Based on the suggestion in Article 63 of UNCAC, the third meeting of the CoSP adopted resolution 3/1 'Review Mechanism'.[172] This resolution consists of the terms of reference for the review of UNCAC implementation. The mechanism establishes a process for reviewing implementation of UNCAC, based on Article 4(1) of UNCAC:

> *States Parties* shall carry out their obligations under this Convention in a manner consistent with the principles of sovereign equality and territorial integrity of States and that of non-intervention in the domestic affairs of other States.[173]

The terms of reference for the mechanism provide an overview of its structure, function, and goals. Throughout the terms of reference, consistent attention is paid to the importance of: state sovereignty; information sharing and cooperation across organisations, between states, regionally, and internationally; political neutrality; and complementarity with other existing international and regional anti-corruption efforts.

Joutsen and Graycar provide an insightful overview of the negotiation process for the review mechanisms.[174] Much like negotiation of UNCAC itself, the process of negotiating the review mechanism required substantial diplomacy and compromise. The terms of reference for the review mechanism of UNCAC reflect a balance between a technocratic approach based on efficient and open review and a politically sensitive approach emphasising the need to protect state sovereignty and avoid co-optation of the mechanism for political objectives, categorisation, and influence.

Chapter IV of the terms of reference discusses the review process in detail. The goals of the process are covered by Chapter IV (A), paragraph 11 (available in Annex B). The general goal of the review process 'shall be to assist *States parties* in their implementation of the Convention'.[175] The mechanism is applicable to all *States Parties.*[176] A participating state must provide information on its compliance and implementation, via a comprehensive self-assessment checklist.[177] The State party is reviewed by two other *States Parties*, with the active involvement of the party under review.[178] One of the two reviewing *States Parties* must be from the same geographical region as the State party under review and have a similar legal system as that State party.[179] The State party under review may request that the drawing of lots to select reviewing states be repeated up to two times.[180]

The reviewing states utilise the responses to the self-assessment checklist and 'any supplementary information provided by the State party under review'.[181] If the state under review is a member of other anti-corruption bodies, mechanism, or intergovernmental organisations, reviewing states can consider information from these bodies in the review process.[182]

The importance of engaging stakeholders outside government is noted in paragraphs 28 and 30 of the terms of reference. Paragraph 28 holds that states under review should prepare responses to the self-assessment checklist 'through broad consultations at the national level with all relevant stakeholders, including the private sector, individuals and groups outside the public sector'.[183] Paragraph 30 continues the support for broad engagement by encouraging states to 'facilitate engagement with all relevant national stakeholders in the course of a country visit'.[184]

Vlassis notes that engagement with outside stakeholders is a positive and substantial element of the review processes.[185] However, the final approach taken was the product of substantial compromise between those parties that supported an 'open' review mechanism and those who favoured a 'closed' review. Supporters of a closed review sought to avoid the use of any information not provided directly by the state under review. Those in favour of an open review supported use of any and all available information on the implementation process conducted by the state under review. In the end, the state under review is still in control of the actors that it chooses to engage in drafting its self-assessment checklist. Furthermore, country visits are optional and involvement of external stakeholders during these visits is at the discretion of the state under review. This compromise is a good example of the continuing importance of domestic political will in securing implementation of multilateral legal instruments such as UNCAC. The approach taken to implementation and review of UNCAC puts into perspective the challenge of non-compliance, noted by Nadelmann and Andreas.[186] Even those states that formally support the global anti-corruption regime and have committed to the approach set out in UNCAC can have significant reservations about a review process designed to evaluate compliance with the regime and its legal tools. Ultimately, the power to implement and enforce the transnational criminal law tools of any global prohibition regime rests with states.

The power of states and the importance of domestic political will is highlighted by the debate and compromise in the review mechanism. However, the important role of international institutions and organisations is also illustrated. The secretariat has a particularly important role. It is tasked with organising training courses for experts who participate in the review process,[187] compiling a thematic implementation report on the most common and relevant successes, good practices, and challenges in implementing UNCAC, and assisting in the preparation of country review reports and executive summaries by supporting and coordinating between reviewing states and states being reviewed.[188] The role of the secretariat in supporting UNCAC implementation reflects the fourth stage of regime evolution discussed in Chapter 1. It provides yet another example of the coordinating role played by international institutions in securing consistent criminal law and enforcement efforts directed at the regime's target activity.[189]

The first cycle of the implementation review mechanism focused on Chapters III (Criminalisation and law enforcement) and IV (International cooperation).[190] This focus reflects the importance of criminalisation in the global anti-corruption regime's approach to combatting corrupt activity, as well as the value placed on a coordinated and cooperative transnational approach, set out in Chapter IV of UNCAC.

Since the review mechanism was adopted, the Implementation Review group has met for eight sessions. The resumed 8th session was held from 7 to 8 November 2017. The first review cycle took place between 2010 and 2015.

The review process resulted in the publication of a UNODC report of the 'State Implementation and Review of UNCAC'. The 2nd Edition, published in October 2017, analyses 156 *States Parties* and their implementation of Chapters III and IV of the Convention.[191] The second cycle of implementation and review began in November 2015, and covers Chapters II and V, on prevention and asset recovery, with the drawing of lots for states reviewed in the first year. The progress report from the sixth session provides some interesting statistics on the review process for the first cycle. Ninety-six % of the countries under review chose to engage in direct dialogue with reviewing states, beyond provision of the self-assessment checklist.[192] Of the 27 *States Parties* reviewed in the first year, 89% arranged for a country visit. Papua New Guinea (PNG) is included in this 89%, being reviewed by Tajikistan and Malawi.[193]

A brief note on the results of the Implementation Review process is useful for illustrating the extensive domestic criminalisation of corrupt acts under UNCAC. The Thematic Report covering Articles 15–29 of Chapter III of UNCAC is insightful.[194] The report 'contains an analysis of the most prevalent challenges in the implementation of chapter III'.[195] It is noted that all *States Parties* have measures to criminalise active and passive bribery of domestic public officials (Article 15), embezzlement (Article 17), and participation (Article 27).[196] Furthermore:

> [M]any had taken steps towards establishing as criminal offences the bribery of foreign public officials and officials of public international organizations . . . Trading in influence, a non-mandatory provision, had been established as a criminal offence in the majority of *States parties* . . . most *States parties* had taken measures towards establishing money-laundering as a criminal offence [and] obstruction of justice had been established as a criminal offence in most *States parties.*[197]

The report emphasises that the main challenges for implementing these articles of UNCAC related to the scope of the domestic legislation. For example, in the case of money laundering, several states' domestic legislation 'covered only part of the conduct described in subparagraphs (1)(a)(ii) and (1)(b)(i) of Article 23, and only minor parts of subparagraphs (2)(a) through (e)'.[198] This illustrates that consistency of approach remains a challenge, perhaps reflecting the unique domestic contexts in which UNCAC must be implemented and ultimately enforced. However, in general, corrupt acts are criminalised in all *States Parties* to UNCAC, illustrating consensus on the need to criminalise corrupt conduct.

Building on the thematic report, the 2017 State Implementation and Review expands on pre-existing findings and emphasises the positive impact that UNCAC has had on domestic anti-corruption frameworks.

> In a considerable number of countries, legislative amendments and structural reforms have produced coherent and largely harmonized criminalization regimes, tangible results in terms of enforcement capabilities and action, and strong frameworks for extradition, mutual legal assistance and

> law enforcement cooperation. In many countries, these legal and policy developments were initiated as a direct result of, or in the context of the implementation reviews.[199]

Substantial engagement in the review mechanism process reflects the strength of UNCAC as a tool of the global anti-corruption regime. It further suggests that the regime can be seen to be in the fourth stage of evolution. Corrupt acts are the subject of criminal law and enforcement measures in almost all countries. A total of 183 states have ratified UNCAC and 156 states have participated in the Implementation Review processes so far. The process of review involves extensive engagement between *States Parties* and allows for facilitation and support from the secretariat. Despite suggestions to further allocate resources to anti-corruption activities and continue to align domestic law with UNCAC, the review process appears to support an adaptable and context specific approach to implementation and enforcement. This may help to counter the risk of inapplicability discussed by critics and reflected in the uneven participation of certain states and regional groups in the negotiation of UNCAC and its review mechanism. However, the 2017 State Implementation and Review document notes that there is still some way to go before all states achieve a coordinated anti-corruption approach in line with UNCAC. Certain mandatory criminalisation measures under UNCAC are often absent in domestic legislation,[200] or are not enforced. Resource and capacity limitations are also raised, especially in terms of implementing preventive measures.[201] However, it should be noted that resource limitations may reflect limited political will, as much as it reflects legitimate technical constraints. Disentangling the legitimate reasons for inaction or ineffectiveness at the domestic level will always be a challenging task.

Conclusion: how has UNCAC evolved within the global anti-corruption regime?

UNCAC is the result of several decades of sustained debate at the international level and a three-year negotiation process. The final instrument represents the primary legal tool of the global anti-corruption regime, supporting a consistent and universal approach to criminalisation, prevention, and punishment of a diverse range of corrupt activities. Extensive ratification of UNCAC, development of and participation in the Review Mechanism, and substantial levels of criminalisation in *States Parties* all illustrate that UNCAC has supported the global anti-corruption regime's evolution to stage four.

Analysis of UNCAC and its Review Mechanism illustrates important issues that will be of continued relevance in the chapters to follow. These issues reflect criticisms and risk factors noted in Chapter 1 including: definitional controversy, criminal law and enforcement focus, the promotion of a link between corruption and other forms of criminality, and potential inapplicability of the global anti-corruption regime in diverse domestic contexts. First, definitional controversy regarding the term corruption was sufficiently strong for states to eliminate any definition of the term in Article 2 of UNCAC. However, the extensive discussion and combination of mandatory and non-mandatory provisions under Chapter III of UNCAC provides options for action while allowing for disagreement on a broad definition.

In the context of this multilateral legal instrument, which seeks to establish effective and actionable measures against corruption, agreement on a definition of corruption would have required extreme breadth. Such a broad definition, for example 'the abuse of public power for private gain', would arguably be of little practical value. Thus, the alternative 'corrupt act' approach may be beneficial to the goal of reducing levels of corruption around the world, thus securing the success of the global anti-corruption regime. While the 'corrupt act' approach allowed for agreement to be reached on UNCAC, failure to 'solve' the challenge of diverse definitions and understandings of the term corruption means criticisms relating to this challenge will remain pertinent in the continued analysis of UNCAC's implementation and enforcement at the national level.

A second issue relates to the centrality of criminal law and enforcement measures. Such measures take centre stage in UNCAC, including through the agenda of the Review Mechanism.[202] Criticisms of the global anti-corruption regime's criminalisation focus will be of continued relevance to the analysis of UNCAC and its domestic implementation and enforcement. However, such criticisms may be tempered by the extensive efforts within UNCAC to include a diverse range of mandatory and optional measures that do not require criminal sanctions. Preventive measures and international cooperation are vital to UNCAC. Thus, the risk of a criminal law and enforcement focus may be balanced by the extensive array of non-criminal measures included in UNCAC.

A final point to note is the under-representation of the South Pacific region in the UNCAC negotiation process. As Joutsen and Graycar note 'the impact of UNCAC is potentially weakened by the fact that it is not self-executing'.[203] UNCAC requires domestic implementation and enforcement in order to have practical impact. Limited involvement by the South Pacific region during the UNCAC negotiation raises concerns regarding the level of implementation and enforcement likely in the region, as well as the extent to which the measures established by UNCAC will be relevant to these unique domestic contexts. This concern reflects the risk factor of inapplicability introduced by critics in Chapter 1.

The 'criminal act' approach taken by UNCAC and the wide range of non-criminal measures established by this multilateral legal instrument may help overcome the risk of inapplicability that results from under-representation. The criminal act approach and its combination of mandatory and non-mandatory provisions, combined with a diverse range of optional prevention measures, may allow states to pick and choose those provisions best suited to their unique contexts. However, this raises concerns regarding the challenge of non-compliant states, noted by Nadelmann and Andreas. If states can pick and choose between provisions, they may do so in a manner that limits the effectiveness of UNCAC, rather than supporting its application domestically. Resource allocation may be another way to limit operational effectiveness of UNCAC. As has been noted already, resource and capacity limits were a reoccurring theme during reviews, but understanding the underlying cause of these limitations is difficult.

Ultimately, UNCAC is the most widely ratified and extensive multilateral legal instrument targeting corruption. It represents the evolution of the global anti-corruption regime to the fourth stage and supports a cooperative and universal approach to the criminalisation and prevention of corrupt acts. Analysis of this multilateral legal instrument suggests that the key risk factors and challenges noted in Chapter 1 are balanced by the structure and scope of UNCAC, but remain relevant to further analysis. Chapter 3 will document the regional context of the South Pacific, before Chapter 4 explores the state level case study of Papua New Guinea in more detail. This preliminary exploration of the regional context is particularly relevant considering the under-representation of the South Pacific region in UNCAC negotiation.

Notes

1 Nadelmann EA and Andreas P, *Policing the Globe: Criminalization and crime control in international relations* (Oxford University Press, 1st Edition, 2006)
2 See Kubiciel M, 'Core Criminal Law Provisions in the United Nations Convention Against Corruption' 9 *International Criminal Law Review* (2009) 139. The author views UNCAC as the peak of international action against corruption, at 140. The Report of the Secretary General, ECOSOC, 2001 'Existing International Legal instruments, Recommendations and other Documents addressing Corruption', E/CN.15/2001/3, notes that other regional and multi-lateral instruments preceding the development of UNCAC tended to focus on the regional sphere (with the exception of the OECD Convention). Thus, UNCAC can be viewed as the first and only instrument dedicated to the prevention and punishment of corruption which has truly international scope
3 General Assembly Resolution 58/4 (2003)
4 *United Nations Convention against Corruption*, opened for signature 9 December 2003, 2349 UNTS 41 (entered into force 14 December 2005) ('UNCAC'), Foreword at iii
5 *UNCAC*, Foreword at iii
6 above n1
7 above n1
8 General Assembly Resolution 34/169, 1997
9 ibid., Annex, at 187
10 ibid.
11 The seminar was convened by the Crime Prevention and Criminal Justice Branch in cooperation with the Department of Technical Cooperation for Development of the Secretariat. The seminar was part of the preparatory work for the 8th Crime Congress and was hosted by the Government of the Netherlands in The Hague. The seminar was attended by officials from 18 developing countries and observers from nine developed countries, NGOs, academic institutions, independent anti-corruption bodies, and ombudsmans' offices.
12 United Nations, '*Travaux Preparatoires* of the Negotiations for the elaboration of the United Nations Convention against Corruption' (2010) at xvii
13 Eighth United Nations Congress on the Prevention of Crime and the Treatment of Offenders, 1990, Resolution 7 'Corruption in Government', A/CONF.144/28/Rev.1
14 above n12 at xvii

15 above n13 at 137
16 ibid. at 136
17 ibid. at 137
18 General Assembly Resolution 46/152, 18 December 1991
19 *United Nations Convention against Transnational Organised Crime,* open for signature 12 December 2000, 2225 UNTS 209 (entered into force 29 September 2003) ('UNTOC') Articles 8 and 9
20 The Commission on Human Rights (March 1992) 'Fraudulent enrichment of top State officials prejudicial to the public interest, the factors responsible for it, and the agents involved in all countries in such fraudulent enrichment', Resolution 1992/50
21 See above n12, quoting the background document of the World Ministerial Conference (E/CONF.88/2, para 121)
22 Boister N, 'Transnational Criminal Law?' 14(5) *EJIL* (2003) 953
23 *Inter-American Convention against Corruption*, opened for signature 29 March 1996, 35 ILM 724 (entered into force 6 March 1997) ('OAS Convention')
24 *Convention on Combating Bribery of Foreign Public Officials in International Business Transactions*, opened for signature 17 December 1997, 37 ILM 1 (entered into force 15 February 1999) ('OECD Convention')
25 *Council of Europe Civil Law Convention on Corruption*, opened for signature 4 November 1999, ETS 174 (entered into force 1 November 2003) ('CoE Civil Law Convention')
26 *Council of Europe Criminal Law Convention on Corruption*, opened for signature 27 January 1999, ETS 173 (entered into force 1 July 2002) ('CoE Criminal Law Convention')
27 above n12, at xxviii–xxix
28 ibid.
29 ibid. at xxvix
30 ibid.
31 Economic and Social Council Resolution 1998/16 'Action against Corruption' (E/1998/30 and Corr.1) adopted 28 July 1998
32 Vlassis D, 'The United Nations Convention against Corruption Origins and Negotiation Process', *Resource Material Series* No. 66 (2005), at 127
33 General Assembly Resolution 55/61, 22 January 2001
34 iIbid.
35 ECOSOC, Secretary General's Report: Existing International Legal Instruments, Recommendations and other Documents Addressing Corruption, E/CN.15/2001/3 ('Secretary-General's Report, 2001')
36 The legal instruments highlighted by the report included: UNTOC, the CoE Criminal and Civil Law Conventions, the EU Convention on PFI and its protocols, the EU Convention on Corruption of European Officials, the EU Joint Action against Corruption in the Private Sectors, the OAS Convention and the OECD Convention
37 Secretary-General's Report (2001) Annex 1 and 2. A full list of relevant legal and non-binding documents reviewed by the Secretary-General in his report can be found in the Annexes of that report
38 OAS Convention, preamble
39 EU Convention on the protection of the European Communities' financial Interests (OJ C 316, 1995), First Protocol (OJ C 313, 1996)
40 EU Convention on the protection of the European Communities' financial interests, Second Protocol (OJ C 221, 1997)
41 General Assembly Resolution 55/25, 2000, 'United Nations Convention against Transnational Organised Crime', at 2
42 ibid.
43 See Chapter 1 at 1.3.1
44 ibid.

45 The *CoE Civil Law Convention against Corruption* does not touch on issues of criminalisation because its purpose is to establish civil remedies for acts of corruption as defined in the *Criminal Law Convention.*
46 OAS Convention
47 EU convention, first protocol
48 EU convention, second protocol
49 OECD Convention, Article 1
50 EU, *Joint Action on Corruption in the Private Sector*, (22 December 1998), *OJ L 358*, preamble
51 CoE Criminal Law Convention (1998), preamble (emphasis added)
52 EU Convention (1997), article 5
53 UNTOC, Article 9
54 OAS Convention
55 OAS Convention, Article III
56 OECD Convention
57 CoE Civil Law Convention, Article 10
58 Secretary-General's Report (2001) at 27
59 Secretary-General's Report (2001)
60 ibid.
61 ibid.
62 ibid.
63 ibid. at 28
64 iIbid.
65 See Chapter 1 at Rish factor four: the limits of a singular solution.
66 Secretary-General's Report (2001) at 28
67 Passas N, 'Globalization and Transnational Crime: Effects of Criminogenic Asymmetries', in Williams P and Vlassis D (Eds), *Combatting Transnational Crime: Concepts, Activities and Responses* (Frank Cass Publishers, 2013) 22 at 47
68 ibid.
69 General Assembly, An effective international legal instrument against corruption', A/Res/55/61 (22 January 2001) at: https://www.unodc.org/pdf/crime/a_res_55/res5561e.pdf (last visited 1 March 2018)
70 An 8th Session was held in 2006 to approve the draft rules of procedure for the convention and submit them to the Conference of *States Parties*
71 *Report of the Meeting of the Intergovernmental Open-Ended Expert Group to Prepare Draft Terms of Reference for the Negotiation of an International Legal Instrument against Corruption* (2001) A/56/402 E/2001/105, Chapter II, para 5 'Terms of Reference for the negotiation of the United Nations Convention against Corruption'
72 ibid.
73 ECOSOC Resolution 2001/46, *Terms of Reference for the negotiation of the United Nations Convention against Corruption*, E/CN.15/2001/3 (ECOSOC Res 2001/46)
74 ECOSOC Res 2001/46
75 ibid.
76 ibid.
77 Ad Hoc Committee for the Negotiation of a Convention against Corruption on its second session (2002) A/AC.261/7, Annex II: List of Participants
78 See Chapter 1 at Risk factor four: the limits of a singular solution
79 above n1
80 *Report of the Meeting of the Intergovernmental Open-Ended Expert Group to Prepare Draft Terms of Reference for the Negotiation of an International Legal Instrument against Corruption* (2001) A/56/402 E/2001/105, Chapter III, para 8
81 ibid., Chapter IV, para 27
82 ibid., Chapter IV, para 14

83 ibid., Chapter IV, para 17
84 ibid., Chapter IV, para 18
85 ibid., Chapter IV, para 31
86 ibid., Chapter IV, para 16
87 ibid., Chapter IV, para 28
88 ibid., Chapter IV, para 16
89 ibid., Chapter IV, para 15
90 ibid., Chapter IV, para 16
91 ibid., Chapter IV, para 17
92 ibid., Chapter IV, para 25
93 ibid., preamble at 2
94 ibid. at 5
95 ibid., preamble
96 United Nations, *Legislative Guide for the Implementation of the United Nations Convention against Corruption* (2006). The Legislative Guide (2006) is not a legal document. 'The guide is not intended to provide definitive legal interpretation of the articles of the Convention.' at iii. Instead, it aims to assist States seeking to ratify and implement UNCAC 'by identifying legislative requirements, issues arising from those requirements and various options available to States as they develop and draft the necessary legislation.' at iii
97 ibid. para 11
98 UNCAC, Chapter VIII, Article 65, para 1, at 53
99 UNCAC, Chapter VIII, Article 65, para 2, at 54
100 above n96 para 18, at 7
101 Joutsen M and Graycar A, 'When Experts and Diplomats Agree: Negotiating peer review of the UN Convention against Corruption' 18 *Global Governance* (2012) 425, at 426
102 UNCAC, Article 30(9) at 23–24
103 above n67 at 39
104 above n67 at 43
105 above n96, para 31, at 12
106 above n12 at 16, footnote 7
107 UNCAC, Article 1(c) at 7
108 See Beare ME, 'Corruption and Organised Crime: Lessons from History' 28 *Crime, Law and Social Change* (1997) 155 and McCulloch J, 'Transnational Crime as Productive Fiction' 24(2) *Social Justice* (2007) 19 regarding the risks of policy laundering
109 above n 67 at 43
110 above n12
111 ibid. at 30, footnote 31
112 In particular, the group of 77 and China, and the Group of African States did not support this method for dealing with the definition of corruption
113 above n12 at 38, footnote 52
114 ibid. at 42, footnote 76
115 ibid. at 42
116 ibid. at 42–43
117 ibid. at 47, footnote 109
118 ibid. at 51, footnote 122
119 ibid.
120 Carr I, 'Corruption, legal solution and limits of law' 3(3) *International Journal of Law in Context* (2007) 227; Farrales M, 'What is Corruption? A history of corruption studies and the great definitions debate', *University of San Diego Working Paper Series* [2005] available at: http://papers.ssrn.com/sol3/papers.cfm?abstract_id=1739962 (last visited 1 March 2018); Reed Q, 'Squeezing a Balloon? Challenging the nexus

between organised crime and corruption' (7) *CMI U4 Issue* (2009); Schloenhardt A, 'Fighting Organised Crime in the Asia Pacific Region: New weapons, lost wars' 2 *Asian Journal of International Law* (2012) 137; Schutte SA, 'Against the Odds: Anti-corruption reform in Indonesia' 32 *Public Admin. Dev.* (2012) 38

121 Above n67 at 47
122 ibid.
123 above n12, at 170
124 above n12
125 UNCAC, Chapter III, Article 30, at 22–23
126 UNCAC, Chapter III, Articles 42(1) and 42(3)
127 UNCAC, Chapter III, Article 42(2)
128 UNCAC, Chapter III, Article 42(2)(c)
129 UNCAC, *Technical Guide to the United Nations Convention against Corruption* (2009), at 132
130 UNCAC, Chapter III, Article 16(2), at 18
131 above n96 at 100, para 273, quoting the UNCAC interpretive note (A/58/422/Add.1, para 28)
132 above n12, at 218, footnote 14
133 UNCAC, Article 23(1), at 19
134 above n12, at 185, footnote 7
135 ibid., at 188, footnote 16
136 ibid.
137 UNCAC, Chapter III, Article 18, at 18
138 above n12, at 196, para 1
139 *Inter-American Convention against Corruption*, opened for signature 29 March 1996, 35 ILM 724 (entered into force 6 March 1997) ('OAS Convention'), Article IX, para 1
140 Carr I, 'Corruption, legal solution and limits of law' 3(3) *International Journal of Law in Context* (2007)
141 Schloenhardt A, 'Palermo on the Pacific Rim: organised crime offences in the asia pacific region' (2009) UNODC Study Series No.1
142 Symeonidou-Kastanidou E, 'Towards a New Definition of Organised Crime in the European Union' (2007) 15(1) *European Journal of Crime, Criminal Law and Criminal Justice* 105
143 above n141 at 15
144 above n12, at 196, para 1
145 ibid., at 197, para 4
146 UNCAC, Chapter III, Article 20
147 ibid., Article 5, at 9
148 above n96 at 19, para 48
149 UNCAC, Chapter II, Article 8, at 11
150 ibid., Article 13(1), at 15
151 See Van der Vyver JD, 'Civil Society and the International Criminal Court' 2 *Journal of Human Rights* 3 (2003) 425; Glasius M, 'Does the Involvement of Global Civil Society Make International Decision-Making More Democratic? The case of the International Criminal Court' 4 *Journal of Civil Society* 1 (2008) 43
152 UNCAC, Chapter II, Article 14(5), at 17
153 above n12 at 341, footnote 1
154 UNCAC, Chapter IV Article 43(1), at 30
155 United Nations, *Technical Guide to UNCAC* (2009) at 141
156 UNCAC, Chapter IV, Article 43(2)
157 above n155 at 141
158 above n12 at 407
159 ibid. at 412

160 ibid.
161 UNCAC, Chapter IV, Article 50, at 41
162 above n1
163 ibid. at 21
164 above n96 at 229, para 660
165 Above n12, at 438
166 ibid. at 439, footnote 4
167 UNCAC, Chapter V, Article 51, at 42
168 UNCAC, Chapter VII, Article 63, at 51
169 ibid. at 52, para 4
170 ibid. at 52, para 5
171 ibid. at 53, para 7
172 *Conference of States Parties to UNCAC*, Res 3/1, (November 2009), V.10–51985
173 UNCAC, Chapter I, Article 4, at 9
174 above n101
175 Terms of Reference of the Mechanism for the Review of Implementation of the United Nations Convention against Corruption (CAC/COSP 3, Resolution 3/1, 2009), Chapter IV(a) para 11, at 6
176 ibid. para 12, at 6
177 ibid. para 15, at 7
178 ibid. para 18
179 ibid. para 19
180 ibid.
181 ibid. para 27(a), at 9
182 ibid. para 27(c)
183 ibid. para 28
184 ibid. para 30, at 9
185 Vlassis D, 'The United Nations Convention against Corruption: A successful example of international action against economic crime' 2(15) *Temida: časopis o viktimizaciji, ljudskim pravima i rodu* (June 2012), at 62
186 above n1
187 above n175, Chapter IV, para 32, at 10
188 ibid., para 35
189 above n1 at 21
190 above n175, para 4
191 UNODC, *State Implementation of the UNCAC: Criminalisation, Law Enforcement and International Cooperation* (Vienna, 2nd Edition, October 2017)
192 CAC/COSP/IRG/2015/2 *Progress report on the implementation of the mandates of the Implementation Review Group*, para 20, at 6 and para 24, at 8
193 UNODC Country Pairings for review, available at: http://www.unodc.org/documents/treaties/UNCAC/WorkingGroups/ImplementationReviewGroup/30May-3June2011/Country_ pairings_-_Year_1-4_rev2011_IRG_rev-FINAL.pdf (last visited 1 March 2018)
194 UNCAC (22 March 2013) *Implementation of Chapters III and IV of the United Nations Convention against Corruption* (review of Articles 15–29) CAC/COSP/IRG/2013/6, available at: https://www.unodc.org/documents/treaties/UNCAC/WorkingGroups/ImplementationReviewGroup/27-31May2013/V1382056e.pdf (last visited 1 March 2018)
195 ibid. at 2
196 ibid. at 5
197 ibid.
198 ibid. at 13
199 UNODC, *State Implementation of the UNCAC: Criminalisation, Law Enforcement and International Cooperation* (Vienna, 2nd Edition, October 2017)

200 ibid.
201 ibid.
202 As noted above, the initial focus of the Review Mechanism has been on Chapters III and IV of UNCAC (Criminalisation and International cooperation)
203 above n101 at 426

References

Beare ME, 'Corruption and Organised Crime: Lessons from History' 28 *Crime, Law and Social Change* (1997) 155.

Boister N, 'Transnational Criminal Law?' 14(5) *EJIL* (2003) 953.

CAC/COSP/2009/3 *Terms of Reference of the Mechanism for the Review of Implementation of the United Nations Convention against Corruption* (9 to 13 November 2009).

CAC/COSP/IRG/2013/6 *Implementation of Chapters III and IV of the United Nations Convention against Corruption* (review of Articles 15–29).

CAC/COSP/IRG/2015/2 *Progress report on the implementation of the mandates of the Implementation Review Group.*

Carr I, 'Corruption, legal solution and limits of law' 3(3) *International Journal of Law in Context* (2007) 227.

Convention on Combating Bribery of Foreign Public Officials in International Business Transactions, opened for signature 17 December 1997, 37 ILM 1 (entered into force 15 February 1999) ('OECD Convention').

Council of Europe Civil Law Convention on Corruption, opened for signature 4 November 1999, ETS 174 (entered into force 1 November 2003) ('CoE Civil Law Convention').

Council of Europe Criminal Law Convention on Corruption, opened for signature 27 January 1999, ETS 173 (entered into force 1 July 2002) ('CoE Criminal Law Convention').

ECOSOC 1998/16 *Action against Corruption*, E/1998/30 and Corr.1.

ECOSOC 2001/46, *Terms of Reference for the negotiation of the United Nations Convention against Corruption*, E/CN.15/2001/3.

Eighth United Nations Congress on the Prevention of Crime and the Treatment of Offenders, 1990, Resolution 7 'Corruption in Government', A/CONF.*144/28/Rev*.1.

EU Convention on the protection of the European Communities' financial Interests (OJC 316, 1995).

EU Convention on the protection of the European Communities' financial Interests (OJC 316, 1995), First Protocol (OJ C 313, 1996).

EU Convention on the protection of the European Communities' financial interests (OJC 316, 1995), Second Protocol (OJ C 221, 1997).

EU, *Joint Action on Corruption in the Private Sector* (OJL 358, 22 December 1998).

Farrales M, 'What is Corruption? A history of corruption studies and the great definitions debate', *University of San Diego Working Paper Series* [2005] available at: http://papers.ssrn.com/sol3/papers.cfm?abstract_id=1739962 (last visited 1 March 2018).

General Assembly Resolution 55/25, 8 January 2001, 'United Nations Convention against Transnational Organised Crime'.

General Assembly Resolution 55/61, 22 January 2001, 'An effective international legal instrument against corruption'.

General Assembly Resolution 58/4, 31 October 2003, 'United Nations Convention against Corruption'.

Glasius M, 'Does the Involvement of Global Civil Society Make International Decision-Making More Democratic? The case of the International Criminal Court' 4 *Journal of Civil Society* 1 (2008) 43.

Inter-American Convention against Corruption, opened for signature 29 March 1996, 35 ILM 724 (entered into force 6 March 1997) ('OAS Convention').

Joutsen M and Graycar A, 'When Experts and Diplomats Agree: Negotiating peer review of the UN Convention against Corruption' 18 *Global Governance* (2012) 425.

Kubiciel M, 'Core Criminal Law Provisions in the United Nations Convention Against Corruption' 9 *International Criminal Law Review* (2009) 139.

McCulloch J, 'Transnational Crime as Productive Fiction' 24(2) *Social Justice* (2007) 19.

Nadelmann EA and Andreas P, *Policing the Globe: Criminalization and crime control in international relations* (Oxford University Press, 1st Edition, 2006).

Passas N, 'Globalization and Transnational Crime: Effects of criminogenic asymmetries', in Williams P and Vlassis D (Eds), *Combatting Transnational Crime: Concepts, Activities and Responses* (Frank Cass Publishers, 2013) 22.

Reed Q, 'Squeezing a Balloon? Challenging the nexus between organised crime and corruption' 7 *CMI U4 Issue* (2009).

Report of the Meeting of the Intergovernmental Open-Ended Expert Group to Prepare Draft Terms of Reference for the Negotiation of an International Legal Instrument against Corruption (2001) A/56/402 E/2001/105.

Schloenhardt A 'Palermo on the Pacific Rim: organised crime offences in the asia pacific region' 1 *UNODC Study Series* (2009).

Schloenhardt A, 'Fighting Organised Crime in the Asia Pacific Region: New weapons, lost wars' 2 *Asian Journal of International Law* (2012) 137.

Schutte SA, 'Against the Odds: Anti-corruption reform in Indonesia' 32 *Public Admin. Dev.* (2012) 38.

Symeonidou-Kastanidou E, 'Towards a New Definition of Organised Crime in the European Union' 15(1) *European Journal of Crime, Criminal Law and Criminal Justice* (2007) 105

UNESC, *Secretary General's Report: Existing International Legal Instruments, Recommendations and other Documents Addressing Corruption*, E/CN.15/2001/3 ('Secretary-General's Report, 2001').

United Nations Convention against Corruption, opened for signature 9 December 2003, 2349 UNTS 41 (entered into force 14 December 2005) ('UNCAC').

United Nations Convention against Transnational Organised Crime, open for signature 12 December 2000, 2225 UNTS 209 (entered into force 29 September 2003) ('UNTOC').

UNODC, '*Travaux Preparatoires* of the Negotiations for the elaboration of the United Nations Convention against Corruption' (UNODC, Vienna, 1st Edition, 2010).

UNODC, *Legislative Guide for the Implementation of the United Nations Convention against Corruption* (UNODC, Vienna, 1st Edition, 2006).

UNODC, *State Implementation of the UNCAC: Criminalisation, Law Enforcement and International Cooperation* (UNODC, Vienna, 2nd Edition, October 2017).

UNODC, *Technical Guide to UNCAC* (UNODC, 1st Edition, 2009).

Van der Vyver, JD 'Civil Society and the International Criminal Court' 2 *Journal of Human Rights* 3 (2003) 425.

Vlassis D, 'The United Nations Convention against Corruption Origins and Negotiation Process', *Resource Material Series No.* 66 (2005).

Vlassis D, 'The United Nations Convention against Corruption: A successful example of international action against economic crime' 2(15) *Temida: časopis o viktimizaciji, ljudskim pravima i rodu* (June, 2012).

3 Corruption and anti-corruption in the South Pacific context – key actors, values, and interests

Introduction and justification

This chapter explores corruption dynamics and anti-corruption efforts in the South Pacific region, providing a background for analysis of the domestic case study of Papua New Guinea (PNG). A regional overview is useful, considering the under-representation of the South Pacific in the negotiation of the United Nations Convention against Corruption (UNCAC). The United Nations Convention against Corruption supports engagement and cooperation between states, regional bodies, and international institutions, with the goal of implementing and enforcing the provisions of the convention. A regional overview therefore assists in illustrating the important actors, values, and interests that will impact implementation and enforcement of UNCAC.

The relevance of the South Pacific region

Criticisms of UNCAC's applicability to the South Pacific region seem particularly poignant, considering the under-representation of the region in negotiating UNCAC. However, the South Pacific region has not been the subject of extensive, analytical, critical, or empirical research on corruption.[1] An opportunity exists to expand and deepen understanding of the interaction between UNCAC and the South Pacific. This includes the role UNCAC plays in shaping the region's regulatory approach to corruption, as well as the unique experiences of the South Pacific with implementation and enforcement of UNCAC.

Chapter structure

This chapter briefly explores the historical and geographical context of the South Pacific region. Geographic heterogeneity, economic challenges, and the dominant state actors and multilateral lending institutions in the region are introduced. The region's colonial history and attempts to balance modern and traditional legal and political systems are discussed.

Following this, the nature of corruption in the South Pacific region is analysed. Corruption impacts the spheres of aid and development, crime and security, and trade and environment. The existence of corrupt activities in these areas is used to justify anti-corruption efforts in the region and motivates engagement by key regional actors, driven by a combination of normative values and interest-based incentives.

Within this context, the chapter moves on to address the regional anti-corruption framework. This framework includes commitments under UNCAC as well as soft law and policy documents, organisational agendas and relationships between states and lending institutions. In most cases, the approach taken to combatting corruption in the South Pacific reflects UNCAC and the global anti-corruption regime.

The chapter concludes by presenting the unique challenges faced by UNCAC and the global anti-corruption regime in the South Pacific region. The regime risk factors and challenges discussed in Chapters 1 and 2 are relevant in the South Pacific context. The regional sphere brings to light the way that risks of co- optation and limited resources and capacity relate to more general regime risk factors and may influence the success of UNCAC and the global anti-corruption regime in the South Pacific. These risks and challenges are further explored in the analysis of the domestic case study of PNG, introduced in Chapter 4 and expanded in Chapters 5 and 6.

Introducing the South Pacific region

The term 'South Pacific' is not precise and the South Pacific region has been subject to diverse classifications. 'Geographical, historical, demographic, constitutional and political factors determine what is and what is not referred to as the "South Pacific"'.[2] The Pacific Islands Forum (PIF) has 16 members,[3] while the Secretariat of the Pacific Community (SPC) includes 22 Pacific Island nations and four 'founding nations': Australia, France, New Zealand, and the USA.[4] The membership of the SPC illustrates the continuing influence of ex-colonial powers in the region.[5]

This chapter focuses on the 16 members of the PIF. This grouping includes the westernised and economically powerful states of Australia and New Zealand. These states make up the westernmost and southernmost points of the grouping, respectively. The other 14 states in this region are categorised by the United Nations (UN) as Small Island Developing States (SIDS).[6] These states are: The Cook Islands, Federated States of Micronesia (FSM), Fiji, Kiribati, Nauru, Niue, Palau, Papua New Guinea (PNG), Republic of Marshall Islands, Samoa, Solomon Islands, Tonga, Tuvalu, and Vanuatu.[7]

Diversity and imbalance: South Pacific geography and economy

From the tropical and mountainous terrain of PNG, to expanses of arable land in New Zealand, and the extensive deserts of Australia,[8] the South Pacific region has substantial geological diversity. In countries with particularly rugged terrain, limited accessibility has been noted as a restriction on the provision of state services.[9] This can impact the level of legitimacy accorded to national governments in the region[10] and may be relevant to the implementation and enforcement of UNCAC in the South Pacific.

Economically, varying histories of resource exploitation have resulted in diverse outcomes for many nations in the region. Generally, Pacific Island countries are or have been resource rich, but struggle to compete in today's global market.[11] Some nations, such as Kiribati and Nauru, have exhausted their supply of natural resources and failed to retain or manage the profits gained from resource exploitation.[12]

In many respects, Australia and New Zealand can be considered the outliers in the South Pacific region, due to their size and economic status. Australia is by far the largest of the South Pacific nations and, although New Zealand has a smaller population than Papua New Guinea, it is the second largest economy in the South Pacific.[13] Australia's GDP is approximately AUD986 billion (USD775 billion). New Zealand's GDP is around NZD134 billion (USD98 billion), with both countries having strong export markets and advanced international trade relationships.[14] Other South Pacific states struggle to compete in the international market due to limited trading power and high levels of debt and unemployment.[15] As an example, Nauru has an estimated unemployment rate of 90%, the highest in the region. Nauru's exports are AUD64,000 (USD50,000) compared to imports of AUD20 million (USD15.7 million).[16] Kiribati, considered one of the least developed South Pacific nations, has a budget deficit of over 29% and receives 25% of its GDP as foreign aid, coming primarily from Australia and New Zealand, as well as the EU, UK, USA, Japan, Canada, Taiwan, and various UN agencies.[17]

Due to the economic imbalance between Australia, New Zealand, and the other 14 South Pacific states, these two countries have a dominant position in the region, supporting other South Pacific countries through the provision of aid, trade, and in some cases security. These roles are intimately connected to political and economic interests in the region and result in substantial influence over law and policy decisions. China and other Asian states and private corporations are also increasingly influential in the region.

Colonial history and post-colonial law and politics

Colonial history is a unifying feature of states in the South Pacific region – Tonga is the only state in the region that avoided colonisation.[18] Australia and New Zealand were the first South Pacific states to attain independence, being former British colonies established between 1788 and 1840. New Zealand has no official date of independence. However, the 1852 New Zealand Constitution Act granted New Zealand citizens the right to self-governance, 12 years after the founding of the colony.[19] Australia became an independent state on 1 January 1901, 61 years before Western Samoa in 1962.[20] Following Western Samoa, the remaining 13 South Pacific states achieved independence during the second half of the 20th Century. Palau was the last state in the region to establish independence, in 1994.

Australia and New Zealand were themselves British colonies, but also acted as colonial powers in the South Pacific region. Australia had varying levels of control over the government of Papua New Guinea from 1906 until PNG's independence in 1975.[21] Historically, New Zealand exerted colonial influence over Western Samoa, Niue, and the Cook Islands.[22]

Colonial histories have impacted the legal systems in South Pacific states. One interesting example is whether a South Pacific state has a Monist or Dualist approach to international law. In a Monist state, 'a legal system of a state is considered to include treaties to which that state has given its consent to be bound. Thus, certain treaties may become directly applicable in that state domestically'.[23] In a Dualist system 'a treaty to which a state has expressed its consent to be bound does not become automatically applicable within that state until appropriate national legislation has been enacted to give the treaty the force of law domestically'.[24]

States in the South Pacific with a British colonial history follow the British legal system and take a Dualist approach. This Dualist approach applies in the clear majority of South Pacific states. Vanuatu, Fiji, Cook Islands, Samoa, Tonga, Tokelau, Nauru, Niue, PNG, Kiribati, Tuvalu, the Solomon Islands, Australia, and New Zealand are all Dualist states in their approach to international law.[25] Former American colonies, including Palau and the Federated States of Micronesia, adopted a Monist approach. In these states, a treaty may be directly applicable in the state, once ratification has occurred. This variation highlights the relevance of colonial influence over states in the region.[26] However, for the purposes of implementation and enforcement of UNCAC, states must adopt domestic legislation regardless of whether they have a Monist or Dualist system. This is because UNCAC is not a self-executing treaty, as noted in Chapter 2.

Constitutional law in the South Pacific provides additional examples of colonial influence. All states in the region, except New Zealand and Fiji, have formal written constitutions.[27] South Pacific constitutions often reflect colonial influence,[28] and in some cases also mirror international discourse[29] popular at the time of drafting. The constitutions of Cook Islands, Fiji, Kiribati, Niue, Solomon Islands, Tuvalu, and Vanuatu were all enacted by the departing colonial power or powers in the region.[30] As an example of the influence of international discourse, the Constitution of Vanuatu, which came into force in 1980, and the 1998 amendments to the 1990 Constitution of Fiji, both include 'provisions which describe conduct which leaders should not undertake, such as use of public office for private gain'.[31] At the time that these constitutional laws were enacted, good governance and anti-corruption discourse was gaining increasing momentum among transnational actors and institutions. During the latter part of the 20th Century, the global anti-corruption regime evolved through the second and third stages. Through this process, corruption came to be viewed as a universal ill with negative impacts on government, economic development, and social stability. This evolution is reflected in the constitutions of Vanuatu and Fiji.

The relationship between colonialism and traditional culture is also notable. Modern legal and political systems in the South Pacific draw on both colonial experiences and local and tribal customs and culture.[32] In many cases, colonial rule established a national layer of government in many South Pacific nations that sits above smaller tribal and community groupings.[33] This national layer was never fully integrated with traditional societal groupings and continues to provide a challenge for state service provision and legitimacy across the region. This challenge is enhanced by the rugged and diverse geography across the South Pacific region.[34]

Traditions and historical practices can also influence corruption in the region. In South Pacific society, 'many basic and necessary organisational principles which were fundamental . . . constitute nepotism, bribery, corruption . . . when applied at a national level'.[35] In certain cases, a combination of increasing transnational interaction, centralisation of government and state power, and sustained cultural values, can result in opportunities for and justification of corrupt activities.[36] These dynamics may further complicate the application of UNCAC and the global anti-corruption regime in the region. The corrupt incentives that result from external influence in the South Pacific are explored further below. However, Barcham suggests that despite clashes between traditional and modern forms of interaction, harnessing traditional cultural structures, institutions, and perspectives may in fact support anti-corruption efforts.[37] This is an important possibility for enhancing implementation and enforcement of UNCAC and securing the final stage of evolution for the global anti-corruption regime. The role of traditional cultural practices and approaches to governance is considered more extensively in the following chapters of this book, being a topic of discussion in some of the interviews documented in Chapter 5.

Understanding corruption in the South Pacific

Corruption as an emergent challenge in the South Pacific region

Corruption has not always been an issue of concern in the South Pacific. In the early stages of independence, South Pacific nations were focused on establishing their own national identities; corruption was not a well-understood concept and was certainly not a central concern of newly emergent governments.[38] While some countries in the region have included aspects of transparency and accountability within their constitutions and domestic legal systems,[39] these developments came late in the 20th Century. They may reflect the evolution of the global anti-corruption regime, which by this time had gained substantial traction through the efforts of multilateral organisations and developed western states. Both groups of actors exert considerable influence in the South Pacific.[40]

Mirroring the evolution of the global anti-corruption regime, corruption has become an increasingly prominent issue on the South Pacific agenda. Regional organisations, including the PIF, have deplored high levels of corruption in the region and adopted recommendations and policy documents in support of good governance.[41] Multilateral institutions and heads of state have also been vocal about stemming corruption in the South Pacific.[42]

Current evidence suggests that corruption is a significant challenge in the South Pacific region.[43] Evidence includes scams in Vanuatu that almost bankrupted the country and links between high-level officials and drug trafficking in Fiji.[44] A report on the logging industry in Papua New Guinea[45] is another illustration of the seemingly endemic nature of corruption in the South Pacific region. Corruption has been found to affect a wide range of sectors in the South Pacific and is linked to aid and development, crime and security, and trade and environment.[46] Each of these sectors involves substantial regional and transnational dynamics, with cross border impact.

Exploring the nature of corruption in each of these sectors helps to illuminate the most substantial challenges the region faces in terms of combatting corruption. This exploration illustrates the role and relevance of diverse actors, institutions, values, and interests that operate in the South Pacific and impact the nature of engagement with UNCAC. These factors will shape UNCAC implementation in the South Pacific, and the extent of the global anti-corruption regime's impact in the region.

Corruption, aid, and development

Corruption related to aid and development is a serious concern in the South Pacific. Australia provides hundreds of millions of dollars in aid to the Pacific Islands, including an estimated AUD547.1 million (USD430.3 million) to PNG for 2017–18.[47] New Zealand also provides extensive aid in the Pacific, with a plan to invest NZD1 billion between 2015 and 2018 (USD730 million) to the Pacific Islands for 2015–2018.[48] As of April 2015, World Bank cumulative lending in the South Pacific was USD473.28million for 55 active projects,[49] directed at the ten South Pacific member states of the World Bank.[50] The Asian Development Bank (ADB) also lends extensively in the South Pacific, approving loans of USD472.2 million in 2013.[51] Despite the influx of aid into Small Island Developing States (SIDS) in the South Pacific, many continue to struggle with crime, poverty, and instability.[52] This fact has led to the suggestion that aid money may itself be the victim of corruption, being siphoned off into private coffers before reaching its intended destination or being used for the designated purpose.[53]

The possibility that aid money is falling victim to corruption has meant that multilateral lending institutions and donor states have taken an active role in promoting anti-corruption and good governance agendas in the South Pacific. These actors have become 'moral entrepreneurs',[54] at the same time supporting their own interest-based agendas in the region. The ADB has been extremely active in this regard. This multilateral lending institution has teamed with the Organisation for Economic Cooperation and Development (OECD) to promote programmes to ratify, implement, and enforce international anti-corruption laws, including UNCAC; promoting principles of good governance, transparency, accountability, and corporate and Civil Society involvement in combatting corruption.[55]

As noted by Crocombe, state and multilateral lenders are motivated by gain and do not operate on pure altruism.[56] Lenders provided aid based on the potential for return on investment, or the desire for that investment to be put towards certain issues of interest to the lender. Issues of interest may include the good governance agenda, to improve the potential of borrowing nations to provide profitable returns on investment, or to prevent degeneration of these nations into increased poverty and instability.

Poverty and instability can have flow-on effects for the region, including increased levels of crime, potential for transnational criminal activity, refugee flows, and the possibility of deploying military personnel to support fragile or failing states.[57] Even if aid is not directed towards the good governance agenda explicitly, if corruption results in the mismanagement of aid then return on investment is likely to be negatively impacted. Any aid money being diverted from its intended location is aid money not being spent on the lender's goal.

Certain commentators view the provision of aid and relationships of aid dependency as having a corrupting influence in and of themselves.[58] The provision of aid frees up other government resources.[59] Ampratwum provides a useful example of how this can result in corrupt outcomes:

> . . . a donor may give aid funds to enable the recipient country to build a school, which the recipient may indeed use for that purpose; however, the availability of aid funds to build the school makes it possible for the recipient to use the resulting savings to buy sophisticated weapons, whose purchase may provide more scope for illegally diverting funds into individuals' pockets than school construction could.[60]

The potential corrupting influence of external actors is substantial. One example is the competition for aid and diplomatic support that has played out in the South Pacific between China, Taiwan, and more 'traditional' lenders in the region.

Sir Mekere Morauta, Prime Minster of PNG from 1999 to 2002 and leader of the review of the Pacific Plan, noted the increased influence of China in the South Pacific region:

> The Pacific Plan is a regional framework. It's a club. And China is not a member of that club . . . China is here to stay. And the leaders are welcoming China staying. The question remains is how do we integrate Chinese aid with other donors, multilateral and bilateral?[61]

The competition between China and Taiwan in the South Pacific region has resulted in the provision of aid with few or no governance-based conditionalities.[62] Instead, these states are seeking diplomatic support at the international level.[63] Some commentators suggest that this dynamic may negatively impact anti-corruption efforts in the region.[64] Aid that is free from good governance conditionalities is now a viable option for South Pacific states. States may choose unconditional aid over aid from traditional lenders such as Australia, New Zealand, and Multinational Development Banks, who tend to require more extensive compliance and reporting around governance and related agendas.

There is a further concern that donors may promote anti-corruption efforts as a means of securing other structural and institutional changes that may be incompatible with regional and domestic contexts. Ampratwum notes the position of the World Bank on combatting corruption, which is that 'the principal way to reduce corruption is to encourage deeper and more thorough economic liberalization and deregulation of borrowers'.[65] However, the author continues by noting:

> . . . experience from developing countries that have undergone some economic liberalization does not provide firm support for the belief that markets can reduce the incidence of corruption. Indeed, economic reforms can have adverse consequences for corruption at least in the short term . . . in the absence of adequate enforcement mechanisms, tax reforms designed to increase government revenues can increase incentives for corrupt practices. Again, privatization, for instance, in the absence of effective regulation has the potential for generating high levels of economic rent . . .[66]

Ampratwum argues against the anti-corruption efforts promoted by multilateral lenders, suggesting that tying aid to 'good governance' represents an attempt to impose 'western' values on developing economies.[67] He argues that:

> . . . the corruption issue is just another means for the [World] Bank to secure its real goal: greater structural adjustment in those states whose adjustment programs have been stymied by political pressures.[68]

Bukovansky supports this view, noting that the broad goals of multilateral financial institutions continue to be liberalisation and economic growth.[69] Bukovansky asserts that:

> In the policy domain, the economic approach to curbing corruption has frequently entailed recommendations to cut the size and scope of the public sector, particularly with respect to privatization and dismantling of state-owned enterprises. But some have argued that cutting the public sector can just as easily inhibit as encourage the development of democratic institutions of governance . . . by advocating smaller government they are not doing much to contribute to – and may inadvertently be undercutting – the positive development of good government.[70]
>
> . . .
>
> By linking the problem of corruption to the problem of under-development,advanced industrial countries implicitly and unjustifiably claim the moral high ground for themselves, and ascribe to the 'developing world' the status of the moral reprobate while simultaneously making vague and possibly unworkable governance demands on developing country governments and societies.[71]

This perspective reflects concerns introduced in Chapter 1, regarding the use of global prohibition regimes and their legal tools as a means of policy laundering.

To summarise, the links between corruption and aid in the South Pacific illustrate the role played by dominant state and multilateral actors, who lend to less developed states in the region. This role is multifaceted. These actors can be seen to contribute to corrupt incentives and may co-opt the anti-corruption agenda for other goals, including the promotion of a western liberal democratic model of economic and social development. At the same time, multilateral donors have an interest in achieving a positive return on their investments and state donors will seek to secure regional stability and develop productive trade partnerships. These incentives may drive state and multilateral lenders to promote anti-corruption efforts in the region, although effectiveness will be limited by contextual relevance and availability of alternative aid providers. Ultimately, aid donors have significant influence in the South Pacific and are well situated to influence the nature of anti-corruption efforts and the approach taken to implementing the global anti-corruption regime in the region.

Corruption, crime, and security

In addition to aid and development, corruption in the South Pacific is often linked to regional security concerns. This link is based on the relationship between corruption and transnational criminal activity. There have been multiple cases, especially relating to the trafficking of drugs, that involve South Pacific nations as both source and transit points for Australian, New Zealand, and even US and Canadian markets.[72] Generally, researchers have illustrated links between transnational organised crime, particularly trafficking of people and drugs, and corruption.[73] Furthermore, trafficking is a border crossing activity by nature and thus brings transnational security dynamics to the fore. Dominant actors in the region, namely Australia and New Zealand, have used these cases to promote anti-corruption initiatives in less developed South Pacific states. By attempting to reduce corruption in less developed South Pacific nations, dominant actors seek to reduce the potential transnational impacts of crime in the region, as well as globally.

Political instability in the region has flow-on effects for Australia and New Zealand. Concerns include refugee flows and provision of military support in conflict. Corruption and political instability have also been linked.[74] The incentive to limit political instability in the South Pacific is similar to that of organised crime. While transnational organised crime may harm powerful actors such as Australia and New Zealand, so political instability in the region may strain military and humanitarian resources that these dominant nations often provide to less developed South Pacific states. Political instability may also foster an environment conducive to increased criminal activity.[75] In this regard, the issues become cyclical. States beyond the South Pacific region may seek to reduce instances of crime and instability, to protect their own borders from illicit inflows. In this context, anti-corruption policies may be viewed as valuable tool for actors seeking to reduce both crime and instability in the region.

Corruption, environment, and economy

As was noted earlier, most states in the South Pacific are economically dependent on a combination of aid and resource extraction. The links between corruption and aid have already been discussed. The role of extractive industries and foreign corporations in the South Pacific should also be explored, with a focus on the provision of corrupt incentives and the possibility for promoting anti-corruption efforts. Illegal logging and corruption in the forestry sector is a particularly good example relevant to the PNG case.

Just as aid may promote corrupt opportunities on the one hand and provide anti-corruption incentives on the other, corporate actors may contribute to corruption in the South Pacific, as well as being motivated by self-interest in their efforts to reduce it. Cases of corruption in the fisheries sector illustrate the ways corporations may be complicit in corruption in the region.

> Alleged and proven cases of corruption through the issue of fishing licenses include Ministers and senior fisheries officials directing license fees into overseas private bank accounts or receiving direct payments from overseas fishing companies in return for favourable license conditions and 'private' licensing by fisheries officials of vessels that do not show up on the government books.[76]

Additional examples of corporate complicity in South Pacific corruption can be seen in relation to the forestry industry in PNG and the Solomon Islands. The Barnett Inquiry report on corruption in PNG found that 'the Secretary for Forests was accepting gifts of golf clubs and cash from a Malaysian timber company'.[77] Additionally, 'In the Solomon Islands, the ombudsman cited evidence that members of area councils deciding on applications from timber companies were given 'Negotiation fees, Employment and Hotel stays in Honiara'.[78] Further, it has been noted that there are risks inherent in the provision of social services by corporations in exchange for extractive contracts.[79]

> Helping local communities by building infrastructure and providing employment as part of the social license to operate can be a complex area. These spending decisions often involve interactions with the very political leaders and government officials who make decisions on issues such as licenses, permits and contracts . . . one has to ask if the mining company won the right to mine because it offered these kinds of 'add-ons.'[80]

Examples like those mentioned above illustrate the risks of corporate complicity in corruption in the South Pacific, highlighting the importance of targeting corporate actors in seeking to prevent corrupt activity.

Passas notes that the operation of transnational corporations can undercut domestic sovereignty in developing countries and contribute to criminogenic power asymmetries where corporations are able to co-opt government actors.[81] The author further argues that in order to reduce harmful asymmetries, corporate actors should be targeted by policies aimed at reducing opportunities to profit from asymmetries, and also through appealing to the 'other selves' of corporate executives, utilising value-based arguments and maximising transparency and accountability 'in both government and economic activities'.[82] Building on this approach, Findlay suggests targeting of corporate actors rather than the states in which they operate may be an effective method for combatting corruption:

> A more effective and commercially long-lasting approach to corruption regulation would be to influence the corporate conscience of the dominant commercial player rather than penalizing a long line of eager recipients of any bribe or corrupt commission. The attack needs to be against the conditions of opportunity.[83]

In addition to appeal to 'other selves', corporate actors may be encouraged to limit their corrupting influence through self-interest. Corruption has been reported to increases the cost of doing business by as much as ten to 25%.[84] Furthermore, the increased criminal activity and low levels of development and stability often associated with corrupt behaviour make business activities challenging, risky, and expensive. Poor, unstable nations make bad trading partners. This reality provides an incentive for other states, and foreign corporates, to combat corruption. The Australian Conservation Foundation and CELCoR report 'Bulldozing Progress' (2006) states:

> Australia and other nations in the region have a deep interest in stopping these abuses (illegal logging and related corruption), aside from any 'good neighbour' obligations. The companies responsible have commercial interests across Asia and Australia. The attendant corruption renders pointless Australia's large aid contributions. The trafficking in guns, timber and workers threatens regional security.[85]

South Pacific corruption is of great importance to powerful states in the region, as well as to corporate actors seeking profitable investment opportunities. Both state and corporate actors should be involved in anti-corruption efforts, on the basis of their contribution to corrupt invectives and their motivation to combat them.

States are concerned with developing strong ties with other Pacific Islands through charitable support and assistance. They also seek to enable productive commercial relationships, ensure effective use of aid, and protect their own borders from crime; all while striving to achieve greater security for the region. While the provision of aid may contribute to corrupt incentives, the motivation to support development in the region drives powerful state actors towards anti-corruption efforts. Similarly, while corporations may act corruptly or provide opportunities for corrupt activity in the region, they may be motivated to reduce corruption overall, decreasing the cost of doing business and limiting opportunities for competitors to engage in corrupt activities at their expense. The importance of these actors must be acknowledged and engaged by the global anti-corruption regime and its legal tools, including UNCAC.

UNCAC and the South Pacific anti-corruption framework

Corruption is a substantial challenge in the South Pacific. External actors play a dual role, contributing to corrupt incentives while having incentives of their own to reduce corruption in the region. In the last two decades, there has been a substantial rise in the level of anti-corruption discourse, law, and policy in the region. This is correlated with the rise of corruption rhetoric at the international level and the emergence of the global anti-corruption regime. However, despite increases in awareness and policy development, corrupt activity continues in the region.[86] This section explores regional anti-corruption efforts and notes the influence of UNCAC and the global anti-corruption regime on these efforts. Understanding anti-corruption efforts in the region will assist the reader when grappling with the continuing challenge of corruption in the South Pacific, and in the PNG case study to follow in Chapter 4.

Introducing the anti-corruption framework in the South Pacific: a 'soft' approach and substantial external influence

UNCAC is the only binding multilateral legal instrument to achieve extensive ratification in the South Pacific region. Australia and New Zealand are the only South Pacific parties to the OECD Convention and there are no regional treaties that target corruption in the South Pacific. UNCAC is therefore the most influential multilateral legal instrument against corruption in the region. Fourteen of the 16 South Pacific states have ratified as of 3 October 2017.

Table 3.1 Pacific States Parties to UNCAC (including year of ratification or accession)

Country	*Signature*	*Ratification or Accession (a)*
Australia	9 Dec 2003	7 Dec 2005
Cook Islands		17 Oct 2011
Fiji		14 May 2008 a
Kiribati		27 Sep 2013 a
Marshall Islands		17 Nov 2011
Federated States of Micronesia		21 Mar 2012 a
Nauru		12 Jul 2012 a
New Zealand	10 Dec 2003	1 Dec 2015
Palau		24 Mar 2009 a
Papua New Guinea	22 Dec 2004	16 Jul 2007
Solomon Islands		6 Jan 2012 a
Vanuatu		12 Jul 2011 a
Niue		3 Oct 2017 a
Tuvalu		4 Sep 2015 a
Samoa		18 Apr 2018 a
Tonga	Non-member	Non-member

The most recent South Pacific ratification was New Zealand on 1 December 2015, with Niue becoming a member by accession on 3 October 2017 and Samoa assenting on 18 April 2018. Tonga remains the only non-member in the region.

In addition to UNCAC, the South Pacific anti-corruption framework consists of programmes and policies initiated through interaction with donor states and multilateral lending groups. The framework also involves agendas and policy documents developed through regional bodies, particularly the PIF, and some statements that may be considered 'soft law'.[87] All South Pacific states have criminalised some acts of bribery and corruption in their domestic criminal codes. In this context, the global anti-corruption regime has achieved the fourth stage of evolution within the South Pacific region. Not all corrupt acts under UNCAC are criminalised in all South Pacific states, however, a partial legal framework exists that supports the regime and its goals.

The approach taken to combatting corruption in the South Pacific reflects the global anti-corruption regime, referencing the language of transnational legal instruments such as UNCAC. The role of external actors is apparent in promoting the global anti-corruption regime's approach. As noted by Hughes, 'much of the agenda of small island states is written elsewhere'.[88] The role of external actors in the region reflects the role of 'regime proponents' in Nadelmann and Andreas' five-stage model.[89] These actors agitate for a consistent and universal approach to combatting the target activity and are usually motivated by a combination of normative values and rationalist interests.[90] In this context, the specific programs, policies and agendas on anti-corruption relevant to the South Pacific context are explored below.

Key policy documents and initiatives: reflecting UNCAC and the global anti-corruption regime

South Pacific states have not yet established legally binding regional or bilateral treaties on the topic of corruption. This section focuses on the limited number of policy documents and agendas that target corruption in the region, discussing the possibility of the PIF Principles of Good Leadership and Accountability as a 'soft law' anti-corruption instrument in the South Pacific. Several additional programmes and projects are also discussed, resulting from engagement with external actors including the UN and ADB/OECD. Unsurprisingly, these projects reflect the method and approach of the global anti-corruption regime and UNCAC. In some cases, these externally driven programmes actively promote UNCAC ratification in the region.

Non-binding programmes and soft law instruments: the Pacific Islands Forum and anti-corruption

The PIF is one of the most active intergovernmental institutions in the South Pacific. The PIF secretariat is an international organisation established by treaty, that produces an annual Communique on issues of relevance to the region. The PIF included 'good governance' as a key objective under the Pacific Plan.[91] This document was endorsed in 2005 by member states of the PIF as 'the region's strategy for strengthening cooperation and integration between Pacific countries'.[92] Although it does not specifically mention ratification of UNCAC, item 12 of the Pacific Plan mirrors the language of UNCAC and seeks 'Improved transparency, accountability, equity and efficiency in the management and use of resources in the Pacific'.[93] The Framework for Pacific Regionalism (FPR) has since superseded the Pacific Plan. This new document is referred to as 'the master strategy for strengthening cooperation and integration between the states and territories of the Pacific region'.[94] The FPR also includes 'governance' as a primary pillar of the overall framework, although the language of transparency and accountability has been removed.

The Principles of Good Leadership and Accountability (2004) are another aspect of the PIF 'good governance' strategy.[95] The PIF Principles reflect the language of UNCAC and promote the recommendations and requirements established by certain key articles of this multilateral legal instrument. The Principles of Good Leadership include: requirements to disclose fraud, corruption, and maladministration (Principle 1(ii)(d)); refraining from exertion of pressure, and abuse of persons carrying out there lawful duties (Principle 1(ii)(e)); proper use of official powers (Principle 4(i)); giving priority to official duties over private interests (Principle (4)(iv)); and ensuring that public resources are not wasted, abused, or used improperly or extravagantly (Principle 6).[96] There is also reference to strengthening the power and capacity of the Ombudsman and Auditor General roles, in those South Pacific nations that have these actors, and of reports and audits to ensure public access to information on government and institutional processes.

The Principles of Accountability establish that reports and data should be presented 'in a way that follows international best practice and allows for internal comparisons'.[97] Principle 4 covers the open advertisement and competitive award of government and public sector contracts, emphasising openness and competition in government contracts. This reflects the approach of the global anti-corruption regime, as documented in Article 9 of UNCAC.[98] Disclosure, audits, and the provision of adequate fiscal resources to Auditor Generals' and Ombudsmen are also highlighted in the PIF Principles of Accountability.[99]

To supplement these principles, the PIF prepares country reports, evaluating the implementation of principles by member states. It is important to note that declarations by the PIF generate no treaty-derived obligation.[100] States cannot hold each other responsible for violation of the rules and norms established by the PIF.

The Principles of Good Leadership and Accountability may be considered 'soft law' instruments. Thurer holds that:

> Soft law as a phenomenon in international relations covers all those social rules generated by state[s] or other subjects of international law which are not legally binding but which are nevertheless of special legal relevance.[101]

Soft law instruments 'can serve as a compromise between sovereignty and the need to establish rules to govern international relations'.[102] '[T]he compliance pull, and as a consequence compliance itself, of a specific soft law norm can be significantly higher than the one of hard law norms'.[103] Therefore, soft law instruments such as the PIF Principles of Good Leadership and Accountability may valuably contribute to South Pacific anti-corruption efforts, reflecting UNCAC and the global anti-corruption regime. However, because the Principles are non-binding, regional actors are not legally obligated to comply with them. This re-emphasises the importance of UNCAC in the South Pacific, as it is the only binding multilateral legal instrument on corruption that applies to a substantial number of South Pacific states.

Externally motivated projects and policies

Transnational, regional, and international organisations have guided the development of several other South Pacific and Asia-Pacific policies aimed at addressing corruption in the region. Relevant institutions include the ADB, OECD, and UN. The policies produced in consultation with these actors are non-binding. However, they can provide a touchstone for best practices and may be used as requirements for certain assistance measures or aid provisions. This reality enhances their persuasive power. The ADB/OECD Anti-Corruption Initiative for the Asia Pacific (2001)[104] and the subsequent Strategic Principles and Operational Activities of the Initiative (2010)[105] are particularly noteworthy.

The original ADB/OECD Anti-Corruption Initiative was endorsed on 30 November 2001 in Tokyo by Bangladesh, Cook Islands, Fiji, India, Indonesia, Japan, Korea, Kyrgyz Republic, Malaysia, Mongolia, Nepal, Pakistan, PNG, Philippines, Samoa, Singapore, and Vanuatu. Since then, the South Pacific nations of Australia, Palau, and Solomon Islands have also joined the initiative. The initiative predates the entry into force of UNCAC but still reflects the language of the global anti-corruption regime. In its preamble, the ADB/OECD Anti-Corruption Initiative holds that: 'corruption is a widespread phenomenon which undermines good governance, erodes the rule of law, hampers economic growth and efforts for poverty reduction and distorts competitive conditions in business transactions.'[106]

This statement draws strongly on the OECD Convention preamble, which holds that bribery 'raises serious moral and political concerns, undermines good governance and economic development, and distorts international competitive conditions'.[107] The Preamble of UNCAC also highlights similar concerns regarding the threat posed by corruption to 'the stability and security of societies, undermining the institutions and values of democracy, ethical values and justice and jeopardizing sustainable development and the rule of law'.[108]

Three pillars of action are established under the ADB/OECD initiative, relating to Public Service, Business Operations, and Public Involvement. Pillar One on Public Service promotes establishment of Codes of Conduct, as is also recommended by UNCAC under Article 7(1)(d). Transparency, accountability, audit procedures, and 'the simplification of the regulatory environment' are also suggested under Pillar One of the ADB/OECD initiative.[109] Under Pillar Two, 'dissuasive sanctions which effectively and actively combat the offence of bribery of public officials' is the first recommendation.[110] The importance of promoting 'corporate responsibility and accountability on the basis of relevant international standards'[111] is also emphasised. Pillar Three covers the promotion of public discussion on corruption, access to information for citizens, and public participation in anti-corruption activities through cooperation with NGOs and other Civil Society groups. Whistleblower protection and NGO monitoring of public sector programmes are also covered by Pillar Three.[112]

The original ADB/OECD initiative clearly reflects the views of the global anti-corruption regime as represented by UNCAC. The ADB/OECD Strategic Principles and Operational Activities of the Pacific Anti-Corruption Initiative further align the initiative with the regime, making explicit the importance of ratification, implementation, and enforcement of UNCAC. The initiative's goal is stated under section B: 'The Initiative is a regional forum for supporting national and multilateral efforts to address and reduce corruption in Asia and the Pacific, primarily through the effective implementation of UNCAC.'[113]

Section 3(1) of the Strategic Plan states that:

> The Initiative's primary goal should be to help its members implement UNCAC. Where appropriate, the Initiative could also address issues not covered by UNCAC, or provisions in the UNCAC that are not mandatory.[114]

To achieve this goal, the initiative states that it will conduct a variety of operational activities, including Steering Group and Advisory Group meetings, Country Self-Reporting on implementation of UNCAC, Capacity Building Seminars, and demand driven Thematic Reviews. Voluntary Country Reviews to identify and address deficiencies in a country's anti-corruption framework are also recommended, as are regional conferences and national and regional awareness-raising activities to promote the initiative and its goals. These operational activities illustrate the coordinating role of multilateral organisations in promoting the evolution of the global anti-corruption regime from stage four onward.

It has already been noted, in Chapter 2, that the UN is an influential coordinating body for the implementation of UNCAC and the promotion of the global anti-corruption regime, especially through the UNCAC Secretariat and the Implementation Review Group. The UN, and specifically UNDP and UNODC, have also been active in the South Pacific, launching a South Pacific focused initiative on corruption, 'The Pacific Regional Anti-Corruption Project' (UN-PRAC), in April 2012.[115] This project seeks to promote continued ratification of UNCAC and focuses on the implementation of sustainable and effective anti-corruption reform. The project recognises that 'external, one-size-fits-all legal and/or institutional responses are rarely effective if they are not calibrated to the small island state contexts'.[116] This is an important acknowledgement of the risk of inapplicability discussed in Chapter 1 as a key factor that may prevent the success of UNCAC and the global anti-corruption regime.

In practice, it is not clear that diverse approaches to combatting corruption are supported by UN-PRAC. The project document suggests a need to reform

South Pacific nations through changing attitudes and incentives, development of 'targeted knowledge products' and increasing understanding among leaders on international anti-corruption standards and the impacts of corruption.[117] Each of these project goals appears to be one directional, promoting a particular anti-corruption approach while at the same time acknowledging that diverse contextual dynamics must be appreciated. Considering this conflict, the risk that this project promotes measures that are inapplicable to unique regional and domestic context appears high. However, recent activities undertaken by the project have focused on raising awareness about UNCAC, particularly with non-state actors in the South Pacific region.[118] This type of engagement may promote positive dialogue between state and non-state actors and could support future implementation of UNCAC in a way that is compatible with unique regional dynamics.

Dominant states in the region, including Australia and New Zealand, are also shaping the South Pacific anti-corruption framework. The extensive aid provided by Australia and New Zealand to other South Pacific nations can be bi-lateral (directly given to another state) or in the form of contributions to larger inter-governmental lending bodies (such as the ADB, OECD, and World Bank).[119] Australia also provides funding for the UN-PRAC project,[120] and both Australia and New Zealand contribute funds to the PIF.

Dobell maintains that these dominant states shape the anti-corruption agenda through their influence. 'Australia wants the Pacific to embrace greater regional integration and the pooling of resources to promote efficiency and transparency of government'.[121] Substantial increases in aid to certain South Pacific nations are often 'subject to meaningful reform and continued improved performance'.[122]

Educational and knowledge-building endeavours are also conducted by dominant states in the region, to promote and align specific values and interests regarding approaches to anti-corruption and good governance. As an example, New Zealand has funded the Pacific Judicial Development Programme, 'intended to support participating Pacific judiciaries to strengthen the rule of law and governance through the provision of training to magistrates and court officials across the region'.[123] New Zealand also provides funding to Transparency International (TI) to produce public presentations on corruption and governance, and disseminate educational material throughout the South Pacific.[124]

'Peak Organisations', consisting of experts from regional member states, work on issues of regional cooperation and governance that often relate to the anti-corruption agenda.[125] Dominant state actors in the South Pacific frequently support these organisations, which include the Regional Ombudsman Association, GOPAC (Global Organisation of Parliamentarians against Corruption), OCO (Oceania Customs Organisation), PIDC (Pacific Immigration Directors' Conference), PCPC (Pacific Chiefs of Police Conference), PILOM (Pacific Island Law Officers' Meeting), and SPASAI (South Pacific Association of Supreme Audit Institutions). GOPAC recently participated in the UN-PRAC workshop on governance and anti-corruption held in Tonga,[126] illustrating the interaction between peak organisations, multilateral institutions, and dominant states in the South Pacific. These actors can cooperate to promote anti-corruption efforts consistent with UNCAC and the global anti-corruption regime.

Private interest groups and NGOs also play a role in shaping the South Pacific anti-corruption framework. The Pacific Basin Economic Council (PBEC) is an economic interest group that has been an active participant in the ADB/OECD anti-corruption initiative.[127] Transparency International is active in the region, tackling issues of corruption and promoting ratification, implementation, and enforcement of UNCAC and other tools of the global anti-corruption regime. Other regional NGOs also work towards anti-corruption goals. Examples include the Pacific Islands News Association (PINA), which promotes freedom of the press, and the Pacific Network on Globalisation (PANG) and the Pacific Conference of Churches, both of which promote good governance, transparency, and accountability in the South Pacific.[128]

The South Pacific anti-corruption framework is based around the global anti-corruption regime and its legal tools, but includes diverse actors with regional, national, and private interests, operating in different ways but articulating a similar agenda. Concerns as to the applicability of the global regime and its tools in the region remain relevant, but active engagement by regional actors with the broader anti-corruption agenda is a positive sign.

Risks and challenges for implementation and enforcement of UNCAC in the South Pacific

UNCAC is the touchstone of the anti-corruption framework in the South Pacific region. The regional policies and programmes mentioned above use discourse consistent with UNCAC and its stated objectives. Some regional policies are designed with the explicit goal of increasing South Pacific ratification of UNCAC and enhancing UNCAC implementation in the region. Certain domestic legislation, including the leadership codes of Papua New Guinea, Solomon Islands, Vanuatu, Fiji, and Tuvalu reflect the recommendations and requirements found in UNCAC. Examples include asset disclosure provisions and statements of conflict of interest regarding public officials and private activities.[129]

The consistency of regional discourse and policy with the approach taken by UNCAC appears to be a positive sign for the potential success of the global anti-corruption regime in the South Pacific. However, as Barcham notes, despite the existence of relevant tools and policies in the region, corruption remains a substantial challenge and implementation of these policies is often limited.[130] Certain regime risk factors and challenges introduced in Chapters 1 and 2 continue to be relevant in the South Pacific context. The South Pacific region does not illustrate an overemphasis on criminal law and enforcement measures. However, the challenges of deviant actors and non-compliant states appear substantial, as does the risk of inapplicability. Such factors may prevent successful implementation of regional anti-corruption policies. These risks will need to be addressed if the global anti-corruption regime is to achieve success in the region through implementation and enforcement of UNCAC.

Deviant actors

Nadelmann and Andreas note the challenge of deviant actors, who limit the possibility of global prohibition regimes achieving the final stage of evolution.[131] In the case of the South Pacific, not all states in the region are parties to UNCAC. Recent ratifications and accessions mean that Samoa and Tonga are the only remaining non-members in the region. Regional anti-corruption efforts are based on non-mandatory policies or 'soft law' instruments. There is a risk that states not party to UNCAC will allow, engage in, or support, corrupt activities without being held accountable through international legal channels. However, regional soft law instruments and policies may still be a powerful compliance tool, especially when combined with external aid conditionalities and pressure from powerful actors.

Inapplicability and non-compliant states

The influence of external actors in the South Pacific region is extensive. When combined with the under-representation of South Pacific states in UNCAC negotiations, this external influence enhances the risk of incompatibility discussed in Chapters 1 and 2. The reasons external actors choose to promote anti-corruption in the region must be viewed critically. If the global anti-corruption regime is promoted out of self-interest, to enhance economic opportunities or as a political tool to achieve other policies' objectives, there is a substantial risk that policies promoted will conflict with the unique dynamics in the region. This incompatibility of external objectives and approaches with regional and local dynamics may ultimately hamper implementation and enforcement of UNCAC and the success of the global anti-corruption regime in the South Pacific.

Promotion of inapplicable anti-corruption policies is also relevant, due to resource and capacity limitations in the South Pacific. These limitations relate not only to limited financial resources, but also to limited human capital, access to technology, and knowledge of the specific features of UNCAC and relevant legal, political, and administrative tools that may support its application. Resource and capacity limitations may contribute to the challenge of non-compliant states and limit the effectiveness of criminal law and enforcement measures.

Many states in the South Pacific region are reliant on external aid and geographic features can prevent consistent penetration of government services. If UNCAC and the global anti-corruption cannot be adapted to function in a context where resources, capacity, and government penetration are limited, the effectiveness of UNCAC and the success of the regime are likely to be compromised.

States in the South Pacific that are parties to UNCAC may support the regime in theory but in practice they may be unable to take necessary steps to combat corrupt activity in line with requirements under UNCAC. Furthermore, if government services are limited in their ability to penetrate the entire state, criminal law and enforcement measures may be of limited effect. The result will be areas immune to sovereign authority in which deviant actors can continue to operate. This reflects the concerns of Nadelmann introduced in Chapter 1.[132]

These risk factors will need to be addressed by UNCAC and the global anti-corruption regime. The success with which they are mitigated will impact the evolution of the global anti-corruption regime to the final stage. The impact of these risk factors and challenges must be explored further in the domestic case study of PNG, as they may operate to limit the effectiveness of UNCAC in the domestic context, as much as in the regional one. Chapter 4 presents the context of the PNG case study in detail, further illustrating the risks and challenges faced by anti-corruption efforts in this unique domestic context.

Notes

1 Larmour has conducted some valuable descriptive studies on corruption in the region, see Larmour P, 'International Action against Corruption in the Pacific Islands: policy transfer, coercion and effectiveness' 15(1) *Asian Journal of Political Science* (2007) and Larmour P, *ANU Policy and Governance Discussion Paper: Culture and Corruption in the Pacific Islands — Some conceptual issues and findings from studies of National Integrity Systems* (2006). However, beyond this, research is limited

2 Crocombe R, *The South Pacific* (University of the South Pacific, 1st Edition, 2001) at 16

3 Pacific Islands Forum Secretariat, *About Us*, available at: http://www.forumsec.org/pages.cfm/about-us/ (last visited 1 March 2018)

4 SPC Website, *Members of the Pacific community*, (2011) available at: http://www.spc.int/en/about-spc/members.html (last visited 1 March 2018)

5 ibid.. Note that the UK and the Netherlands were historically members but are no longer part of the SPC.

6 SPC Website, *History*, (2011) available at: http://www.spc.int/en/about-spc/history.html (last visited 1 March 2018)

7 UN-OHRLLS Website, *Country Profiles*, (2015) available at: http://unohrlls.org/about-sids/country-profiles/ (last visited 1 March 2018)

8 Geoscience Australia, *Deserts* (1994) available at: http://www.ga.gov.au/scientific-topics/national-location-information/landforms/deserts (last visited 1 March 2018). It is noted that *70% of Australia's land mass is classified as arid or semi-arid.*

9 UNDP and Barcham M, Corruption in Pacific Island Countries (2007)

10 ibid.

11 Findlay M, 'Misunderstanding Corruption and Community: Comparative Cultural Politics of Corruption Regulation in the Pacific' 2 *Asian Criminology* (2007) 47, at 52

12 CIA Library, *The World Fact Book: Nauru* (2014), available at: https://www.cia.gov/library/ publications/resources/the-world-factbook/geos/nr.html and *The World Fact Book: Kiribati* (2014), available at: https://www.cia.gov/library/publications/resources/the-world-factbook/geos/kr.html (last visited 1 March 2018)

13 CIA Library, *The World Fact Book: New Zealand* (2014), available at: https://www.cia.gov/library/publications/the-world-factbook/geos/nz.html (last visited 1 March 2018)

14 ibid.; CIA Library, *The World Fact Book: Australia* (2014), available at: https://www.cia.gov/library/publications/the-world-factbook/geos/au.html (last visited 1 March 2018)

15 Inferred from a general overview of the 16 South Pacific states conducted on the CIA Library, *The World Fact Book* (2014) available at: https://www.cia.gov/library/publications/the-world-factbook/ (last visited 1 March 2018)

16 CIA Library, *The World Fact Book: Nauru* (2014), available at: https://www.cia.gov/library/ publications/resources/the-world-factbook/geos/nr.html (last visited 1 March 2018)

17 CIA Library, *The World Fact Book: Kiribati* (2014), available at: https://www.cia.gov/library/publications/resources/the-world-factbook/geos/kr.html (last visited 1 March 2018)
18 Larmour P, 'International Action against Corruption in the Pacific Islands: policy transfer, coercion and effectiveness' 15(1) *Asian Journal of Political Science* (2007) at 4
19 Constitutional Advisory Panel, *New Zealand's Constitution: A report on a conversation*, (November 2013) at Appendix E
20 above n2 at 442
21 National Archives of Australia, *Records of Papua New Guinea 1883–1942: Fact sheet 148* (2015) available at: http://www.naa.gov.au/collection/fact-sheets/fs148.aspx (last visited 1 March 2018)
22 Ministry of Culture and Heritage, *New Zealand History: Capture of German Samoa* (13 April 2015) available at: http://www.nzhistory.net.nz/war/capture-of-samoa (last visited 1 March 2018)
23 Pacific Islands Treaty Series, *How Treaties become Law* (2014) available at: http://www.paclii.org/pits/en/domestication.shtml (last visited 1 March 2018)
24 ibid.
25 ibid.
26 Corrin J and Patterson D, *Introduction to South Pacific Law* (Palgrave Macmillan, 3rd Edition, 2011)
27 ibid. at 4 and 62. Fiji abolished the most recent written constitution in 2009 and it has not yet been replaced.
28 ibid. at 70
29 ibid. at 95
30 ibid. at 4
31 ibid. at 95
32 ibid. at 5
33 Above n9; above n11
34 Above n9 at 10; Above n18 at 4
35 Above n2 at 546. Note also above n9; Babu RR, 'The United Nations Convention against Corruption: A critical overview' *SSRN* (2006) available at: http://ssrn.com/abstract=891898 (last visited 1 March 2018)
36 Nicholls R, 'Corruption in the South Pacific: the potential impact of the UN Convention against Corruption on Pacific Island States' 2 *NZYB Int'l L* (2005) 207; Above n9 at 34. The increased corrupt incentives provided by aid and trade relationships in the South Pacific are explored further below at Chapter 3: Understanding corruption in the South Pacific
37 Above n9
38 Above n2 at 515
39 Leadership codes are perhaps the best example. Annex C provides a complete list of the relevant laws in the South Pacific
40 Huffer E, 'Governance, Corruption, and Ethics in the Pacific' 17(1) *The Contemporary Pacific* (2005) 118
41 Pacific Islands Forum Secretariat, *The Pacific Plan for Strengthening Regional Cooperation and Integration*, (2005) ('The Pacific Plan, 2005'); Pacific Islands Forum Secretariat, *The Framework for Pacific Regionalism* (2014)
42 One example is the ADB/OECD, *Anti-Corruption Action Plan for Asia and the Pacific* (2001)
43 Above n2; Barcham M, 'Cleaning up the Pacific: anti-corruption initiatives' 63(2) *Australian Journal of International Affairs* (2009) 249; Chene M, *Corruption Challenges in Small Island Developing States in the Pacific region*, U4 Expert Answer No.255 (2010)
44 Above n2, at 168

45 PNG Ombusman, Commission of Inquiry into Aspects of the Forestry Industry, Vol.1, 1990 ('The Barnett Report')
46 Chene M, *Corruption Challenges in Small Island Developing States in the Pacific region*, U4 Expert Answer No.255 (2010)
47 Statistic from Department of Foreign Affairs and Trade website: http://dfat.gov.au/geo/papua-new-guinea/development-assistance/pages/papua-new-guinea.aspx (last visited 1 March 2018)
48 Statistic a summary based on information provided at the New Zealand Department of Foreign Affairs website: https://www.mfat.govt.nz/en/aid-and-development/our-work-in-the-pacific/ (last visited 1 March 2018)
49 World Bank, *Programs and Projects* (2015) available at: http://www.worldbank.org/en/country/pacificislands/projects (last visited 1 March 2018)
50 Federated States of Micronesia, Fiji, Kiribati, Marshall Islands, Palau, Samoa, Solomon Islands, Tonga, Tuvalu, and Vanuatu. See The World Bank, *Pacific Islands Overview* (2015) available at: http://www.worldbank.org/en/country/pacificislands/overview (last visited 1 March 2018)
51 ADB, *Statement of Operations* (2013) at Appendix 1
52 Above n9
53 ibid.
54 See Nadelmann EA and Andreas P, *Policing the Globe: Criminalization and crime control in international relations* (Oxford University Press, 1st Edition, 2006)
55 ADB OECD, *Anti-corruption initiative for Asia Pacific,* (2010) available at: http://www.oecd.org/site/adboecdanti-corruptioninitiative/ (last visited 1 March 2018); n43
56 Above n2 at 552
57 The regional assistance mission in the Solomon Islands (RAMSI), beginning in 2003, is one example of costly intervention in the South Pacific, with estimates of Australian expenditure of AUD2.6 billion on the mission. Lowy Institute, Hayward-Jones J, *Australia's Costly Investment in Solomon Islands: The lessons of RAMSI* (8 May 2014) available at: http://www.lowyinstitute.org/publications/lessons-ramsi (last visited 1 March 2018)
58 Williamson CR, 'Exploring the Failure of Foreign Aid: The role of incentives and information' (2010) 23(1) *The Review of Austrian Economics* 17; Moyo D, *Dead Aid: Why Aid Is Not Working and How There Is a Better Way for Africa* (Farrar, Strauss and Giroux, 1st Edition, 2009); Passas N, 'Globalization and Transnational Crime: Effects of Criminogenic Asymmetries', in Williams P and Vlassis D (eds), *Combatting Transnational Crime: Concepts, Activities and Responses* (Frank Cass Publishers, 2013) 22, at 37
59 Ampratwum EF, 'The Fight Against Corruption and its Implications for Development in Developing and Transition Economies' 1(11) *JMLC* (2008) 76 at 83
60 ibid. at 83
61 Devpolicy Blog, Morauta and Cain, *In Conversation with Sir Mekere Morauta* (8 April 2013) available at: http://devpolicy.org/in-conversation-with-sir-mekere-morauta-20130408/ (last visited 1 March 2018)
62 Dobell G, 'China and Taiwan in the South Pacific: Diplomatic chess versus Pacific political rugby', *1 CSCSD Occasional Paper* (May 2007) 10
63 Vltchek A, 'Wooing the Islands: China and Taiwan high stakes bid for Pacific Island support' (20 April 2008) *The Asia-Pacific Journal: Japan Focus,* available at: http://www.japanfocus.org/-Andre-Vltchek/2727/article.html (last visited 1 March 2018)
64 above n62
65 above n59 at 82
66 ibid.
67 ibid.
68 iIbid. at 84
69 Bukovansky M, 'The Hollowness of Anti-Corruption Discourse' 13(2) *Review of International Political Economy* (2006) 181 at 194

70 ibid. at 195
71 ibid. at 198
72 McCusker R, 'Transnational crime in the Pacific Islands: real or apparent danger?' 308 *Trends & Issues in Crime and Criminal Justice* (2006); Briggs G, 'Organised Crime Groups: A transnational security threat to the region north of Australia' *Future Directions International Strategic Analysis Paper* (2010); Windybank S, 'The illegal Pacific, Part 1: organised crime' 24(1) *Policy* (2008) 32
73 Bales K, 'What Predicts Human Trafficking?' 31(2) *International Journal of Comparative and Applied Criminal Justice* (2007) 269; UNODC, *Issue Paper: The Role of Corruption in Trafficking in Persons* (2011)
74 Henshaw C, 'Strengthening the Rule of Law in the Pacific through International Crime Cooperation' 15 *Australian International Law Journal* (2008) 109; above n9
75 ibid.; above n9
76 Tsamenyi BM and Hanich QA, *Addressing Corruption in Pacific Islands Fisheries: A report prepared for IUCN PROFISH law enforcement, corruption and fisheries project* (2008), at 10
77 Larmour P, 'Corruption and Governance in the South Pacific' 20(3) *Pacific Studies* (1997) 1, at 6
78 ibid. at 6
79 Ernst and Young, *Managing Bribery and Corruption Risks in the Mining and Metals Industry* (EY, 2013) at 14
80 ibid. at 14
81 Passas N, 'Globalization and Transnational Crime: Effects of Criminogenic Asymmetries', in Williams P and Vlassis D (eds), *Combatting Transnational Crime: Concepts, Activities and Responses* (Frank Cass Publishers, 2013) 22 at 42
82 ibid. at 50
83 above n11 at 51
84 International Chamber of Commerce, Transparency International, UN Global Compact, World Economic Forum Partnering against Corruption Initiative, *Clean Business is Good Business: The business case against corruption* (2008) [ICC et al, 2008]
85 ACF and CELCoR, *Bulldozing Progress: Human rights abuses and corruption in Papua New Guinea's large scale logging industry* (2006) ('CELCoR Report, 2006') at 4
86 In addition to continuing cases of corrupt conduct raised in the media, an aggregate of South Pacific countries' scores in the 2014 World Bank Governance Indicators for Control of Corruption put the region in the 54th percentile, excluding Australia, with a score of 95.2, and New Zealand, with perfect score of 100. Data gathered from World Bank, *World Wide Governance Indicators* (2015) available at: http://info.worldbank.org/governance/wgi/ (last visited 1 March 2018)
87 The term 'soft law' refers in this context to those documents that do not result in any legal obligation but may have legal relevance due to their 'proximity to the law'; in this case UNCAC and other multilateral legal instruments that support the global anti-corruption regime. An overview is provided by Thurer D, 'Soft Law', *Max Planck Encyclopedia of Public International Law* (March 2009) at 4
88 Hughes R, 'Corruption', in Jowitt A and Cain TN (Eds), *Passage of Change: Law, society and governance in the Pacific* (Pandanus Books, 2003) 35 at 47
89 Chapter 1: Introducing the five-stage model: the theory of Nadelmann and Andreas
90 Abbott KW and Snidal D, 'Values and Interests: International legalization in the fight against corruption' 31 *Journal of Legal Studies* (2002) 141 as introduced in Chapter 1
91 The Pacific Islands Forum Secretariat, *The Pacific Plan for Strengthening Regional Cooperation and Integration*, (2005) ('The Pacific Plan, 2005')
92 Pacific Islands Forum Secretariat, *The Framework for Pacific Regionalism* (2014) at 11
93 n92 at 18

94 Pacific Islands Forum Secretariat Website, *The Framework for Pacific Regionalism* (2014) available at: http://www.forumsec.org.fj/pages.cfm/strategic-partnerships-coordination/framework-for-pacific-regionalism/ (last visited 1 March 2018)
95 Pacific Islands Forum Secretariat, *Principles of Good Leadership and Accountability* (2004) available at: http://www.forumsec.org/pages.cfm/political-governance-security/good-governance/forum-principles-of-good-leadership-accountability.html (last visited 1 March 2018) (‘*PIF Principles of Good Leadership and Accountability, 2004*’)
96 These ideals reflect the criminal acts established in UNCAC under Articles 17–19 relating to embezzlement, misappropriation, or other diversion of property, trading in influence and abuse of functions.
97 PIF Principles of Good Leadership and Accountability, 2004 (n96)
98 *United Nations Convention against Corruption*, opened for signature 9 December 2003, 2349 UNTS 41 (entered into force 14 December 2005) (‘UNCAC’), Article 9
99 This reflects UNCAC, Article 10 and Article 6(2)
100 Boister N, ‘New Directions for Regional Cooperation in the Suppression of Transnational Crime in the South Pacific' 9(2) *Journal of South Pacific Law* (2005) available at: http://www.paclii.org/journals/fJSPL/vol09no2/1.shtml (last visited 1 March 2018)
101 Thurer (n88) at section 3(8)
102 ibid. at section 2(6)
103 ibid.
104 ADB/OECD, *Anti-Corruption Action Plan for Asia and the Pacific* (2001) (n43)
105 ADB/OECD, *Anti-Corruption Initiative for the Asia Pacific: Strategic principles and operational activities of the initiative* (2010) (‘ADB/OECD *Strategic Principles*, 2010’)
106 ADB/OECD *Strategic Principles*, 2010 (n106) Preamble
107 *Convention on Combating Bribery of Foreign Public Officials in International Business Transactions*, signed 17 December 1997, 37 ILM 1 (entered into force 15 February 1999) (‘OECD Convention’), Preamble
108 UNCAC, Preamble
109 ADB/OECD, *Anti-Corruption Action Plan for Asia and the Pacific* (2001) (n43), Pillar One, at 3
110 ibid. at 4
111 ibid.
112 ibid. at 5. This reflects UNCAC Article 13 on Participation of Society
113 ADB/OECD *Strategic Principles*, 2010 (n106) at 2
114 ibid.
115 UNODC/UNDP, UN Pacific Regional Anti-Corruption (UN-PRAC) Project Document (20 April 2012) (‘UN-PRAC’)
116 UN-PRAC, at 7
117 UN-PRAC
118 United Nations Information Centre: Canberra, *Pacific Journalists Learn about UNCAC at Combating Corruption Workshop*, 18 August 2015, available at: http://un.org.au/2015/08/18/pacific-journalists-learn-about-uncac-at-combating-corruption-workshop/ (last visited 1 March 2018)
119 As of 31 December 2014 Australia had committed AUD8.90 billion in capital subscription to the ADB and New Zealand had committed NZD2.36 billion. See ADB Country Factsheets (April 2015) available at: http://www.adb.org/publications/new-zealand-fact-sheet and http://www.adb.org/publications/australia-fact-sheet (last visited 1 March 2018)
120 UNDP in Asia and the Pacific, *UN Gears up to Fight Corruption in the Pacific* (7 August 2013), available at: http://www.asia-pacific.undp.org/content/rbap/en/home/presscenter/pressreleases/2013/08/07/un-gears-up-to-fight-corruption-in-the-pacific.html (last visited 1 March 2018)

121 above n62 at 15
122 ibid.
123 above n9 at 49
124 ibid.
125 ibid. at vii
126 UNDP Press Release, *Tonga Parliament aims to Boost anti-Corruption Efforts*, (13 May 2015) available at: http://www.asia-pacific.undp.org/content/rbap/en/home/presscenter/pressreleases/2015/05/13/tonga-parliament-aim-to-boost-anti-corruption-efforts.html (last visited 1 March 2018)
127 PBEC, *PBEC Participates in the 11th ADB-OECD Anti-Corruption Initiative in Manila* (2008) available at: http://www.pbec.org/21-strategic-partners/adb-oecd-anti-corruption-initiative/302-adb (last visited 1 March 2018)
128 PINA, *About Us*, available at: http://www.pina.com.fj/index.php?p=pina&m=about-us (last visited 1 March 2018); Eldis, *Pacific Network on Globalisation* available at: http://eldis.org/go/home&id=40938&type=Organisation (last visited 1 March 2018)
129 See Annex C of this book
130 Barcham M, 'Cleaning up the Pacific: anti-corruption initiatives' 63(2) *Australian Journal of International Affairs* (2009) 249
131 above n54
132 ibid.

References

Abbott KW and Snidal D, 'Values and Interests: International legalization in the fight against corruption' 31 *Journal of Legal Studies* (2002) 141.

ACF and CELCoR, *Bulldozing Progress: Human rights abuses and corruption in Papua New Guinea's large scale logging industry* (2006) ('CELCoR Report, 2006').

ADB /OECD, *Anti-Corruption Initiative for the Asia Pacific: Strategic principles and operational activities of the initiative* (2010) ('ADB/OECD *Strategic Principles*, 2010').

ADB Country Factsheets (April 2015) available at: http://www.adb.org/publications/new-zealand-fact-sheet and http://www.adb.org/publications/australia-fact-sheet (last visited 1 March 2018).

ADB OECD, *Anti-corruption initiative for Asia Pacific* (2010) available at: http://www.oecd.org/site/adboecdanti-corruptioninitiative/ (last visited 1 March 2018).

ADB/OECD, *Anti-Corruption Action Plan for Asia and the Pacific* (2001).

ADB, *Statement of Operations* (2013) available at: https://www.adb.org/documents/statement-asian-development-banks-operations-2013 (last visited 1 March 2018).

Ampratwum EF, 'The Fight Against Corruption and its Implications for Development in Developing and Transition Economies' 1(11) *JMLC* (2008) 76.

Australian Department of Foreign Affairs and Trade website: http://dfat.gov.au/geo/papua-new-guinea/development-assistance/pages/papua-new-guinea.aspx (last visited 1 March 2018).

Geoscience Australia, *Deserts* (1994) available at: http://www.ga.gov.au/scientific-topics/national-location-information/landforms/deserts (last visited 1 March 2018).

Babu RR, 'The United Nations Convention against Corruption: A critical overview', *SSRN* (2006) available at: http://ssrn.com/abstract=891898 (last visited 1 March 2018).

Bales K, 'What Predicts Human Trafficking?' 31(2) *International Journal of Comparative and Applied Criminal Justice* (2007) 269.

Barcham M, 'Cleaning up the Pacific: anti-corruption initiatives' 63(2) *Australian Journal of International Affairs* (2009) 249.

Barcham M, *Corruption in Pacific Island Countries* (UNDP Pacific Centre, 2007).

Boister N, 'New Directions for Regional Cooperation in the Suppression of Transnational Crime in the South Pacific' 9(2) *Journal of South Pacific Law* (2005).

Briggs G, 'Organised Crime Groups: A transnational security threat to the region north of Australia' *Future Directions International Strategic Analysis Paper* (2010).

Bukovansky M, 'The Hollowness of Anti-Corruption Discourse' 13(2) *Review of International Political Economy* (2006) 18.

Chene M, *Corruption Challenges in Small Island Developing States in the Pacific region* (U4 Expert Answer No.255, 2010).

CIA Library, *The World Fact Book: Australia* (2014), available at: https://www.cia.gov/library/publications/the-world-factbook/geos/print_as.html (last visited 1 March 2018).

CIA Library, *The World Fact Book: Kiribati* (2014), available at: https://www.cia.gov/library/publications/resources/the-world-factbook/geos/kr.html (last visited 1 March 2018).

CIA Library, *The World Fact Book: Nauru* (2014), available at: https://www.cia.gov/library/publications/resources/the-world-factbook/geos/nr.html (last visited 1 March 2018).

CIA Library, *The World Fact Book: New Zealand* (2014), available at: https://www.cia.gov/library/publications/the-world-factbook/geos/nz.html (last visited 1 March 2018).

Constitutional Advisory Panel, *New Zealand's Constitution: A report on a conversation* (November 2013) at Appendix E.

Convention on Combating Bribery of Foreign Public Officials in International Business Transactions, opened for signature 17 December 1997, 37 ILM 1 (entered into force 15 February 1999) ('OECD Convention').

Corrin J and Patterson D, *Introduction to South Pacific Law* (Palgrave MacMillan, 3rd Edition, 2011).

Crocombe R, *The South Pacific* (University of the South Pacific, 1st Edition, 2001).

Dobell G, 'China and Taiwan in the South Pacific: Diplomatic chess versus Pacific political rugby', 1 *CSCSD Occasional Paper* (May 2007) 10.

Eldis, *Pacific Network on Globalisation* (2017) available at: http://eldis.org/go/home&id=40938&type=Organisation (last visited 1 March 2018).

Ernst and Young, *Managing Bribery and Corruption Risks in the Mining and Metals Industry* (EY, 2013).

Findlay M, 'Misunderstanding Corruption and Community: Comparative Cultural Politics of Corruption Regulation in the Pacific' 2 *Asian Criminology* (2007) 47.

Hayward-Jones J, *Australia's Costly Investment in Solomon Islands: The lessons of RAMSI* (8 May 2014) available at: http://www.lowyinstitute.org/publications/lessons-ramsi (last visited 1 March 2018).

Henshaw C, 'Strengthening the Rule of Law in the Pacific through International Crime Cooperation' 15 *Australian International Law Journal* (2008) 109.

Huffer E, 'Governance, Corruption, and Ethics in the Pacific' 17(1) *The Contemporary Pacific* (2005) 118.

Hughs R, 'Corruption', in Jowitt A and Cain TN (eds) *Passage of Change: Law, society and governance in the Pacific* (ANU Press, 2003) 35.

ICC et al, *Clean Business is Good Business: The business case against corruption* (2008).

Larmour P, 'International Action against Corruption in the Pacific Islands: policy transfer, coercion and effectiveness' 15(1) *Asian Journal of Political Science* (2007).

Larmour P, 'Corruption and Governance in the South Pacific' 20(3) *Pacific Studies* (1997).

Larmour P, *ANU Policy and Governance Discussion Paper: Culture and Corruption in the Pacific Islands — Some conceptual issues and findings from studies of National Integrity Systems* (ANU Press, 2006).

McCusker R, 'Transnational crime in the Pacific Islands: real or apparent danger?' 308 *Trends & Issues in Crime and Criminal Justice* (2006).

Ministry of Culture and Heritage, *New Zealand History: Capture of German Samoa*, (13 April 2015) available at: http://www.nzhistory.net.nz/war/capture-of-samoa (last visited 1 March 2018).

Moyo D, *Dead Aid: Why Aid Is Not Working and How There Is a Better Way for Africa* (Farrar, Straus and Giroux, 1st Edition, 2009).

Nadelmann EA and Andreas P, *Policing the Globe: Criminalization and crime control in international relations* (Oxford University Press, 1st Edition, 2006).

National Archives of Australia, *Records of Papua New Guinea 1883–1942: Fact sheet* 148 (2015) available at: http://www.naa.gov.au/collection/fact-sheets/fs148.aspx (last visited 1 March 2018).

New Zealand Department of Foreign Affairs website: https://www.mfat.govt.nz/en/aid-and-development/our-work-in-the-pacific/ (last visited 1 March 2018).

Nicholls R, 'Corruption in the South Pacific: the potential impact of the UN Convention against Corruption on Pacific Island States' 2 *NZYB Int'l L* (2005) 207.

Pacific Islands Forum Secretariat, *About Us*, available at: http://www.forumsec.org/pages.cfm/about-us/ (last visited 1 March 2018).

Pacific Islands Forum Secretariat, *Principles of Good Leadership and Accountability*, (2004) available at: http://www.forumsec.org/pages.cfm/political-governance-security/good-governance/forum-principles-of-good-leadership-accountability.html (last visited 1 March 2018).

Pacific Islands Forum Secretariat, *The Framework for Pacific Regionalism* (PIF, 2014) available at: http://www.forumsec.org/pages.cfm/strategic-partnerships-coordination/framework-for-pacific-regionalism/ (last visited 1 March 2018).

Pacific Islands Forum Secretariat, *The Pacific Plan for Strengthening Regional Cooperation and Integration*, (2005) ('The Pacific Plan 2005').

Pacific Islands Treaty Series, *How Treaties become Law* (2014) available at: http://www.paclii.org/pits/en/domestication.shtml (last visited 1 March 2018).

Passas N, 'Globalization and Transnational Crime: Effects of criminogenic asymmetries', in Williams P and Vlassis D (Eds), *Combatting Transnational Crime: Concepts, Activities and Responses* (Frank Cass Publishers, 2013) 22.

PBEC, *PBEC Participates in the 11th ADB-OECD Anti-Corruption Initiative in Manila* (2008) http://www.pbec.org/21-strategic-partners/adb-oecd-anti-corruption-initiative/302-adb (last visited 1 March 2018).

PINA, *About Us*, available at: http://www.pina.com.fj/index.php?p=pina&m=about-us (last visited 1 March 2018).

PNG Ombusman, *Commission of Inquiry into Aspects of the Forestry Industry*, Vol.1 (1990).

SPC Website, *History* (2011) available at: http://www.spc.int/about-us/history/ (last visited 1 March 2018).

SPC Website, *Members of the Pacific community* (2011) available at: http://www.spc.int/our-members/ (last visited 1 March 2018).

Devpolicy Blog, Morauta and Cain, *In Conversation with Sir Mekere Morauta* (8 April 2013) available at: http://devpolicy.org/in-conversation-with-sir-mekere-morauta-20130408/ (last visited 1 March 2018).

Thurer D, 'Soft Law' (at March 2009) in Oxford University Press, *Max Planck Encyclopedia of Public International Law*.
Tsamenyi BM and Hanich QA, *Addressing Corruption in Pacific Islands Fisheries: A report prepared for IUCN PROFISH law enforcement, corruption and fisheries project* (2008).
UN-OHRLLS Website, *Country Profiles* (2015) available at: http://unohrlls.org/about-sids/country-profiles/ (last visited 1 March 2018).
UNDP in Asia and the Pacific, *UN Gears up to Fight Corruption in the Pacific* (7 August 2013), available at: http://www.asia-pacific.undp.org/content/rbap/en/home/presscenter/pressreleases/2013/08/07/un-gears-up-to-fight-corruption-in-the-pacific.html (last visited 1 March 2018).
UNDP Press Release, *Tonga Parliament aims to Boost anti-Corruption Efforts*, (13 May 2015) available at: http://www.asia-pacific.undp.org/content/rbap/en/home/presscenter/pressreleases/2015/05/13/tonga-parliament-aim-to-boost-anti-corruption -efforts.html (last visited 1 March 2018).
United Nations Convention against Corruption, opened for signature 9 December 2003, 2349 UNTS 41 (entered into force 14 December 2005) ('UNCAC'), Article 9.
United Nations Information Centre: Canberra, *Pacific Journalists Learn about UNCAC at Combating Corruption Workshop*, 18 August 2015, available at: http://un.org.au/2015/08/18/pacific-journalists-learn-about-uncac-at-combating-corruption-workshop/ (last visited 1 March 2018).
UNODC, *Issue Paper: The Role of Corruption in Trafficking in Persons* (UNODC, 2011).
UNODC/UNDP, *UN Pacific Regional Anti-Corruption (UN-PRAC) Project Document* (20 April 2012) ('UN-PRAC').
Vltchek A, 'Wooing the Islands: China and Taiwan high stakes bid for Pacific Island support' 6(4) *The Asia-Pacific Journal: Japan Focus* (1 April 2008).
Williamson CR, 'Exploring the Failure of Foreign Aid: The role of incentives and information' 23(1) *The Review of Austrian Economics* (2010) 17.
Windybank S, 'The illegal Pacific, Part 1: organised crime' 24(1) *Policy* (2008) 32.
World Bank, *Pacific Islands Overview*, (2015) available at: http://www.worldbank.org/en/country/pacificislands/overview (last visited 1 March 2018).
World Bank, *Programs and Projects*, (2015) available at: http://www.worldbank.org/en/country/pacificislands/projects (last visited 1 March 2018).
World Bank, *World Wide Governance Indicators* (2015) available at: http://info. worldbank.org/governance/wgi/ (last visited 1 March 2018).

4 The case study of Papua New Guinea

Introduction and chapter structure

Chapter 3 demonstrated the consistency of approach between the regional framework and the global anti-corruption regime, encapsulated by the United Nations Convention against Corruption (UNCAC). The relevance of external interest actors and the promotion of various value and interest-based agendas under the ambit of anti-corruption was documented. The challenges of deviant states and non-compliant states, and the risks of inapplicability and criminal law and enforcement focus were noted, especially regarding limited resources and capacity in the region and the possibility of co-optation of the anti-corruption agenda for other objectives.

Regional dynamics are an important aspect of the context in which UNCAC and the global anti-corruption regime must operate. However, the 'soft' non-mandatory nature of regional anti-corruption programmes and policies in the South Pacific emphasise the central importance of action at the state level. This reflects the reality for UNCAC and the global anti-corruption regime, which require domestic implementation and enforcement to secure a consistent anti-corruption approach and ultimately reduce corrupt activity globally.

Given the importance of the domestic context, this chapter focuses on the case study of Papua New Guinea (PNG) and analyses how international and regional laws and policies interact in this domestic context. Key features of the domestic context include domestic laws and policies, social norms, and political institutions. The cultural, economic, and societal dynamics at play and the influential actors that promote their values and interests in this context are also relevant. Ultimately, the dynamic interaction of these features shapes the nature and operation of domestic law and policy and therefore influences the implementation and enforcement of international instruments such as UNCAC.

This chapter first introduces the importance of the PNG case study. An historical overview of PNG is provided, introducing the legal, political, and cultural features of the PNG context, relevant to implementation and enforcement of UNCAC. The nature of corruption in PNG is then explored, referencing the unique challenges that emerge in this context. The legal and institutional anti-corruption framework is outlined, including documentation of the dominant values and interests influencing this framework and the challenges that have arisen in ensuring the effective functioning of the framework.

Papua New Guinea's interaction with the global anti-corruption regime is documented, through analysis of PNG's engagement with UNCAC. Participation in the initial UNCAC negotiations was limited in PNG's case, but since its signature and ratification of this multilateral legal instrument PNG has engaged more extensively through the implementation review process. PNG is a participant in the first round of UNCAC Implementation Review (2010–15) and the country is currently in the process of establishing an Independent Commission against Corruption (ICAC). The extent to which PNG has incorporated UNCAC into its domestic anti-corruption framework is evaluated in this chapter. Challenges to the implementation and enforcement of UNCAC in the PNG context are also explored and analysed. Preliminary findings are presented regarding PNG's experiences with UNCAC and the key challenges facing implementation and enforcement of the global anti-corruption regime. This allows for initial evaluation of criticisms relating to the application of the regime, within the context of PNG. Ultimately, the analysis in this chapter provides preliminary answers to the second and third research questions:

1 What impact has UNCAC had on PNG's approach to combatting corruption?
2 Does PNG's experience with implementation and enforcement of UNCAC support the existing theoretical and practical criticisms of UNCAC and the emergent global anti-corruption regime more generally?

Chapter 5 explores these questions further, drawing on material from interviews with a range of actors involved with UNCAC at the national, regional, and international levels.

The value of the PNG case study

A national case study is useful in order to explore the challenges of implementing and enforcing UNCAC and the global anti-corruption regime domestically. To achieve the fifth stage of evolution, the regime must secure consistent support and enforcement across diverse domestic contexts.[1] The goal is to eradicate the target behaviour through consistent legal frameworks, requiring enforcement across all states, regardless of diverse legal, political, economic, or cultural dynamics.

In Chapter 3, the regional sphere was presented as a useful intermediate point of analysis. Interaction at the regional level illustrated the dominant actors, values, and interests at play in the South Pacific. Most Small Island Developing States (SIDS) in the region have a strong colonial history and are aid-dependent, susceptible to the values and interests of nations such as Australia and New Zealand, as well as multilateral lending institutions and, increasingly, China and states in South-East Asia. A regional framework targeting corruption has been developed in the South Pacific. However, application of this framework is not mandatory and the risks of misuse and continual non-compliance by state actors are relevant concerns.

The PNG case study is not intended as a complete or generalised picture of the dynamics experienced in all South Pacific states. In many ways, PNG is a unique case in the region. However, focusing analysis on PNG helps to illustrate many of the challenges and complexities that arise when implementing and enforcing a global prohibition regime domestically. Furthermore, some facets of the PNG case reflect the context of other SIDS in the region, and perhaps also developing nations elsewhere in the world. The PNG case has many of the attributes considered to limit applicability of transnational law and success of the global anti-corruption regime.[2] Insights gained from analysis of the PNG case will therefore be informative for enhancing the implementation and enforcement of UNCAC and securing success of the global anti-corruption regime.

There are several key issues relevant to PNG that may be generalised to other SIDS, both regionally and globally. First, PNG has a history of colonial rule and has since adopted political and legal frameworks that reflect this history. These frameworks and the values that underly them often clash with traditional modes of societal organisation. Conflict between modern and traditional modes of societal organisation has been cited as a risk factor for corruption, and was discussed in Chapter 3.

A second issue is that PNG is a resource rich country, but has not fully utilised its resources to secure social development or sustainable economic growth. This failure can be linked in part to global and domestic power asymmetries, which coalesce to limit developmental opportunities. As Lasslett notes, PNG's natural resource reserves have provided 'the most immediate means for attracting international flows of capital'.[3] However, landowners have often been frustrated by the failure of the state to share benefits from these projects.[4] Passas notes that Transnational Corporations (TNCs) have: '. . . often co-opted national leaders, who then oppressed their own people and allowed TNCs to pollute the countryside, exploit local labour, disregard safety regulations, avoid taxes, etc'.[5]

This has certainly been a trend in PNG. The case of the Bougainville conflict is perhaps the most extreme illustration of power asymmetries between transnational corporations and the state, and between the state and citizens, having a fundamentally destabilising effect, both domestically and regionally.[6]

In addition to complex power dynamics, a colonial history and limited domestic capacity have resulted in aid reliance and susceptibility to external interests and influences (both state and corporate). Substantial inflows of aid and international corporate competition for resource extraction rights can provide corrupt incentives for domestic government officials. Conditional aid can also be used to promote governance frameworks such as those suggested under UNCAC, however, compatibility with regional and domestic contexts is not guaranteed.[7] Furthermore, PNG has limited influence within international institutions. This is a common reality for many less developed nations.

This lack of influence has been linked to risks of inapplicability, as well as other related harms stemming from the implementation and enforcement of multilateral legal instruments such as UNCAC. Lack of international influence means that multilateral legal instruments such as UNCAC risk being unsympathetic to local contexts and challenges, despite promotion of a universal approach.[8]

Each of the points noted above is relevant to numerous developing nations globally, not just PNG. Engagement with these issues in the PNG context may provide insight relevant to other developing and less developed nations seeking to regulate corruption and engage with the global anti-corruption regime. Aside from the potential for generalisation, exploring domestic dynamics is an essential element of understanding the risks and challenges faced by the global anti-corruption regime and UNCAC.

Historical background and context of corruption in Papua New Guinea

Papua New Guinea is a nation state with a population of between 7.3 and 7.8 million.[9] The country gained independence from Australia in 1975, becoming a member of the Commonwealth. With a landmass of 462,840 square kilometres, its geography includes the eastern half of the world's second largest island (New Guinea), which borders the Indonesian province of Irian Jaya, as well as 600 small islands to the north and east of this main landmass.[10]

PNG is part of the Melanesian sub-region of the South Pacific, along with Vanuatu, the Solomon Islands, and Fiji. However, PNG is unique in that its indigenous population is extremely heterogeneous: 'In ethnolinguistic terms, Papua New Guinea is probably the most fragmented society in the world, being home to over 800 separate languages and thousands of small, competitive micro-ethnic polities.'[11]

PNG is also relatively new to centralised governmental control. Before colonial settlement, towns did not exist in PNG. 'The traditional PNG economy comprised of small self-sufficient villages'[12] and infighting amongst tribal groups was common.[13] Following colonisation, towns were established and governed by foreign actors, existing for their convenience.[14]

Independence came to PNG by way of steady international pressure and a global trend of decolonisation. 'Despite some nationalist stirrings, the impetus for self-government has its origins more in Australia then in PNG'.[15] External pressure on Australia to relinquish control of PNG resulted in a relatively hasty transition. The 1960 United Nations General Assembly Declaration on the Granting of Independence to Colonial Countries and Peoples 'culminated in a dramatic reversal of the old Australian colonial approach to self-government'.[16] However, it was not until 1964, after publication of a critical UN Mission Report, that universal suffrage was introduced in PNG and the process of decolonisation was set in motion.[17] The first House of Assembly elections were held that year and a further two elections were held before independence.

Government structure and political dynamics

The PNG Constitution was developed by an entirely Papua New Guinean Constitutional Planning Committee. The country's colonial history is reflected in the Westminster style of government established by the Constitution.[18] The Papua New Guinean government consists of three independent branches: the executive, the legislature, and the judiciary. The judiciary consists of the Supreme Court, National Court, and various local courts. Under the executive branch, the head of state is the Queen of Great Britain and the United Kingdom, represented by the Governor General who is nominated by parliament for the Queen's approval. Executive power is vested in the Prime Minister and National Executive Council (NEC), comprising 28 members appointed by the Governor General on advice of the Prime Minister. The legislative branch is made up of 111 seats comprising a unicameral parliament elected for five-year terms by a Limited Preferential Voting system (LPV). Administratively, PNG consists of 22 provincial administrative divisions (including the national capital district and the autonomous region of Bougainville); each of these divisions holds a seat in parliament, with the remaining 89 seats filled from open electorates.[19]

Competition for government office is fierce, with a record 3,435 candidates running for the mere 111 seats in the 2012 election.[20] Alliances are often based on village, clan, or provincial ties, rather than on political ideology.[21] This fluid system can be linked to the heterogeneous nature of PNG society and the clash between modern western liberal democratic modes of governance and traditional alliances and localised models of societal organisation. Lack of strong political alliances between groups has resulted in dynamic shifts in government. PNG has followed constitutional process for all governmental changes, except for the 2011 coup that resulted in the election of the current Prime Minister, Peter O'Neill.[22] Constitutional process allows for changes in leadership, which are commonplace. Parliamentary votes of no confidence are a frequent occurrence.[23] Limitations have been placed on this procedure, with votes of no confidence precluded in the first 18 months following an election. A no confidence vote in the last 12 months before a new election triggers an election immediately. This is a significant disincentive for a vote of no confidence, as political turnover is high and elections are a risky choice for those seeking to maintain power.[24]

Political volatility can contribute to corruption. The attempt to topple Prime Minister Namaliu in 1989 is illustrative. Two years after the Prime Minister assumed office, the opposition tabled a vote of no confidence.

> In the centre of the ensuing scramble for advantage was a group of disgruntled government backbenchers, four of whom had recently been dropped from the cabinet. But the group stayed loyal to Namaliu, and the vote was withdrawn. It was later revealed that each of the former ministers had demanded K400,000 to keep from crossing the floor. Indeed, the Times of Papua New Guinea claimed (but the government vehemently denied) that some K2.5 million had been distributed to government MPs just before the scheduled vote.[25]

In this case, political fluidity and the subsequent maintenance of stability turned on attempts to secure financial gain. It has been suggested that lack of opportunities in the private sector in PNG may contribute to the increased desirability of public sector positions. A political position may secure wealth both for the political candidate, and for their family and community.

> Public and political positions give access to significant amounts of wealth, from natural resource revenue and aid, which can be redistributed to a leader's kin and constituency to maintain power and influence.[26]

In the context of PNG, incentives to engage in political corruption are driven by the fluid political structure in the country and the limited private sector opportunities available. Both factors make the political sphere attractive to individuals seeking personal gain.

Aid and external influence

Chapter 3 introduced the possible influence of aid dynamics on corruption in the South Pacific region. In PNG, Australia and China are powerful aid donors and are involved in the resource extraction and forestry sectors of the PNG economy. Australia is the primary aid donor to PNG, providing an estimated 547.1 million AUD between 2016 and 2017.[27] China is reluctant to reveal the extent and nature of its aid programme. However, it was the first country to provide assistance after PNG suffered a violent national election and major political and economic crisis in 2002. Chinese assistance and interaction increased substantially following this, and 'by 2005, China had become Papua New Guinea's top trading partner and the largest buyer of its lumber'.[28] In January 2013, China and PNG signed the Grant-In-Aid of Economic and Technical Cooperation Agreement. As part of this agreement, China pledged PGK23 million (USD7.13 million) to PNG for various projects.[29] More recently, there have been allegations that private infrastructure projects in PNG have in fact been funded by the government-run China Development Bank. The lack of transparency around transnational development activities between PNG and China makes it difficult to evaluate the full extent of China's influence. Certainly, the interests and incentives that underlie the provision of aid by Australia and China vary significantly. The first objective noted by the Department of Foreign Affairs and Trade (DFAT) in relation to the Australian aid programme in PNG is 'promoting effective governance', with direct reference to preventing and combatting corruption.[30] The PNG-Australia Aid Partnership Arrangement 2016–2017 places 'governance' under its objectives and priorities at 2.3(e). Further, the document notes at 2.7: 'Australia has a zero tolerance of fraud in the aid program. As such fraud and anti-corruption will also be cross-cutting components of all sectoral programs.'[31]

Similar statements are absent from the limited documentation available regarding China's aid and assistance programmes. This variation reflects broader differences in approach between Asian and Western actors.

Australia and the western liberal democratic agenda

Immediately following the award of independence, Australia provided aid to PNG in the form of grants without substantial ties to specific projects or conditionalities.[32] These large capital inflows, combined with the mismatch between modern centralised government and traditional tribal and family relationships, provided significant incentives for corruption and personal gain through appointment to public positions.[33] Beginning in the late 1980s and 1990s Australia aligned with the position of other western donors, especially multilateral lending institutions such as the World Bank and IMF, and began increasingly to tie aid to specific projects and an agenda of neoliberal governance and privatisation.[34]

In 1990 the World Bank offered PNG a USD50 million loan based on structural adjustment, reflecting neoliberal policies targeted at shrinking the state and expanding private enterprise.[35] Australian aid was also directed towards this neoliberal agenda, supporting IMF recommendations of government restructuring and privatisation.[36] In 2006, Australia threatened to ban imports of timber from PNG, after World Bank accusations of corruption and illegal logging in the PNG forestry sector.[37] Conditional aid has significant potential to promote and facilitate the global anti-corruption regime and implementation and enforcement of UNCAC. However, private sector relationships between Australia and PNG mean that economic incentives may conflict with the goals of promoting governance reform.

Australia has been cited as a significant importer of illegally logged timber from PNG[38] and has been accused more recently of acting as the 'Cayman Islands' for corrupt PNG officials seeking to launder the profits of their plunder.[39] Furthermore, the privatisation agenda and promotion of neoliberal policies supported by Australian aid has opened PNG's financial sector, enabling the outflow of corrupt profits and increasing foreign investment in domestic production and the services.[40] Both free capital flows and increased foreign investment present risks for corruption.

The PNG Department of Finance scandal illustrates the extent of domestic corruption in PNG and the risks posed by free flowing capital between PNG and Australia. A commission of inquiry report produced in October 2009 found that 'between 1st January 2000 and 1st July 2006 not less than K572,591,348.70 (249,578,713 AUD) was paid out by the Department of Finance in satisfaction of some 539 claims against the State'.[41] It was concluded that 'in all but a handful of claims the statutory process has been grossly abused, allowing illegitimate and improper claims and excess payments and excessive payouts to be legitimised'.[42] Paul Paraka and other lawyers were responsible for filing these improper claims on behalf of various public servants, including the former Finance Secretary Gabriel Yer. Yer used his son's name to falsely claim extensive compensation from the state. The lawyer responsible for filing these claims (Mr Paraka) was then hired for PGK41 million (USD12.7 million) to defend the state against similar claims filed by other lawyers.[43] The transnational nature of the scandal was enhanced when Mr Paraka was found to be 'regularly transferring large sums of money to several contacts on the Gold Coast and in New South Wales'.[44] The transnational transfer of capital by an individual embroiled in an extensive corruption scandal is concerning, especially as Australia has never assisted PNG in repatriating corruptly obtained funds.[45]

The Department of Finance scandal demonstrates the interaction between public and private actors engaged in corruption in PNG and illustrates how transnational interactions can facilitate corrupt activity. The role of transnational dynamics in facilitating corrupt activity in PNG reflects the views of Passas regarding the criminogenic asymmetries that result from globalisation.[46] The promotion of further liberalisation through western aid should be viewed cautiously in this context, as it may promote corrupt opportunities.

China as an alternative partner in PNG aid and trade

The increasingly conditional nature of aid from Australia and other Western and international donor agencies has resulted in China's rising influence in PNG. China provides an 'interest free, no-strings-attached, open-ended style of financial support to countries in the South Pacific with development assistance often coming in the form of grants, not loans'.[47]

Grant-based aid does not need to be repaid and is therefore appealing to less developed nations seeking to gain capital input without becoming stuck in a cycle of dependency.[48] Grant-based aid is also less likely to be tied to broad economic reform, as the interest is not to regain investment but to serve other mutually beneficial goals.[49]

The interests of China in PNG, and more broadly in the South Pacific region, differ from the security and governance interests of Western states and institutions. China is more interested in the development of 'on the ground' business relationships and the establishment and maintenance of support for its position within the international sphere. China is especially interested in securing continued support for its position on Taiwan.

The Chinese approach to aid in PNG has its own set of corruption challenges. The grant-based aid approach has some advantages in terms of the receiving state's independence, but it allows funds to be more easily diverted by government officials and bureaucrats for personal gain. The political nature of such aid can also be problematic. One example is the clash of diplomatic interests between China and Taiwan, which has provided corrupt incentives in PNG:

> In 1999, Taiwan secretly gave $30 million to two brokers to bribe PNG ministers to cut diplomatic ties with Beijing in favour of Taipei . . . It is widely believed that at least $20 million was given to six senior PNG politicians before the deal collapsed. In January 2009, former Taiwan National Security Council General Secretary Chiou I-jen and former Foreign Minister James Huang Chi-fang were charged in Taiwan in connection with the scandal. In May, one of the brokers, a Singaporean, was sentenced and jailed for two years and four months by the Taiwan Supreme Court.[50]

This example illustrates the way contests for political favour can provide corrupt incentives for government officials.

Increased diplomatic relations between China and PNG have come alongside growing private sector interaction, and sometimes the two are not clearly delineated. Chinese migration to PNG has been on the rise and, in combination with Chinese corporate activity, corruption scandals have triggered domestic unrest. In 2009, PNG experienced extensive anti-Chinese rioting. The riots were the result of resentment toward Chinese migrants seen to be displacing indigenous businesses.[51] Suggestions were made that Chinese workers, especially those employed at the Ramu nickel mine, had corruptly obtained visas via relations between PNG officials and 'Asian Mafia'.[52] In the same year, the owner of Malaysian logging company Rimbunan Hijau was knighted in PNG. This action caused outrage among Civil Society groups. Rimbunan Hijau is the largest logging company in PNG. The knighting of the owner (Tiog Hiew King) in PNG raised questions about the relationship between foreign corporations and the PNG government. The company has been implicated in illegal logging of PNG forests and facilitation of organised criminal activity through smuggling of workers and trafficking of women for purposes of prostitution in mining camps. Furthermore, Rimbunan Hijau 'has consistently been implicated in bribing key politicians from all parties'.[53]

The above examples illustrate the nature and patterns of corruption in PNG. While corruption in PNG takes many forms, corrupt incentives can be related to certain key contextual and historical features, including PNG's colonial history; the country's fluid political structure; the nature and extent of external influence in aid and commercial spheres; and increasing transnational interaction and the free flow of capital. Many of these features also reflect the risks, challenges, and incentives discussed in Chapter 3 relating to corruption in the South Pacific region.

Political dynamics and resource and capacity limitations

Domestic dynamics in PNG are also relevant to corruption risks and incentives. The PNG Department of Finance scandal and the China/Taiwan diplomacy conflict both illustrate the limited resources and capacity provided to anti-corruption efforts in the country, as well as the susceptibility of these efforts to political interests.

In the case of the PNG Department of Finance scandal, the commission of inquiry established in August 2006 was suspended five times due to political opposition and lack of financial resources.[54] Once the Commission completed its report in 2009 and presented it to Parliament in February 2010, Mr Paraka and former Solicitor General Zachary Gelu had an injunction placed on the report. It was not until December 2013 that a High Court judge overturned the injunction, allowing for the publication of the report.[55] Mr Paraka was later arrested by Task Force Sweep and remains on bail.[56] As the case continued to evolve, Task Force Sweep sought the arrest of current Prime Minister Peter O'Neill. This arrest warrant subsequently triggered a chain of events that left Task Force Sweep without government funding or political support.[57] Attempts were made to keep the Task Force operational, including an initial stay on the Prime Minister's order to disband. However, its lack of independence from the executive branch of government meant that it was at the whim of the same Prime Minister that initially created it.[58] Task Force sweep is no longer in operation, it was ordered to transfer all cases and investigations to the Independent Commission Against Corruption (ICAC) body, which has not yet been formally created.

The China/Taiwan diplomacy scandal further illustrates how a lack of political will and resource and capacity limitations can coalesce to limit anti- corruption efforts in PNG. No PNG nationals were ever charged regarding this case. Although, former PNG Minister Paul Tiensten, who was implicated in this corruption scandal, has since been convicted of corrupt acts related to the embezzlement of USD million designated for a development project. Mr Tiensten was the first individual to be investigated by PNG's Task Force Sweep and has been sentenced to nine years of jail with hard labour.[59] This conviction is a significant milestone for anti-corruption efforts in PNG. However, the investigation was not without controversy.

Mr Tiensten was an elected member of the PNG parliament until 'a mass defection of MPs saw the government of Sir Michael Somare thrown out of office.'[60] Task Force Sweep was set up by the new Prime Minister, Mr O'Neill, leading to allegations that the investigation of former MP Mr Tiensten was politically motivated. It is difficult to discern with certainty the incentives behind the investigation. However, the court emphasised that 'misappropriation of public funds by public officials in positions of trust is a serious crime.'[61] The case appears to illustrate an effort on the part of the courts to tackle corruption and establish a disincentive for future corrupt activities by MPs. It is possible that the success of the case was related in part to the political support provided by the incumbent government, as Mr Teinsten was a member of the opposition. However, the case itself was prosecuted through standard legal channels and the outcome appears to be positive for anti-corruption efforts in PNG. Regardless of the motivation, the successful prosecution demonstrates the power of political will for anti-corruption efforts.

Papua New Guinea as an influential South Pacific state

The above discussion depicts a grim picture of the state of corruption in PNG society. However, despite significant domestic corruption challenges and susceptibility to external influence, PNG has been playing an increasingly influential role in guiding other South Pacific nations. In comparison to other small island nations in the South Pacific, PNG has one of the most developed economies. PNG was also the first South Pacific Island to ratify UNCAC and participate in the Implementation Review mechanisms. PNG has also been an active member of various regional bodies, including the Pacific Island Forum and Melanesian Spearhead Group. In terms of corruption and the promotion of good governance, PNG was responsible for assisting Vanuatu in the development of its Leadership Code. By providing assistance in this regard PNG has illustrated its emerging role in the promotion of a regional anti-corruption agenda.

If PNG's influence in the South Pacific is combined with, and promoted through, the global anti-corruption regime, the state may set an example for others in the region. This example would be valuable because other South Pacific states may struggle with similar domestic challenges, seeking to balance corrupt incentives and traditional/modern conflict with economic and social development goals. Through South-South policy transfer and sharing of experiences between PNG and other South Pacific nations, external interests and agendas may be balanced with unique and contextually relevant experiences and knowledge. This approach may support anti-corruption objectives in the region and help to overcome the risk of inapplicability that has been raised throughout analysis in this book.

The experience of PNG with implementation and enforcement of UNCAC, and insight gained through interaction with other developing states in the region, could be valuably disseminated through regional institutions, back to the international organisations involved in development of the global anti-corruption regime. This process could provide insight into new methods for engagement that may enhance the values and success of the regime and its legal tools. This idea reflects Koh's concept of feedback loops and norm internalisation introduced in Chapter 1 and could be facilitated through the UNCAC Implementation Review process.

Certainly, corruption appears to be a substantial concern for PNG and the role of powerful external actors continues to be relevant in this context. Additionally, PNG suffers from resource and capacity limitations and variations in political will with regard to anti-corruption efforts. Exploring these issues and their impact on the implementation and enforcement of UNCAC is essential for evaluating the potential success of the global anti-corruption regime in PNG. Such exploration provides valuable insight into the challenges and opportunities facing the regime in other similar contexts.

The Anti-corruption framework in Papua New Guinea

The nature of corrupt activities in PNG and the challenges faced by domestic anti-corruption efforts have not precluded attempts to combat corruption in PNG. Both the public sector and Civil Society in PNG are aware of corruption as a challenge to government legitimacy and economic and social development. In fact, anti-corruption has been a popular campaign platform in PNG politics. The anti-corruption agenda has even been used by candidates that have previously been accused of corrupt activity. Several candidates for the 2002 election even campaigned from jail, serving time for the misappropriation of public funds.[62]

In PNG, awareness of corruption and its harms does not necessarily translate into zero tolerance for corruption behaviour. Citizens condemn corruption, especially amongst high level officials and foreign actors, but they are often willing to justify corrupt behaviour when it benefits them or their family or interest group.[63] This justification is based in part on the failure of government institutions to provide necessary goods and services and the lack of connection between central government and the broader PNG society.

Despite some ambivalence regarding corrupt activities, a range of laws and institutions exist and continue to emerge in PNG to prevent, investigate, and punish corrupt activities. The legal framework for combatting corruption in PNG is primarily contained within the *Criminal Code Act 1974*.[64] Other relevant legal documents include the *Constitution* and the Leadership Code contained in Division 2, as well as the associated *Organic Law on the Duties and Responsibilities of Leadership 1975*.[65] *The Organic Law on the Integrity of Political Parties and Candidates 2003*[66] and the change from a First Past the Post (FPP) to a Limited Preferential Vote (LPV) system are also relevant developments, as is the establishment of the *Proceeds of Crime Act 2005 (POCA)*.[67] In addition to this legal framework, various organisational and institutional elements of the PNG anti-corruption framework are introduced below. These include the efforts of Task Force Sweep, attempts to establish an Independent Commission against Corruption (ICAC), the role of the Ombudsman, and the activities of various NGOs and Civil Society groups.

The Leadership Code and the Organic Law on the Duties and Responsibilities of Leadership (OLDRL)

Section III Division 2 of the *Constitution* establishes the Leadership Code. This Code gives the Ombudsman Commission extensive investigative powers and sets out the application of the division to a list of 14 public officials and types of persons holding public office.[68] The Ombudsman Commission retains final discretion in the event of doubt as to whether or not the code applies to a particular person.[69] Subsection 27 sets out the responsibilities of office. It can be found in Annex D of this book. Responsibilities under the leadership code include avoiding any conflicts of interest or engagement in activities that may 'endanger or diminish respect for or confidence in the integrity of government of Papua New Guinea'.[70] This section of the code illustrates awareness of the negative impact that corruption can have on perceptions of government legitimacy. The code also establishes that no person covered by the code shall use his office for personal gain.[71] This requirement reflects the 'Public Office' definition of corruption discussed in Chapter 1: 'the misuse of public office for private gain'.

The *OLDRL* is the organic law established to implement the Leadership Code. Organic laws in PNG get their authority from section 12 of the *Constitution*. Organic laws can only be altered by other organic laws or the *Constitution* itself.[72] Furthermore, all Acts of Parliament and subordinated legislation are to be read and construed subject to the organic laws. Relevant sections of the *OLDRL* are included in Annex D of this book. The *OLDRL* establishes the responsibilities of leadership in PNG, including the requirement that relevant persons disclose their income and assets to the Ombudsman Commission within three months of assuming office.[73] Failure to disclose or explain income or assets, or the intentional falsification of disclosure documents, will result in an offence of misconduct in office.[74] The misuse of office for personal benefit is also covered under *OLDRL*. Any person covered by the law who accepts 'any benefit in relation to any action (past, present or future) in the course of his duties, or in the course of or by reason of his official position, is guilty of misconduct'.[75] The benefit need not be directly intended for the relevant person.[76]

Other offences established under the *OLDRL* include 'Acceptance of Bribes',[77] 'Acceptance of Loans',[78] and 'Misappropriation of Funds'.[79] Liability of the relevant person for an offence under *OLDRL* is based on express or implied consent, express or implied authority, and even extends to acts committed by a spouse, relative, or associate 'from whose actions he could have disassociated himself'.[80]

The *OLDRL* gives the Ombudsman investigative power over the offences established by this law.[81] The Ombudsman may initiate an investigation independently, or upon complaint by any person.[82] Having completed an investigation, the Ombudsman Commission must refer the individual to the Public Prosecutor. The Public Prosecutor is then responsible for prosecution before the appropriate tribunal. If the Public Prosecutor fails to initiate prosecution, the Ombudsman Commission can refer the matter to the appropriate tribunal.[83]

The Leadership Code and supplementary *OLDRL* establish the offences of misconduct in office relating to personal benefit, passive bribery, and misappropriation of funds committed by the relevant individual or an agent of that individual. The *Criminal Code Act (CCA)* establishes a range of other corruption related offences – relevant sections of the *CCA* can be found in Annex D.

The Criminal Code Act

The *CCA* was based on the Queensland Criminal Code,[84] reflecting the influence of Australia as an ex-colonial power in PNG and demonstrating the extent to which this influence is reflected in the legal framework of PNG.[85] Part III Division 2 of the *CCA* covers offences related to corruption and abuse of office, including both active and passive bribery of a public official. The Leadership Code and *OLDRL* only cover passive bribery by a public official. There is some internal overlap between the various corruption related crimes in the *CCA*. For example, section 87 covers 'Official Corruption' and section 88 establishes the misdemeanour of 'Extortion by Public Officers'. The misdemeanour under section 88 refers only to passive extortion, that is, acceptance of a reward or promise thereof for performance of duties. This misdemeanour overlaps with 'Official Corruption' covered under section 87(1)(a)(ii). It is unclear what the difference is between 'property or benefit' under section 87 and 'reward' under section 88; or between 'receives or obtains' in section 87 and 'takes or accepts' in section 88.

Additional overlap exists between section 87, section 88 and section 97(b). Section 97(b) covers bribery of a member of public service. It covers much of the same conduct covered under sections 87 and 88, adding specific language related to voting or abstaining from voting in Parliament, and the granting of contracts. Section 97(b) covers supply side or active commission as well as demand side or passive commission, in the same manner as section 87.

The Leadership Code, *OLDRL* and *CCA* provide a comprehensive legislative framework for combatting corruption in PNG, with some overlap within and between the laws. This overlap may be a challenge for implementation and enforcement, especially considering the challenge of limited resources and capacity that have already been mentioned in the PNG context. If the investigative and prosecutorial bodies involved in a case do not have access to sufficient financial or human resources, having to cover a range of overlapping acts, or investigating a case alongside other investigating bodies, may put unnecessary strain on the judicial processes and related institutions, ultimately limiting its effectiveness.

The Organic Law on the Integrity of Political Parties *(*OLIPPAC*) and changes to the electoral system*

In addition to the corruption-specific laws introduced above, PNG has policies in place that affect the structure of government and in turn may influence the nature and frequency of corrupt activity. In addition to those laws introduced above, focusing specifically on regulating corrupt activities, it is useful to discuss developments and legislation that affects the structure of government in PNG. The change from FPP to the LPV system in 2007 and the enactment of *OLIPPAC*, are both important features of PNG's anti-corruption framework. These legal and political features demonstrate that the anti-corruption framework in PNG is not exclusively focused on criminalisation. Much as UNCAC recommends both criminal and non-criminal measures, so PNG has in place a range of criminal and institutional measures to combat corrupt activities and incentives for corrupt behaviour.

The LPV system was instituted in 2007 to improve the representativeness of the PNG Government. Under LPV 'most winning candidates achieved victory on only a small minority of the vote'.[86]

> The general consensus seems to be that LPV has been a qualified success, though it has not, at this stage, done much to change deeply rooted patterns of behaviour in much of the country . . . More dramatic improvements in electoral performance will require not just changes in electoral procedures, important though these may be, but radical shifts in deeply rooted patterns of behaviour.[87]

Despite these limitations, attempts to improve the representativeness of government in PNG should be viewed positively as they may have flow-on effects for government legitimacy and accountability.

In addition to LPV, *OLIPPAC* seeks to promote 'the emergence of a more consolidated and less fragmented party system'.[88] As noted earlier in this chapter, political fragmentation and fluidity creates corrupt incentives in PNG. Historically, ministers have been bribed and coerced into the formation and reformation of political parties after elections.[89] Politicians may see short-lived and volatile nature of politics as an excuse for quick use and abuse of government resources.[90] The *OLIPPAC* was designed to address some of these challenges.

Initially, *OLIPPAC* appeared to have provided greater stability for the PNG government. The *OLLIPAC* requirement to register parties substantially reduced the number of parties put forward.[91] The first government to be elected following the introduction of *OLIPPAC* was also the first government since independence to maintain office for an entire term.[92] However, this stability did not translate to reduced corruption levels relating to elections and government alliances. Following the 2007 election, the Ombudsman Commission launched an inquiry into more than PGK90 million (USD27.65 million) of Parliamentary funding that had been expended in 'questionable procedures' leading up to the election.[93] There have also been concerns that *OLIPPAC* may entrench unpopular governments and prevent a free democratic process.[94]

In 2012, a Supreme Court ruling deemed several *OLIPPAC* provisions unconstitutional and therefore null and void.[95] This ruling was based on findings that key sections of *OLIPPAC* were in conflict with sections 47 and 50 of the *Constitution*.

Article 47 of the *Constitution* provides for freedom of assembly and association and 'gives every citizen the right to freedom of peaceful assembly and association and to form or belong, to or not to belong to, political parties.'[96] The court noted:

> Under s 57(2) [of OLIPPAC], a Member is given the right to resign from a party if the party or the executive officer of the party has committed a serious breach of the constitution of the party, or the party has been adjudged insolvent under any applicable law. These are the only grounds under which a Member would have a right to resign from a party. In our opinion, this is a clear prohibition on the Member from exercising his freedom of association under s 47.[97]

The court also held that sections 58, 59, 60 and 61 of *OLIPPAC* prevent MPs from exercising their freedom of association under section 47 of the *Constitution*.[98]

There is a qualification to the right under section 47 of the *Constitution*, as provided in section 38. However, the court was not satisfied that *OLIPPAC* was 'the only way available to the government to bring about political stability'[99] or 'that the restrictions or prohibitions imposed by all these provisions are justified in a democratic society having a proper regard to the right and dignity of mankind.'[100] It was held that 'OLIPPAC, ss 57, 58, 59, 60, 61, 65, 66 and 67 are inconsistent with s 47 of the *Constitution*, and are therefore unconstitutional.'[101]

Section 50 of the *Constitution* enshrines the rights of a citizen to 'take part in the conduct of public affairs . . . vote for and be elected to, elective public office . . . and to hold public office and exercise public functions.'[102] Section 50(2) of the *Constitution* allows these rights to be regulated as 'is reasonably justifiable for the purpose in a democratic society that has proper regard for the rights and dignity of mankind.'[103] The court acknowledges these provisions in their judgment on the constitutionality of *OLIPPAC* and concluded, on the basis of section 47 and section 50 of the *Constitution*, that numerous *OLIPPAC* provisions were unconstitutional and therefore null and void.[104]

The Supreme Court ruling was unanimous. However, some aspects of the judgment have been criticised. One commentator notes:

> The considerations in support of the OLIPPAC provisions were highlighted but not discussed. Obviously, the Supreme Court dismissed them but, given that this is an important decision, the reasons for rejecting them should have been discussed in full.[105]

The Court presented some suggestions for improving political stability without restricting the rights of MPs. Suggestions included better education of MPs to behave appropriately and voter election of responsible MPs. These suggestions were criticised as naïve, considering that 'the reality of PNG politics is presently not attuned to either [option]'.[106] From a legal perspective however, these suggestions help the court to illustrate that *OLIPPAC* restrictions were not the only method Parliament could have chosen to deal with the challenges of corruption and political instability. This undermined the argument in favour of OLIPPAC's validity, based on section 38 of the *Constitution.*

The above example demonstrates the challenges of balancing democratic freedoms with concern for corrupt activity in the public sphere. The enactment of *OLIPPAC*, and the provisions later deemed unconstitutional, illustrate that fear of corrupt activity may result in laws and policies that are harmful to the rights and freedoms of citizens. Balancing these rights and freedoms against the harms of corruption is an ongoing legal and political challenge that will impact all states seeking to implement and enforce UNCAC.

Papua New Guinea has in place an extensive legal framework targetting corrupt activities and the structure of government, including legislation to combat corrupt incentives in public office. However, corruption remains a substantial challenge. Okele argues:

> Much of the concern relating to poor governance and administrative problems in Papua New Guinea, just as in any country in the world, is about behavioural issues . . . no amount of legislation or regulation will be sufficient to address problems when the very people who are expected to abide by the remedial steps are bent on undermining them.[107]

Acknowledging the role of individual autonomy in proliferating corrupt activity, it seems reasonable to suggest that successful implementation of UNCAC will require moving beyond criminal measures, and engaging with other preventive, procedural, and institutional approaches covered by the Convention. This is especially important considering the limited resources and capacity available in PNG for implementation and enforcement efforts. Additionally, many of the measures recommended or required under the criminalisation chapters of UNCAC have existed in domestic legislation in PNG for decades. The realities in PNG suggest that the risk factor of a criminal law enforcement focus will be highly relevant.

Unless this risk is overcome, UNCAC is unlikely to achieve success in PNG and the success of the global anti-corruption regime will remain limited.

The extent to which UNCAC has supported alternative anti-corruption measures in PNG is explored later in this chapter.

Anti-corruption institutions

It is useful to present the key institutions and actors responsible for combatting corruption in PNG. Often, these actors and institutions derive their power from the legal framework discussed above, but they are important in their own right as they actively apply and engage with this framework and the success of their activities influences anti-corruption outcomes. There are several government bodies working to combat corruption and implement the laws discussed above. The role of the Ombudsman Commission has already been noted. The Ombudsman Commission is responsible for investigations of misconduct in office established under the Leadership Code and *OLDRL*. The Public Prosecutor is also an important government body. Reports produced by the Ombudsman Commission are forwarded to the Public Prosecutor for referral and prosecution in the relevant tribunal. The Royal Papua New Guinea Constabulary also plays a role in preventing and investigating corruption in PNG. Each of these bodies aims to ensure compliance with relevant anti-corruption law or related legislation.

In 2004, a National Anti-Corruption Alliance (NACA) was established in PNG. This organisation became operational in 2006. The aim of NACA is to effectively coordinate investigation and prosecution of corruption cases by bringing together representatives from ten government institutions.[108] The National Anti-Corruption Alliance was developed with financial and technical assistance provided by the Australian government. The organisation appears to be an attempt to streamline departmental interaction and improve efficiency of investigation and prosecution. However, more than a decade after its creation, details on the functional activities and outcomes associated with NACA are hard to find. Research was conducted through electronic databases and at the National Library in PNG, with limited success. Discussion with interview participants in PNG led to the conclusion that NACA was a positively viewed ad hoc arrangement and has fallen into disuse in recent years.

Papua New Guinea does not currently have an operational ICAC. The case of Task Force Sweep provides an interesting illustration of the political dynamics of anti-corruption bodies in PNG. The Task Force was established in 2011 by the NEC under direction of the Prime Minister.[109] The organisation was headed by Sam Koim, a member of the Solicitor General's Office. Other members were drawn from the Royal PNG Constabulary, Public Prosecutors Office, Department of Treasury, Office of the Auditor General, Internal Revenue Commission, and Department of Provincial and Local Level Government Affairs. Between 2011 and 2014 the Task Force put 77 cases before the PNG courts and convicted the former minister Paul Tiensten, mentioned earlier. However, in 2014, the

Prime Minister disbanded the Task Force. The events that resulted in the ultimate disbandment of Task Force Sweep illustrate the continuing challenges faced by anti-corruption institutions operating in the PNG context.

The catalyst for the disbandment was the investigation of lawyer Paul Paraka. During this investigation, evidence of a letter of authorisation from Prime Minister Peter O'Neill emerged, regarding payment of claims. Shortly after this evidence emerged, Task Force Sweep made statements that the letter was not legitimated and suggested that there would be no further investigation into the Prime Minister.[110] However, on 16 June 2014, the Task Force issued an arrest warrant for Prime Minister O'Neill, citing his relationship with the Paraka case.[111] The issuing of this warrant resulted in an immediate action to disband the Task Force. The Prime Minister stated that the organisation had been politically compromised.[112] A court ruling initially stayed the the order to disband,[113] however it was ultimately ruled that Task Force Sweep's authority was the result of the NEC and therefore it could be disbanded by the same individual who created it. This series of events reflects the continual challenge posed by the political dynamics behind corruption and anti-corruption efforts in PNG.

Despite the obvious challenges and political limitations faced by anti-corruption institutions in PNG, attempts have been made to establish an Independent Commission against Corruption (ICAC). The first draft ICAC Bill was tabled in 1997.[114] In 2014, steps were taken to amend the *Constitution* and allow for the possibility of an organic law to create and govern ICAC. The constitutional amendment provides ICAC with a legal basis and institutional powers. The amendment creates a new division of the constitution under Part VIII Division 3. Under section 220B(4), an organic law will further detail and operationalise the ICAC, the purpose of which will be 'to contribute, in cooperation with other agencies, to preventing, reducing and combating corrupt conduct'.[115] The Bill for the organic law passed its first reading in Parliament in 2015, but remains with the Parliamentary Committee on Constitutional Laws, Acts and Subordinate Legislations, as of March 2018. The reasons for the delay are unclear. Until the organic law is passed, PNG remains without and ICAC. The delay with establishment of ICAC and the disbanding of Task Force Sweep raise concerns about political will for anti-corruption efforts in PNG. The long-term National Anti-Corruption Strategy (NACS, 2010–2030) and Mid-term Action Plan developed by the government, suggest continuing commitment to anti-corruption objectives. However, without material outcomes and transparency of processes, the true level of commitment is difficult to evaluate.

The PNG NACS 2010–2030 was designed as:

> [A] strategic driver, providing both impetus for action and strategic direction for political, public service and business leaders, state actors, non-state actors, Civil Society, development partners and citizens to rally their institutional and individual actions to fight corruption in a more systematic and integrated way.[116]

The strategy document uses similar language to that of the international and regional framework, including UNCAC. The strategy focuses on reducing corruption and enhancing 'good governance' in order to secure better development outcomes and comply with obligations established under UNCAC. It highlights the importance of transparency, accountability, and streamlining of relevant agencies and the participation of Civil Society in addressing corruption. The strategy also adopts the uniquely domestic view of anti-corruption as a means of securing government legitimacy and restoring faith in public institutions that have been undermined by consistent scandal. The document suggests that donor agencies are key stakeholders in the development and functioning of the anti-corruption strategy.[117] The overall vision of the NACS is to:

> Establish a self-sustaining national system of integrity in which corruption is eliminated and the principles of honesty and ethical conduct, effective application of the rule of law, fair play, and openness and accountability are established and practiced in PNG.[118]

Eight Key Action Areas (KAAs) are identified for the achievement of the above vision. These are: honest leadership, transparency and public exposure, effective people management, integrity of the public financial management system, accountability and oversight, compliance and enforcement, public awareness and education, and coordination and partnership. The strategy suggests five approaches to securing outcomes in each of these KAAs: prevention, criminalisation and law enforcement, international cooperation, leadership and coordination, and monitoring.[119] The focus appears to be on non-legal, normative, value-based approaches to changing 'culture' and establishing 'personal integrity'. Within the transnational framework, this focus fits with the preventive discourse that emphasises a reduction of incentives for corrupt behaviour within existing systems of government. The NACS also seeks to institute structural change and establish reporting mechanisms and disclosure requirements.

Several legal initiatives are also suggested, specifically the establishment of illicit enrichment and freedom of information laws. Illicit enrichment is a recommended criminal measure under UNCAC[120] and freedom of information laws align with the global anti-corruption regime and its support for enhanced transparency and diverse stakeholder engagement. The National Anti-Corruption Strategy also discusses strengthening of the Leadership Code to ensure effective investigation and prosecution. Amending legislation to support investigation and prosecution based on Commission of Inquiry findings is a further suggestion under NACS. One of the weaknesses of the NACS framework is that it is a non-binding policy document with no mechanisms in place to formally evaluate government performance. It also does not seem to be actively referenced in government or Civil Society debate around anti-corruption issues. However, the document does show that the PNG government is aware of the importance of anti-corruption efforts, at least discursively, and is willing to draw on the language of the global anti-corruption regime and UNCAC. For example, acknowledgement of the role played by foreign actors illustrates awareness of the transnational nature of corruption and anti-corruption efforts.

Generally, anti-corruption laws, policies, and institutions in PNG appear to support enforcement of the domestic legal framework against corruption, in line with the approach taken by UNCAC. These anti-corruption institutions and policies seek to enhance the legitimacy of the PNG government while simultaneously struggling to overcome political obstacles and resource and capacity limitations. Transparency of processes and political will remain substantial obstacles.

In addition to the legal and institutional framework in PNG, non-government and Civil Society actors are also engaged in combatting corruption domestically. These actors are perhaps the most vocal regarding the importance of reducing corruption in PNG, and may be powerful catalysts for action if they are able to motivate government and hold existing institutions to account.

Non-government efforts

Extensive NGO and Civil Society engagement in PNG has pushed forward the anti-corruption agenda. Transparency International PNG (TI PNG) is an active interest group on anti-corruption issues. ActNow! PNG and the Centre for Environmental Law and Community Rights (CELCOR PNG) are other notable national NGOs. All three of these groups promote public awareness of corruption scandals and argue for strengthening of the anti-corruption framework in PNG. TI PNG and ActNow! PNG have provided feedback on the proposed organic law for implementation of ICAC. This feedback process was part of the government's call for public submissions on the topic. TI PNG and CELCOR were also involved in the drafting of NACS.[121]

The media in PNG is an important non-governmental force with potential to influence government and society on a range of issues, including corruption and anti-corruption efforts. Freedom House notes that 'news media in Papua New Guinea (PNG) remain among the most vibrant in the South Pacific'.[122] The Media Council for PNG is often cited as a key Civil Society stakeholder in anti-corruption initiatives. However, while PNG media has been active in uncovering corruption scandals, one of the top selling newspapers in the country, *The National*, is owned by the logging giant Rimbunan Hijau. In 2011 a civil suit was filed against *The National*'s competition, *The Post Courier*, due to allegations by the latter of police corruption associated with Rimbunan Hijau and its treatment of local landowners. In the same year, a corruption scandal emerged within the PNG Media Council. Executive director Nimo Kama was suspended in June 2011, after an independent audit of Australian government funding to the organisation found evidence of fraud.[123] Even those organisations that can empower anti-corruption efforts are not immune to corrupt activity or manipulation by external interests.

Papua New Guinea's anti-corruption framework has substantial legal and institutional support, but struggles to secure effective implementation and enforcement. The challenges limiting success of PNG's anti-corruption efforts include variable political will, diverse interests, and resource and capacity limitations. These challenges are likely to influence the success of UNCAC in the PNG context. Approaches to addressing and overcoming these challenges are explored further in the following chapters. However, it is necessary to first evaluate the extent of UNCAC's influence on the current anti-corruption framework in PNG.

Placing the international into the domestic: UNCAC and Papua New Guinea

The domestic challenges explored above have limited the effectiveness of the PNG anti-corruption framework and are also likely to impact the effectiveness of UNCAC in PNG. Without effective domestic implementation and enforcement, the global anti-corruption regime will be unable to shift to the fifth and final stage of evolution. It is therefore necessary to explore the current level of engagement with UNCAC in PNG. This provides a starting point for analysis of the experiences of specific actors involved in UNCAC implementation and enforcement in PNG.

It is difficult to establish the extent of UNCAC's influence on PNG's anti-corruption laws and policies, or the exact nature of PNG's interaction with UNCAC and the global anti-corruption regime. Much of PNG's anti-corruption framework predates the negotiation of UNCAC and PNG's ratification of the Convention. Most documentation of PNG's engagement with UNCAC comes from the country's involvement in the first round of the implementation review cycle.

PNG signed UNCAC on 22 December 2004 and ratified the Convention on 16 July 2007. Following ratification, PNG became one of the first South Pacific nations to take part in the first round of the UNCAC Implementation Review process. This process seeks to evaluate the compliance of *States Parties* with Chapter III on Criminalisation and Law Enforcement, and Chapter IV on International Cooperation.[124] The process has three phases, beginning with self-assessment, followed by peer review, finishing with a country review report and executive summary drafted with the assistance of the United Nations Office on Drugs and Crime (UNODC).[125] As noted in Chapter 2, PNG was not involved in the negotiation of UNCAC. Therefore, criticisms regarding the applicability of UNCAC to the PNG context seem highly relevant. Despite these concerns, and despite ranking 144 on the Transparency International Corruption Perception Index in the same year, PNG received a generally positive country report from the UNCAC review process.

The PNG Executive Summary (ES) from the Implementation Review Group notes several good practices regarding domestic compliance with UNCAC's criminalisation and law enforcement provisions.[126] The combination of general and particular offences of corruption under the *CCA* was commended by the ES. The potential of the *POCA* to combat money laundering was noted and the move to establish an ICAC was seen in a positive light. Existing coordination of domestic anti-corruption agencies under NACA was also commended, and the development of NACS was considered noteworthy.[127]

The UNCAC Review presented some suggestions to improve PNG's compliance. The need to consolidate existing anti-corruption law, 'preferably in a separate statute', was emphasised.[128] The review noted provisions within existing laws that covered most aspects of bribery, trading in influence, embezzlement, and abuse of functions in PNG. However, suggestions were made that such laws could be strengthened through use of language that conformed directly with the language used in UNCAC. The review also suggested that criminalisation could be extended to the public sector and to bribery of foreign public officials. The potential to establish the crime of illicit enrichment under PNG law (in line with UNCAC Article 20) was also noted.

The review group recognised developments towards the establishment of a domestic whistle-blower protection law and suggested amendments to the *Corrupt Conduct Disclosure (Protection) Bill 2011* to 'take into consideration the broader scope of UNCAC Articles 32 and 33'.[129] Operational independence was an issue raised by the review group. One example is the current Financial Intelligence Unit (FIU) in PNG, which is not independent from the Royal PNG Constabulary more generally. Independence of corruption-specific bodies from other branches of government has been a controversial issue in parliamentary debate in PNG, especially on the topic of ICAC and its powers.[130]

The review suggested that improved compliance with UNCAC could be secured through technical assistance directed at drafting legislative bills, capacity building with respect to whistle-blower protection, and the function and development of specialised anti-corruption agencies including the FIU and future ICAC. Interestingly, there was no discussion in the review document of the limited effectiveness of domestic legislation in PNG, especially in regard to low prosecution rates, political co-optation, or compatibility of the legal framework with traditional systems.

When discussing implementation of the International Cooperation Chapter of UNCAC (Chapter IV), the recommendations were again highly technical. Resource limitations were not addressed, although there was some mention of capacity building to increase the expertise of magistrates, prosecutors, and police involved in investigations of corruption. The use of electronic communication channels by the Department of Justice and Attorney General's Office was commended. Acceptance by PNG authorities of urgent extradition requests via ICPO-INTERPOL was also viewed positively.

The recommendations for improved implementation of Chapter IV of UNCAC in PNG were extensive. Some examples include establishing minimum penalties for all UNCAC offences criminalised domestically; streamlining existing policy with a focus on extradition; engaging in bi- and multi-lateral agreements on extradition, transfer of sentenced persons, mutal legal assistance, and joint investigations. The review suggested amending the *Mutual Legal Assistance in Criminal Matters Act 2005* ('*MACMA*') and the *Extradition Act 2005*, to ensure compliance with Articles 44(11) and 44(12) of UNCAC. As of 2017, there is little evidence of compliance with these recommendations and documentation of progress is limited. The failure of PNG to implement recommendations of the implementation and review mechanism raises important questions about the validity of the UNCAC framework to the PNG context, as well as the extent of political will to make changes to domestic law and policy in line with UNCAC. These questions are addressed further in the following chapters, through the insights from actors working on implementation and enforcement of UNCAC in PNG.

Beyond engagement with the UNCAC review mechanism, various UN agencies have been actively contributing to PNG anti-corruption policy. NACS makes note of the important role that UNDP played in 'enlightening the Inter-departmental Committee [responsible for coordinating and putting the document together] on the provisions of the United Nations Convention against Corruption'.[131] This illustrates the active role that UN bodies are playing on the ground in PNG, assisting with understanding of obligations under UNCAC. Within NACS, some discursive links are made to the approach promoted by UNCAC and the global anti-corruption regime. Under the KAA, 'Compliance and Enforcement', the need to 'review existing legislation to ensure relevant legal instrument are in place to support . . . PNG's UNCAC obligations' is highlighted.[132] The role for donors and the need to 'ensure effective donor coordination in support of government anti-corruption initiatives' is also raised. Strengthening international cooperation is mentioned within NACS, alongside the coordination of national, provincial, and local level anti-corruption mechanisms domestically.[133]

The United Nations Country Program for Papua New Guinea 2008–2012 makes no mention of combatting corruption or implementing UNCAC, even under the heading of 'governance'.[134] This omission reflects that the document was published in 2007, following PNG's signature to UNCAC in 2004 but preceding its ratification in July 2007. A follow-up document produced in 2011 includes extensive references to anti-corruption efforts, including use of corruption ranking as a progress indicator.[135] However, no direct reference is made to UNCAC. This development illustrates how engaging with UNCAC may allow for more open discussion of corruption issues between international organisations like the UN and state actors. If such discussion leads to a shift in government agendas that are then implemented effectively, UNCAC could be seen to play an active role in reshaping domestic law and policy to target corruption.

Papua New Guinea also signed up to the joint UNDP/UNODC Pacific Regional Anti-Corruption Project (UN-PRAC). A document published on this project notes that PNG has been provided with funding to support its attendance at a number of UNDP Asia Pacific Community of Practice (COP) meetings 'designed to bring together UNDP country staff with national government and CSO anti-corruption practitioners'.[136] The third meeting in February 2010 focused specifically on implementation of UNCAC and PNG attended, along with Palau and the Solomon Islands.[137] Through UN-PRAC, the agenda of the global anti-corruption regime is being promoted, coordinated, and facilitated through international organisations, including the UN. This reflects the role of these organisations as coordinating actors during the fourth stage of regime evolution.

Direct engagement with UNCAC and promotion through UNCAC's influence on donor states, may in turn affect PNG's anti-corruption policy. This is likely when donor states are parties to UNCAC, or multilateral donor agencies support UNCAC's approach and the broader agenda of the global anti- corruption regime. In the latter case, PNG's involvement with the ADB/OECD Anti-Corruption Initiative for Asia and the Pacific is noteworthy. Hakobyan states that 'the UN Convention and the ADB/OECD Anti-Corruption Action Plan for Asia–Pacific have important similarities in terms of involved actors, thematic coverage and means to achieve their common goal to eliminate corruption'.[138] PNG endorsed the action plan in November 2001, even before UNCAC had entered into force.[139] In the endorsement, the representative of PNG held that endorsement was based on recognition that 'corruption in public places is a serious problem affecting development in the country',[140] and that PNG's interest in the initiative 'demonstrates the Government's priority and commitment to fight corruption'.[141] In 2013 PNG received a total of USD305.7 million from the ADB. Between 2016 and 2017, the total financing amount increased to USD743.7 million between ADB and PNG.[142] This funding is loaned for specific projects, mostly based on investments in the economy but also for some policy and technical and advisory support operations.[143] The ADB and the ADB/OECD initiative combine promotion of the global anti-corruption regime, with tangible funding opportunities for nation states, including PNG.

Papua New Guinea appears to be working towards legal and institutional compliance with UNCAC and the global anti-corruption regime. However, the slow pace at which domestic legal and institutional change is progressing illustrates the gap between discursive and practical compliance. Legal and institutional compliance, combined with discursive alignment in policy documents, is not in itself sufficient to catalyse the global anti-corruption regime into the fifth and final stage of evolution.[144]

There appears to be a lack of connection between technical compliance, promoted through the UNCAC review mechanism and associated institutions, and the practical challenges of implementation and enforcement within the unique domestic context addressed earlier in this chapter. It is difficult to assess the actual impact of UNCAC on PNG, as much of PNG's anti-corruption framework was in place before signature and ratification of the Convention and post UNCAC changes have not resulted in actionable outcomes. Documents discussing PNG's anti-corruption policies primarily refer to domestic issues and national development, rather than expressly referencing compliance with international legal frameworks. Chapters 5 and 6 of this book provide greater insight into the extent of UNCAC's impact in PNG, drawing on the personal experiences of key actors engaged in anti-corruption efforts at the international, regional, and domestic levels.

Initial hypotheses and points for further exploration

Before moving on to an analysis of the fieldwork and interview process, several key points should be noted in relation to the domestic context of PNG and the relationship between this context and the risks and challenges noted in Chapter 1.

The PNG context reflects several of the primary risk factors and challenges discussed in Chapters 1 to 3. Of particular relevance are the risks of inapplicability and criminal law and enforcement focus, and the challenges of deviant actors and non-compliant states. Additionally, the above overview of the PNG context illustrates some generalisable challenges regarding the prevention and punishment of corruption in PNG, which may be generalised to other developing states.

PNG struggles with resource and capacity limitations which present a substantial hurdle to the successful enforcement of legal regimes and institutional policies. This is often the reality for developing or less developed nations globally, and highlights the relevance of non-compliant states and inapplicability, especially when combined with a criminal law and enforcement focus. Colonial history is also a common feature of many developing states, including PNG. This history can manifest in the conflict between modern and traditional norms and methods of societal organisation. In the context of corruption, such conflict can result in a wealth of corrupt incentives, which may be justified based on culture and tradition, or ignored due to the apathy of the citizenry and primacy of other concerns within community groups.

The influence of external actors is a corruption concern in PNG. Many other developing nations rely on foreign aid and industry to support their economies, so this external influence and its impact may also be generalisable. In PNG, there has been some competition between Western and Asian donors. In some cases, the political dimensions of aid and aid conditionalities can affect the approach taken to combatting corruption, or can even provide incentives for corrupt behaviour. One example of this is the competition between China and Taiwan for PNG's support in the international arena. Foreign corporate influence in the resource extraction sector of the PNG economy has also lent itself to corruption of government and police. These examples reflect the risks of inapplicability if external interests are promoted through anti-corruption objectives without regard to the unique domestic context. Additionally, deviant actors can support the continuation of corruption domestically, through the provision of corrupt incentives.

The diverse nature of PNG society, its extreme ethno-linguistic heterogeneity and traditionally small societal groups, pose a challenge to the governance agenda and domestic anti-corruption framework. This unique aspect of PNG society manifests itself in the fluidity of political organisation. This fluidity provides opportunities for bribery within government as various factions seek to forge alliances or shift their position based on individual gain. There are further incentives to capitalise on opportunities for material gains while in office, as political positions are often short lived. In this way, deviant actors remain a challenge domestically in PNG. Limited resources and capacity, intertwined with issues of political will, mean that existing legal and institutional frameworks appear limited in their prohibitive effect on deviant actors.

UNCAC must operate within this unique domestic context. However, interaction between PNG and UNCAC appears to be based on technical compliance, ignoring more complex political and socioeconomic challenges. Having ratified UNCAC in 2007, PNG's engagement with the Implementation Review Mechanism has resulted in recommendations focused on amendments to legislation and technical assistance on issues such as extradition and mutual legal assistance. Even these technical recommendations have been slow to implement. It is also difficult to gauge the full extent of UNCAC's influence on PNG, as the domestic anti-corruption framework is premised on national development rather than international obligation. The relationship between UNCAC and domestic anti-corruption efforts in PNG is explored further in the following chapters, which document fieldwork and findings from interviews with actors seeking to implement and enforce UNCAC and the domestic anti-corruption regime in PNG.

Notes

1 Nadelmann E and Andreas P, Policing the Globe: Criminalization and Crime Control in International Relations (Oxford University Press, 1st Edition, 2006)
2 See Chapter 1: Transnational criminal law: concerns and critique
3 Lasslett K, 'State Crime by Proxy: Australia and the Bougainville Conflict' 52 *British Journal of Criminology* (2012) 705, at 707
4 ibid.
5 Passas N, 'Globalization and Transnational Crime: Effects of criminogenic asymmetries', in Williams P and Vlassis D (Eds), *Combatting Transnational Crime: Concepts, Activities and Responses* (Frank Cass Publishing, 2013) 22 at 42
6 Lasslett K, *State Crime: On the margins of empire, Rio Tinto, the war on Bougainville and resistance to mining* (Pluto Press, 1st Edition, 2014). This book explores the Bougainville conflict in detail and discusses the various state actors, corporate interests, and power dynamics that coalesced to produce a civil war and autonomy for Bougainville from PNG.
7 Chapter 3
8 Nicholls R, 'Corruption in the South Pacific: The Potential Impact of the UN Convention against Corruption on Pacific Island States' 2 *New Zealand Yearbook of International Law* (2005) 207; Roberts SM, Wright S and O'Neill P, 'Good Governance in the Pacific? Ambivalence and possibility' 38 *Geoforum* (2007) 967
9 CIA Library, *The World Factbook: Papua New Guinea* (2015) available at: https://www.cia.gov/library/publications/the-world-factbook/geos/pp.html (last visited 1 March 2018)
10 ibid.
11 Reilly B and Phillpot R, '"Making Democracy Work" in Papua New Guinea: Social capital and provincial development in an ethnically fragmented society' 42(6) *Asian Survey* (2002) 906, at 907
12 Premdas RR, 'Papua New Guinea: Internal problems of rapid political change' 15(12) *Asian Survey* (1975) 1054, at 1056
13 ibid. at 1062
14 ibid. at 1056
15 Hawksley C, 'Papua New Guinea at thirty: Late decolonisation and the political economy of nation-building' 27(1) *Third World Quarterly* (2006) 161, at 164
16 above n12 at 1066
17 ibid
18 May RJ, 'Turbulence and Reform in Papua New Guinea' 14(1) *Journal of Democracy* (2003) 154, at 155
19 CIA Library, *The World Factbook: Papua New Guinea* (2015) available at: https://www.cia.gov/library/publications/the-world-factbook/geos/pp.html (last visited 1 March 2018)
20 Standish B, 'Governance is Political in Papua New Guinea' 6 *IBS Journal of Business & Research* (2013) at 3
21 above n18 at 156
22 May RJ, 'Papua New Guinea: From coup to reconciliation' 24(1) *Journal of Democracy* (2013) 165. From independence until 2011 all government changes in

PNG were achieved by constitutional means. However, on 2 June 2011 the PNG parliament ignored constitutional process and declared the position of Prime Minister open. Peter O'Neill was elected as Prime Minister and retained that position despite Supreme Court rulings against it until he was ultimately voted in, following the scheduled elections in 2012

23 ibid. at 166

24 May RJ, 'Political Parties in Papua New Guinea', in Rich R, Hambly L and Morgan MG (Eds), *Political Parties in the Pacific Islands* (Pandandus, 1st Edition, 2008) at 98–99

25 Wesley-Smith T, 'Papua New Guinea in 1990: A year of crisis' 31(2) *Asian Survey* (1991) 188, at 195

26 Wickberg S, 'Papua New Guinea: Overview of corruption and anti-corruption', *U4 Expert Answer No.370* (2014) at 2

27 DFAT, 'Overview of Australia's Aid Program to Papua New Guinea', available at: http://dfat.gov.au/geo/papua-new-guinea/development-assistance/Pages/papua-new-guinea.aspx (last visited 1 March 2018)

28 Shie TR, 'Rising Chinese Influence in the South Pacific: Beijing's "Island Fever"' 47(2) *Asian Survey* (2007) 307, at 315

29 PNG Today, *China Grants K23m Aid to PNG* (10 January 2013) available at: http://news.pngfacts.com/2013/01/china-grants-k23m-aid-to-png.html (last visited 1 March 2018)

30 DFAT, 'Overview of Australia's Aid Program to Papua New Guinea', available at: http://dfat.gov.au/geo/papua-new-guinea/development-assistance/Pages/papua-new-guinea.aspx (last visited 1 March 2018)

31 DFAT, *Papua New Guinea-Australia Aid Partnership Arrangement 2016–2017* (3 March 2016), available at: http://dfat.gov.au/about-us/publications/Pages/papua-new-guinea-australia-aid-partnership-arrangement-2016-2017.aspx (last visited 1 March 2018)

32 above n12 at 1060

33 above n26

34 above n15 at 169

35 World Bank, *Papua New Guinea — Structural Adjustment Loan* (10 May 1990) available at: http://documents.worldbank.org/curated/en/1990/05/737208/papua-new-guinea-structural-adjustment-loan (last visited 1 March 2018); see also Feeny S, 'The Impact of Foreign Aid on Poverty and Human Well-being in Papua New Guinea' 10 *Asia-Pacific Development Journal* 2 (2003) 73 at 86

36 above n15 at 169

37 Chin J, 'Papua New Guinea in 2006: Somare's U-Turn and Legacy' 47(1) *Asian Survey* (2007) 200, at 204

38 It has been noted that 'Around $400 million worth of illegally logged timber products are imported into Australia every year' CELCoR Report, 2006, at 6

39 Devpolicy Blog, *Pacific Buzz: Australia 'the Cayman Islands' for PNG* (17 October 2012) available at: http://devpolicy.org/pacific-buzz-october-17-2012-20121017/ (last visited 1 March 2018)

40 Business Advantage PNG, *Ten-Fold growth in foreign companies investing in Papua New Guinea* (9 September 2015) available at: http://www.businessadvantagepng.com/ten-fold-growth-in-foreign-companies-investing-in-papua-new-guinea/ (last visited 1 March 2018)

41 Papua New Guinea, *Commission of Inquiry Generally into the Department of Finance: Final Report* (October 2009) at 12

42 ibid at 23

43 ibid at 29

44 The Sydney Morning Herald, *PNG 'dirty money' trail leads to Australia* (19 June 2013) available at: http://www.smh.com.au/national/png-dirty-money-trail-leads-to-australia-20130618-2oguz.html (last visited 1 March 2018)

45 Devpolicy Blog, *Pacific Buzz: Australia 'the Cayman Islands for PNG* (17 October 2012) available at: http://devpolicy.org/pacific-buzz-october-17-2012-20121017/ (last visited 1 March 2018)
46 above n5 at 28–29
47 above n28 at 315
48 ibid.
49 This is important considering the self-interested agendas of lenders discussed in Chapter 3.
50 Chin J, 'Papua New Guinea in 2009: Anti-Chinese Rioting and the Liquefied Natural Gas Deal' 50(1) *Asian Survey* (2010) 247, at 251–52
51 ibid at 247
52 Gridneff I, 'The Chinese Connection in PNG' *Pacific Islands Report* (June 2009) available at: http://archives.pireport.org/archive/2009/June/06-03-com.htm (last visited 1 March2018)
53 above n50 at 249. See also Papua New Guinea, Barnett TE, Asia-Pacific Action Group, *The Barnett Report: A summary of the report of the Commission of Inquiry into Aspects of the Timber Industry in Papua New Guinea* (1990). This report documents much of the corruption and bribery between Rimbunan Hujau and the PNG government
54 Above n41 at 8
55 ActNOW! PNG, *Read the Finance Inquiry Commission of Inquiry Report* (11 January 2014) available at: http://www.actnowpng.org/content/read-finance-inquiry-commission-inquiry-report (last visited 1 March 2018)
56 Despite the ongoing charges, Mr Paraka registered a political party and participated, unsuccessfully, in the 2017 elections
57 ABC News, *PNG Anti-Corruption Taskforce Broke after Making Allegations Against Prime Minister Peter O'Neill* (5 February 2015) available at: http://www.abc.net.au/news/2015-02-04/png-anti-corruption-taskforce-starved-of-funding/6070170 (last visited 1 March 2018)
58 ABC News, *PNG court finds abolition of corruption watchdog Taskforce Sweep was legal* (5 December 2016) available at: http://www.abc.net.au/news/2016-12-05/court-finds-abolition-of-png- corruption-watchdog-was-legal/8092774 (last visited 10 March 2018)
59 The Australian, Callick R, *Ex-PNG Minister Paul Tiensten gets Nine Years Jail* (1 April 2014) available at: http://www.theaustralian.com.au/news/world/expng-minister-paul-tiensten-gets-nine-years-jail/story-e6frg6so-1226870122116 (last visited 1 March 2018)
60 ABC, *PNG Politician Says He is a Victim of a Witch-Hunt* available at: http://www.abc.net.au/news/2011-11-02/png-politician-claims-he27s-victim-of-witch-hunt/3615672 (last visited 1 March 2018)
61 Lowy Interpreter, 'A Victory over Corruption in PNG' available at: http://www.lowyinterpreter.org/post/2014/04/04/A-victory-over-corruption-in-PNG-paul-tiensten.aspx (last visited 1 March 2018)
62 Chin J, 'Political Reviews: Papua New Guinea' 15(2) *Contemporary Pacific* (2003) 457 at 458
63 Walton GW, 'Is All Corruption Dysfunctional? Perceptions of corruption and its consequences in Papua New Guinea' 33(3) *Public Administration and Development* (2012)
64 *Criminal Code Act 1974*, Part III, Division 2 ('*CCA*')
65 *Organic Law on the Duties and Responsibilities of Leadership 1975* ('*OLDRL*')
66 *Organic Law on the Integrity of Political Parties 2003* ('*OLIPPC*')
67 *Proceeds of Crime Act 2005* ('*POCA*')
68 *Constitution of Papua New Guinea 1975*, Section III Division 2, s 26(1) ('*Constitution*')
69 ibid. s 26(4)
70 ibid. s 27(1a) and (1d)

71 ibid. s 27(2)
72 ibid. s 12(2)
73 *OLDRL* Part II (4)
74 ibid. Part II (4)
75 ibid. Part II (5)
76 ibid. Part II (5)
77 ibid. Part II (11)
78 ibid. Part II (12)
79 ibid. Part II (13)
80 ibid. Part II (16)
81 ibid. Part III (17)
82 ibid. Part III (17d)
83 *OLDRL* Part V (27)(3)
84 Colvin E, 'Criminal procedure in the South Pacific' 8(1) *Journal of South Pacific Law* (2004) at 16
85 It is interesting to note the history of Queensland in PNG, as it attempted to annex a section of Papua New Guinea on 4 April 1883, in response to the expanding power of European nations in the region. However, the British Government strongly rebuked this act. It was not until 1902 that the British protectorate of 'British New Guinea' was placed under the authority of Australia, until its independence in 1975
86 Reilly B, 'Political reform in Papua New Guinea: Testing the evidence' 21(1) *Pacific Economic Bulletin* (2006) 187, at 189
87 May RJ, Wheen K and Haley N, 'Assessing the Shift to Limited Preferential Voting' Chapter 13 in May RJ, Anere R, Haley N and Wheen K (Eds), *Election 2007: The shift to limited preferential voting in Papua New Guinea* (ANU E Press, 2013) 193, at 203
88 above n86 at 190
89 Okelo (2012/5) *SSGM Discussion Paper*: A Critical Review of Papua New Guinea's Organic Law on the Integrity of Political Parties and Candidates: 2001–2010, at 4
90 above n24 at 98
91 above n89
92 ibid. The Somare government was elected on 5 August 2002 and stayed in office for that entire term, being re-elected again in 2007
93 Report of the Commonwealth Pacific Islands Forum, *Election Assessment Team: Papua New Guinea National Elections*, June–August 2007, at 11
94 Above n89
95 Supreme Court of Papua New Guinea, *Special Reference Pursuant to Constitution, Section 19*, SC1057 Ref No. 11 (2008). At paragraph 120, the court held that the following provisions of *OLIPPAC* were in conflict with the Constitution: ss 59 to 61, ss 69 to 73, and s 81.
96 ibid. para 130
97 ibid. para 165
98 ibid. paras 167, 170, 172, 175
99 ibid. para 187
100 ibid. para 188
101 ibid. para 189
102 *Constitution* s50(1)(c-e)
103 ibid. s 50
104 above n95 paras 225–230
105 Nongorr J, 'Explaining the Integrity Law' available at: http://www.pngblogs.com/2010/07/explaining-intergrity-law_9.html (last visited 1 March 2018)
106 ibid.
107 Above n89 at 12
108 The institutions included in NACA are: Department of Treasury, Auditor-General's Office, Customs, Internal Revenue Commission, Department of Personnel Management,

Public Prosecutor, Solicitor General, Ombudsman Commission, Police, and the Department of Provincial and Local Government Affairs
109 NEC Decision No. NG03/2011
110 ABC News, *Task Force Sweep says Papua New Guinea Prime Minister O'Neill has no Corruption Case to* Answer (17 January 2014) available at: http://www.abc.net.au/news/2014-01-16/an-taskforce-says-png-pm-has-no-corruption-case-to-answer/5203948 (last visited 1 March 2018)
111 ABC News, *Papua New Guinea Prime Minister Peter O'Neill Axes Anti-Corruption Taskforce Sweep* (19 June 2014) available at: http://www.abc.net.au/news/2014-06-18/an-png-pm-axes-anti-corruption-task-force-sweep/5533400 (last visited 1 March 2018)
112 ibid.
113 Papua New Guinea Today, *Task Force Sweep Permanently Stayed* (28 July 2014) available at: http://news.pngfacts.com/2014/07/task-force-sweep-permanently-stayed.html (last visited 1 March 2018)
114 Bengo P, 'Corruption in Papua New Guinea', in ADB/OECD, *Regional Strategies and International Instruments to Fight Corruption* (1999)
115 Constitutional Amendment (No.40) (Independent Commission Against Corruption) Law 2014 s220C
116 Papua New Guinea, National Anti-Corruption Strategy 2010–2030 (2010) ('NACS') at 3
117 ibid.
118 ibid. at 14
119 ibid. at 35–36
120 Illicit enrichment is recommended under Article 20 of UNCAC
121 above n116 at 38
122 Freedom House, *Papua New Guinea*, (2012) available at: http://www.freedomhouse.org/report/freedom-press/2012/papua-new-guinea#.U1W2f_mSw8o (last visited 1 March 2018)
123 ibid.
124 UNCAC Coalition, *UNCAC Review Mechanism*, available at: http://www.uncaccoalition.org/en/uncac-review/uncac-review-mechanism (last visited 1 March 2018)
125 ibid.
126 CAC/COSP/IRG/2013/CRP.7, *Executive Summary: Papua New Guinea* (23 May 2013)
127 ibid.
128 ibid. at 6
129 ibid. at 7
130 ABC News, *Concerns that changes to PNG's ICAC Bill will undermine its effectiveness* (20 September 2017) available at: http://www.abc.net.au/news/programs/pacific-beat/2017-09-20/concerns- that-changes-to-pngs-icac-bill-will/8964862 (last visited 1 March 2018)
131 above n116 at 38
132 ibid. at 29
133 ibid. at 32
134 UNDP, *United Nations Country Program Papua New Guinea 2008–2012: A Partnership for Nation Building* (10 April 2007) ('UN Country Program PNG')
135 UNDP, *Common Country Programme Document for Papua New Guinea 2012-2015* (28 November 2011)
136 UNDP, *United Nations Pacific Regional Anti-Corruption Project* (2012), at 7
137 ibid.
138 Hakobyan A, 'Implementing UNCAC' *U4 Expert Answer* (22 October 2005) at 7
139 ADB/OECD, *Formal Endorsement of the Anti-Corruption Action Plan for Asia-Pacific: Papua New Guinea* (30 November 2001)

140 ibid.
141 ibid.
142 ADB, *Asian Development Bank & Papua New Guinea Fact Sheet* (April 2014) available at: https://www.adb.org/publications/papua-new-guinea-fact-sheet (last visited 1 March 2018)
143 ibid.
144 above n1

References

ABC News, *Concerns that changes to PNG's ICAC Bill will undermine its effectiveness* (20 September 2017) available at: http://www.abc.net.au/news/programs/pacific-beat/2017-09-20/concerns-that-changes-to-pngs-icac-bill-will/8964862 (last visited 1 March 2018).

ABC News, *Papua New Guinea Prime Minister Peter O'Neill Axes Anti-Corruption Taskforce Sweep* (19 June 2014) available at: http://www.abc.net.au/news/2014-06-18/an-png-pm-axes-anti-corruption-task-force-sweep/5533400 (last visited 1 March 2018).

ABC News, *PNG Anti-Corruption Taskforce Broke after Making Allegations Against Prime Minister Peter O'Neill* (5 February 2015) available at: http://www.abc.net.au/news/2015-02-04/png-anti-corruption-taskforce-starved-of-funding/6070170(last visited 1 March 2018).

ABC News, *PNG court finds abolition of corruption watchdog Taskforce Sweep was legal* (5 December 2016) available at: http://www.abc.net.au/news/2016-12-05/court-finds-abolition-of-png-corruption-watchdog-was-legal/8092774 (last visited 1 March 2018).

ABC News, *Task Force Sweep says Papua New Guinea Prime Minister O'Neill has no Corruption Case to* Answer (17 January 2014) available at: http://www.abc.net.au/news/2014-01-16/an-taskforce-says-png-pm-has-no-corruption-case-to-answer/5203948 (last visited 1 March 2018).

ABC News, *PNG Politician Says He is a Victim of a Witch-Hunt* (2 November 2011) available at: http://www.abc.net.au/news/2011-11-02/png-politician-claims-he27s-victim-of-witch-hunt/3615672 (last visited 1 March 2018).

ActNOW! PNG, *Read the Finance Inquiry Commission of Inquiry Report* (11 January 2014) available at: http://www.actnowpng.org/content/read-finance-inquiry-commission-inquiry-report (last visited 1 March 2018).

ADB, *Asian Development Bank & Papua New Guinea Fact Sheet* (April 2014) available at: https://www.adb.org/publications/papua-new-guinea-fact-sheet (last visited 1 March 2018).

ADB/OECD, *Formal Endorsement of the Anti-Corruption Action Plan for Asia-Pacific: Papua New Guinea* (30 November 2001).

Bengo P, 'Corruption in Papua New Guinea', in ADB/OECD, *Regional Strategies and International Instruments to Fight Corruption* (1999).

Business Advantage PNG, *Ten-Fold growth in foreign companies investing in Papua New Guinea* (9 September 2015) available at: http://www.businessadvantagepng.com/ten-fold-growth-in-foreign-companies-investing-in-papua-new-guinea/ (last visited 1 March 2018).

CAC/COSP/IRG/2013/CRP.7, *Executive Summary: Papua New Guinea* (23 May 2013).

Chin J, 'Papua New Guinea in 2006: Somare's U-Turn and Legacy' 47(1) *Asian Survey* (2007) 200.

Chin J, 'Political Reviews: Papua New Guinea' 15(2) *Contemporary Pacific* (2003) 457.

Chin J, 'Papua New Guinea in 2009: Anti-Chinese Rioting and the Liquefied Natural Gas Deal' 50(1) *Asian Survey* (2010) 247.

CIA Library, *The World Factbook: Papua New Guinea* (2015) available at: https://www.cia.gov/library/publications/the-world-factbook/geos/pp.html (last visited 1 March 2018).

Colvin E, 'Criminal procedure in the South Pacific' 8(1) *Journal of South Pacific Law* (2004).

Constitution of Papua New Guinea 1975 ('*Constitution*').

Constitutional Amendment (No.40) (Independent Commission Against Corruption) Law 2014.

Criminal Code Act 1974 ('*CCA*').

Devpolicy Blog, *Pacific Buzz: Australia 'the Cayman Islands for PNG* (17 October 2012) available at: http://devpolicy.org/pacific-buzz-october-17-2012-20121017/ (last visited 1 March 2018).

DFAT, 'Overview of Australia's Aid Program to Papua New Guinea', available at: http://dfat.gov.au/geo/papua-new-guinea/development-assistance/Pages/papua-new-guinea.aspx (last visited 1 March 2018).

Feeny S, 'The Impact of Foreign Aid on Poverty and Human Well-being in Papua New Guinea' 10(2) *Asia-Pacific Development Journal* (2003).

Freedom House, *Papua New Guinea* (2012) available at: http://www.freedomhouse.org/report/freedom-press/2012/papua-new-guinea#.U1W2f_mSw8o (last visited 1 March 2018).

Gridneff I, 'The Chinese Connection in PNG', *Pacific Islands Report* (June 2009) available at: http://www.pireport.org/articles/2009/06/03/chinese-connection-png (last visited 1 March 2018).

Hakobyan A, 'Implementing UNCAC', *U4 Expert Answer* (22 October 2005).

Hawksley C, 'Papua New Guinea at thirty: Late decolonisation and the political economy of nation-building' 27(1) *Third World Quarterly* (2006) 161.

Lasslett K, 'State Crime by Proxy: Australia and the Bougainville Conflict' 52 *British Journal of Criminology* (2012) 705.

Lasslett K, *State Crime: On the margins of empire, Rio Tinto, the war on Bougainville and resistance to mining* (Pluto Press, 1st Edition, 2014).

Lowy Interpreter, *A Victory over Corruption in PNG* (4 April 2014) available at: https://www.lowyinstitute.org/the-interpreter/victory-over-corruption-png (last visited 1 March 2018).

May RJ, 'Political Parties in Papua New Guinea', in Rich R, Hambly L and Morgan MG (eds), *Political Parties in the Pacific Islands* (Pandandus, 1st Edition, 2008) 98.

May RJ, 'Turbulence and Reform in Papua New Guinea' 14(1) *Journal of Democracy* (2003) 154.

May RJ, Wheen K and Haley N, 'Assessing the Shift to Limited Preferential Voting' in May RJ, Anere R, Haley N and Wheen K (Eds), *Election 2007: The shift to limited preferential voting in Papua New Guinea* (ANU E Press, 2013) 193.

May RJ, 'Papua New Guinea: From coup to reconciliation' 24(1) *Journal of Democracy* (2013) 165.

Nadelmann E and Andreas P, *Policing the Globe: Criminalization and Crime Control in International Relations* (Oxford University Press, 1st Edition, 2006).

NEC PNG, *Decision No. NG03/2011.*

Nicholls R, 'Corruption in the South Pacific: the potential impact of the UN Convention against Corruption on Pacific Island States' 2 *New Zealand Yearbook of International Law* (2005) 207.

Nongorr J, 'Explaining the Integrity Law', *PNG Blogs* (9 July 2010) available at: http://www.pngblogs.com/2010/07/explaining-intergrity-law_9.html (last visited 1 March 2018).

Okelo HT, 'A Critical Review of Papua New Guinea's Organic Law on the Integrity of Political Parties and Candidates: 2001–2010', *SSGM Discussion Paper* 5 (2012).

Organic Law on the Duties and Responsibilities of Leadership 1975 ('*OLDRL*').

Organic Law on the Integrity of Political Parties 2003 ('*OLIPPC*').

Papua New Guinea Today, *Task Force Sweep Permanently Stayed* (28 July 2014) available at: http://news.pngfacts.com/2014/07/task-force-sweep-permanently-stayed.html (last visited 1 March 2018).

DFAT, *Papua New Guinea-Australia Aid Partnership Arrangement 2016–2017* (3 March 2016), available at: http://dfat.gov.au/about-us/publications/Pages/papua-new-guinea-australia-aid-partnership-arrangement-2016-2017.aspx (last visited 1 March 2018).

Papua New Guinea, Barnett TE, Asia-Pacific Action Group, *The Barnett Report: A summary of the report of the Commission of Inquiry into Aspects of the Timber Industry in Papua New Guinea* (1990).

Papua New Guinea, *Commission of Inquiry Generally into the Department of Finance: Final Report* (October 2009).

Papua New Guinea, *National Anti-Corruption Strategy 2010–2030* (2010) ('NACS').

Passas N, 'Globalization and Transnational Crime: Effects of criminogenic asymmetries', in Williams P and Vlassis D (Eds), *Combatting Transnational Crime: Concepts, Activities and Responses* (Frank Cass Publishers, 2013) 22.

PNG Today, *China Grants K23m Aid to PNG* (10 January 2013) available at: http://news.pngfacts.com/2013/01/china-grants-k23m-aid-to-png.html (last visited 1 March 2018).

Premdas RR, 'Papua New Guinea: Internal problems of rapid political change' 15(12) *Asian Survey* (1975) 1054.

Proceeds of Crime Act 2005 ('*POCA*').

Reilly B and Phillpot R, '"Making Democracy Work" in Papua New Guinea: Social capital and provincial development in an ethnically fragmented society' 42(6) *Asian Survey* (2002) 906.

Reilly B, 'Political reform in Papua New Guinea: Testing the evidence' 21(1) *Pacific Economic Bulletin* (2006) 187.

Pacific Islands Forum Secretariat, *Report of the Commonwealth Pacific Islands Forum Election Assessment Team: Papua New Guinea National Elections* (June–August 2007).

Roberts SM, Wright S and O'Neill P, 'Good Governance in the Pacific? Ambivalence and possibility' 38 *Geoforum* (2007) 967.

Shie TR, 'Rising Chinese Influence in the South Pacific: Beijing's "Island Fever"' 47(2) *Asian Survey* (2007) 307.

Standish B, 'Governance is Political in Papua New Guinea' 6 *IBS Journal of Business & Research* (2013).

Supreme Court of Papua New Guinea, *Special Reference Pursuant to Constitution, Section 19*, SC1057 Ref No. 11 (2008).

The Australian, Callick R, *Ex-PNG Minister Paul Tiensten gets Nine Years Jail* (1 April 2014) available at: http://www.theaustralian.com.au/news/world/expng-minister-paul-tiensten-gets-nine-years-jail/story-e6frg6so-1226870122116 (last visited 1 March 2018).

The Sydney Morning Herald, *PNG 'dirty money' trail leads to Australia* (19 June 2013) available at: http://www.smh.com.au/national/png-dirty-money-trail-leads-to- australia-20130618-2oguz.html (last visited 1 March2018).

UNCAC Coalition, *UNCAC Review Mechanism*, available at: http://www.uncaccoalition.org/en/uncac-review/uncac-review-mechanism (last visited 1 March 2018).
UNDP, *Common Country Programme Document for Papua New Guinea 2012–2015* (28 November 2011).
UNDP, *United Nations Country Program Papua New Guinea 2008–2012: A Partnership for Nation Building* (10 April 2007) ('UN Country Program PNG').
UNDP, *United Nations Pacific Regional Anti-Corruption Project* (2012).
Walton GW, 'Is All Corruption Dysfunctional? Perceptions of corruption and its consequences in Papua New Guinea' 33(3) *Public Administration and Development* (2013).
Wesley-Smith T, 'Papua New Guinea in 1990: A year of crisis' 31(2) *Asian Survey* (1991) 188.
Wickberg S, 'Papua New Guinea: Overview of corruption and anti-corruption', *U4 Expert Answer No.370* (2014).
World Bank, *Papua New Guinea — Structural Adjustment Loan* (10 May 1990) available at: http://documents.worldbank.org/curated/en/1990/05/737208/papua-new-guinea-structural-adjustment-loan (last visited 1 March 2018).

5 Experience from the field – insight into the implementation and enforcement of the United Nations Convention against Corruption in Papua New Guinea

Introduction

This chapter introduces key findings from fieldwork conducted in Papua New Guinea (PNG), including 17 interviews with actors from the international, regional, and domestic spheres, working on the implementation and enforcement of UNCAC. Participants included members of the United Nations (UN), Australian government departments, the Pacific Islands Forum (PIF), Transparency International (TI), local NGOs, PNG government departments, and PNG public institutions. The chapter provides an introductory overview of the interviews and fieldwork conducted, both in PNG and remotely. It summarises the findings from the fieldwork through categorisation of key points and common themes. Seventeen interviews were conducted, with actors from international, regional, and domestic spheres.

Interviewees were selected based on their involvement with UNCAC and anti-corruption projects and programmes. Thirty participants were recruited and 17 respondents were secured. Although the sample size is not large, the area of exploration is highly specialised and the interviewees represent a valuable cross-section of relevant geographic spheres, sectors, and experiences. Interviews were conducted remotely with actors at the international level, including the chief of the Corruption and Economic Crime Branch of the UN Office on Drugs and Crime (UNODC), who is also the Secretary of the Conference of *States Parties* to UNCAC. Most interviews with domestic actors in PNG were conducted in person in the capital city, Port Moresby, over a nine-day period from 3 to 11 June 2014. Reference to interview participant roles and positions refer to those held by the participant at the time the interview took place, unless otherwise stated.

Eleven interviews were conducted with actors from PNG, including those from central government departments, specialist anti-corruption agencies, Royal PNG Constabulary, and various legal offices including the Department of Justice and Attorney General, and the Office of the Public Prosecutor.[1] Time was also spent in government archives and libraries, as well as networking 'off-the-record' with knowledgeable individuals in the public service and the university.

Interviews were conducted using a semi-structured method. The details of the questions varied depending on the flow of the dialogue, knowledge, and background of the participant and willingness of the participant to expand on a topic. However, certain key areas were targeted by the interview questions for all participants. Annex F provides the general framework for interview questions. Participants were first asked to provide background information on their position and experience. Following this, questions explored participant views on corruption and then the participant's experiences with combatting corruption. Finally, questions were directed towards the participant's awareness and engagement with UNCAC.

Participant responses and additional insight from open-ended discussion illustrate a range of key points valuable for answering the research questions presented at the outset of this book. Challenges facing anti-corruption efforts were a common topic, as was the relationship between PNG's efforts and the regional and transnational context. Interviews also provide insight into the values and interests at play, that influence the political, economic, social, and legal environment in which anti-corruption programmes must operate.

Key findings from the empirical research

Ultimately, the findings from this empirical research illustrate that, in the context of the PNG case study, UNCAC has had limited influence and impact. Of the 17 interview participants, 14 were aware of UNCAC, but only eight had been actively engaged with it, either through the implementation process, or through reference to UNCAC in their own anti-corruption efforts. Of those eight who had directly engaged, four were domestic actors from the PNG government, who had taken part in the Implementation Review process or utilised UNCAC as part of a Mutual Legal Assistance (MLA) request. Of the remaining four actors, one was a member of TI PNG and the other three were UN officials.

UNCAC's coercive influence in PNG, and the impact of treaty obligations more generally, appear limited in the context of interview responses. This suggests that the consequences for non-compliance under UNCAC are not considered substantial enough to motivate extensive implementation and enforcement, in the absence of additional value or interest-based motivation. This reflects the point made by Dimitri Vlassis of the UNODC and UNCAC secretariat:

> Sanctions are the prerogative of the security council. You will not find conventions where there are sanctions for non-compliance. With the exception of the security council this is not the way that this organization works.[2]

The approaches of UNCAC and of *States Parties* in the Pacific appear normatively aligned. *States Parties* seem to have undertaken anti-corruption efforts in line with UNCAC, not because of the coercive power of the Convention and the obligation to enforce it, but because the Convention allows for a diverse range of possible actions in order to combat corruption, reflecting the diverse contexts in which such actions must be taken.

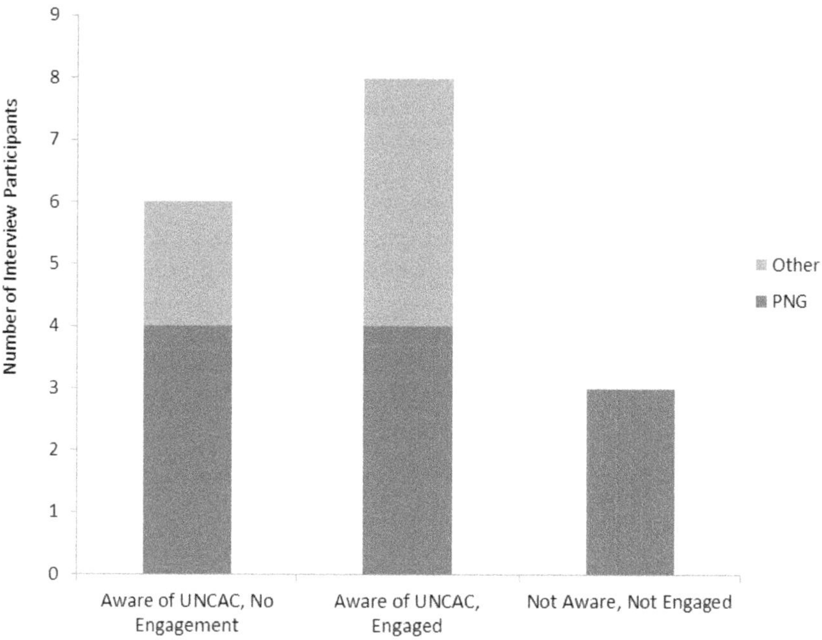

Figure 5.1 Awareness of and engagement with UNCAC

Domestically, PNG government officials were quick to highlight that UNCAC provided a framework that was mutually supportive of their own domestic, localised efforts to combat corruption. UNCAC was seen as a reflection of existing impetus to combat corruption at the national level:

> . . . you can see from our strategy we are focused on our situation . . . It [UNCAC] doesn't defer from our circumstances here at all. It is a good thing to get PNG to address corruption here. Becoming a member gives us the responsibility to make sure it gets implemented and this is an opportunity to look at our own circumstances.[3]

A high level official within the PNG Office of the Public Prosecutor (OPP) put forward this view:

> . . . it [UNCAC] is going to add value to what we already have. We already have corruption and fraud, all of these offences we have, some we are adding but most of the basic offences for corruption have been in place for some time, but I would say that UNCAC is going to add value to this current regime that we have.[4]

From a more critical standpoint, some participants presented the view that UNCAC may be a poorly understood document requiring resource expenditure without providing meaningful assistance and support. For example, a now retired senior official with extensive experience working for AusAID in the South Pacific, noted:

> A lot of these conventions have reporting requirements attached and we are dealing with situations in which there are no working computers, in some places there are no lights for half the day, no air con – how are you expecting engagement with the community let alone creation of complex reports back to the UN.[5]

This perspective reflects some of the critique about unintentional side effects and negative consequences of the global anti-corruption regime.[6] However, national actors who have engaged with the UNCAC Implementation Review process in PNG stated that the experience had provided positive insights and unique perspectives for combating corruption.

While the financial burden of fulfilling obligations under UNCAC was noted,[7] in general the process was seen as productive and informative:

> Most useful is the Country Review . . . other countries share their experience in terms of how they went about implementing for example Chapter II on criminalisation. So when it comes to our own legislation we can draw on those experiences . . . from the Sri Lanka review, they shared their experience on how they criminalised the bribery offences and so we are looking at developing this.[8]

The potential for UN assistance resulting from the Implementation Review process was highlighted as a positive benefit of engagement:

> . . . if we as a country identify areas where we need assistance we can ask them to provide technical assistance in those areas. We could ask for someone to come and assist us who has broad experience in that aspect of the Convention and they can also provide some funding.[9]

The view of UNCAC from those engaged with the Convention emphasises that it is a framework that supports the goals and agendas of domestic anti-corruption campaigners. In the words of a UNDP Official who worked in PNG and assisted with the development of their National Anti-Corruption Strategy:

> UNCAC is a politically negotiated document. It's not enforceable, but I just needed it as a framework. It is a great document because of the range of issues that it covers.[10]

These perspectives conflict with criticisms of UNCAC and the global anti-corruption regime which highlight its coercive potential and inapplicability, as well as the burden placed on domestic actors in the context of limited resources and capacity.[11] Interview findings suggest that these concerns of coercion and inapplicability are limited, but do enhance concerns regarding non-compliant states and the challenge of securing domestic compliance with UNCAC.

The supporting, rather than central, role of UNCAC in PNG does not imply that anti-corruption efforts in the country, and across the South Pacific region, operate in isolation from transnational dynamics. Approaches taken and challenges faced by actors combatting corruption in PNG and regionally illustrate points of convergence with the approach promoted by UNCAC, even where acknowledgement of this connection is absent. Furthermore, national and regional perspectives provided insight on areas where UNCAC could enhance its positive influence and contribute more substantially to the reduction of corrupt acts in PNG, the South Pacific region, and globally.

Interview participants at the domestic, regional, and transnational levels were all aware of the extensive challenge posed by corruption. In PNG, corruption was viewed as 'endemic'[12] and of increasing concern, with ever growing incentives and limited effectiveness of anti-corruption measures.[13] A member of the PNG Eco Forestry Forum (EFF) noted:

> Corruption is ingrained in this system . . . people are beginning to accept that that's the way of life here . . . At the higher levels, it's not being dealt with effectively.[14]

Participants were generally aware of and had experienced some aspects of each of the risk factors identified by critics of UNCAC and the global anti-corruption regime. Awareness of these risk factors existed even in cases where engagement with international actors and laws was limited. However, these risk factors were viewed not as fundamental flaws or sticking points related to the anti-corruption approach, instead they were viewed as inevitable challenges that required innovative action within the domestic context. This perspective diverges from the view of critics, who see the risk factors as resulting from flaws in the current anti-corruption approach.

Critical risk factors in the context of Papua New Guinea

The four regime risk factors introduced in Chapter 1 are: (1) definitional complexity; (2) links to other forms of criminality; (3) criminal law and enforcement focus; and (4) inapplicability. It has been suggested that the complexity of the concept of corruption, and the resultant failure of UNCAC and the global anti-corruption regime to establish a definition, may allow for abuse and potentially contribute to harmful policy rather than effective reductions in corrupt activity.[15] Regarding links between corruption and other forms of criminality, it is argued that such links can be used as a tool for 'policy laundering', especially when combined with a lack of clear definition and focus on criminal and law enforcement solutions. Policy laundering is the activity of promoting foreign state agendas through the lens of international best practice and global cooperation.[16]

Critics also argue that global prohibition regimes tend to focus on criminal law and enforcement measures at the cost of other relevant contextual factors that may contribute to, or be the underlying cause of, the target activity.[17] This leads to the final risk factor of inapplicability. This risk factor draws on the other three noted above. The concern is that application of a regime that avoids addressing definitional uncertainty, links corrupt activity to other forms of criminality, and overemphasises criminal law and enforcement measures, is unlikely to achieve success in domestic contexts where resources and capacity are limited, values and interests are diverse, and the relevance of other forms of criminality vary substantially. The unique way that these risk factors were discussed by interview participants is illustrated below.

Definitional complexity

Regarding definitional complexity, variations in understandings of corruption were often noted in response to the question 'how would you define corruption?' Reasons for this variation were cited as relating to cultural norms and education. For example, the director of the Institute of National Affairs in PNG noted: 'TI PNG undertook a little survey on perception, corruption perceptions, a few years ago. There is certainly a lot of variation.'[18] In response to the same question, the executive director of TI PNG stated:

> We have done surveys in PNG and the definitions have ranged from adultery to drugs, a whole range of things, depending on the backgrounds of the people answering. But overall people regard it as being people in official role receiving or demanding entitlement for acting in an official capacity, that's just how it is seen.[19]

Expanding on the issue of defining corruption and the role of culture in PNG, a member of the PNG National Executive Council (NEC)[20] explained it in this way:

> Sometimes perceptions are culturally defined, we are a communal society . . . if I know Mark [a friend] . . . and he runs a printing company with a government contract . . . Mark gives me 20 bucks . . . it's a gift, it's a gesture, but it doesn't go to reinforce that his contract is maintained. For us, we would understand when someone is seeking a favour.[21]

Cultural dynamics and variation in perceptions were generally acknowledged by participants, but there was a view that this did not prevent effective prosecution of corruption. A member of the Department of Justice and Attorney-General, pointed out 'it comes down to circumstance'.[22] In the words of an official working for the National Fraud and Anti-Corruption Office 'the law is the law'.[23]

In this context, the benefits of the 'corrupt act' approach taken by UNCAC seems highly relevant. It was pointed out by some UN practitioners that the flexibility provided by the range of corrupt acts that could be criminalised under UNCAC may be advantageous for countries like PNG, where unique and dynamic cultural contexts must be considered. Dimitri Vlassis of UNODC stated that this approach allows UNCAC to be 'a dynamic instrument', avoiding the risk that UNCAC will be a snapshot of the views on corruption at a single point in time.[24] Tying this back to the domestic context and PNG's anti-corruption activities, a member of the PNG Department of Justice and Attorney-General noted:

> there are a couple [programmes and activities] that come from the recommendations from internationals but most we have developed . . . basically, what the UNCAC requires is its *States Parties* to implement a strategy [to combat corruption].[25]

Building on this, Mr Asa of the NEC pointed out:

> Becoming a member [of UNCAC] gives us the responsibility to make sure it gets implemented and this is an opportunity to look at our own circumstances . . . it doesn't defer from our circumstances here at all.[26]

Criminal law and enforcement focus

Moving on to the second risk factor, criminal law and enforcement was highlighted as an important part of the anti-corruption framework in PNG, and more broadly in the region. All interview participants agreed that, for the most part, the legal framework that currently exists for combatting corruption was sufficient. Ms Rodrigues of the UNDP stated that: 'A lot of countries have a majority of the criminal provisions on the books already, it's not the criminal code that's the problem, it's many other things.'[27]

As noted in Chapter 4, the PNG *Criminal Code Act* and Leadership Code have existed since independence in 1975, pre-dating any international action on corruption. Failure to enforce the criminal framework through investigation, arrest, and prosecution was highlighted as a key issue for anti-corruption efforts in PNG. Lawrence Stephens of TI PNG made the point:

> We have a huge number of laws, laws that if they were applied and policed work. We spent a hell of a lot of time legislating and not enough time policing. Some may need improvement but overall they are there and they need to be enforced.[28]

This was mirrored in statements by a representative of the EFF. She argued that, while international pressure was a powerful tool for motivating political will, 'the only thing that would bring total change, would be the enforcement and resourcing of available mechanisms, and policies and laws'.[29]

Even within the government framework, the challenge of enforcement and resource and capacity limitations was highlighted:

> The legal framework is sufficient. The laws are there. They have been there since independence. The sentences are quite tough. The challenge is for police to investigate every case, bring all the evidence before the court and prosecute it . . . the legal system is sufficient but the challenge is properly resourcing the institutions.[30]

The criminal law and enforcement approach is insufficient to secure anti-corruption objectives. A legal framework is an essential element of any prohibition regime. However, if this framework is unable to secure necessary political support and related allocation of resources then its applicability and effectiveness will remain limited. If implementation and enforcement of UNCAC in PNG is based on a criminal law and enforcement approach, it is unlikely to achieve greater success than has previously been had domestically. Applying UNCAC using a criminal law and enforcement approach may have harmful consequences, including overworking institutions and misallocating limited resources to inapplicable projects.

Criminal law and enforcement was not the only method contemplated by interview participants. Criminal measures were viewed more as a deterrence mechanism, rather than a solution in and of themselves. Participants highlighted a range of social, economic, political, and cultural factors that contribute to corrupt activities in PNG. Accordingly, participants suggested a wide array of mechanisms, beyond revised or enhanced enforcement of criminal law measures, to address these underlying issues and combat corruption in PNG. Additional mechanisms included educational initiatives and improved public service delivery.[31]

Enhanced public service delivery relates to an expansion of the provision of government services to the public, as a means of strengthening government legitimacy and enhancing the interaction between public and private spheres. This approach is related to overcoming the risks associated with limited government influence and relevance in remote areas of PNG, as noted in Chapter 4. Interestingly, many of these non-criminal factors and anti-corruption mechanisms were emphasised by actors within law enforcement, illustrating general support for a multifaceted anti-corruption approach.[32]

Links to other forms of criminality

Links with other forms of criminality were not explored extensively in interviews. In the context of transnational organised crime, the then director of the Australian Federal Police Transnational Crime Unit (AFP TNCU) in PNG noted corruption as a key facilitator of organised crime. The focus, however, was on the need to improve the functioning of institutions and address challenges of limited political will, capacity limitations, lack of expertise and underdevelopment of social and economic systems. From this perspective, corruption and organised crime are not directly linked, but the impact of corruption on domestic institutions and systems was related to the challenges of combatting organised crime.

Participants noted two additional contributing factors for domestic corruption in PNG: (1) foreign aid and its impact on the functioning of government agencies; and (2) the role played by foreign investment within the context of limited rural opportunities for work and income. In relation to the provision of aid, the director of AFP TNCU detailed a useful example in terms of aid provided to the PNG Police force by Australia:

> What has evolved, either by design or just by evolution, you find that we might put 1000 Kina [AUD470] towards their operations, knowing they have 1000 Kina from their own organisation, what we find is that the 1000 Kina from their own organisation gets diverted, so they still only have 1000 Kina . . . They have sufficient funds; they just don't want to spend it. They would rather spend ours.[33]

This reflects the discussion in Chapter 3, regarding the corrupt incentives provided by aid despite the intention that this aid support good governance or capacity building objectives.

Regarding the role of foreign investment, several participants noted the risks and incentives for corruption that arise in the PNG context:

> The development model we currently pursue is based on capitalism and it is totally contrary to the culture of Papua New Guineans . . . the companies and the government too is taking advantage of this. A lot of government departments are pushing things through and working for the company more than the interests of the country.[34]

Lawrence Stephens, of TI PNG, provided details of corruption in the logging sector in PNG, and the issuing of short term agriculture and business leases. This is an issue that resulted in a Commission of Inquiry:[35]

> Rimbunan Hijau is a logging company from Malaysia that also owns business interests, the Vision City Mall here in Waigani and also the National newspaper. In PNG 97% of the land is traditionally owned but there are ways around this . . . the laws were changed so that the land owner group was able to register the land and lease it for special purposes business agriculture and development . . . what happened is that people with particular interests became involved and 10% of PNG land was covered by these leases in a way that did not comply with the rules in which they were issued . . . It was clearly a case of commercial logging interest. Promises are made to land owners to get them to commit the land and then they do not follow through. They promise roads that last until the timber is gone . . . Many of the companies get very wealthy and it becomes apparent that legislation and politics are done not in government but behind closed doors with private groups involved.[36]

More generally, the participant noted one risk resulting from external perceptions of corruption and the kind of investment likely to be attracted:

> Investors whose home governments regulate better will be less inclined to invest and we will end up with investors that are less inclined to conform . . . We keep having trade groups coming in from places like Australia and New Zealand. I don't notice much investment coming from those directions. I do see a large level of engagement from generally Asian countries in forestry here, and a large level of investment by Asian companies in oil and gas.[37]

An employee with the National Fraud and Anti-Corruption Directorate, a branch of the Royal PNG Constabulary, noted the role played by increases in financial capital and investment in the country generally:

> Corruption, in the last 10–15 years has grown from what it used to be. Going back some years . . . soon after independence, at the time I joined the police . . . We never had any problem with corruption. But late 80s early 90s we started seeing some evidence of corruption and since then it has gone beyond our imaginations . . . Now we have a lot of money in the country from natural gas, and when we have a lot of money we are going to have more corruption because the incentive is there.[38]

National and regional challenges were the subject of extensive concern for interview participants. However, some regime risk factors were also identified, based on participants' domestic and regional experiences. Interview participants provided unique perspectives on how such regime risk factors might be addressed. Significantly, these risks were generally perceived more as standard challenges to be reckoned with, rather than fundamental flaws in the existing anti-corruption approach, domestically or transnationally.

Awareness of the challenges faced in combatting corruption, combined with the apparently weak coercive influence of UNCAC, limits the relevance of much of the traditional critique of UNCAC and the global anti-corruption regime. However, as will be explored in the following section, domestic and regional approaches to corruption highlight areas where UNCAC could be more effectively engaged.

If UNCAC can be utilised by civil society within the domestic and regional context, and if its positive potential to assist national and regional efforts through technical and financial assistance is mobilised, UNCAC may strengthen its influence and contribute to enhancing anti-corruption outcomes. This type of engagement may assist in overcoming the challenges of deviant actors and non-compliant states noted by Nadelmann and Andreas and may provide a partial solution to the risks of inapplicability related to domestic irrelevance and limited resources and capacity. Through engagement with UNCAC, actors in PNG and regionally may be able to shape the application of the Convention in a way that is contextually relevant, while also ensuring some action is taken in line with international commitments. If such engagement remains limited, inapplicability is likely to remain as a substantial challenge. The possibility of effective implementation and enforcement of UNCAC will thus be limited in PNG. This, in turn, will limit the ultimate success of the global anti-corruption regime. The possible role of UNCAC in supporting domestic anti-corruption efforts in PNG is explored further below.

Domestic approaches to anti-corruption in Papua New Guinea – is there a place for UNCAC?

The legal framework in PNG was considered by participants to be sufficient to combat corruption.[39] Attempts to enhance or expand the existing legal framework through further legislation or policy were not widely supported by government officials and others involved in the implementation and enforcement of anti-corruption efforts domestically. This general view can be summarised in relation to concerns surrounding the development of an Independent Commission against Corruption (ICAC) in PNG.

The establishment of a PNG ICAC was mostly viewed in a positive light by interview participants. The point was made that if the ICAC was established in an appropriate manner and was properly resourced with human and financial capital, the development would be beneficial.[40] Mr Asa of the NEC highlighted the rationale behind a PNG ICAC:

> We have beautiful systems and procedures in place; it's us that don't make them work . . . So putting ICAC in place means something to specifically focus on making the systems work and combatting corruption.[41]

However, concerns were raised regarding the extent of ICAC's powers and the risks of developing further anti-corruption legislation in relation to the institution. Fears about the creation of 'another white elephant'[42] were noted. One commentator stated that: 'I am supportive of an ICAC, but I am equally of the view that if they don't do it properly it will never work.'[43] Sam Koim, then director of Task Force Sweep, noted:

> We have to identify inter-agency territorial conflict and the correct space for interagency cooperation . . . we are trying to create ICAC but it is not the solution, it is one of the solutions and a lot of other agencies must also be in play.[44]

He continued, explaining:

> There is some appetite to include in the structure [of ICAC] an offense of corruption . . . but corruption itself cannot be exhausted and defined . . . if they try to define corruption they will end up taking the crime already under the criminal code, some of the are already under the leadership code . . . this is the problem that they will have where conflict will occur . . . when there is overlap, you bring the various organisations to conflict.[45]

The issue of over-criminalisation and conflicting domestic laws reflects concerns of states during negotiation of UNCAC, as discussed in Chapter 2.

Additional dimensions of overlapping organisational purview and competition for case leadership and resource allocation are important in the context of PNG. The head of the AFP TNCU in PNG notes that one of the biggest challenges faced in the context of his work is ensuring that various institutions work together:

> What they have to do is get over this hurdle of not sharing information . . . they don't understand that if they share it out they would be much more powerful. They need to share it amongst themselves and share it regionally.[46]

Another interesting dimension of this issue is the relationship between the Leadership Code and the *Criminal Code Act* in PNG. A member of the EFF sums up the conflict:

> You have prosecutions now under the Leadership Code . . . The only penalties they get are they lose office, or they are suspended from duties, which is not effective punishment. There is this separation between the leaders and the common people. The common people are prosecuted under the Criminal Code and leaders get away under the Leadership Code . . . the mechanisms are available. We need to, as a government, invest in these mechanisms and get them up and running . . . The police say they don't have the capacity, but it's a matter of building up the capacity. You have a Fraud and Anti-Corruption unit, so build it up.[47]

Aside from the technical overlap and institutional challenges introduced above, a variety of other domestic factors were raised as obstacles to effective implementation and enforcement of the existing anti-corruption framework. These included inconsistent political will, resource and capacity limitations, cultural challenges, lack of education, apathy, limited government accountability, and insufficient access to necessary goods and services. Figure 5.2 illustrates the prevalence of views on each of these domestic risk factors, which affect the success of anti-corruption and impede ability to implement and enforce the existing legal framework.

Lack of political will was referenced by most participants as a limiting factor for anti-corruption efforts, and a contributor to continued corrupt activity. Greed was noted specifically by actors from PNG, while apathy and a lack of education were highlighted by most participants. Interestingly, participants from PNG saw limited accountability as more of an issue than lack of education. Finally, references to culture were primarily made by participants from PNG, and those outside of the UN.

Ideas to combat these domestic risk factors included information sharing and cross-agency cooperation, enhanced auditing systems to enforce administrative frameworks, adjustments to government structure to increase political accountability, and educational initiatives. Education initiatives were suggested to target

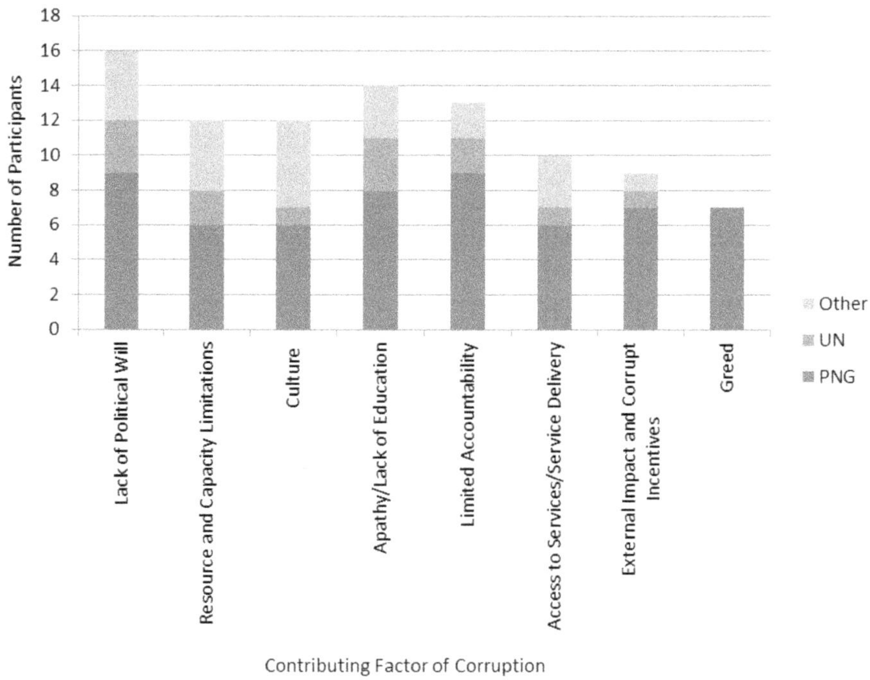

Figure 5.2 Factors contributing to corruption and hampering anti-corruption

the general public, as well as specific public sectors and anti-corruption agencies. Additionally, some targeted legal measures were suggested, such as the adoption of whistleblower protection law, access to information legislation, and a means test for unjust enrichment.

The desire to engage in a multifaceted anti-corruption approach is a positive dimension of the PNG context. Such an approach is also supported by UNCAC. As discussed in Chapter 2, UNCAC has considerable scope, covering a range of measures beyond criminal law and enforcement. Many optional provisions of UNCAC align with ideas raised by the actors engaged in PNG and the South Pacific region. The similarities between the approach promoted domestically by interview participants and the approach of UNCAC and the global anti-corruption regime are explored in more detail in Chapter 6.

Engagement with UNCAC in Papua New Guinea: missed opportunity?

Knowledge of UNCAC and its provisions was limited in PNG. The Department of Justice and Attorney-General and the NEC had some understanding of the Convention, developed through engagement in the Implementation Review process. Other actors had limited awareness of UNCAC and its relevance in PNG.

The following is a question and response from the Director of the NEC in PNG:

> Q: What do you see as the primary purpose of the Convention?
>
> A: Good governance. We are really into this.[48]

Most of the actors involved in the initial process of UNCAC signature and ratification were no longer working in PNG at the time the research was conducted. The exception was a high level official within the Office of the Public Prosecutor (OPP), who had been involved in early stages of UN engagement in the South Pacific. His response to the above question about the purpose of UNCAC was: 'Basically, to combat corruption, short answer. To put in place everything that is necessary to combat corruption.'[49]

The purpose of UNCAC was seen from a very practical perspective by those in PNG. Another interesting aspect of PNG government involvement with UNCAC was the perceived irrelevance of PNG's lack of involvement in the negotiation phase. A member of the Department of Justice and Attorney-General stated: 'Basically, it [UNCAC] is relevant to PNG. I don't think there would be anything to negotiate on.'[50] Mr Asa added that: 'There are checks and balances in our system, you don't just go off and sign a convention.'[51] However, he could not expand on the process leading up to signature, as he was not involved with the PNG government at that time.

Several transnational and regional actors commented that the South Pacific region is generally under-represented in multilateral legal negotiations.[52] However, from a different perspective, UNDP Official Ms Rodrigues stated:

> . . . at the end of the day a lot of the countries involved in negotiation water it down and then don't sign. They negotiate and then don't ratify . . . I am much more understanding of conventions as a goal or guiding document . . . institutions are just people and people need to change their behaviour and that is very difficult. Corruption is about getting people to understand behaviour.[53]

The pertinent point here is that involvement in the negotiation process may not necessarily lead to a document that reflects the values and interests held by that actor or the state they represent. However, if the final document is sufficiently broad and flexible, it may be used as a framework, which can be expanded based on the unique context in which it must operate.

Aside from TI PNG, NGO actors and civil society participants from PNG were not aware of the substance of UNCAC. This lack of awareness was common, even when the participant was active on anti-corruption issues and engaged with other transnational NGOs and international legal mechanisms. The primacy of domestic anti-corruption concerns may help to explain limited awareness of UNCAC within civil society and NGO actors in PNG. Lack of engagement with UNCAC may be a missed opportunity, both for the successful implementation and enforcement of UNCAC and for those actors seeking to motivate domestic change and combat corruption domestically. On this point, Paul Barker of the Institute of National Affairs pointed out that international agencies seeking domestic civil society insight need to look beyond a single catchall organisation:

> Q: When a United Nations Branch seeks to discuss UNCAC, what aspects are they trying to engage with you on?
>
> A: They sometimes have a focus that INA [Institute of National Affairs][54] is the go to civil society voice . . . we certainly don't want to be seen as representative of everyone else. We can pass on messages and views but we cannot be the civil society box that these organisations tick.[55]

Expanding the level of domestic engagement with UNCAC has the potential to broaden and deepen domestic understandings and, importantly, also enhance the understandings of the international community, regarding the application of this framework in the domestic contexts in which it must operate.

A number of actors emphasised the importance of public perception and the image politicians seek to project, both domestically and internationally.[56] The head of the AFP TNCU in PNG made the following statement:

> I think a lot of the legislation they put in place there [in PNG] is for the UN, to look like they are doing the right thing, so they can be seen to be doing the right thing on the public stage.[57]

This desire to be seen to be 'doing the right thing' was raised in a number of discussions. This behaviour was referred to as 'smoke and mirrors' by the head of the AFP TNCU. Another participant noted that legislative change or institutional development, in line with international 'best practice', could be a means to distract from continued corrupt behaviour.[58] Acknowledging these issues, civil society and NGO engagement with UNCAC may be one way to utilise this political interest productively, enhancing tangible action on corruption in compliance with obligations under UNCAC. If domestic civil society groups are informed about and engage with the UNCAC framework, they will have greater potential to hold governments to account for failures to comply and give effect to their international commitments. This would in turn enhance the value of UNCAC by limiting its use as a 'smoke screen' for continued inaction.

The interviews did not reveal any stigma against utilising UNCAC. However, proposed solutions to domestic corruption were generally presented in terms of domestic action and the importance of domestic ownership. Participants emphasised the importance of national and local solutions that reflected the need to make internal changes in response to the specific challenges and cases of corruption occurring domestically. Participants did not view corruption as an activity that could be solved by external intervention. Despite this, many of the approaches and suggestions put forward by participants aligned with those found in UNCAC. For example, education measures and enhanced accountability frameworks, as well as freedom of information, unjust enrichment and whistleblower protection laws are encompassed by UNCAC.[59] These points of convergence between domestic approaches and the approach of UNCAC are expanded upon in Chapter 6.

Government actors in particular, were inclined to focus on the domestic efforts and home grown nature of the anti-corruption framework in PNG:

> . . . we are focused on our situation. How can we make things work, how can we get services to our rural communities. Almost 90% live in a rural community. Our basic approach is from the perspective. How can we improve circumstances; schools, roads, hospitals, participation in business, in the economy? That is where we sit and where we want to go.[60]

Transnational and regional actors were also keen to emphasise that domestic political will and ownership are key to the success of anti-corruption efforts. Ms Rodrigues of the UNDP discusses her involvement with the development of the PNG anti-corruption framework, following UNCAC ratification:

> There was no question about the importance of tackling corruption in PNG. They came to me . . . Governance programming is special . . . It is possible to extend the time frame to achieve goals . . . With a flexible time frame it is possible to build a relationship of trust and mutual support and also allows countries to adopt policies they are ready for and are willing to take ownership of . . . PNG is a great example of genuine local ownership in terms of an anti-corruption framework.[61]

In cases where actors were aware of or had engaged with UNCAC, the idea of the Convention as a framework for action, rather than an obligatory tool, was popular among both the transnational and regional development practitioners and government actors in PNG. This is illustrative of the limited coercive power of UNCAC, mentioned earlier.

Findings from interviews illustrate that membership of UNCAC is not a coercive obligation in and of itself. Government actors see UNCAC as an opportunity to promote a positive image of their commitment to anti-corruption. This reality limits the possible harms that may result from enforcement of measures ill-suited to a particular domestic context, however, it also presents a challenge for securing efficient implementation and enforcement domestically. This challenge is furthered by limited awareness of and engagement with among civil society actors and NGOs in PNG. Lack of awareness and engagement may present an avenue for enhancing UNCAC's influence domestically and, if utilised effectively, may enhance the relevance and potential success of the global anti-corruption regime.

Other transnational dynamics

As well as illustrating UNCAC's limited influence and the possibilities for enhanced interaction between domestic and regional efforts and the UNCAC framework, interview participants provided unique perspectives on the dynamic nature of transnational influence, including the role of foreign corporations and foreign legal representatives.

A member of the EFF noted that corporations often become the law in remote areas.[62] When isolation and limited education combine with the failure of government to provide public services and basic infrastructure, corporations can manipulate communities for their own financial benefit. This situation reflects the criminogenic potential of power asymmetries discussed by Passas.[63] Such imbalances can make contracts in PNG profitable, which may motivate corporate actors to bribe and collude with government officials to secure profitable resource extraction opportunities. Asymmetries can even result in civil conflict, as was the case with the conflict in Bougainville from 1988 to 1998.[64]

Foreign legal representatives are another type of transnational actor viewed critically in the PNG context. Several commentators noted that PNG is an extremely litigious society.[65] Government officials and wealthy individuals are able to call on foreign legal specialists to defend their cases in court. The expertise of these actors often results in skewed outcomes when the prosecution lacks necessary resources, capacity, expertise, and experience. Mr Wilson of the AFP TNCU points out this inequality:

> What you have now is that the crooks up there [in PNG] are using Australian lawyers to fight the case and they are using local prosecutors who are not up to the same speed.[66]

Foreign advisors have been put in place to assist the OPP in PNG. However, these advisors cannot actively participate in court proceedings. Despite this, 'the defence can have an expat stand up and be the mouth piece' for their case.[67]

In Chapters 3 and 4, the potentially dominating influence of large, ex-colonial, states in the region was highlighted as a risk factor for countries like PNG trying to develop a domestically relevant anti-corruption framework. In the case of the establishment of the *Proceeds of Crime Act 2005* (*PCA*) and Financial Intelligence Unit (FIU) in PNG, this influence was substantial. Despite external influence, the development of the *PCA* and FIU was viewed positively by practitioners in PNG. The FIU appears to have been well resourced and adapted to the national context.

The power of international and domestic perceptions in motivating action on corruption was discussed earlier. In the PNG context, international influence is definitely relevant, but the value of this influence compared to the related risks is difficult to evaluate with certainty. Often, actors in PNG have engaged in some way with foreign actors and institutions as part of their anti-corruption efforts. As discussed in Chapter 1, this supports the five-stage model of regime evolution, emphasising the role played by values and interests from domestic, regional, and international spheres. However, in the context of PNG, there are limitations to the power of external state pressure. In certain cases, the limitations of foreign state influence were highlighted as a contributing to continued corruption. This is a cause for serious concern, especially considering the corrupt incentives provided by foreign aid, which is often tied to donor desire to preserve economic interests.

Effrey Dademo, of ActNow! PNG states:

> In terms of how the international community can combat corruption in the country, I think that something should be done about . . . the fact that there is aid money coming in and those moneys are being used by people who have access to it without it trickling down to the people it is supposed to reach.[68]

When discussing the reason why aid was not always tied to the anti-corruption agenda, the challenges of balancing politics with governance were noted by several actors. In the context of the Australian Aid Program (AusAid) and the role of the Department of Foreign Affairs and Trade (DFAT), one interview participant noted:

> We do expressly engage with corruption, but particularly with PNG, we're just very cautious about it. Given public discourse about senior individuals, there's a degree of nervousness. The AusAid DFAT structural change will impact on this as well. DFAT's role is a diplomatic one and talking about this stuff doesn't make friends.[69]

Sam Koim, then director of Task Force Sweep, was very pragmatic about the issue:

> Some countries although corruption is a real worry, there are other strategy considerations that they give higher priority than fighting corruption in PNG . . . So it is hard to strike a balance.[70]

When asked to expand on the interests that may override anti-corruption, Mr Koim stated 'it depends on which country you are looking at'.[71] Generally, security and economic interests were viewed as primary concerns.

Paul Barker, of the Institute of National Affairs (INA) in PNG, noted a reversal of power in the negotiation around the Manus Island Regional Processing Centre. Prime Minister O'Neill negotiated with Australia on a deal that Australia was very keen to secure. Once secured, this deal provided the Prime Minister with 'useful leverage . . . the Australian government couldn't criticise him on corruption or anything else'.[72] It is noteworthy that there have been no formal investigations or prosecutions in Australia, of Australian nationals or corporations for charges of corruption, money-laundering, or bribery engaged in PNG, despite evidence of such activities.[73] Whether this lack of action is due to diplomacy, the low priority of such issues for the Australian government, or a lack of substantial evidence, is difficult to assert.

Relating to the issue of diplomatic limitations, multilateral organisations have the potential to neutralise political challenges, including diplomatic limits faced in bilateral interactions. Tony Prescott of the UNDP notes the following:

> Donors are always very mindful of their reputations working in partner countries. Anti-corruption is so politically sensitive . . . That's where organisations like the United Nations, because of their impartiality, can work in spaces that bilateral donors can't.[74]

The dynamic interaction between international, regional, and domestic actors may provide innovative solutions to anti-corruption challenges. The impact of such dynamic interactions is explored in greater depth in Chapter 6.

Preliminary summary and implications

Introductory findings from interviews and fieldwork in PNG suggest that criticisms of UNCAC and the global anti-corruption regime overstate its coercive power and influence, especially in the context of the South Pacific region and particularly in PNG. Criticisms fail to acknowledge the complex power dynamics that exist in the South Pacific region and in PNG. Domestic interests often 'trump' transnational concerns and bilateral politics may limit the capacity of foreign nations to engage with issues of corruption. However, some risk factors raised by critics are still relevant in the PNG context. In many ways, these risk factors are not regime specific, but reflect the challenges of combatting corruption more generally.

Diverse understandings of corruption, extensive focus on criminal law and enforcement efforts, and links to other forms of crime all reflect domestic challenges. Domestic challenges include: limited resources, isolated access to public goods and services, and diverse cultural practices. It is encouraging that, in this context, interview participants presented innovative possibilities for promoting anti-corruption objectives. Many of these approaches, while not directly related to UNCAC, provide opportunities for greater engagement with the global anti-corruption regime and suggest possibilities for enhancing UNCAC's relevance in PNG, and regionally. This is an important finding, as limited domestic influence of UNCAC in *States Parties* is a significant concern for the regime. Without domestic implementation and enforcement, it is not possible to reach the fifth and final stage of evolution.[75]

Fieldwork and interviews illustrate several key points, including the importance of domestic political will in the enforcement of anti-corruption law and policy, the strong role played by external interest actors through their influence on public perceptions, the subsequent impact of such perceptions, and the challenges of balancing limited resources and capacity with a diverse range of issues and challenges arising in all geographic spheres. Preliminary analysis suggests that critical views of UNCAC and the global anti-corruption regime may misunderstand the role of UNCAC and over-emphasise its rigidity. It appears the limited coercive influence of UNCAC allows for state actors to draw on the wide range of mandatory and optional measures within the Convention, in a manner that is applicable to the values, interests, and challenges that exist domestically. This finding calls into question the actuality of several regime risk factors, including co-optation of the regime for unrelated political agendas, misuse of resources to implement and enforce laws that are ill-suited to domestic context, and the potential erosion of legal norms (including the rule of law and human rights), in the name of reducing corruption.

Interview participants generally viewed UNCAC as complementary and supportive of their endeavours, rather than being a strict set of legal obligations enforced vertically from the international sphere down to the local level. Participants understood UNCAC as a broad framework that could be drawn on in domestic and regional anti-corruption endeavours. Most participants regarded membership of UNCAC as a tool to assist key actors, especially governments, in promoting a positive public image regarding anti-corruption efforts. This view illustrates the supporting role and flexibility of the UNCAC framework. However, it also presents the risk that membership of UNCAC may be misused as 'smoke and mirrors', promoting an external image of anti-corruption as high on the political agenda, while masking a lack of political will to implement and enforce anti-corruption policies domestically. This risk of misuse is not unique to UNCAC, however, it could be a substantial obstacle to reductions in the target activity globally, delegitimising the regime and its legal tools, and preventing a shift to the fifth and final stage of evolution.[76]

Extensive implementation and enforcement of UNCAC cannot occur if membership is used as a tool for positive public perceptions of government, rather than a tool to support anti-corruption objectives. Even if political will exists, lack of capacity can present limitations for successful implementation and enforcement of UNCAC, both regionally and in PNG. Again, this is not a challenge unique to UNCAC. Capacity limitations are a general challenge for implementation and enforcement of any legal framework. These challenges are especially relevant in less developed and developing countries.

In PNG, implementation and enforcement of a wide range of anti-corruption laws and policies were hampered by limited financial and human resources. Such tangible challenges have the potential to prevent effective implementation and enforcement of UNCAC, presenting a hurdle for successful achievement of the final stage of regime evolution. The above challenges are even more likely to hamper in contexts where other domestic concerns, such as economic development or specific health and education goals, are given higher priority than those of the global prohibition regime.

Limited resources and capacity are not insurmountable barriers to the success of UNCAC. In fact, UNCAC may be able to support and build increased interest in and capacity for combatting corruption. For example, some interview participants within the PNG government mentioned opportunities provided by UNCAC for assistance and education on technical matters related to implementation and enforcement. These opportunities appear to be underutilised at present. Interview responses regarding the specifics of UNCAC illustrate that understanding was extremely limited, especially amongst actors not directly involved with the Implementation Review process. There was also a lack of continuity between government actors involved in the early stages of negotiation and ratification of UNCAC and those responsible for its implementation and enforcement.

Transnational actors including corporations, NGOs, and multilateral lenders were active in promoting their interests in PNG. These actors appear to have a significant, though varied, impact on corrupt incentives and the nature of anti-corruption efforts. For example, the profit-based interests of multinational corporations in PNG provide incentives for corrupt behaviour on the part of government actors, who seek contracts from these organisations despite popular disapproval for the proposed activities. Additionally, influential states, multilateral lending institutions, intergovernmental groups, and NGO and civil society actors, all have varying degrees of domestic influence. Either explicitly or implicitly, these actors can influence perceptions of corruption, approaches to combatting corruption, and opportunities for corrupt activities in PNG.

These findings are expanded and further analysed in Chapter 6, providing answers to the second and third research questions, introduced in Chapter 1:

2 What impact has UNCAC had on PNG's approach to combatting corruption?
3 Does PNG's experience with implementation and enforcement of UNCAC justify existing criticisms of this multilateral legal instrument and the emergent global anti-corruption regime?

Chapter 7 draws on the PNG case study, to suggest potential future directions for UNCAC, the global anti-corruption regime, and regional and national approaches to engagement with this regime. These suggestions will address the fourth and final research question:

4 What insights does the PNG case study provide in terms of potential improvements to UNCAC and approaches to the Convention, with the goal of securing the final stage of evolution for the global anti-corruption regime?

Chapter 7 also discusses possibilities for continued research and exploration, to further develop understanding of the global anti-corruption regime.

Notes

1 A complete list of interview participants and their institutional affiliations at the time the research was conducted is available in Annex E
2 Vlassis [Transcript No.1]
3 Asa [Transcript No. 10]
4 [Transcript No.15] Anonymity requested. Office of the Public Prosecutor PNG (OPP PNG)
5 [Transcript No.16] Anonymity requested. AusAID Senior Official
6 See Chapter 1: Criticisms of UNCAC and the global anti-corruption regime
7 [Transcript No.9] Anonymity Requested. Attorney General's Department PNG, Legal Policy and Governance Branch (AG Department)
8 ibid..
9 ibid.
10 Rodrigues [Transcript No. 2]
11 See Chapter 1: Criticisms of UNCAC and the global anti-corruption regime

12 [Transcript No. 15] Individual Anonymity requested. OPP PNG.
13 [Transcript No. 7] Anonymity requested. Royal PNG Constabulary; Stephens [Transcript No.8]
14 [Transcript No. 12] Anonymity requested. PNG Eco Forestry Forum (EFF PNG).
15 See Chapter 1: Criticisms of UNCAC and the global anti-corruption regime. In particular, see Williams JW and Beare ME, 'The Business of Bribery: Globalization, economic liberalization, and the "problem" of corruption', in Beare ME (Ed), *Critical Reflections on Transnational Organized Crime, Money Laundering, and Corruption* (University of Toronto Press, 1st Edition, 2003) 88
16 above n14; Wonders N, 'Globalization, Border Reconstruction Projects, and Transnational Crime' 34(2) *Social Justice* (2007) 33
17 Reed Q, 'Squeezing a Balloon? Challenging the nexus between organised crime and corruption' 7 *CMI U4 Issue* (2009); Snider TR and Kidane W, 'Combating Corruption Through International Law in Africa: A Comparative Analysis' 40 *Cornell Int'l L.J.* (2007) 691; Beare ME, 'Corruption and Organised Crime: Lessons from History' 28 *Crime, Law and Social Change* (1997) 155
18 Barker [Transcript No. 13]
19 Stephens [Transcript No.8]
20 The NEC is the executive branch of the PNG government made up of the Prime Minister and Cabinet Ministers
21 Asa [Transcript No.10]
22 [Transcript No.9] AG Department
23 [Transcript No. 7] Anonymity requested. Royal PNG Constabulary
24 Vlassis [Transcript No.1]
25 [Transcript No.9] AG Department
26 Asa [Transcript No.10]
27 Rodrigues [Transcript No.2]
28 Stephens [Transcript No.8]
29 [Transcript No. 12] Anonymity Requested. EFF PNG
30 [Transcript No.15] Anonymity Requested. OPP PNG
31 Vlassis [Transcript No.1]; Stephens [Transcript No.8]; [Transcript No.9] Anonymity Requested. AG Department; Asa [Transcript No.10]; [Transcript No.12] Anonymity Request. Eco Forestry Forum PNG (EFF PNG); Wilson [Transcript No.14]; [Transcript No. 7] Anonymity requested. Royal PNG Constabulary; [Transcript No.15] Anonymity Requested. OPP PNG
32 Such suggestions came from participants in both PNG law enforcement and Australian law enforcement with experience in PNG. Wilson [Transcript No.14]; [Transcript No. 7] Anonymity requested. Royal PNG Constabulary
33 Wilson [Transcript No. 14]
34 [Transcript No.12] Anonymity Requested. Eco Forestry Forum PNG (EFF)
35 Papua New Guinea, Mirou, *Commission of Inquiry into Special Agriculture and Business Leases (SABL): Report* (June, 2013) ('SABL Report 2013')
36 Stephens [Transcript No.8]
37 ibid.
38 [Transcript No. 7] Anonymity requested. Royal PNG Constabulary
39 Ten of the 17 respondents were questioned specifically on the sufficiency of PNG's legal framework
40 Dademo [Transcript No.3]; Prescott [Transcript No.4]; Koim [Transcript No. 6]; [Transcript No. 7] Anonymity requested. Royal PNG Constabulary; Stephens [Transcript No.8]
41 Asa [Transcript No.10]
42 ibid.
43 Prescott [Transcript No.4]
44 Koim [Transcript No.6]

45 ibid
46 Wilson [Transcript No.14]
47 [Transcript No.12] Anonymity Request. Eco Forestry Forum PNG (EFF PNG)
48 [Transcript No.9] AG Department
49 [Transcript No.15] Individual Anonymity Requested. OPP PNG
50 [Transcript No.9] AG Department
51 Asa [Transcript No. 10]
52 Prescott [Transcript No.4]; Wilson [Transcript No.14]
53 Rodrigues [Transcript No.2]
54 The INA is a 'privately funded non-profit policy research institute' founded in 1976. For more information see PNG Institute of National Affairs, *About Us* (2015) available at: http://www.inapng.com/# (last visited 1 March 2018)
55 Barker [Transcript No.13]
56 Koim [Transcript No.6]; Stephens [Transcript No.8]; [Transcript No.12] Anonymity Request. Eco Forestry Forum PNG (EFF)
57 Wilson [Transcript No.14]
58 Dademo [Transcript No.3]; Wilson [Transcript No.14]; [Transcript No.15] Anonymity Requested. PNG OPP
59 Note in particular Articles 7, 9, 10, 13, 20, 32 and 33
60 Asa [Transcript No.10]
61 Rodrigues [Transcript No. 2]
62 [Transcript No.12] Anonymity Request. Eco Forestry Forum PNG (EFF PNG)
63 Passas N, 'Globalization and Transnational Crime: Effects of Criminogenic Asymmetries', in Williams P and Vlassis D (eds), *Combatting Transnational Crime: Concepts, Activities and Responses* (Frank Cass Publishers, 2013) 22
64 See Lasslett K, *State Crime: On the margins of empire, Rio Tinto, the war on Bouganville, and resistance to mining* (Pluto Press, 1st Edition, 2014) for an in depth exploration
65 Dademo [Transcript No.3]; Wilson [Transcript No.14]
66 Wilson [Transcript No.14]
67 ibid
68 Dademo [Transcript No.3]
69 [Transcript No.5] Anonymity requested. Australian Law Enforcement Agency with Experience in PNG
70 Koim [Transcript No.6]
71 ibid
72 Barker [Transcript No.13]
73 see for example Global Witness briefing on Brisbane based lawyers who discuss on camera the specifics of laundering corrupt money out of PNG, available at: https://www.globalwitness.org/en/campaigns/corruption-and-money-laundering/png-lawyers/ (last visited 1 March 2018)
74 Prescott [Transcript No.4]
75 Nadelmann EA and Andreas P, *Policing the Globe: Criminalization and crime control in international relations* (Oxford University Press, 1st Edition, 2006)
76 See Chapter 1: The global anti-corruption regime for a full discussion of the five-stage model

References

Beare ME, 'Corruption and Organised Crime: Lessons from History' 28 *Crime, Law and Social Change* (1997) 155.

Global Witness, *Briefing: corruption and money laundering PNG*, available at: https://www.globalwitness.org/en/campaigns/corruption-and-money-laundering/png-lawyers/ (last visited 1 March 2018).

Lasslett K, *State Crime: On the margins of empire, Rio Tinto, the war on Bougainville and resistance to mining* (Pluto Press, 1st Edition, 2014).

Nadelmann EA and Andreas P, *Policing the Globe: Criminalization and crime control in international relations* (Oxford University Press, 1st Edition, 2006).

Papua New Guinea, Mirou, *Commission of Inquiry into Special Agriculture and Business Leases (SABL): Report* (June, 2013) ('SABL Report 2013').

Passas N, 'Globalization and Transnational Crime: Effects of criminogenic asymmetries', in Williams P and Vlassis D (Eds), *Combatting Transnational Crime: Concepts, Activities and Responses* (Frank Cass Publishers, 2013) 22.

PNG Institute of National Affairs, *About Us* (2015) available at: http://www.inapng.com/pages.php?pid=94 (last visited 1 March 2018).

Reed Q, 'Squeezing a Balloon? Challenging the nexus between organised crime and corruption' 7 *CMI U4 Issue* (2009).

Snider KR and Kidane W, 'Combating Corruption Through International Law in Africa: A comparative analysis' 40 *Cornell Int'l L.J.* (2007) 691.

Williams JW and Beare ME, 'The Business of Bribery: Globalization, economic liberalization, and the "problem" of corruption', in Beare ME (ed), *Critical Reflections on Transnational Organized Crime, Money Laundering, and Corruption* (University of Toronto Press, 1st Edition, 2003) 88.

Wonders N, 'Globalization, Border Reconstruction Projects, and Transnational Crime' 34(2) *Social Justice* (2007) 33.

6 Seeking answers – understanding the United Nations Convention against Corruption and its role in Papua New Guinea

Introduction

This chapter expands on the findings and analysis presented in Chapter 5. It utilises the theoretical framework established in Chapter 1 to synthesise insights from the fieldwork with key points developed in earlier chapters. This chapter provides answers to the second and third research questions, presented in Chapter 1. Chapter 7 further expands analysis and answers the fourth and final research question. Chapter 7 also presents possibilities for increasing the domestic relevance of the United Nations Convention against Corruption (UNCAC), advancing the global anti-corruption regime, and improving regional and national approaches to engaging with this regime.

The primary goal of this book has been to understand why extensive ratification and implementation of UNCAC has so far failed substantially to reduce instances of corrupt activity in *States Parties.* Four key research questions were presented in Chapter 1.

First, how has UNCAC evolved within the global anti-corruption regime? This question was answered in Chapter 2. Essentially, UNCAC is the primary tool of the global anti-corruption regime, and represented the evolution of the regime to the fourth stage. The second question involves the impact UNCAC has had on Papua New Guinea's approach to combatting corruption. Chapter 5 provided some perspective on this question. To answer it in full, this chapter will link findings from Chapter 5 with those of Chapters 3 and 4, within the theoretical framework established at the outset of this thesis.

Third, does the Papua New Guinea (PNG) case support existing critique of UNCAC and the global anti-corruption regime? Answering this question is an essential goal for this chapter. If existing criticisms appear accurate in the case of PNG, possibilities for the future should be based upon such findings, combined with further expansive research. However, if criticisms do not appear accurate, alternative hypotheses will be necessary to explain the continued failure of UNCAC and the global anti-corruption regime. Once these three questions have been answered in their entirety, Chapter 7 will focus on suggestions for the future.

The fourth and final research question will be left to Chapter 7: what insights does the PNG case study provide in terms of potential improvements to UNCAC and its implementation and enforcement, with the goal of securing the final stage of evolution for the global anti-corruption regime?

What impact has UNCAC had on Papua New Guinea's approach to combatting corruption?

Key findings

In seeking to understand the impact, if any, UNCAC has had on PNG's approach to combatting corruption a number of key insights from earlier chapters are relevant. These are:

1 Participation in the negotiation of UNCAC involved a range of states from diverse regions. However, PNG and the South Pacific region more generally were not strongly represented (Chapter 2).
2 UNCAC has played a supporting, rather than leading, role in PNG's anti-corruption efforts (Chapter 2).
3 PNG's criminal code has included provisions equivalent to those of UNCAC since before the country gained independence, predating UNCAC negotiations by 30 years. This is also true of many other South Pacific nations (Chapters 3 and 4).
4 Additional criminal law provisions promoted by UNCAC have been implemented in PNG, for example the recent addition of the *Proceeds of Crime Act 2005* ('*POCA*').[1] Despite this, enforcement remains a constant challenge (Chapters 4 and 5).
5 Understanding of UNCAC's provisions is limited in PNG beyond engagement by certain government officials involved in the Implementation Review process (Chapter 5).
6 UNCAC is primarily viewed as a framework that reflects domestic anti-corruption priorities set by the government (Chapter 5).

When these findings are synthesised with reference to the interaction of key actors, values, and interests, the following conclusions can be drawn:

1 The direct impact of UNCAC on domestic anti-corruption efforts is limited.
2 A primary motivator for UNCAC engagement domestically is supporting positive public perceptions at the national, regional, and transnational levels.
3 The importance of public perception means that UNCAC's potential impact on domestic law and policy may be a result of attempts by domestic and external actors to promote compliance and to support both value and interest-based agendas, rather than being the direct result of *States Parties*' rights and obligations established by the Convention.
4 The Implementation Review Mechanism allows for communication between the domestic and transnational spheres in which UNCAC operates and may be a mechanism for facilitating more productive engagement and impact.

Each of these statements is expanded upon and justified in the following sections, drawing on theoretical concepts and findings identified and developed in preceding chapters.

Placing UNCAC within the theoretical framework of transnational law

Chapter 1 outlined the theoretical framework for this thesis based on the work of transnational legal scholars, emphasising Nadelmann and Andreas' work on the evolution of global prohibition regimes. This framework was supplemented by the work of Passas, Abbott and Snidal, Boister, Koh, Twining, and Zumbansen.[2] Each of these theorists builds on the concept of transnational law, not as a globally enforceable doctrine, but as a dynamic normative process occurring across transnational, regional, and domestic spheres and involving diverse actors.

Nadelmann and Andreas establish the concept of 'global prohibition regimes', which represent the substance and process of enforcing norms that prohibit state and non-state actors from engaging in a targeted activity.[3] This book has documented the evolution of the global anti-corruption regime, building on this concept. The global anti-corruption regime has reached the fourth stage of norm evolution, but is struggling to achieve the fifth and final stage. Nadelmann and Andreas note a range of challenges that must be overcome, for the final stage to be achieved. These include: political will, deviant actors, the sustaining influence of prohibitionist arguments, technological developments, the nature of the target activity, and the activity's susceptibility to criminal law and enforcement measures.[4]

Nadelmann and Andreas point to the role of 'moral entrepreneurs' in catalysing and developing any global prohibition regime. Moral entrepreneurs are actors who 'redefine the activity as a problem and as evil'.[5] With regard to corruption, this book has shown that, in the early stages of norm evolution, relevant actors included members of the US business community, concerned with competitiveness in the global market following the enactment of the *FCPA*, as well as individuals from multilateral institutions opposed to the pre-existing view of corruption as an unavoidable and even 'necessary evil'.[6] The US also played the role of 'moral entrepreneur', presenting normative arguments for collective action against corruption on the basis of its harmful effect on societies, economies, and governments globally.[7] The diverse perspectives represented by these actors illustrate the view of Abbott and Snidal, that the evolution of a transnational legal regime involves the interaction of actors not only motivated by normative values, but also by rationalist interest.[8]

As the normative discourse of the global anti-corruption regime took hold, it became more difficult for other states to protest against the need for a unified approach to combatting corruption, and transnational legal instruments were subsequently developed.[9] UNCAC emerged as the primary international legal tool of the global anti-corruption regime. The reliance of UNCAC on domestic implementation and enforcement reflects the arguments of Passas that efforts to combat transnational crime in a globalised world are still firmly in the hands of states.[10]

Notably, during the early stages of UNCAC negotiation the representative of the Group of Asian and Pacific States insisted that the definition of corruption established by the Convention should not infringe on the integrity of domestic legal systems. This argument is based on the view that states should remain free to decide for themselves how best to define corruption, avoiding any definition that may conflict with societal norms in that country. Sovereignty was also raised as a concern during negotiation of topics such as reversal of the burden of proof and bank secrecy, as well as with regard to a review mechanism for the Convention. This reality aligns with Boister's argument that state sovereignty is the key restrictive factor in the success of transnational criminal law.[11] It further reflects the argument of Passas, that state actors are ultimately responsible for criminogenic asymmetries that can result in corrupt incentives and other transnational criminal activity.[12] Both Boister and Passas assert that, if states are not willing to compromise, or do not see the relevant law as aligned with their own domestic legal system, the law in question has little chance of being effectively implemented or enforced.[13]

As discussed in Chapter 1, Boister views transnational criminal law as a unique sphere of law that includes international instruments such as UNCAC. This sphere of law is more restrictive than international criminal law *stricto sensu*, in both the nature of the perceived threat and extent of jurisdiction.[14] Although this interpretation may be limited, it provides a range of useful insights regarding the limitations and challenges faced by transnational criminal law, many of which appear relevant to UNCAC. For example, Boister notes the potential challenge of legal overlap in the implementation and enforcement of transnational criminal law. When external laws are implemented domestically, it is challenging to enforce them effectively if other existing domestic laws cover the same or similar acts. This challenge of legal overlap is relevant to the PNG case, as was shown in Chapter 5. Resource and capacity limitations further the impact of this issue.

Transnational legal overlap was addressed by the UN Secretary-General Report on existing transnational legal mechanisms.[15] Legal overlap in the domestic context was not given the same level of attention. This failure was noted with concern earlier in the thesis, especially considering that bribery and related crimes have existed as offences in most states since long before the negotiation of UNCAC. Boister's work provides insight into the nature of legal tools such as UNCAC, suggesting some challenges that may limit effectiveness and, in the case of UNCAC, could prevent evolution of the global anti-corruption regime to the fifth and final stage. The work of Zumbansen, Koh, and Twining expands on Boister's analysis, further emphasising the importance of the domestic context and the interaction between domestic, regional, and international spheres. The work of Passas on criminogenic asymmetries is also useful in this regard.

Passas argues that criminogenic asymmetries, including inequalities in the spheres of politics, culture, the economy, and law, can generate demand for illegal goods and services, generate incentives for criminal activity, and reduce the ability of authorities to combat such activities.[16] Acknowledging that globalisation 'multiplies, intensifies or activates asymmetries',[17] Passas emphasises that 'it is through policies decided on and carried out at the national level that asymmetries materialize their criminogenic potential'.[18] However, the author also highlights that state actors can influence asymmetries transnationally. Due in large part to power asymmetries, domestic policies can result in asymmetrical outcomes in foreign states.[19] A good illustration of this is the influential role of dominant states, multilateral lending institutions and corporations in shaping the nature of corrupt activity and anti-corruption efforts in the South Pacific region.

Koh highlights the importance of state and non-state actors in shaping global prohibition regimes.[20] Rather than focusing on the development of the regime at the international level, Koh explores the role of these actors in solidifying global prohibition regimes through domestic norms and practice.[21] Koh also suggests that the implementation and enforcement of transnational legal norms is not a one-way process but involves dynamic interaction and feedback loops between domestic and international spheres. This implies that nation states influence the nature of a global prohibition regime by shaping the manner in which it is applied domestically.

Twining helps to explain this dynamic relationship by focusing on the principle of 'interlegality'. He argues that 'law is rarely introduced into a vacuum' and therefore it is essential to understand the relationship between multiple legal and normative processes that shape responses to, and ultimately the solidification of, new norms.[22] When a global prohibition regime is introduced domestically this regime will interact with existing laws, as well as cultural and social norms, which will shape the nature and effectiveness of the regime in that context. Zumbansen too supports this perspective, holding that 'domestic experience is a crucial point of orientation' when exploring global prohibition regimes and their domestic implementation and enforcement.[23]

The most extreme outcome of this concept, within the five-stage model, is the power of states to secure or prevent evolution of a global prohibition regime to the final stage, through willingness or failure to effectively implement and enforce the regime domestically. In the same way that consistent implementation and enforcement can secure a regime (as with the anti-slavery movement), if a regime consistently fails to achieve domestic implementation and enforcement then the regime itself may be deemed impossible or irrelevant and cease to exist (one example being the prohibition of alcohol in the 1920s).

The theories recapped above emphasise the role and interaction between the international, regional, and domestic spheres through actors who promote their own values and interests regarding a particular norm. The importance of the regional and domestic, as well as the transnational context, in understanding norm evolution motivated the exploration of the regional (South Pacific) and domestic (PNG) context to UNCAC in the third and fourth chapters of this thesis. Findings from these chapters suggest that feedback loops were limited in the regional and domestic context. Feedback loops refer to flows of information, ideas, values, and interests back and forth between two or more spheres. In general, it appeared that the South Pacific, and PNG, had adopted the transnational approach with little alteration or input. This raised concerns regarding the relevance of the global prohibition regime to the South Pacific context, especially when combined with limited involvement by South Pacific states during the negotiation process. Additionally, Chapters 3 and 4 suggested that the impact of non-state actors was substantial within the South Pacific and PNG context. This mirrors the views of transnational legal theorists, discussed above, who emphasise that transnational law is not the sole concern of states, but in fact involves a diverse range of competing and collaborating actors, values, and interests.

Of note in the South Pacific region, and within PNG, was the role of multilateral lending institutions. These actors promote the global anti-corruption regime through targeted funding and provision of 'technical expertise' to governments and regional bodies in the South Pacific. Funding and technical expertise is provided for specific anti-corruption initiatives such as the Pacific Plan, the ADB/OECD Anti-Corruption Initiative for the Asia Pacific, and the UN-PRAC programme.[24] Conversely, funding can also be withheld from projects deemed to be at odds with the global anti-corruption regime, thus adding a coercive element to the influence of these actors.

The role of aid and investment more generally was also noted in earlier chapters. In many less developed and developing South Pacific nations there is a substantial need for external funding, both in the form of aid and also through foreign investment. Donor states are therefore in a position to influence the application of the global anti-corruption regime. However, their influence does not always support the regime, as is discussed further below. Corporate actors also complicate the regional and domestic framework. While the desire for investment motivates states to adopt corporate friendly policies, these policies may not always be in the interest of citizens and thus may facilitate corrupt relationships between government officials and corporations. Furthermore, the power of corporations may allow for hijacking of domestic policy initiatives in a corrupt manner. A good example from the case study of PNG relates to the Special Agricultural Business Leases (SABL) granted to corporations for resource extraction. As discussed in the introduction to this thesis, this programme was initially developed to promote economic empowerment, support customary landowners, and provide opportunities for the development of small scale agricultural projects. The majority of these leases however were given to large multinational corporations who often engaged in corrupt activities and used SABLs for unsustainable forestry practices.[25] Furthermore, only four of 42 leases examined were issued with consent from landowners.[26] The report of the commission of inquiry held that in the case of SABLs:' Greed and corruption at all levels; political, government bureaucracy, landowner agents /representatives, and developers have tainted a noble landowner empowerment initiative.'[27]

Despite this damning report, the SABL programme has still not been cancelled, even after the Prime Minister pledged to do so in May 2014.[28] More recently, an official statement from the Secretary for Department of Justice and Attorney General held that 'cancelling SABL leases is not something easy . . . The State has already incurred liabilities totalling [PGK]8 billion'.[29] This case demonstrates the potentially harmful influence of foreign corporate actors and corporate friendly policies in countries like PNG. Programmes developed with the objective of enabling and supporting economic development domestically, can be hijacked by foreign actors with an interest in securing profitable opportunities for themselves, at the expense of the local actors that the programmes were designed to support.

Certain influential actors, including the World Bank and other multilateral lending institutions, have argued that corruption should be targeted by states because it will reduce foreign investment due to the increased cost of doing business. However, the cash flows generated from foreign investment can equally encourage corrupt activities. In some cases, it may be that perceptions of corruption can result in limited options for investment. Corporations domiciled in countries with strict anti-corruption laws may avoid investing in countries perceived to be highly corrupt, while those corporations willing to pay bribes will continue to engage in these countries, further perpetuating the corrupt environment. These dynamic relationships are discussed further below.

The limited impact of UNCAC in the context of Papua New Guinea

At the outset of this book, it was suggested that UNCAC might have had a negative impact in PNG and the South Pacific region, based on the limited involvement of these actors during the negotiation process and the associated lack of relevance that UNCAC would have to the regional and domestic context. This lack of relevance was based on the critique explored in Chapter 1 and presented by authors including Corva, Beare, Reed, and Henshaw.[30] However, the fieldwork and interview insights presented in Chapter 5 illustrate that a more nuanced interpretation is necessary. An unspoken assumption of the critical hypothesis is that ratification and implementation of UNCAC would involve wholesale adoption of all policies of the global anti-corruption regime, including those that were irrelevant or poorly suited to the domestic context. In PNG, UNCAC appears to have played a supporting rather than central role in the development of domestic anti-corruption law and policy. Furthermore, UNCAC itself is a politically negotiated document. The negotiation process resulted in a text that is careful to protect the concerns of state sovereignty, as noted in Chapter 2.

The anti-corruption framework in PNG reflects the global anti-corruption regime in many ways, but it also emphasises context-specific efforts to combat corruption. The PNG National Anti-Corruption Strategy 2010–2013 (NACS) notes the need to 'ensure compliance with the United Nations Convention against Corruption' and promotes the enactment of illicit enrichment legislation in line with Article 20 of UNCAC.[31] However, PNG has also developed unique anti-corruption policies and practices that appear 'home-grown'. These range from school education programmes promoting integrity and 'zero tolerance of corruption', to the establishment of a specific branch within the judiciary to hear corruption cases.[32] These two initiatives target the contextual challenges of apathy towards corrupt activity and inefficiency and lethargy of the judiciary in dealing with corrupt cases. These challenges were raised by several interview participants, as noted in Chapter 5.

The supporting rather than central role of UNCAC in PNG is further illustrated by the lack of understanding regarding specific provisions of the Convention, even amongst those government actors directly engaged with implementation and enforcement of treaty obligations. One reason for this may be the fluidity of domestic politics in PNG: the actors involved in the initial decision to sign and ratify UNCAC are no longer active in PNG government and thus the processes lack continuity. Simplistic and general responses to the question 'What do you see as the purpose of UNCAC' are particularly telling.[33]

Overall, the view of government actors in PNG was that UNCAC was a supporting framework for existing domestic anti-corruption efforts, providing international credibility to these efforts and supporting positive perceptions of PNG within the international community. This perspective seems at odds with PNG's lack of involvement in the negotiation of UNCAC, but it is more easily understood through the theory of Zumbansen and Twining. Both of these authors emphasise that law cannot be introduced into a vacuum.[34] Domestic experience and socio-legal history are important factors shaping the nature and effectiveness of any transnational legal regime. UNCAC's supporting role reflects the history of law in PNG where anti-corruption measures have been in place since independence. The *Criminal Code Act 1974* ('*CCA*') includes the offences of corrupt procurement and bribery, abuse of office, extortion, and official corruption.[35] A number of administrative measures also exist on the statute books with the aim of limiting corrupt incentives within the public sector.[36] Ratification of UNCAC required limited action domestically, at least in the short term, and had extensive potential benefit in terms of promoting a positive view of the country internationally.

Points of engagement with UNCAC: international perceptions

The desire to promote a positive image of PNG internationally highlights the importance of transnational values and interests within the domestic context of PNG. The state's reliance on aid and external investment makes it extremely susceptible to international opinions of donor states, corporations, and non-state actors.

It is possible that the influence of UNCAC was under-emphasised by domestic actors who participated in the research, keen to highlight domestic ownership of the anti-corruption agenda. Perhaps the points of convergence between the PNG approach and the global anti-corruption regime do not illustrate synergy between the two spheres, but in fact reflect a power imbalance between transnational actors and domestic governments. The impact of UNCAC in PNG may be more substantial than domestic actors were willing to admit. Instead of reflecting the aligned interests of PNG with the global prohibition regime, it may reflect the overbearing influence of external actors on the policies and practices in PNG.

The PNG NACS acknowledges the role of development partners, including AusAid, New Zealand High Commission and UNDP, which contributed to the document by providing perspective 'on the link between corruption and development and how the strategy should be tailored'.[37] However, as noted earlier, the pre-existing legal framework in PNG supports a long history of anti-corruption efforts in line with the transnational framework. Furthermore, the *Proceeds of Crime Act 2005*, developed following UNCAC ratification, has proven relatively successful. A range of cases have been brought under the new law and some successful prosecutions have been achieved. This suggests that even though the law itself was developed in response to external pressure,[38] there was sufficient domestic political will to secure effective implementation and enforcement.

The supporting role played by UNCAC contradicts some criticisms levelled at the global anti-corruption regime and may reduce the relevance of associated risks and harmful side effects. However, corruption is still a substantial problem in PNG, despite the development of a broad anti-corruption strategy combining domestic programmes with compatible elements of UNCAC. Based on the above findings, three possibilities emerge.

One possibility is that, despite aligned rhetoric and complementary domestic efforts, political will remains limited in PNG. In this scenario, anti-corruption developments will amount to little more than public image exercises, using anti-corruption rhetoric as 'smoke and mirrors' to secure aid and transnational investment, detract from criticism, and distract from continued corrupt behaviour.

The second possibility is that the foundations have been laid for a successful, multifaceted anti-corruption framework. Due to the complex nature of the challenge posed by corruption, patient, persistent and dynamic efforts must continue at the domestic, regional, and transnational levels before corrupt activity can be substantially reduced in any State party to UNCAC, including PNG. Only with such dynamic and consistent effort – involving actors, values, and interests at the international, regional, and domestic levels – can the global anti-corruption regime hope to achieve the fifth stage of norm evolution. As Nadelmann and Andreas note, the establishment of a global prohibition regime is not in itself sufficient to secure a substantial reduction in the target activity. To achieve the fifth and final stage of evolution, the regime must contend with a range of risks and challenges. The nature and impact of criminogenic asymmetries on efforts to harmonise anti-corruption law and policy must also be addressed.[39] The impact of state policies on transnational dynamics should be acknowledged. Efforts must be made to 'diminish or eradicate undesirable asymmetries and to reduce the criminogenic effect of those we wish to preserve or cannot do much about'.[40]

The third possibility is that a combination of general challenges and limited political will have prevented the successful reduction of corrupt activities in PNG. This possibility allows the most breadth for discussion of actions and solutions to enhance the success of the global anti-corruption regime. It is difficult to establish with certainty whether political will, or the complexity of the target activity, are more substantial challenges to the implementation and enforcement of UNCAC and the evolution of the global anti-corruption regime. By addressing both, solutions are likely to be more robust.

Engagement with UNCAC in PNG, on the basis of promotion of positive public image and the influence of external actors, may be seen as positive, but also as potentially harmful to the ultimate goals of the regime. Such motivation may lead to implementation and enforcement, but it is equally possible that the appearance of implementation and enforcement domestically may shroud a lack of genuine political will. In either case, the role of the Implementation Review Mechanism and PNG's engagement with this mechanism is cause for optimism. Engagement with this mechanism supports a positive public image of engagement with UNCAC, and may also assist in overcoming any lack of genuine political will. The mechanism has the potential to support implementation and enforcement of UNCAC in a manner that acknowledges unique domestic challenges, as well as providing a means for promoting genuine engagement and motivating continued support for the regime, where it may otherwise be lacking.

Points of engagement with UNCAC: the implementation and review process

The bulk of PNG's domestic engagement with UNCAC appears to have come by way of the Implementation Review process. As discussed in Chapter 2, this mechanism was negotiated subsequent to UNCAC's entry into force. The mechanism is now in its second cycle. Interview participants highlighted that the review process was useful, as it provided access to the experiences of other *States Parties* who were also in the process of implementing and enforcing UNCAC.[41]

The role played by the Implementation Review Mechanisms mirrors activity in the fourth stage of regime evolution, where international institutions and conventions emerge to play a coordinating role.[42] Situated within this fourth stage, the global anti-corruption regime is faced with a range of challenges including deviant states, *States Parties* that are unable (due to lack of resources and capacity) or unwilling (due to lack of political will or conflicting interests) to enforce the regime, and deviant individuals and criminal organisations that elude enforcers and continue to engage in the target activity.[43] In addition to these challenges, Nadelmann and Andreas hold that success in attaining the fifth stage of regime development depends primarily on the nature of the criminal activity and its susceptibility to criminal justice measures, both of which can be strongly influenced by technological developments.[44] State engagement with the Implementation Review Mechanism may assist in overcoming many of these challenges.

Deviant states are, by their nature, unlikely to be members of UNCAC. Therefore, the Implementation Review process is limited in its ability to overcome this hurdle. However, if the process engages *States Parties* in productive dialogue and documents positive outcomes for a diverse number of member states, dissemination of these positive case studies may encourage non-members to ratify UNCAC. The likelihood of this outcome will of course depend on the rationale for non-membership. In cases where states had specific concerns about a particular provision of the Convention, positive examples of that provision's use in practice may reduce reservations. If successful cases documented through the review process are disseminated, certain actors within deviant states may be able to leverage these cases to motivate political action; whether through membership of UNCAC or via changes to domestic law and policy in line with the proven approach. The most likely actors to motivate such action are civil society groups and NGOs. However, corporate actors and individual moral entrepreneurs may also play a role. The type and number of actors likely to engage in promotion of UNCAC in deviant states will depend on the social, legal, political, and economic context within that state. The more examples that exist, demonstrating positive outcomes resulting from engagement, the easier it will be for actors to promote adherence and motivate action.

Within *States Parties* the review process may be harnessed by non-state actors to motivate continued action and combat lack of political will within member States. The Implementation and Review process emphasises the importance of engagement with civil society and relevant stakeholders. If engagement was facilitated through the Implementation Review process, the power of such actors would be enhanced. Potential for non-state actors to provide their perspective on anti-corruption efforts within the UNCAC forum may motivate collaboration between these actors and governments. While some States may not be swayed by value-based arguments in support of UNCAC, their participation as *States Parties* makes them vulnerable to interest-based incentives driven by non-state actors who have the potential to 'name and shame' states for failure to adequately implement and enforce their obligations.

The Implementation Review process may be most helpful in the case of *States Parties* that have limited resources and capacity to enforce obligations. The process is designed to illustrate areas in which the state party has met or exceeded obligations under UNCAC, and identify areas where the state party needs to increase efforts or should consider additional or different measures. Suggestions will usually involve expending more resources, both human and financial. This may be a burden on states, but the UNCAC Implementation Review framework is designed so that assistance can be requested from the UN to meet goals suggested by the review process. This potential contribution of financing and technical assistance and expertise acts to stimulate state participation in the review mechanism. It has been noted that implementation and enforcement of UNCAC obligations is costly in terms of both time and resources.[45] The possibility of securing fiscal and technical support for UNCAC-related activities makes participation in the Implementation Review process appealing. Targeted aid from the UN to *States Parties*, may reduce instances of selective funding or intentional underfunding that were noted by some interview participants regarding anti-corruption work in PNG.[46] It has been noted that a lack of political will to target corruption could be a reason for underfunding certain key institutions and programmes in PNG. Some interview participants suggested that funding was often provided for the development of new policies, programmes, and institutions, that appear to target corruption in line with UNCAC but may not be given the necessary support to actually enforce anti-corruption laws.[47] This was a particular concern in PNG with regards to the development of an Independent Commission against Corruption (ICAC), despite the existence of numerous other agencies and branches already tasked with investigation and prosecution of corruption.[48]

Finally, while the Implementation Review process cannot alter the nature of corruption, it can be utilised as a mechanism to consolidate and disseminate valuable experiences and expertise. This can include information on both legal and technological developments that have been proven to assist states in combatting corruption, as well as expertise in designing and using such tools. In the case of PNG, it was noted that participation in the Implementation Review processes had provided useful examples of how to draft whistleblower protection laws.[49] PNG has also established an Open Parliament Project, with the goal of increasing public awareness and engagement with parliament and subsequently reducing corruption in government. Although this project was developed in collaboration with the European Union and not through the UNCAC Implementation Review process, it illustrates the value of transnational collaboration. Utilising transnational interaction, governments are able to stay abreast of technological, legal, and procedural developments that may assist them in combatting corruption. This could counter the possibility that corrupt actors continue to develop more complex methods for achieving corrupt goals and disguising corrupt activities. As Nadelmann and Andreas note, the technology race between criminals and law enforcement actors is a substantial challenge in securing the fifth and final stage of norm evolution.[50] This was certainly a concern for actors in PNG, who noted that corrupt activity had increased substantially in recent decades and was becoming increasingly complex and difficult to detect and prosecute.[51]

UNCAC as a flexible tool

The United Nations Convention against Corruption appears to have had limited direct impact on PNG's approach to combatting corruption. However, UNCAC has the potential to support other actors engaged in anti-corruption activities, or those actors concerned about the impact of such activities. Donor states and multilateral lending institutions including the Asian Development Bank (ADB), Organisation for Economic Cooperation and Development (OECD), and World Bank may call upon PNG's obligations under UNCAC to support their efforts to shape PNG's approach to combatting corruption or, more specifically, to ensure that corruption does not adversely impact their activities in PNG. If efforts are undertaken to enhance the level of educated engagement with UNCAC domestically, the Convention could also be used as a valuable tool to combat window dressing by local political elite, at the same time countering risks of coercion by external actors equipped to utilise UNCAC to their advantage.

In the case of Australian engagement in PNG, it was noted during interviews that corruption was a difficult issue to tackle.[52] It is challenging to maintain stable political and economic relationships in PNG while mitigating the potential harmful impact of corruption. An interview participant with experience coordinating criminal law and enforcement efforts between PNG and Australia summarised this point by stating, 'talking about this stuff doesn't make friends'.[53] Another interviewee noted that, in this regard, UNCAC can be a useful tool. The UN can work in spaces that bilateral donors cannot, thanks to the institution's political neutrality.[54]

Multilateral lending institutions have more flexibility to promote specific programmes and courses of action than do bilateral donors, as the relationship is largely one way. Lending institutions provide aid to countries in need and are able to put certain conditions on this aid, without the risk of harming future diplomatic relations and losing potential political or economic opportunities. Both the ADB/OECD and the World Bank have included anti-corruption efforts in their approaches to lending. Papua New Guinea continues to receive funding from the World Bank. One project, initiated in 2008, involves the development of a Mineral Resource Authority Anti-Corruption Plan, as a key output of the USD17 million loan.[55] The alignment between the World Bank approach and that of UNCAC is further illustrated by the StAR initiative, a joint World Bank UNODC programme for the return of stolen assets, in line with Chapter V of UNCAC, which focuses on asset recovery.[56]

Transparency International (TI) and many other NGOs at the international, regional, and domestic levels, have utilised UNCAC to support their recommendations and motivate government action. The UNCAC Coalition is perhaps the most notable grouping in this regard. This coalition is specifically focused on 'promoting the ratification, implementation and monitoring of the UN Convention against Corruption'.[57] The coalition includes more than 250 civil society organisations in more than 100 countries, although none of the members are from PNG and few members represent the South Pacific region.[58]

In the context of PNG, calls to comply with obligations under UNCAC are limited, in large part due to limited understanding of the Convention. Interview participants from local level NGOs showed significant interest in harnessing UNCAC as a tool for motivating state action.[59] The obligations UNCAC places on *States Parties* were viewed as having the potential to influence government behaviour, due to the substantial power of public perceptions, especially between actors at the international level. Expanding awareness and knowledge of UNCAC amongst non-government actors in PNG would enhance UNCAC's value as a tool to support home-grown anti-corruption efforts. This would reduce the risk of coercion by external actors who may manipulate UNCAC to support their own agendas. If local actors are aware of the nature of the Convention, they can use their position to support beneficial interpretations of UNCAC and prevent misapplication in conflict with the domestic context.

The majority of UNCAC's impact occurs through pressure by specific actors and institutions that support the goals of the Convention, either for value-based or interest- based reasons. UNCAC can be utilised as a tool to support the anti-corruption goals of donor states, multilateral lending institutions, NGOs and potentially domestic civil society groups. In the case of PNG, UNCAC has been promoted as a tool that reflects existing political will to combat corruption domestically, in line with the transnational approach. Whether this is in fact the case, or simply an effort to promote a positive public image, it allows UNCAC to be utilised as a tool of diplomacy when external actors attempt to engage with this sensitive issue. The use of UNCAC by these actors may assist in promoting the global anti-corruption regime and catalysing further regime evolution. However, certain risks should be noted.

There is a distinct possibility that UNCAC could be used to support diverse goals and agendas. If the actors utilising UNCAC are predominantly powerful donor states and multilateral lending institutions, there is a risk that UNCAC may be used to promote policies that are ill-suited to the domestic context. This concern was raised by many critics. Many small island developing nations in the South Pacific are extremely reliant on external aid; this is the case even in the larger, resource rich, country of PNG. When this aid is tied to donor driven reforms and supported by obligations under UNCAC, the coercive power is likely to be strong. Utilising such coercive power may help the global anti-corruption regime to proliferate, promoting legal and policy changes. However, if these changes do not align with the unique domestic context in which they operate, there is a substantial risk that they will be misapplied, ignored, or have harmful repercussions. This will not assist in securing large-scale global reductions in corrupt activity, which is the goal of the global anti-corruption regime and the requirement for the final stage of norm evolution.

Despite the risks of manipulation and misapplication, UNCAC was drafted with enough flexibility to operate in diverse contexts and adapt to unique national and local dynamics. For this adaption to take place, it is essential that utilisation by external actors is balanced with utilisation by national and local actors. These national and local actors will be able to maximise the relevance of UNCAC based on their understanding of the unique contexts in which the Convention must operate. This understanding and engagement will counter possible manipulation of the structure and obligations of the Convention, either in support of external agendas, or as window dressing by domestic political actors.

Summary

The United Nations Convention against Corruption is the primary tool of the global anti-corruption regime; it evolved within a context of extensive debate and concern regarding the transnational nature of corruption and the need to target corrupt activity homogeneously across borders. However, the political negotiation process that produced UNCAC resulted in a multifaceted instrument that extends beyond unified criminalisation measures. The Convention covers a diverse range of preventive measures and possibilities for transnational cooperation, all paying close attention to the fundamental norm of state sovereignty. Although the negotiation process did not involve all relevant actors from all nations, its flexibility allows it to be used as a tool to support home grown anti-corruption efforts, at least in theory.

The PNG case illustrates that government actors see UNCAC as a supportive and complementary framework for assisting domestic anti-corruption policy, rather than as a coercive or obligatory document. The most attractive aspect of UNCAC for these actors was its promotion of a positive public image for PNG, demonstrating to the world that PNG was committed to anti-corruption efforts in line with the global anti-corruption regime. Additionally, the information sharing element of the Implementation Review process was highlighted as a useful aspect of UNCAC, although the time and resource costs of participating in the review mechanisms were also noted.[60] The provision of technical assistance was viewed positively, as a means of attaining support for homegrown initiatives in line with the Convention.

Domestic actors outside government were critical of UNCAC's relevance, suggesting that PNG's membership was not sufficient to secure the sustained political will necessary to combat corruption in the country. They suggested that UNCAC had little relevance to PNG and noted the risk that membership could be used as 'smoke and mirrors', promoting an image of commitment to anti-corruption goals, while corrupt activities continue unabated in both the government and private sectors.[61]

When UNCAC is viewed in relation to external actors, including donor states and multilateral lending institutions, an alternative view emerges. In this context, powerful actors who seek to coerce law and policy changes could use UNCAC as a tool for their objectives. Calling upon obligations under UNCAC, in combination with conditional aid, it may be possible for such actors to promote action that is in line with the global anti-corruption regime but may not necessarily apply well in a given domestic context. An example of this kind of policy change, motivated by combined power of UNCAC obligations and international consequences, is the *POCA*. This piece of legislation was developed in PNG as a result of pressure from the Financial Action Task Force (FATF). Interestingly, this new law was viewed positively by the majority of interview participants and does not appear to have had any harmful consequences yet. However, its positive impact also appears limited, as corrupt activity continues to be a major issue in PNG.

Ultimately, UNCAC is a flexible instrument open to diverse interpretations. It can be used productively and shaped to fit the context in which it must operate, but its flexibility presents two challenges that exist at opposite ends of the spectrum. If either challenge is not dealt with effectively, the result will be negative outcomes for the successful reduction in corrupt activities. First, governments that lack political will to change may utilise UNCAC to promote a positive public image, while failing to effectively implement and enforce UNCAC obligations. This will result in maintenance of the status quo and potential delegitimation of UNCAC and the global anti-corruption regime. Second, use of UNCAC obligations by external actors may motivate domestic action, when combined with other incentives. However, it may also result in the application of reforms that are inappropriate to the domestic context in which they must operate. In this case, such reforms will fail to achieve a reduction in corruption levels, and could potentially have harmful consequences. One possible approach to overcoming these challenges involves greater awareness, understanding, and engagement, by local actors both within and outside of the government sphere. Additional possibilities are explored in Chapter 7.

Answering question three: evaluating the critique of UNCAC and the global anti-corruption regime

How do the above findings contribute to answering the third research question, relating to the actuality of existing critiques of UNCAC and the global anti-corruption regime? It appears that some critics overstate the influence of

UNCAC and their warnings about the harmful side effects of implementation and enforcement may not be entirely warranted. If UNCAC is viewed as a neutral tool, as appears to be the case in the context of PNG, criticism of the harmful potential of UNCAC may be overstated. Further analysis is necessary, in order to develop this hypothesis fully and address alternative explanations for why ratification and implementation of UNCAC has not resulted in achievement of the fifth and final stage of regime evolution. In other words, if aspects of the critique do not play out in practice, what alternative possibilities present themselves? Possibilities have already been presented regarding the use of UNCAC as 'smoke and mirrors' by uncommitted governments, and the manipulation of this tool for agendas and programmes ill-suited to domestic contexts.

A brief recap of critiques is presented, followed by analysis of their value, limitations, and alternative possibilities. Analysis draws heavily on the experiences of PNG with implementation and enforcement of UNCAC. This analysis is open to criticisms, as the subject matter is specific. However, the experiences of PNG fit well with the theoretical framework established at the outset of this research and many of the challenges faced by this country reflect the concerns of critics. Papua New Guinea is therefore a highly relevant case study. Furthermore, many of the underlying issues and challenges faced in PNG can be generalised to other nations seeking to combat corruption. The findings themselves may thus be cautiously generalised to provide insight into the future of the regime and possible approaches to enhancing it.

Reintroducing the critique

At the broadest level, critiques of UNCAC and the global anti-corruption regime are presented either as explanations for failure or warnings of potential harms that may result from large scale implementation and enforcement. Often, critiques act as both explanation and warning. Critics argue that the regime and its legal tools are ill suited to application across the diverse domestic contexts in which they must operate to achieve 'success'. This leads critics to predict that UNCAC, and the global anti-corruption regime, will never reach stage five: the substantial reduction in corrupt activity globally.

Critical perspectives of regime evolution build on the model established by Nadelmann and Andreas and the challenges presented in that model. Nadelmann and Andreas do not directly address the crime of corruption and the evolution of the global anti-corruption regime. Drawing on additional critique provides insight into regime specific risks. Additional critique also expands on the general risks raised by Nadelmann and Andreas. The authors note the importance of political will, technological developments, and the nature of the target activity, which all affect the success of a regime. However, Nadelmann and Andreas do not detail how these factors influence the likelihood of securing application of a regime domestically. It is here that the additional critique is again useful, providing expanded analysis and understanding of the restrictions that limit evolution of the global anti-corruption regime.

Drawing from this critique, four key risk factors are identified. These risk factors relate to: (1) the regime's avoidance of a definition of corruption; (2) the relationship promoted by the regime between corruption and other forms of criminality, particularly transnational crime; (3) the focus on criminal law and enforcement measures as the best tool to combat corruption; (4) the potential inapplicability of a universal anti-corruption approach, considering the myriad of unique contextual factors existing domestically. Each of these risk factors is interrelated, and the fourth is the most general and the most substantial. It reflects the underlying challenge of balancing transnational harmonisation with domestic relevance across diverse contexts. Utilising the language of Passas,[62] the fundamental challenge of the global anti-corruption regime is to limit relevant criminogenic asymmetries between states, while also reducing them within a state. Additionally, Boister highlights the 'doctrinal weaknesses' of global prohibition regimes.[63] Even if the regime's approach is deemed appropriate, reliance on domestic implementation and enforcement remains a challenge and potential weakness. This concern reflects the concern of Passas, who emphasises that states are ultimately in control of, and capable of limiting, international efforts at harmonisation.[64] This is especially pertinent in cases of legal overlap, resource and capacity limitations, and institutional deficits, which often exist in states required to implement and enforce the regime.[65]

The above risk factors have the potential to both limit the success of the regime, and result in harmful outcomes within states that attempt to apply this regime. Potential harmful outcomes include co-optation, coercion and 'policy laundering' by powerful actors who can manipulate the regime to suit their political agendas. Such outcomes are possible if the regime fails to clearly define the target activity.[66] Another harmful effect is that of 'squeezing the balloon', or shifting the target activity from one area to another, without addressing underlying causes of corruption. Such causes may be unique to the context in which the activity takes place.[67] If the regime does not address the underlying causes of corruption within a unique context, a further harmful result may be that valuable and often limited resources are wasted on anti-corruption policies that do not have the desired effect. This last argument is especially relevant to criminal law and enforcement efforts, which stem from the criminalisation focus of the global anti-corruption regime. Critical authors, including Bridenthal, argue that corruption is a symptom rather than a cause and therefore the criminal law approach is misguided and doomed to failure.[68]

Finally, several authors argue that, through the global anti-corruption regime's focus on the relationship between corruption and other forms of criminal activity, the criminal law and law enforcement focus is able to extend the limits of established norms of human rights, due process, and the rule of law.[69] Such extensions, justified on the basis of the potential harm posed by corrupt activity, are certainly concerning. Nadelmann and Andreas discuss many of the above noted risks and harms raised by critics in the context of the global prohibition regime against drugs. The authors argue that the criminalisation approach is not well suited to the nature of the target activity, namely drug trafficking. They argue this on the basis that – unlike other activities, such as currency counterfeiting – producing drugs does not require substantial expertise; the activity is more easily concealed, than for example human trafficking; and it 'produces few victims who have an interest in notifying criminal justice authorities'.[70] Ultimately, Nadelmann and Andreas argue that, like other vice activities such as gambling and prostitution, transnational prohibition regimes 'can powerfully affect the nature of the activity and the market, but they cannot effectively deter or suppress most of those determined to participate in the activity'.[71] Andreas is particularly vocal on the harmful side effects of attempting to enforce the global prohibition regime against drug trafficking in Central and South America. These efforts have resulted in increased violence and conflict between civilians and law enforcement authorities without substantially reducing the extent of the target activity, or the harms related to drug use.[72] Nadelmann and Andreas also point to the role of moral entrepreneurs, who condemn alternative approaches that do not align with the global prohibition regime against drug trafficking. The authors note that:

> US drug enforcement officials have persistently criticized foreign governments . . . for their emphasis on public health approaches to the drug problem, and pressured them to change, despite substantial evidence that these countries have proven far more successful than the United States in dealing with illicit drug addiction.[73]

If the global anti-corruption regime takes a singular approach to combatting corruption, without acknowledging alternative possibilities and underlying causes, similar outcomes could occur. Each risk factor is addressed individually below, based on findings from earlier chapters and particularly from the fieldwork and interview insights.

Risk factor one: definition

Critics present the lack of a clear definition of corruption as a risk factor for the regime. However, analysis of UNCAC in the context of PNG suggests that the 'corrupt act' approach and avoidance of a general definition of corruption may be a strength, rather than a weakness. If a State party to UNCAC is generally committed to reducing corruption levels domestically, then such an approach allows UNCAC to provide a framework for action which can focus on the corrupt acts deemed most harmful or prevalent within that State party. Because the nature of corruption differs from one country to another, a single definition of corruption is unlikely to be relevant to all nations. Furthermore, as Larmour notes, 'the diagnosis suggests the cure'.[74] A narrow and specific definition of corruption would result in narrow and specific suggestions regarding appropriate methods for combatting corruption. Such methods established and promoted in UNCAC would only be relevant in cases where the nature of corruption fitted the restrictive definition established by the Convention. In alternative situations, application of the same methods would likely fail to achieve the desired goals and may have additional harmful effects, as noted by Nadelmann and Andreas in the case of the 'war on drugs'.[75] The corrupt act approach adopted by UNCAC may in fact mitigate the risk of harmful outcomes such as 'squeezing the balloon', misallocation of resources, and the harmful social outcomes that concern many critics.[76]

From a practical standpoint, a restrictive definition was impossible to develop within the political context of international legal negotiations. During UNCAC negotiations, a wide range of diverse actors promoted differing values, interests, and beliefs. Actors sought to establish a legal framework that supported their goals and was the least detrimental to their international position. Within this context, the only way for a singular definition of corruption to be established would have been through broadening the concept to incorporate the views of all relevant actors. Such a definition would be tantamount to no definition at all and would not contribute to developing relevant methods to combat corruption.

Another risk is that a general definition of corruption would involve a substantial moral component that could be misapplied or used to coerce action from *States Parties* that may not be in their best interests. The corrupt act approach also involves a moral component, in so much as it inherently supports a criminalisation and criminal law enforcement focus. UNCAC requires that certain acts be criminalised in *States Parties* and that criminalisation of additional acts is considered. If the view is taken that criminalisation is in fact not an appropriate method for combatting corruption then this approach may be viewed in a negative light. However, this critique does not adequately address two important factors, both of which have been illustrated by this research and the case study of PNG.

First, most of the corrupt acts that require criminalisation under UNCAC have been part of domestic law since long before the Convention was negotiated. In PNG, bribery, trading in influence, and a range of other corrupt acts have been part of the *CCA* since independence. It was noted in Chapter 4 that this was the case in the majority of South Pacific nations. Bribery, in one form or another, has existed as a crime in almost all states for centuries, in some cases millennia.[77] In this way, the approach taken in UNCAC merely reflects existing practices in much of the world. This was indeed the view of government actors in PNG, who saw UNCAC as reflecting their own anti-corruption methods and goals in line with international best practice.[78]

The second point, which has been alluded to above, is that the alternative to a corrupt act approach is unlikely to produce better outcomes. A broad and general definition of corruption has little value for an international instrument that is ultimately focused on universalising efforts to combat corrupt activities. Equally, a restrictive and specific definition of corruption is likely to result in a restrictive and specific method for combatting corruption. Such a restrictive approach is unlikely to secure widespread support and, if applied across diverse contexts, is likely to fail, while potentially exacerbating harms. While the criminalisation of a diverse range of corrupt acts illustrates a criminal law and enforcement focus, the alternatives appear to be untenable. In the context of PNG, the outcomes of the corrupt act approach appear to be a flexible framework that supports existing practices and provides insight into additional possibilities.

Risk factor two: links to other forms of criminality

Criticisms of the global anti-corruption regime are concerned with the relationship between corruption and other forms of criminality. This relationship helped to justify the establishment of the regime and emphasises the importance of criminal law and enforcement measures within the regime. In the context of PNG, links to other forms of criminality did not appear to be a substantial concern or driving force for action. The link may still be relevant in other contexts where, for example, drug and human trafficking are a more pressing concern to both the implementing country and neighbouring states. Connections between corruption and other transnational criminal regimes may appear stronger in alternative contexts, raising the risk that value-based arguments may be co-opted to support interest-based agendas. In these situations, moral entrepreneurs interested in suppressing a certain transnational criminal activity may promote the suppression of corruption as a means to combat the other targeted act, regardless of the relevance of corruption or applicability of the promoted approach. However, a substantial transnational criminal element exists and is supported by corrupt activity, acknowledging this connection may assist in establishing effective anti-corruption measures. In such a situation, it is essential that domestic actors remain empowered to choose elements of the regime that best suit their situation.

Links to other forms of criminality, especially transnational organised crime, money laundering, and terrorist financing, informed debate surrounding UNCAC. If such threats evolve and become of greater concern to PNG, their relationship to corruption could be emphasised and criminal law and enforcement measures may subsequently play a more dominant role. If this occurs, the concerns raised by Boister,[79] Beare,[80] Corva,[81] and Bridenthal[82] regarding potential violations of human rights and the fundamental rule of law, would be of increased relevance. When anti-corruption efforts are focused on criminal law and enforcement measures, in reaction to other transnational criminal threats, the potential to enact and enforce aggressive laws and support extensive police action is concerning. Such steps are likely to be ill suited to the underlying nature of corrupt activity and its causes. Conversely, a pre-emptive and rational approach to combatting corruption, focused equally on prevention, enforcement, and concern for unique domestic contexts, may reduce corrupt activities and simultaneously reducing opportunities for engagement in other forms of related transnational crime.

Risk factors three and four: criminal and law enforcement focus and incompatibility

In response to the third and fourth risk factors, three points must be made. First, as noted above, the criminal measures presented in UNCAC reflect the approaches of domestic legal systems. This is unsurprising, considering the primacy of domestic concerns during the UNCAC negotiation processes. Throughout this process, participants consistently raised arguments for the protection of state sovereignty and the integrity of domestic law.

Second, the criminal law measures under Chapter III of UNCAC were developed using a flexible approach, as discussed in Chapter 2. Certain key criminal law provisions of UNCAC are mandatory, requiring *States Parties* to implement them domestically. However, the more controversial measures are optional. It falls on the *States Parties* to decide whether or not to enact domestic legislation in line with these optional measures. This flexible approach reduces the risk of inapplicability and related harms, especially considering that most mandatory measures under Chapter III of UNCAC have a history of domestic criminalisation that pre-date the Convention. Additionally, UNCAC is wholly reliant on domestic implementation and enforcement, even in regard to 'mandatory measures'. It is therefore unlikely the criminal measures will be implemented or enforced without domestic support.

A final point on this issue is that criminal law measures under UNCAC represent only part of the overall approach of the Convention. Chapter III of UNCAC focuses on criminalisation and is the most substantial chapter (consisting of Articles 15–42). However, Chapter II is dedicated to preventive measures and Chapter IV focuses on international cooperation – neither of which emphasise criminalisation. Chapters V–VIII are also focused on obligations of *States Parties*, which do not relate directly to criminalisation. Furthermore, the Implementation Review Mechanism allows for information sharing and development of approaches beyond mere homogenisation of criminal codes in *States Parties.*

Development of a whistleblower protection law in PNG emerged out of PNG's engagement with the Implementation Review Mechanism. This is a legal measure that is not focused on criminalisation, but instead on the protection of witnesses and potential victims of corrupt activity. This example is insightful, considering that the first round of the Implementation Review process focused explicitly on criminalisation and international cooperation. The next round of Implementation Review focuses on Chapter IV, the preventive chapter, and may further expand discussion and dissemination of methods for combatting corruption beyond criminalisation. Certainly, in the context of PNG, criminal law and enforcement measures do not eclipse alternative approaches. The PNG NACS expressly supports preventive measures above criminalisation of corrupt conduct.[83] As noted in Chapter 2, the preventive measures covered by UNCAC are more expansive than those in any other multilateral convention targetting corruption. Chapter IV includes almost all suggestions put forward by participating states during the negotiation process. The flexible approach to criminalisation further reduces the risk of inapplicability, with states having ultimate control over implementation and enforcement of criminal measures.

Seeking answers: a summary of UNCAC critique

The above analysis suggests that all three of the risk factors presented by critics are of limited concern in practice, at least in the case of PNG. However, corruption does remain a challenge in PNG. One possible reason for the continued challenge posed by corruption, is that it results not from inherent flaws in the transnational approach, but instead from unavoidable complexities of the target activity and general challenges that arise with enforcement of criminal law more generally, especially in less developed nations.

One such challenge, that appears relevant in the case of PNG, is lack of political will. When political will is lacking, existing criminal laws may not be enforced. Adequate resources may not be provided, or in certain cases, may be withheld from the relevant institutions. This was an issue raised by interview participants engaged in enforcement of existing anti-corruption law in PNG, including members of the Office of the Public Prosecutor.[84] The challenge of political will is illustrated by the case of Task Force Sweep in PNG. At the time interviews were conducted, Task Force Sweep has just achieved its first successful conviction for corruption, against a member of the opposition government. However, following attempts to investigate the Prime Minister, the Task Force was disbanded, re-established, forced to operate without any access to funding, and ultimately dissolved, without the establishment of an operational replacement body.

An additional challenge is resource and capacity limitations. Even where political will is sufficiently strong, a country's economic context is relevant to the effective enforcement of criminal law measures. Resources are finite and may not be sufficient to tackle the large number of cases that occur. Additionally, technology plays a substantial role, as noted by Nadelmann who highlights technological development as key to securing, or failing to secure, the fifth and final stage of norm evolution.[85] If deviant actors are able to use technology to their advantage, and those tasked with enforcing criminal law measures cannot keep up with these technological advances, then deviant actors will gain the upper hand. In PNG, it was noted that instances of corruption have become increasingly complex. This poses a substantial challenge for those seeking to combat corrupt activity through criminal law measures, without adequate resources.[86]

Political will and resource and capacity limitations are certainly not unique to anti-corruption efforts, nor can they be attributed to flaws in the approach established by UNCAC. However, they do illustrate the importance of a holistic approach to combatting corruption. Sole reliance on criminal law enforcement measures will not be effective in this context. It appears that, despite critiques, UNCAC allows for a broad range of additional preventive and non-criminal measures against corruption. In the case of PNG, many such measures are being undertaken or considered. Within this context, the critique of the global anti-corruption regime and UNCAC's focus on criminal law and enforcement is not convincing. While there are certainly risks and limitations inherent in criminal law and enforcement efforts, UNCAC appears to support existing domestic legal approaches and practices. Criticisms may reflect inherent policing challenges, more than flaws in the regime and its approach.

An additional risk factor? The role of public perceptions, reputation and external interest actors

The findings above bring to light another risk factor that may help to explain the continued challenges facing UNCAC and the global anti-corruption regime. The nature of transnational interactions, both between sovereign states and between state and non-state actors, may be the major risk factor. The role of corporations, multilateral lending bodies, NGOs, and civil society groups, has been substantial throughout analysis in this book. These actors were highlighted by many interview participants as influencing the nature of corrupt activity and possibilities for combatting corruption in the PNG context. The interaction between diverse actors with capacity to influence corruption and anti-corruption efforts presents two opposing risks. On the one hand, there is potential for co-optation of the global anti-corruption regime by actors outside of the implementing state. Conversely, the importance of reputation may encourage governments to appear compliant with UNCAC and the global anti-corruption regime, despite limited or non-existent domestic commitment and political will. This, in turn, will undermine the effectiveness of the global anti-corruption regime and ultimately the legitimacy of UNCAC as a tool for combatting corruption globally.

The first risk, of co-optation, was noted by the critique introduced in Chapter 1, with reference to the lack of definitional clarity provided by the regime. Subsequent chapters have established that the corrupt act approach is a strength, rather than a weakness. However, UNCAC's neutrality may be manipulated through interaction between external actors, public perceptions, and the importance of reputation in transnational politics. Further analysis is necessary. Based on insights from the PNG case, several relationships deserve further exploration. First, states with economic and political interests in PNG may have incentives to influence the approach to anti-corruption in the country. This was a point made in Chapters 3 and 4, where the role of powerful ex-colonial nations was noted. Several interview participants, however, argued that corruption is a difficult issue to tackle when economic and political interests are at stake.[87]

The reality of interstate relations is not so much vertical, with powerful states providing conditional aid and policy advice, but more horizontal: economically or politically powerful States are able to use their assets to gain mutually beneficial outcomes through engagement with less powerful, less developed actors. To do this effectively, powerful states must utilise diplomatic channels. Increasing competition between donor states contributes to this structure. In recent years, more countries have shown an interest in exerting external influence. China is an especially notable player, emerging in the South Pacific region. Less developed and developing nations have increasingly more options for bilateral aid and investment. Powerful state actors seeking to take advantage of opportunities in developing countries must maintain strong diplomatic ties, or risk losing out to other competing states. This dynamic appears especially relevant in the context of PNG, which has substantial primary resources available for exploitation and is itself exerting increasingly more influence in the South Pacific region.[88] Opportunities for aid and investment are increasing for PNG from countries including China, India, and Taiwan. This is a recent development, historically aid and investment came predominantly from Australia.[89]

In this context, the potential for co-optation by foreign states is limited by diplomatic concerns, including political support and economic opportunity. This may be viewed positively, as it allows countries to shape their own anti-corruption policies in a contextually relevant manner. However, it also means that the possibility of enforcing obligations under UNCAC through bilateral action is limited. Therefore, the potential for member states to use UNCAC as a public relations tool, without actual political will for enforcement, remains substantial.

Other actors including multilateral lending institutions, professional and expert groups, NGOs, civil society actors, and corporations, illustrate the potential for co-optation, as well as the limitations of coercion. Ultimately, implementation and enforcement of UNCAC remains in the hands of *States Parties*.

Multilateral lending institutions may have more power than individual states to influence the nature of anti-corruption policy and therefore also to co-opt the global prohibition regime for alternative objectives. These institutions often provide loans in situations where no alternatives exist. Unlike the environment amongst potential donor states, there is little to no competition amongst multilateral lending institutions. These institutions share the same goals and promote the same value-based agenda for achieving them. Levinson explains:

> The basic business of Multilateral Financing Agencies (MFAs) is to lend money for specific projects and programs to borrowing member countries which will, in turn, stimulate higher economic growth rates. As part of the conditions for such lending, the MFAs increasingly require that institutions (and their governments) which borrow the money implement economic reforms. Thus, multilateral lending institutions are not only concerned with assuring repayment of the loans; they are also concerned with how a particular loan impacts the country's economy and the government's implementation of economic policies.[90]

The economic policies that such institutions have historically supported are those of decentralisation, privatisation, and limited government intervention. The vague concept of 'good governance' is often associated with reducing corrupt activity in the discourse of these actors. To use Abbott and Snidal's language of values and interests, multilateral lending institutions are interested in securing repayment of loans, which they deem most likely if countries adopt policies that reflect the values of neoliberalism.[91] The literature criticising the appropriateness of neoliberal policies in developing countries is extensive.[92] It is not within the purview of this book to explore this literature in depth. However, it is important to recognise that the existence of a specific value-based agenda amongst multilateral lending institutions, which may provide incentives for co-optation of existing obligations, such as those established under UNCAC. Manipulation of the global anti-corruption regime may result in harmful social outcomes, if the values promoted by the lending institution are ill-suited to the domestic context in which they are to be applied and are focused on economic growth over socially sustainable development.

It is important to note the role of corporations in promoting neoliberal policies, due to the benefit that these policies provide, in terms of access to investment opportunities and reduced operation costs. Walton emphasises that the role of corporations in contributing to corruption, especially in developing countries, should not be overlooked simply because modern discourse supports the involvement of corporate actors in combatting corrupt activities. The author cites Holmes, stating that:

> The spread of neoliberalism since the 1970s, which accelerated in the late 1980s, has significantly contributed to the apparent rise in corruption. Neoliberalism's focus on ends over means, flexibility, competition, homo economicus, consumption, free trade, and reducing the role of the state (state 'downsizing', monetarism rather than Keynesianism) helps to explain that connection.[93]

Walton continues, noting:

> PNG's ranking on the Control of Corruption component of the World Bank's WGI index, shows that the country's ability to address corruption has diminished significantly since the mid 1990s . . . with PNG's perceived control of corruption reducing significantly from 1996 to 1998, and again from 2002 to 2003 after the period of significant privatization (1999 to 2002).[94]

The author argues that anti-corruption efforts are not always focused equally on the private and public sectors, especially when it comes to the discourse of multilateral actors and their engagement in developing countries. Walton concludes:

> AusAID and TI PNG have acknowledged, and have taken steps to address, corruption in the private sector. But while campaigns against the government are aggressive and, particularly for AusAID, well funded, businesses are by and large considered anti-corruption champions. Those associated with these organisations consider private sector corruption as a failure of government regulation, rather than a key part of doing business. When anti-corruption activities are aimed at business they often assume that the private sector–particularly Western transnational corporations–are capable of self-regulation.[95]

In the context of PNG, several interview participants noted that the 'capitalist' or 'neoliberal' model of development, based on privatisation, decentralisation, and extraction of primary resources, was in conflict with the culture of PNG, understood to be largely collective and collaborative.[96] Promotion of neoliberal policies by multilateral lending institutions may in this context contribute to the disempowerment of citizens and motivate corrupt acts by government officials seeking to circumvent constitutionally established rights.[97] However, this may not always be the case. In some situations, aid conditionalities may align with the goals of UNCAC and the global anti-corruption regime, without substantial risks or side effects. For example, the World Bank and the ADB/OECD both require transparency in the use of funds and effective accounting measures to ensure funds are tracked and effectively spent. Aside from any additional conditionalities, such policies complement UNCAC. Obligations under the Convention could be drawn on to further strengthen the power of such requests by multilateral lenders. As one interview participant noted, UNCAC can be a useful tool, due to its political neutrality.[98] Member states have already agreed to the terms of UNCAC. Requests that are based on compliance with UNCAC are therefore less susceptible to arguments of conflict with domestic policies.

Extensive government corruption is likely to have a negative impact on the ability of countries to effectively apply for and use loan funds from multilateral institutions. Corruption increases the risk that these institutions will be unable to secure repayment. Due to the interests of multilateral lending institutions, such institutions may be motivated to promote compliance with UNCAC as a coercive tool. This action may assist in securing implementation and enforcement of the anti-corruption agenda. However, implementation and enforcement based on coercion remains limited. Ultimately, the government of the receiving state is in control of implementation and enforcement of domestic laws and policies. While external actors may attempt to motivate compliance, the possibility remains that governments can promote compliance discursively to secure funding, but fail to follow through on obligations in practice. In this situation, the only recourse for multilaterals is to withhold further aid. An unfortunate side effect of this outcome is that potentially valuable development projects go unfunded. This side effect could further result in the continuation, and potentially the expansion, of corrupt activity. It may also lead to states looking to more unscrupulous sources for funding.

Corporations, as well as states and multilateral lending institutions, play an influential role in both shaping incentives for corrupt activity and influencing compliance with anti-corruption programmes and policies. Increased competition between corporate actors from various countries affects the nature of this influence, in a manner similar to the case of bilateral donors. On the one hand, corporations that are bound by anti-corruption laws in the jurisdictions in which they are domiciled are likely to attempt to play by the rules in foreign jurisdictions. Therefore, countries seeking foreign investment may be required to comply with anti-corruption and good governance policies in order to secure potential investors. However, as with bilateral donors, competition between corporations has increased in recent years, increasing investment options available to states. Governments that are not committed to anti-corruption objectives, or that lack the capacity to comply with the requirements for investment from a specific corporation, may choose to work with corporations ambivalent about corruption. These corporations may not be bound by strict anti-corruption regulation in their own jurisdictions. An additional dynamic is that countries perceived to be corrupt may struggle to attract investment from corporations worried about corruption. This limits the available options in countries perceived to be corrupt. These countries may end up interacting with corporations that either have no scruples about corruption, or even promote corrupt activities to benefit their own profit generation. This is a concern in PNG.

One interview participant noted the increasing presence of Chinese corporates working on construction projects in Port Moresby. These corporates have won government contracts and should be bound by domestic labour laws, but they appear to be violating many laws and regulations.[99] The Malaysian logging company Rimbunan Hijau also holds extensive contracts in PNG, despite their long record of corrupt activity.[100] The company is believed to control the majority of logging operations in PNG.[101] Rimbunan Hijau has a track record of corruption outside of PNG, however, it has never been investigated or prosecuted for such activities in its country of domicile (Malaysia). Despite allegations of corruption, it continues to operate transnationally, not only in PNG, but also in Indonesia and the Solomon Islands.[102]

Donor states, multilateral lending institutions, and corporations can all influence the application of anti-corruption law domestically, through promotion of their own interest-based agendas. The outcomes of such interaction will vary, depending on the domestic political context in which the interaction occurs. The most powerful transnational influence may come, not from the interest-based actors discussed above, but through organisations whose focus is on the promotion of specific value-based agendas. Two such examples are the FATF and TI.

The FATF is a multilateral institution that seeks to:

> set standards and promote effective implementation of legal, regulatory and operational measures for combating money laundering, terrorist financing and other related threats to the integrity of the international financial system.[103]

In the context of PNG, this external actor motivated the development of domestic law, in the form of the *POCA*. Such action was secured by the threat of placing PNG on its blacklist. The related negative impact of this blacklisting on the international reputation of the country motivated action. As noted in interviews with key government actors in PNG, it was the government's desire to avoid the negative reputation that would accompany FATF blacklist status that drove the development of the new legislation to comply with FATF recommendations.[104] The combined international influence of the FATF and its independence from diplomatic or economic constraints make it a powerful force for influencing domestic action. The *POCA* in PNG is generally viewed positively, however, the risk of limited political will in such situations of coercive pressure is substantial.

Transparency International is another actor motivated by a specific value-based agenda unattached to any diplomatic or economic dependencies. This NGO can be appropriately termed a 'moral entrepreneur'.[105] The self-proclaimed mission of this institution is 'to stop corruption and promote transparency, accountability and integrity at all levels and across all sectors of society'.[106] It aims to achieve this mission through educational activities, as well as the dissemination of research and, most notably, the publication of the Corruption Perceptions Index (CPI), which ranks countries according to their perceived levels of corruption. The index was mentioned several times, during interviews with government actors in PNG. These actors noted its motivating effect on anti-corruption efforts in the country.[107] Transparency International has been criticised for the negative impact the index can have on investment and development opportunities. The influential nature of the index illustrates the power of reputation and perceptions for motivating government action.

Due to the substantial number of actors that shape the implementation and enforcement of UNCAC, the flexibility discussed earlier as a strength, may in fact contribute to the risk of co-optation. Furthermore, the above analysis illustrates that the ultimate power to implement and enforce UNCAC remains within the domestic sphere. This brings with it an unexpected challenge. Attempts by various interest- and value-based actors to influence domestic action may encourage use of UNCAC's flexibility to benefit *States Parties*, while bypassing the need for genuine political will. Laws and policies may be put in place that align with UNCAC and the values and interests of external actors, absent any intent to adequately implement and enforce these measures. External pressure and coercion are unlikely to be a sound solution to this misuse by states, as such pressure may have harmful side effects. Instead, one possibility stands out above others.

A potential solution to the double-edged risk of co-optation and lack of political will is empowerment and increased collaboration among diverse domestic actors in UNCAC member states. Empowerment and collaboration may be achieved through a variety of methods, involving domestic, regional, and transnational actions. These possibilities are discussed further in the final chapter of this book.

Summary: the reality of UNCAC in Papua New Guinea

The United Nations Convention against Corruption is the primary tool of a global anti-corruption regime, which is currently in the fourth stage of normative regime evolution. The goal of the regime is to secure a substantial reduction in instances of corruption globally, resulting in achievement of the fifth and final stage of regime evolution. To date, corruption remains a substantial challenge, both in PNG and around the globe. The fifth stage of regime evolution has proven elusive. A survey of regime critiques suggests that the three key risk factors believed to have contributed to the failure of the regime may overstate the coercive power of the regime and its legal tools, especially in the context of PNG. Ultimately, *States Parties* to UNCAC retain the power to implement and enforce the Convention domestically, or allow it to remain underutilised. Therefore, UNCAC is best understood as a relatively neutral tool capable of supporting a range of approaches to combatting corruption, depending on the unique domestic context in which it must operate.

The Convention's neutrality enables it to be applied across a diverse range of domestic contexts, but also presents two substantial risks that, until now, were only partially addressed by critique. First, due to complex transnational power dynamics, membership of UNCAC may be manipulated by external actors promoting their own interests or value-based agendas, ill-suited to domestic contexts. This risk was noted by some critics. However, the research conducted for this book has shown that such coercive power is often limited by competitive global environments and concerns for economic interests and diplomacy. Conversely, with no way to ensure domestic action from outside of the domestic sphere, there is a risk that governments may use membership of UNCAC to promote an image of compliance, while lacking the political will to implement and enforce the regime.

In the context of PNG, these two factors pose the biggest threat to successful evolution of the global anti-corruption regime. Practical challenges of resource and capacity limitations further entrench the problem. These risks and challenges need to be overcome, in order to secure successful evolution of the global anti-corruption regime. If such risks are not adequately addressed, the regime and its legal tools will be gradually delegitimised and ultimately rendered ineffective.

Addressing the limitations of the research: an explanation of broad relevance

Before addressing possibilities for combatting the above noted risks, the limitations of this research and its findings should be noted. Having focused primarily on a single case study it is important to acknowledge that findings may reflect unique aspects of this case, and may not be generalisable to all other cases. It would certainly be beneficial for future research to explore additional cases and evaluate whether the findings are replicated in these alternative contexts. It is argued that, although the PNG case is unique, several findings are indeed generalisable to other states and the global context. Papua New Guinea has a history of colonial rule but maintains a strong and unique cultural tradition. The country is a relatively young democracy and despite its resource wealth it remains reliant on external aid and investment. As noted in Chapter 4, such conditions also characterise many other less developed and developing nations, many of which also struggle with corruption.

Furthermore, the findings from this research relate to a broader interpretation of UNCAC as a multilateral legal instrument and to a multifaceted understanding of the role of diverse actors from the international, regional, and domestic spheres. While findings are well illustrated by the PNG case study, they also provide guidance for analysing and understanding alternative cases. With this in mind, Chapter 7 answers the fourth and final research question:

4 What insights does the PNG case provide in terms of improvements to the global anti-corruption regime and domestic, regional and transnational approaches to this regime?

Notes

1 *Proceeds of Crime Act (2005) ('POCA')*
2 In particular, see Passas N, 'Globalization and Transnational Crime: Effects of Criminogenic Asymmetries', in Williams P and Vlassis D (eds), *Combatting Transnational Crime: Concepts, Activities and Responses* (Frank Cass Publishers, 2013) 22; Abbott KW and Snidal D, 'Values and Interests: International legalization in the fight against corruption' 31 *Journal of Legal Studies* (2002) 141; Boister N, 'Transnational Criminal Law?' 14(5) *EJIL* (2003) 953; Koh H, 'Transnational

Legal Process' 75 *Neb. L. Rev.* (1996) 181; Zumbansen P, 'Defining the Space of Transnational Law: Legal Theory, Global Governance, and Legal Pluralism' 21 *Transnational Law & Contemporary Problems* (2012) 305; Twining W, 'Normative and legal pluralism' 20 *Duke Journal of Comparative & International Law* (2010) 473

3 Nadelmann EA and Andreas P, *Policing the Globe: Criminalization and crime control in international relations* (Oxford University Press, 1st Edition, 2006) at 17

4 ibid. at 14

5 ibid. at 21

6 Carr I, 'Corruption, legal solution and limits of law' 3(3) *International Journal of Law in Context* (2007) 227

7 See Chapter 1: Applying the five-stage model to the global anti-corruption regime

8 Abbott KW and Snidal D, 'Values and Interests: International legalization in the fight against corruption' 31 *Journal of Legal Studies* (2002) 141

9 ibid.

10 Passas N, 'Globalization and Transnational Crime: Effects of Criminogenic Asymmetries', in Williams P and Vlassis D (eds), *Combatting Transnational Crime: Concepts, Activities and Responses* (Frank Cass Publishers, 2013) 22 at 39

11 Boister N, 'Transnational Criminal Law?' 14(5) *EJIL* (2003) 953

12 above n10

13 ibid. at 43

14 above n13

15 ECOSOC, Secretary General Report: Existing International Legal Instruments, Recommendations and other Documents Addressing Corruption, E/CN.15/2001/3, (2001), ('Secretary General Report, 2001')

16 Above n10, introduced in Chapter 1: The global anti-corruption regime

17 ibid at 28

18 ibid

19 ibid at 40. Passas discusses how domestic protectionism and outward promotion of liberalisation 'impair the efforts of less developed countries to narrow the gaps'.

20 Koh H, 'Transnational Legal Process' 75 *Neb. L. Rev.* (1996) 181

21 ibid.

22 Twining W, 'Normative and legal pluralism' 20 *Duke Journal of Comparative & International Law* (2010) 473 at 516–517

23 Zumbansen P, 'Defining the Space of Transnational Law: Legal Theory, Global Governance, and Legal Pluralism' 21 *Transnational Law & Contemporary Problems* (2012) 305 at 324

24 The Pacific Islands Forum Secretariat, *The Pacific Plan for Strengthening Regional Cooperation and Integration*, (2005) ('The Pacific Plan, 2005'); ADB /OECD, *Anti-Corruption Initiative for the Asia Pacific: Strategic Principles and Operational Activities of the Initiative*, (2010); UNODC/UNDP, *UN Pacific Regional Anti-Corruption (UN-PRAC) Project Document* (20 April 2012) ('UN-PRAC')

25 Papua New Guinea, Mirou N, *Commission of Inquiry into Special Agriculture and Business Leases (SABL): Report* (June, 2013), ('SABL Report, 2013')

26 ibid.

27 ibid.

28 ActNOW!PNG *Government Should Not Shift the Blame on SABL Land Grab* (10 April 2015) available at: http://www.actnowpng.org/blog/government-should-not-shift-blame-sabl-land-grab (last visited 1 March 2018)

29 ibid.

30 Corva D, 'Neoliberal globalization and the war on drugs: Transnationalizing illiberal governance in the Americas' 27 *Political Geography* (2008) 176; Beare ME, 'Corruption and Organised Crime: Lessons from history' 28 *Crime, Law and Social Change* (1997) 155; Beare ME, 'North America: A perspective on the globalisation of organised crime' 6(1) *Journal of Financial Crime* (1993) 81; Reed Q, 'Squeezing a Balloon? Challenging

the nexus between organised crime and corruption' 7 *CMI U4 Issue* (2009); Henshaw C, 'Strengthening the Rule of Law in the Pacific through International Crime Cooperation' 15 *Australian International Law Journal* (2008) 109

31 Papua New Guinea, *National Anti-Corruption Strategy 2010–2030* (2010) ('NACS') at 3 and 19; *United Nations Convention against Corruption*, opened for signature 9 December 2003, 2349 UNTS 41 (entered into force 14 December 2005) ('*UNCAC*'), Article 20

32 Asa [Transcript No.10]

33 Participant responses were covered in Chapter 5

34 above n22 at 516; above n 23 at 344

35 Independent State of Papua New Guinea, *Criminal Code Act,* (1974) (*'CCA'*), Division 2, Article 97A, 97B, 92, 88 and 87

36 Asa [Transcript No.10]

37 Papua New Guinea, *National Anti-Corruption Strategy 2010–2030* (2010) ('NACS') at 38

38 [Transcript No.9] Anonymity Requested. Attorney Generals Department, Legal Policy and Governance Branch (AG Department). This participant discussed the FATF Grey-listing of PNG and the desire to be removed from the list

39 above n10

40 ibid. at 46

41 [Transcript No.9] Anonymity Requested. AG Department

42 above n3, discussed in Chapter 1 of this book

43 above n3 at 21

44 ibid.

45 Barker [Transcript No.13]; [Transcript No.15] Anonymity Requested. PNG OPP

46 [Transcript No.15] Anonymity Requested. PNG OPP; Koim [Transcript No.6]

47 [Transcript No.15] Anonymity Requested. PNG OPP; Koim [Transcript No.6]; Barker [Transcript No.13]

48 Koim [Transcript No.6]; [Transcript No.15] Anonymity Requested. PNG OPP

49 [Transcript No.9] Anonymity Requested. AG Department

50 Above n3

51 Note Koim [Transcript No.6]; [Transcript No.15] Anonymity Requested. PNG OPP

52 Wilson [Transcript No.14]

53 [Transcript No.5] Anonymity Requested. Member of Australian Law Enforcement Agency with Experience in PNG (Aus Law Enforcement)

54 Prescott [Transcript No.4]

55 World Bank, *Second Mining Sector Institutional Strengthening*, (TA P102396) available at: http://worldbank.org/projects/search?lang=en&searchTerm=corruption (last visited 1 March 2018)

56 UNODC, World Bank, *Stolen Asset Recovery Initiative*, available at: http://star.worldbank.org/star/ (last visited 1 March 2018)

57 UNCAC Coalition, *About Us,* available at: http://www.uncaccoalition.org/en/about-us/about-the-coalition (last visited 1 March 2018)

58 The only national members that represent the South Pacific region are three Australian based groups: TI Australia; Mitigating Endemic Democratic Problems (MED-P) and Uniting Church Australia. For details see UNCAC Coalition, *Members List,* available at: http://www.uncaccoalition. org/en/about-us/members-list (last visited 1 March 2018)

59 See discussion in Chapter 5

60 Barker [Transcript No.13]; Prescott [Transcript No.4]

61 Wilson [Transcript No.14]

62 above n10

63 above n11

64 above n10 at 39

65 above n11, discussed in Chapter 1

66 above n11; Henshaw C, 'Strengthening the Rule of Law in the Pacific through International Crime Cooperation' 15 *Australian International Law Journal* (2008) 109; McCulloch J, 'Transnational Crime as Productive Fiction' 24(2) *Social Justice* (2007) 19; Williams JW and Beare ME, 'The Business of Bribery: Globalization, economic liberalization, and the "problem" of corruption', in Beare ME (ed), *Critical Reflections on Transnational Organized Crime, Money Laundering, and Corruption* (University of Toronto Press, 1st Edition, 2003) 88

67 Reed Q, 'Squeezing a Balloon? Challenging the nexus between organised crime and corruption' 7 *CMI U4 Issue* (2009); Corva D, 'Neoliberal globalization and the war on drugs: Transnationalizing illiberal governance in the Americas' 27 *Political Geography* (2008) 176

68 Bridenthal R, 'Special Issue: The hidden history of crime, corruption, and states' 45(3) *Journal of Social History* (2012) 575

69 above n6; above n11

70 above n3 at 45

71 ibid. at 46

72 Andreas P, 'Illicit Globalization: Myths, misconceptions, and historical lessons' 126(3) *Political Science Quarterly* 3 (2011) 403

73 above n3 at 43

74 Larmour P, 'Corruption in REDD+ Schemes: a framework for analysis', Chapter 8 in Graycar A and Smith RG, *Handbook of Global Research and Practice in Corruption* (Edward Elgar, 2011) 157 at 162

75 above n3

76 Including Reed Q, 'Squeezing a Balloon? Challenging the nexus between organised crime and corruption' 7 *CMI U4 Issue* (2009); Corva D, 'Neoliberal globalization and the war on drugs: Transnationalizing illiberal governance in the Americas' 27 *Political Geography* (2008) 176; Henshaw C, 'Strengthening the Rule of Law in the Pacific through International Crime Cooperation' 15 *Australian International Law Journal* (2008) 109; above n6

77 Farrales M, 'What is Corruption? A history of corruption studies and the great definitions debate', *University of San Diego Working Paper Series* [2005] available at: http://papers.ssrn.com/sol3/papers.cfm?abstract_id=1739962 (last visited 1 March 2018)

78 [Transcript No.9] Anonymity Requested. AG Department; Asa [Transcript No.10]

79 Above n11

80 Beare ME, 'Corruption and Organised Crime: Lessons from history' 28 *Crime, Law and Social Change* (1997) 155; Beare ME, 'North America: A perspective on the globalisation of organised crime' 6(1) *Journal of Financial Crime* (1993) 81

81 Corva D, 'Neoliberal globalization and the war on drugs: Transnationalizing illiberal governance in the Americas' 27 *Political Geography* (2008) 176

82 above n72

83 above n37 at ii

84 [Transcript No.15] Anonymity Requested. PNG OPP

85 Nadelmann EA, 'Global prohibition regimes: The evolution of norms in international society' 44(4) *International Organization* (22 May 1990) 479

86 Koim [Transcript No.6]; [Transcript No.7] Anonymity Requested. Royal PNG Constabulary

87 Rodrigues [Transcript No.2]; Prescott [Transcript No.4]; [Transcript No.16] Anonymity Requested. AusAID

88 Lowy Interpreter, Hayward-Jones J *PNG Backs Up Its Pacific Leadership Claims* (10 July 2015) available at: http://www.lowyinterpreter.org/post/2015/07/10/PNG-backs-up-its-Pacific-leadership-claims.aspx (last visited 1 March 2018)

89 See Chapter 4 for discussion of the role played by Australia historically in PNG

90 Levinson J, 'Multilateral Financing Institutions: What form of accountability?' 8(1) *American University International Law Review* (1992) 39, at 39–40
91 See discussion of interest based aid incentives in Chapter 3
92 For an introduction see Bayliss K, Fine B, Waeyenberge EV, *Political Economy of Development: The World Bank, Neoliberalism and Development Research* (Pluto Press, 1st Edition, 2011)
93 Walton GW, 'The Limitations of Neoliberal Logic in the Anti-Corruption Industry' 60(2) *Crime Law and Social Change* (2013) at 150
94 ibid. at 153–154
95 ibid. at 160
96 [Transcript No.12] Anonymity Requested. Eco Forestry Forum PNG (EFF PNG); Dademo [Transcript No.3]
97 The SABLs in PNG are a good example of this, discussed earlier in this chapter
98 Rodrigues [Transcript No.2]
99 Stephens [Transcript No.8]
100 ibid.
101 See ActNOW!PNG, *Rimbunan Hijau Logging Operations* available at: http://www.actnowpng.org/project/Rimbunan%20Hijau%20logging%20operations (last visited 1 March 2018)
102 Green Peace (2006) Forest Crime File, *Rimbunan Hijau Group: Thirty Years of Forest Plunder*, available at: http://www.greenpeace.org/eu-unit/Global/eu-unit/reports-briefings/2009/3/rimbunan-hijau-group-thirty-y.pdf (last visited 1 March 2018)
103 FATF Online, *About Us*, available at: http://www.fatf-gafi.org/pages/aboutus/ (last visited 1 March 2018)
104 Asa [Transcript No.10]
105 Nadelmann EA and Andreas P, *Policing the Globe: Criminalization and crime control in international relations* (Oxford University Press, 1st Edition, 2006)
106 TI, *Who We Are*, available at: http://www.transparency.org/whoweare/organisation/mission_vision_and_values (last visited 1 March 2018)
107 Asa [Transcript No.10]

References

Abbott KW and Snidal D, 'Values and Interests: International legalization in the fight against corruption' 31 *Journal of Legal Studies* (2002) 141.

ActNOW! PNG *Government Should Not Shift the Blame on SABL Land Grab* (10 April 2015) available at: http://actnowpng.org/node/25531 (last visited 1 March 2018).

ActNOW! PNG, *Rimbunan Hijau Logging Operations* (23 April 2010) available at: http://actnowpng.org/watch/Rimbunan%20Hijau%20logging%20operations (last visited 1 March 2018).

ADB /OECD, *Anti-Corruption Initiative for the Asia Pacific: Strategic principles and operational activities of the initiative* (2010) ('ADB/OECD Strategic Principles, 2010').

Andreas P, 'Illicit Globalization: Myths, misconceptions, and historical lessons' 126 *Political Science Quarterly* 3 (2011) 403.

Bayliss K, Fine B, Waeyenberge EV, *Political Economy of Development: The World Bank, Neoliberalism and Development Research* (Pluto Press, 1st Edition, 2011).

Beare ME, 'Corruption and Organised Crime: Lessons from History' 28 *Crime, Law and Social Change* (1997) 155.

Beare ME, 'North America: A perspective on the globalisation of organised crime', 6(1) *Journal of Financial Crime* (1993) 81.

Boister N 'Transnational Criminal Law?' 14(5) *EJIL* (2003) 953.

Bridenthal R, 'Special Issue: The hidden history of crime, corruption, and states' 45(3) *Journal of Social History* (2012) 575.

Carr I 'Corruption, legal solution and limits of law' 3(3) *International Journal of Law in Context* (2007) 227.

Corva D, 'Neoliberal globalization and the war on drugs: Transnationalizing illiberal governance in the Americas' 27 *Political Geography* (2008) 176.

Criminal Code Act 1974 ('*CCA*').

Farrales M, 'What is Corruption? A history of corruption studies and the great definitions debate', *University of San Diego Working Paper Series* [2005] available at: http://papers.ssrn.com/sol3/papers.cfm?abstract_id=1739962 (last visited 1 March 2018).

FATF Online, *About Us*, available at: http://www.fatf-gafi.org/pages/aboutus/ (last visited 1 March 2018).

Green Peace, *Rimbunan Hijau Group: Thirty Years of Forest Plunder* (May 2006) available at: http://www.greenpeace.org/eu-unit/Global/eu-unit/reports-briefings/2009/3/rimbunan-hijau-group-thirty-y.pdf (last visited 1 March 2018).

Henshaw C, 'Strengthening the Rule of Law in the Pacific through International Crime Cooperation' 15 *Australian International Law Journal* (2008) 109.

Koh H, 'Transnational Legal Process' 75 *Neb. L. Rev.* (1996) 181.

Larmour P, 'Corruption in REDD+ Schemes: a framework for analysis', in Graycar A and Smith RG (Eds), *Handbook of Global Research and Practice in Corruption* (Edward Elgar, 2011) 157.

Levinson J, 'Multilateral Financing Institutions: What form of accountability?' 8(1) *American University International Law Review* (1992) 39.

Lowy Interpreter, Hayward-Jones J, *PNG Backs Up Its Pacific Leadership Claims* (10 July 2015) available at: https://www.lowyinstitute.org/the-interpreter/png-backs-its-pacific-leadership-claims (last visited 1 March 2018).

McCulloch J, 'Transnational Crime as Productive Fiction' 24(2) *Social Justice* (2007) 19.

Nadelmann EA and Andreas P, *Policing the Globe: Criminalization and crime control in international relations* (Oxford University Press, 1st Edition, 2006).

Nadelmann EA, 'Global prohibition regimes: The evolution of norms in international society' 44(4) *International Organization* (22 May 1990) 479.

Papua New Guinea, Mirou, *Commission of Inquiry into Special Agriculture and Business Leases (SABL): Report* (June, 2013) ('SABL Report 2013').

Papua New Guinea, *National Anti-Corruption Strategy 2010–2030* (2010) ('NACS').

Passas N, 'Globalization and Transnational Crime: Effects of criminogenic asymmetries', in Williams P and Vlassis D (Eds), *Combatting Transnational Crime: Concepts, Activities and Responses* (Frank Cass Publishing, 2013) 22.

Proceeds of Crime Act 2005 ('*POCA*').

Reed Q, 'Squeezing a Balloon? Challenging the nexus between organised crime and corruption' 7 *CMI U4 Issue* (2009).

Pacific Islands Forum Secretariat, *The Pacific Plan for Strengthening Regional Cooperation and Integration*, (2005) ('The Pacific Plan 2005').

TI, *Who We Are*, available at: http://www.transparency.org/whoweare/organisation/mission_vision_and_values (last visited 1 March 2018).

Twining W, 'Normative and Legal Pluralism' 20 *Duke Journal of Comparative & International Law* (2010) 473.

UNCAC Coalition, *About Us*, available at: http://uncaccoalition.org/en_US/about-us/about-the-coalition/ (last visited 1 March 2018).

UNESC, *Secretary General Report: Existing International Legal Instruments, Recommendations and other Documents Addressing Corruption*, E/CN.15/2001/3 ('Secretary General Report, 2001').

United Nations Convention against Corruption, opened for signature 9 December 2003, 2349 UNTS 41 (entered into force 14 December 2005) ('*UNCAC*').

UNODC, World Bank, *Stolen Asset Recovery Initiative*, available at: http://star.worldbank.org/star/ (last visited 1 March 2018).

UNODC/UNDP, *UN Pacific Regional Anti-Corruption (UN-PRAC) Project Document* (20 April 2012) ('UN-PRAC').

Walton GW, 'The Limitations of Neoliberal Logic in the Anti-Corruption Industry', 60(2) *Crime Law and Social Change* (2013).

Beare ME, 'The Business of Bribery: Globalization, economic liberalization, and the "problem" of corruption', in Beare ME (ed), *Critical Reflections on Transnational Organized Crime, Money Laundering, and Corruption* (University of Toronto Press, 1st Edition, 2003) 88.

World Bank, *Second Mining Sector Institutional Strengthening* (TA P102396, 26 June 2008) available at: http://projects.worldbank.org/P102396/pg-second-mining-sector-inst-strengthening-ta?lang=en (last visited 1 March 2018).

Zumbansen P, 'Defining the Space of Transnational Law: Legal theory, global governance, and legal pluralism' 21 *Transnational Law & Contemporary Problems* (2011) 305.

7 The final question – possibilities for the future and concluding remarks

Introduction

The United Nations Convention against Corruption (UNCAC) is the primary legal tool of the global anti-corruption regime. The Convention plays a coordinating role for the regime, supporting consistent criminalisation of specific acts across all Member States and facilitating interaction between *States Parties*, through operation of the Implementation Review Mechanisms. The regime is currently in the fourth stage of norm evolution and must overcome a range of challenges to achieve success. Success is defined as evolution of the regime to the fifth and final stage, resulting in a substantial reduction in corrupt activity globally. To achieve the final stage, the joint challenge of government manipulation and limited political will must be overcome, along with practical challenges of resource and capacity limitations. Some other risks and challenges noted by critics appear less relevant, particularly in the PNG context.

The extent of UNCAC's impact on PNG is difficult to gauge. The PNG government emphasises UNCAC's role as a representation of PNG's existing commitment to anti-corruption. In this way, the power of membership to promote positive public perceptions is clear. While the PNG approach to corruption is consistent with UNCAC, practical understanding of the Convention is limited, especially outside the executive branch of government directly involved in the Implementation Review process. This raises concerns of co-optation and inapplicability. However, in the context of PNG such criticisms appear to overemphasise the coercive power of UNCAC and the global anti-corruption regime. Political dynamics and the flexibility of the UNCAC framework support a view of the Convention as a neutral tool, rather than a coercive and potentially harmful set of obligations. External actors' ability to use UNCAC coercively are limited by economic or diplomatic interests, especially as the number of external actors increases while the number of opportunities to engage domestically remains roughly the same.

Findings from this research illustrate the complexity of corruption and of anti-corruption efforts. By analysing the interaction between actors, values, and interests in the context of PNG some key insights have emerged regarding the nature of UNCAC and challenges faced in implementing and enforcing the global anti-corruption regime. While some criticisms and challenges were found to be of limited relevance in the PNG context, others have emerged as substantial hurdles. Continued research is certainly warranted to address the relevance of these challenges beyond the PNG context. It would be especially useful to apply Nadelmann and Andreas' model,[1] combined with a focus on actors, values, and interests,[2] to other domestic case studies around the world. In the meantime, addressing the hurdles presented by this research in the context of PNG may provide valuable possibilities for enhancing domestic relevance of UNCAC in a number of Member States. This enhanced relevance may in turn support the global anti-corruption regime in attaining the fifth and final stage of norm evolution.

The two most substantial risk factors limiting the implementation and enforcement of UNCAC in PNG are: (1) co-optation of the global anti-corruption regime by external actors, and (2) manipulation and misuse of the regime by domestic governments. The practical challenges of resource and capacity limitations and keeping up with the technical advances of perpetrators are also highlighted by the fieldwork. These practical challenges reflect the risks noted by Nadelmann and Andreas with regard to implementation and enforcement of any global prohibition regime.[3] The possibility of co-optation by external actors was noted by critics including Carr, Beare, Scholenhardt, and Schutte, in Chapter 1. Potential manipulation of UNCAC membership by domestic states was not directly addressed by the theoretical framework. This challenge emerges from the fieldwork findings and subsequent analysis. However, this challenge is well understood by looking to Nadelmann and Andreas' model and the implicit emphasis of this model on the power of perceptions.

This research supports the view that UNCAC is a powerful tool to promote anti-corruption efforts and support the successful evolution of the global anti-corruption regime. While the risks and limitations of UNCAC and the global anti-corruption regime are not insignificant, the potential for UNCAC to support anti-corruption efforts at the international, regional, and domestic levels should not be overlooked. In order to improve UNCAC and secure the fifth and final phase of norm evolution for the global anti-corruption regime, it is necessary to address all of the challenges noted above and present possible solutions to each of them.

It is argued in this chapter that meaningful engagement and interaction between diverse actors, particularly domestic actors, on the issue of corruption and application of UNCAC could address each of these obstacles simultaneously. Meaningful engagement may allow the global anti-corruption regime to gain and maintain legitimacy and avoid the risks of co-optation by external actors, or manipulation by uncommitted governments. Ultimately, such steps may catalyse the global anti-corruption regime into the fifth and final phase of evolution and result in the substantial reduction in corrupt activity globally. Such an approach may be usefully applied to other existing or emerging global prohibition regimes.

Nadelmann and Andreas demonstrate that most prohibition regimes evolve through a similar five-stage pattern.[4] The latter stages of evolution require genuine and sustained commitment by domestic governments to secure effective implementation and enforcement.[5] Therefore, the same challenges are likely to be relevant to most global prohibition regimes. If measures that enhance the engagement of diverse domestic actors assist in limiting the risks of manipulation and coercion, such measures may be a valuable tool for any global prohibition regime.

Fieldwork in PNG demonstrates that general domestic understanding of the substance of UNCAC is limited. Non-state actors had the least exposure to UNCAC, despite substantial interest in engaging government on corruption issues and utilising obligations under international law.[6] All interview participants acknowledged the importance of reputation in influencing state action. Government actors in PNG recognised that international perceptions were important,[7] NGO actors highlighted the desire of governments to promote a positive image of their anti-corruption efforts, and members of foreign states and multilateral institutions noted the diverse impact that perceptions can have on political and economic opportunities.[8] As explored in Chapter 6, the power to influence UNCAC's application ultimately rests with the governments of *States Parties*. When this assertion is combined with the power of perceptions to motivate government action, it appears that domestic actors outside government may have substantial power to shape the application of UNCAC in a way that is consistent, context specific, and relevant to the unique conditions of the State party.

If domestic NGOs, civil society actors, private organisations, and individual citizens are empowered to engage with their governments on the topic of corruption and are aware of state obligations under UNCAC, it may be possible to simultaneously combat discursive manipulation stemming from a lack of political will, as well as the potential for external influence and co-optation. Furthermore, engagement by diverse non-state actors in domestic anti-corruption efforts and with UNCAC's Implementation and Review process may support a more context-relevant approach. This approach will be less susceptible to resource and capacity limitations, that currently pose a threat to the success of the regime.

Domestic engagement could be facilitated in a variety of ways, each of which is documented below. In addition to engaging diverse actors in the process of UNCAC evaluation and application, technological developments and targeted financial and technical assistances through the Implementation Review process have the potential to alleviate some of the more practical challenges, such as resource and capacity limitations, that are preventing successful enforcement of UNCAC. These tools may also assist in enhancing levels of engagement between actors engaged in effective application of the regime.

The current state of the global anti-corruption regime

Before expanding on the above ideas, a summary of the current state of the regime is presented. This summary situates the reader within the broader theoretical framework of global prohibition regime evolution, enhancing the relevance of suggestions for the future.

Despite large scale ratification and implementation of UNCAC, and participation in the Implementation Review process, corruption remains a substantial problem globally. The global anti-corruption regime has failed to achieve the fifth and final phase of norm evolution. Nadelmann and Andreas note a range of challenges that may limit the successful evolution of a global prohibition regime. These challenges include dissident and deviant actors that refuse to participate in or comply with the regime; formally compliant states that are unable or unwilling to fully implement and enforce the regime; and the nature of the target activity.[9] The nature of the target activity relates to the following features: (1) the level of technical sophistication required; (2) the resources and expertise necessary; (3) the likelihood of the activity being reported; (4) the ability to conceal the activity and its profits and the extent of demand for the activity; and (5) substitutability of the activity for a legitimate alternative.[10]

Corruption as a target activity has a unique combination of the above traits. On the one hand, it does not require a high level of sophistication or expertise to commit a corrupt act, on the other hand it does require a position of power or access to someone in a position of power. The resources necessary to commit corruption depend on the nature of the corrupt act, the actors involved, and the desired outcome. Because corruption, by its nature, involves relatively powerful actors and is generally an act that requires two consenting parties, it is often easily concealed. The participants directly involved in a corrupt transaction certainly have a disincentive to report the activity. However, technological advancements and increasing financial regulation are making it more difficult to conceal the often large sums of money used in corrupt transactions. Furthermore, developments that allow for anonymous tip offs and protection of witnesses may enhance the likelihood of reporting corruption.

Corrupt activity does not lend itself easily to discussions about demand and substitutability as it is not a commodity-based crime, compared with trafficking crimes or vice activities. However, as opportunities for foreign investment and aid increase in both number and size, the incentive for those in positions of power to act corruptly is also likely to increase. Furthermore, there does not appear to be an easy substitute for corrupt activity, from the perspective of the actors engaged, because corruption involves inappropriate use of power and influence. In cases where pay scales for government actors are low and do not cover the cost of living, a substitute for corrupt behaviour would be better compensation. However, in cases of grand corruption involving actors who are simply seeking to improve their position, no real substitute exists. In this regard, increasing the likelihood of being caught and the penalty for committing the activity may be the only way to reduce demand. An alternative would be to target supply. If the number of actors willing to pay bribes was reduced, perhaps the level of corruption would also be reduced. However, if one actor is unwilling to engage in a particular activity but demand remains constant, another actor is likely to step up and fill that demand.[11]

This discussion illustrates that corruption is a complex activity and in many ways does not appear to be well suited to a criminal law and enforcement approach. Despite this, Nadelmann and Andreas illustrate their model using a mix of successful and failed regimes, each with its own unique combination of attributes. In the case of successful regimes, piracy and slavery are particularly illustrative. Piracy was not easily substitutable activity. Once delegitimised, piracy was effectively robbery on the high seas and the alternative was not to engage in robbery.[12] However, the regime was still successful in greatly reducing the levels of piracy, in large part because regime proponents were able to harness technology to their advantage.[13] When considering piracy and slavery, no substantial expertise was required to commit either activity. However, the strength of moral arguments against slavery mobilised sufficient commitment and action by state and non-state actors, resulting in near complete eradication of the activity.[14] An interesting parallel exists between slavery and corruption. Both activities require a unique institutional structure to exist. Nadelmann holds that:

> The most important vulnerability of slavery . . . involves its substantial dependence on legal institutions to sustain itself . . . slavery typically involves an ongoing coercive relationship between private individuals . . . without the support of a legal institution, slavery can only persist where nonlegal social norms in support of slavery are strong, where the state is sufficiently disinterested in eradicating slavery that it ignores the efforts of slave owners to retain their slaves, or where slaves acquiesce, in one way or another, to their enslavement.[15]

As already noted, corruption relies on the uniquely powerful position of at least one actor in the transaction. In this way, corruption relies on an institutional structure that allows for power without accountability, suggesting that targeting the institutional structures that provide individual actors with power, and increasing the levels of accountability required in those positions, may help to combat corruption.

In addition to the challenges presented by Nadelmann and Andreas, critics of the global anti-corruption regime present more specific risks. From the critique of the global anti-corruption regime and UNCAC, four key risk factors were extracted and presented in Chapter 1. These risk factors were: (1) the lack of definitional clarity regarding the target activity; (2) the links between corruption and other forms of transnational criminal activity; (3) the use of this connection to promote a focus on criminal law and enforcement measures to combat corruption; and (4) the potential inapplicability of the regime and its legal tools with the diverse contexts in which it must operate.

The research presented by this book has shown that limited political will and resource and capacity limitations are highly relevant restrictive factors in the implementation and enforcement of UNCAC domestically. Additionally, the PNG case suggests that some risk factors misinterpret the role of UNCAC and overemphasise the coercive power of this transnational legal tool.

Three specific findings emerge from the PNG case. First, the risk of external manipulation due to lack of definitional clarity fails to acknowledge complex relationships between domestic and external actors. This risk factor was based on the assumption that flexibility is open to manipulation by actors seeking to hijack the regime for their own interest. In the case of PNG, the complex relationship between domestic and external actors illustrates that such coercive influence is limited by diplomatic concerns and competition between external actors, who seek access to domestic economic and political opportunities.

The criticism that the global anti-corruption regime overemphasises criminal law and enforcement measures, failing to acknowledge the causes of corrupt activity within unique domestic contexts, was also of limited value. In PNG, and in many other UNCAC Member States, criminal law measures against corruption have existed since long before the evolution of the global anti-corruption regime. It is inappropriate to view these measures as the product of the global prohibition regime. Furthermore, criminal law and enforcement measures require concerted domestic effort to implement and enforce. When political will, resources, and capacity are lacking, such measures will remain under-utilised, regardless of external pressure or coercion. Additionally, UNCAC provides a range of additional measures beyond criminalisation, including preventive measures and measures to enhance cooperation between states, which enhance its value as a flexible tool for domestic anti-corruption efforts.

Finally, in the case of PNG, the links between corruption and other forms of transnational crime were weak. This illustrates that, despite discursive adherence to the regime as whole, UNCAC Member States emphasise those aspects of the Convention that are relevant to their values and interests.

Lack of definitional clarity, raised as a risk factor by critics, does not account for the diverse values and interests that shape and constrain engagement between states and other powerful actors. From a different perspective, the flexibility of UNCAC can be viewed as a strength, allowing the regime to be implemented and enforced in a way that was contextually relevant and thus more likely to achieve long-term support, both in terms of political will and resources. However, the PNG case also illustrated that the flexibility of the UNCAC framework may present opportunities for a new risk, not addressed by earlier critique. This risk stems from domestic manipulation by governments seeking to promote politically and economically profitable relationships with external actors. The implicit importance of perceptions in Nadelmann and Andreas' model helps to explain the existence of this risk.

Nadelmann and Andreas view moral entrepreneurs as central to shaping the nature and application of any global prohibition regime. This influence is illustrated by the success of the anti-slavery regime. Despite substantial economic interests that supported the continuation of the slave trade:

> The spread of abolitionist principles . . . strongly influenced elite opinion in countries that had developed the strongest dependencies on African slavery. Both Spain . . . and Brazil . . . were strongly influenced by the violent fate of slavery in the United States and by the growing sense of moral isolation that followed . . . especially among the laggards, the consciousness of being perceived as deviant surely weighed heavily in the decisions of local rulers to abolish slavery.[16]

In the PNG case, government actors were certainly concerned about being perceived as deviant.[17] The reasons for this preoccupation with perception are not simply because of vanity, but because of the consequences related to this perception. As noted in Chapter 6, the appearance of corruption domestically can limit options for aid and investment.

Preoccupation with perceptions usefully empowers moral entrepreneurs to promote the internalisation of a particular approach to the target activity. However, if moral entrepreneurs do not succeed in changing the views of dominant actors within a specific domestic context, there may be an opportunity for subversive misuse of the regime by governments seeking to maintain an outward image of compliance, while remaining disinterested in combatting the target activity. It could be argued that this dynamic is the reason for the challenge of 'non-compliant' states, noted by Nadelmann and Andreas.[18] This challenge is separate to the challenge of 'deviant states and individuals', but can equally result in the failure of a regime to achieve the final stage.[19] While deviant states and individuals actively oppose the regime, unwilling states may outwardly support it, while inwardly avoiding meaningful compliance.

Possible improvements to UNCAC

The primary challenges faced by the global anti-corruption regime are limited resources and capacity, combined with potential misuse and manipulation of UNCAC membership by domestic governments. Misuse and manipulation may result in a failure to implement, and certainly to enforce, the regime. Despite outward support for the regime and its goals, through membership of UNCAC and participation in the Implementation Review process, governments may avoid application of UNCAC in practice. This avoidance will ultimately prevent the success of the global anti-corruption regime, by limiting its impact domestically. In addition, the risk of external co-optation of the regime cannot be ruled out. However, practical constraints on external actors, which must maintain positive relationships with domestic governments in order to achieve their goals, limit the extent of this risk in practice. Ultimately, the power to enforce a regime remains with individual states and their governments.

These findings help to explain why the global anti-corruption regime is struggling to reach the final stage of evolution, despite near universal ratification of UNCAC and extensive participation in the Implementation Review processes. The suggestions presented below are targeted at overcoming these challenges, which may in turn assist the regime to achieve the final stage.

Enhanced engagement: a general suggestion for improvement

The first suggestion for supporting the evolution of the global anti-corruption regime is a general one. 'Enhanced engagement' is a concept that leverages the power of perceptions, which appear fundamental to the process of norm internalisation and adherence to prohibition regimes. Perceptions are an important factor in empowering moral entrepreneurs. However, if domestic governments are unwilling to actively implement and enforce the regime, they may subversively avoid taking necessary action, despite outward support. In this context, the power of moral entrepreneurs, especially in the form of external actors and organisations, may be limited.

A second concern is that powerful external actors, including states, multilateral institutions, and transnational moral entrepreneurs, may promote action in line with the regime in a way that does not suit the domestic context. In this case, willing governments that seek to implement and enforce the regime may fail to achieve the desired outcome of substantially reducing the target activity. This situation also increases the risk of harmful side effects, as discussed by critical authors in Chapter 1.[20]

Enhancing engagement of domestic actors in the process of UNCAC's implementation and enforcement, as well as facilitating increased interaction between diverse actors on the issue of anti-corruption and methods for combatting anti-corruption, may help to overcome the challenges of unwilling governments and the application of inappropriate and potentially harmful approaches. Some possibilities for enhancing engagement are discussed below, noting how this approach fits with the findings from the research on the nature of UNCAC and the current dynamics of implementation and enforcement illustrated by the PNG case.

Improving working knowledge of UNCAC domestically

Education is one method for enhancing engagement to support UNCAC and the global anti-corruption regime. Domestic non-state actors must be aware of and understand the nature of state obligations under UNCAC, if they are going to hold governments to account based on their commitments as *States Parties* to the Convention. As illustrated in Chapter 5, awareness of the substance of UNCAC was extremely limited in the case of PNG. The United Nations (UN) may be a useful institutional channel for providing relevant information to domestic actors, taking on the supporting and coordinating role noted by Nadelmann and Andreas.[21]

The educative process should be presented in as neutral and technical a manner as possible, to allow domestic actors to shape their own approach to UNCAC. This will help to ensure that governments implement and enforce UNCAC in a manner that is relevant to the domestic context. The UN may be at a unique advantage in providing educational assistance, because of both its expertise on the details of UNCAC and its perceived neutrality, compared with other actors such as states and multilateral lenders.[22] Domestic non-state actors that should be engaged in the process include NGOs and civil society groups, the general public, and private organisations. Targeting the media will likely have powerful effects, as news media shape public perceptions. Therefore, the media is in a unique position to apply pressure to governments.

Gaining access to these domestic actors may be challenging. Some *States Parties* are likely to oppose the UN taking on this educative role. The perceived neutrality of the UN stems from its ability to work with diverse Member States based on common goals, illustrated by state membership to the UN and to a particular convention.[23] While all *States Parties* to UNCAC have acknowledged their support for the objective of eliminating corruption, the extent to which these states see a role for civil society and other non-state actors in this process varies considerably.[24] The United Nations Convention against Corruption provides for the involvement of civil society groups in Article 13,[25] but there is a risk that efforts to promote inclusion may weaken the working relationship between the UN and Member State governments. This outcome should be avoided.

A possible solution to this challenge is for the educative role to be taken up by those non-government actors already informed and engaged with UNCAC. A good example of such an actor is Transparency International (TI), an organisation that has a strong international presence, and has established more than 100 domestic chapters.[26] Transparency International is perhaps the foremost moral entrepreneur for the global anti-corruption regime. It has performed this role through lobbying foreign governments and creating an international presence that has elevated corruption on the international agenda. Domestically, TI chapters are seeking to raise the profile of corruption and target government weakness to perceptions of corruption. Common methods used by TI chapters include public criticism and awareness building activities. In PNG, the TI Anti-Corruption Walk is one such example of awareness building.[27] However, at least in PNG, there was no substantial interaction between the national TI chapter and other NGOs interested in combatting corruption domestically. TI PNG appeared to be focused primarily on government and private sector engagement.

Increasing the level of interaction between TI and other non-government actors domestically may help to raise the level of awareness and education regarding UNCAC as a tool for these actors. This would assist in dissemination of educative documents, such as those produced by TI in cooperation with the UNCAC civil society Coalition. These documents are a good example of attempts to expand knowledge and understanding of UNCAC and its value to domestic non-government actors. They include the titles 'Using the UN Convention against Corruption to advance anti-corruption efforts: A guide'[28] and 'civil society Guide: UNCAC and the Private Sector'.[29] Both publications cover the structure of UNCAC, methods for engaging with the Convention, and ways to use the framework to achieve positive outcomes when combatting corruption. The publications highlight the powerful opportunity for engagement presented by civil society participation in the Implementation Review process of UNCAC.[30]

Supporting dialogue through the Implementation and Review process

Domestic non-government actors may use knowledge about UNCAC and *States Parties* obligations under the Convention to lobby for government action. These actors may motivate meaningful action in situations where governments would otherwise have left their obligations unimplemented or under-enforced. This approach will assist in combatting the challenge of manipulation and misuse. Domestic accountability will limit the ability of governments to use UNCAC to promote a positive image of anti-corruption efforts, despite lack of political will to implement and enforce obligations. If domestic non-state actors are directly involved in the Implementation Review process, the power of these actors to illustrate areas of success and failure will be strengthened substantially. Domestic actors may also present alternative suggestions for combatting corruption, conforming to the UNCAC framework, but responding to unique domestic challenges. In addition to taking on an adversarial role, domestic non-state actors have the power to support enhanced relevance of UNCAC domestically, targeting the risks of external co-optation and regime inapplicability.

Unfortunately, a lack of political will may limit access of domestic non-state actors to the Implementation Review process. Justification for engagement, on the basis that domestic non-state actors may limit the potential for governments to manipulate UNCAC membership, may encourage these governments to avoid such engagement. Governments that seek to use membership of UNCAC to promote a particular image are unlikely to support involvement of actors that may undermine this image. It is important that a continued effort be made to promote the importance of non-state actor engagement. This could be done through recourse to specific provisions of UNCAC, in particular Article 13, as well as through the Implementation Review mechanism directly. Resolution 4/1 'Mechanism for the Review of Implementation of the United Nations Convention against Corruption', adopted by the Conference of *States Parties* to UNCAC:

> *[U]rges States parties*, in accordance with article 13 of the Convention, to continue promoting the participation of individuals and groups outside the public sector, such as civil society, non-governmental organizations and community- based organizations, in the prevention of and the fight against corruption, and encourages *States parties* to enhance their capacity in this regard.[31]

Targeted assistance from the UN, in terms of both technical and financial support, could assist in promoting government/non-government interaction. States may be encouraged to include domestic non-state actors in the UNCAC Implementation Review process if inclusion resulted in increased access to support. Another motivating factor could be the argument that engaging diverse domestic actors in the Implementation Review process may assist governments to enhance the relevance and applicability of UNCAC. Actors involved in the Implementation Review process in PNG noted the importance of domestic efforts based on a unique understanding of national and local contexts and challenges.[32] Domestic non-state actors also have a unique perspective on domestic challenges and possibilities for action. In this regard, these actors could be promoted as partners for governments seeking to successfully combat corruption domestically. Partnership between government and non-government actors could assist in reducing external pressure to adopt particular measures that may be costly and are unlikely to succeed based on peculiarities of the domestic context.

Adapting UNCAC based on domestic experience

Education and access are two elements of engagement that may facilitate enhanced effectiveness of UNCAC and support the global anti-corruption regime to reach the final stage of evolution. A third element of engagement is 'adaptability'. This element refers to state and non-state engagement with the Implementation Review process, not only in terms of supporting implementation of UNCAC, but also in terms of contributing to the evolution of the Convention in a way that enhances its effectiveness. The engagement of diverse domestic actors in the Implementation Review process of UNCAC provides an opportunity for feedback loops between domestic and international spheres, as envisioned by Koh.[33]

UNCAC may be able to utilise the experiences of diverse actors across all *States Parties* to enhance the Convention and the broader global anti-corruption regime. This transformative potential could be grounded in the text of UNCAC, which allows for the possibility of alteration and amendment, under Article 69.[34] Feedback from domestic government and other non-government actors could contribute to positive enhancement and alteration of the regime, based on domestic experiences. This adaptability would help to overcome the challenge of inapplicability and external co-optation, making allowance for changes to be made to UNCAC that either enhance the effectiveness of provisions, or replace provisions that have proved to be particularly ineffective or even harmful.

Facilitating adaptability of UNCAC, based on domestic engagement, reduces the chances of harmful side effects related to inapplicability. This adaptability could also increase the power of the global anti-corruption regime to combat corrupt activity. Corruption is likely to continue to evolve, utilising technological developments and reacting to anti-corruption measures. Adaptability of regime tools such as UNCAC, limits the opportunities for deviant actors to gain the upper hand.

The possibility of a complaints mechanism

Finally, it is worth mentioning the possible development of an international complaints mechanism for UNCAC. If domestic non-state actors are educated about UNCAC and are aware of their governments' obligations under the Convention, they will be empowered to act as whistle-blowers, drawing attention to government failures and leveraging the power of perceptions to motivate government action. However, in extreme cases, perceptions alone may not be a significant incentive for governments to take action or amend their actions to conform to their international obligations. In these cases, an international complaints mechanism may be a useful way to hold governments accountable.

A complaints mechanism could be developed based on the existing model in international human rights law.[35] However, such a mechanism would require substantial human and financial resources and may promote an adversarial relationship between government and non-government actors. Such a relationship would undermine the trust necessary to facilitate the former suggestions for positive engagement and interaction. Further research should be conducted on this topic, to establish whether a complaints mechanism would add value to UNCAC and the broader global anti-corruption regime, or contribute to unproductive conflicts between actors.

External assistance and technological development: a supporting role for the UN and other external actors

Technology plays an important role in anti-corruption efforts. In addition to enhanced engagement, technology may be harnessed to combat challenges of government misapplication on the one hand, and regime inapplicability and external co-optation on the other. Nadelmann notes that 'technological developments can strongly influence the vulnerability of an activity to suppression efforts'.[36] Technology can benefit corrupt actors and complicate anti-corruption efforts, as noted by participants in the fieldwork documented in Chapter 5.[37] However, technology also has the potential to benefit anti-corruption efforts. Enhancing technology and its use in anti-corruption efforts may reduce the cost of such efforts, in terms of both financial and human capital. Technology may also support the success of UNCAC and the global anti-corruption regime through facilitation of engagement between diverse actors. The establishment of the Open Parliament project provides an example of this:

> The Open Parliament Project (OPP) is a partnership between Transparency International (PNG), European Union and Parliament to support the Speakers vision to 'restore, reform and modernize' parliament. The OPP has established a database of information on the parliament and its members which can be accessed through variety of means including website www.parliament.gov.pg and SMS by texting to 70000300 the first and last name of the MP or the district name. The project is not designed to criticize the Members of Parliament or the institution of Parliament itself. The overarching goal of the project is to build the integrity of parliament.[38]

This example demonstrates that technological solutions can be combined with the engagement-based solutions to extend the value of both.

Harnessing technology can also enhance research and evaluation mechanisms. Given that corruption is inherently difficult to measure,[39] efforts to evaluate the effectiveness of UNCAC and the global anti-corruption regime remain challenging. Technological developments should be utilised to enhance transparency of government processes, and increase the quality and extent of records covering corruption cases and outcomes. Increased data will enhance understanding of corrupt activity and the strengths and weaknesses of anti-corruption methods. These insights could be used to improve approaches to corrupt activity and reshape anti-corruption efforts to enhance their effectiveness.

Summary: the future of UNCAC and the global anti-corruption regime

To conclude, this research has embarked on an extensive analysis of UNCAC and the global anti-corruption regime. Through empirical research and fieldwork in PNG, it has shown that some criticisms of UNCAC and the global anti-corruption regime are overstated. In particular, the risks of inapplicability and external co-optation fail to acknowledge UNCAC's flexibility and do not account for the ultimate power of states to implement and enforce the regime. However, substantial challenges remain.

The PNG case illustrates an additional risk factor that may limit the success of UNCAC and the global anti-corruption regime. While UNCAC's flexibility can be seen as a strength, it also presents an opportunity for misuse. States seeking to promote outward compliance with UNCAC, without possessing genuine political will to implement and enforce the Convention, may ratify UNCAC and participate in the Implementation Review process, without taking meaningful enforcement steps. This limits the effectiveness of UNCAC and reduces the possibility of success for the global anti-corruption regime.

Considering the above findings, enhanced education about and engagement with UNCAC is suggested as a tool for improving UNCAC relevance domestically and increasing the global anti-corruption regime's chance of success. Engagement should be facilitated through interaction within states, between state and non-state actors, and between states and other transnational actors at the regional and international levels. Engagement must address inherent power asymmetries, political interests, and diverse values held by participating actors.

Law, transnational or otherwise, cannot operate in isolation of social and political dynamics. The PNG case study illustrates the limits of external co-optation, due to interest-based agendas and diplomatic concerns. However, future efforts to prevent manipulation and window-dressing on the part of national governments must be careful to avoid coercive methods that fail to account for the complexities of domestic contexts. If the global anti-corruption regime is to succeed, UNCAC must be utilised by a diverse range of actors with a deep understanding of the Convention and the challenges and limitations facing application of the Convention in Member States.

Enhanced understanding of UNCAC and Member State obligations can be a tool to neutralise the risk of domestic manipulation and the risks of external coercion. Both risks must be neutralised if the regime is to succeed. As one risk is mitigated, the possibility of the opposing risk is enhanced. This reality demonstrates the value of UNCAC as a tool of the global anti-corruption regime, and highlights the limitations of purely domestic, or purely international, approaches to combatting corruption.

A balance must be struck between supporting contextually relevant approaches to anti-corruption and ensuring meaningful action is taken across diverse contexts. The United Nations Convention against Corruption may provide a framework to achieve this balance. However, opportunities for meaningful engagement must be enhanced at all levels and adaptability of the regime should be supported. Most importantly, power imbalances between actors must be addressed, ensuring that engagement and adaption lead to positive anti-corruption outcomes and avoid the risks of manipulation and co-optation. If these steps are not taken, success of the global anti-corruption regime will remain elusive, the regime will be delegitimised, and corrupt activity will continue to proliferate transnationally.

Notes

1 Nadelmann EA and Andreas P, *Policing the Globe: Criminalization and crime control in international relations* (Oxford University Press, 1st Edition, 2006)
2 Abbott KW and Snidal D, 'Values and Interests: international legalization in the fight against corruption' 31 *Journal of Legal Studies* (2002) 141
3 above n1. The concept of global prohibition regimes is introduced in Chapter 1 of this book
4 above n1
5 ibid.
6 [Transcript No.12] Anonymity Requested. Eco Forestry Forum PNG (EFF PNG); Dademo [Transcript No.3]
7 See discussion in Chapter 5
8 [Transcript No.5] Anonymity Requested. A Member of an Australian Law Enforcement Agency with Experience in PNG (Aus Law Enforcement); Prescott [Transcript No.4]
9 above n1
10 ibid.
11 This reflects criminogenic asymmetries discussed by Passas N, 'Globalization and Transnational Crime: Effects of Criminogenic Asymmetries', in Williams P and Vlassis D (Eds), *Combatting Transnational Crime: Concepts, Activities and Responses* (Frank Cass Publishing, 2013) 22
12 above n1
13 ibid.
14 ibid.
15 Nadelmann E, 'Global prohibition regimes: the evolution of norms in international society' 44(4) *International Organization* (22 May 1990) 479, at 498
16 above n1 at 30–31
17 Asa [Transcript No.10] referring to civil society criticism 'it is not productive . . . it does affect the international perception of PNG'
18 above n1
19 ibid.
20 See Chapter 1, in particular Reed Q,'Squeezing a Balloon? Challenging the nexus between organised crime and corruption' 7 *CMI U4 Issue* (2009)
21 above n1
22 Rodrigues [Transcript No.2]
23 ibid.
24 See debate covered in Chapter 2
25 *United Nations Convention against Corruption*, opened for signature 9 December 2003, 2349 UNTS 41 (entered into force 14 December 2005) ('*UNCAC*'), Art 13
26 TI, Our Chapters, available at: http://www.transparency.org/whoweare/organisation/our_chapters (last visited 1 March 2018)
27 Stephens [Transcript No.8]
28 TI, UNCAC civil society Coalition, *Using the UN Convention against Corruption to Advance Anti-Corruption Efforts: A guide* (2014)
29 TI, UNCAC civil society Coalition, *civil society Guide: UNCAC in the Private Sector* (2013)
30 TI, UNCAC civil society Coalition, *civil society Guide: UNCAC in the Private Sector* (2013) at 18; TI, UNCAC civil society Coalition, *Using the UN Convention against Corruption to Advance Anti-Corruption Efforts: A guide* (2014) at 55
31 CAC/COSP 4/1 *Mechanism for the Review of Implementation of the United Nations Convention against Corruption* (24 to 28 October 2011)
32 Prescott [Transcript No.4]; Kershaw [Transcript No.17]
33 Koh H, 'Transnational Legal Process' 75 *Neb. L. Rev.* (1996) 181
34 UNCAC, Art 69

35 A useful introduction is provided by Harrington AR, 'Don't Mind the Gap: The rise of individual complaint mechanisms within international human rights treaties' 22(2) *Duke Journal of Comparative & International Law* (2012) 153; for an overview of existing mechanisms see UNHR, *Human Rights Bodies-Complaints Procedures* (2015) available at: http://www.ohchr.org/EN/HRBodies/TBPetitions/Pages/HRTBPetitions.aspx (last visited 1 March 2018)
36 above n15 at 526
37 Koim [Transcript No.6]; [Transcript No.7] Anonymity Requested. Royal PNG Constabulary
38 *Open Parliament Project Papua New Guinea* (2015) available at: http://www.openparliamentproject.org/ (last visited 1 March 2018)
39 Graycar A and Smith RG, 'Research and practice in corruption: an introduction, in Graycar A and Smith RG (eds), *Handbook of Global Research and Practice in Corruption* (Edward Elgar, 1st Edition, 2011) 3 at 6

References

Abbott KW and Snidal D, 'Values and Interests: International legalization in the fight against corruption' 31 *Journal of Legal Studies* (2002) 141.

CAC/COSP 4/1 *Mechanism for the Review of Implementation of the United Nations Convention against Corruption* (24 to 28 October 2011).

Graycar A and Smith RG, 'Research and practice in corruption: an introduction, in Graycar A and Smith RG (eds), *Handbook of Global Research and Practice in Corruption* (Edward Elgar, 1st Edition, 2011) 3.

Harrington AR, 'Don't Mind the Gap: The rise of individual complaint mechanisms within international human rights treaties' 22(2) *Duke Journal of Comparative & International Law* (2012) 153.

Koh H, 'Transnational Legal Process' 75 *Neb. L. Rev.* (1996) 181.

Nadelmann EA, 'Global prohibition regimes: The evolution of norms in international society' 44(4) *International Organization* (22 May 1990) 479.

Nadelmann EA and Andreas P, *Policing the Globe: Criminalization and crime control in international relations* (Oxford University Press, 1st Edition, 2006).

Open Parliament Project Papua New Guinea (2015) available at: http://www.openparliamentproject.org/ (last visited 1 March 2018).

Passas N, 'Globalization and Transnational Crime: Effects of criminogenic asymmetries', in Williams P and Vlassis D (Eds), *Combatting Transnational Crime: Concepts, Activities and Responses* (Frank Cass Publishers, 2013) 22.

Reed Q, 'Squeezing a Balloon? Challenging the nexus between organised crime and corruption' 7 *CMI U4 Issue* (2009).

TI, *Our Chapters*, available at: http://www.transparency.org/whoweare/organisation/our_chapters (last visited 1 March 2018).

TI, UNCAC Civil Society Coalition, *Civil Society Guide: UNCAC in the Private Sector* (2013).

TI, UNCAC Civil Society Coalition, *Using the UN Convention against Corruption to Advance Anti-Corruption Efforts: A guide* (2014).

UNHR, *Human Rights Bodies-Complaints Procedures* (2015) available at: http://www.ohchr.org/EN/HRBodies/TBPetitions/Pages/HRTBPetitions.aspx (last visited 1 March 2018).

United Nations Convention against Corruption, opened for signature 9 December 2003, 2349 UNTS 41 (entered into force 14 December 2005) ('UNCAC').

Annex A: multilateral anti-corruption instruments

OAS Convention – *Inter-American Convention against Corruption*, opened for signature 29 March 1996, 35 ILM 724 (entered into force 6 March 1997)

OECD Convention – *Organisation for Economic Cooperation and Development Convention on Combating Bribery of Foreign Public Officials in International Business Transactions*, opened for signature 17 December 1997, 37 ILM 1 (entered into force 15 February 1999)

CoE Criminal Law Convention – *Council of Europe Criminal Law Convention on Corruption*, opened for signature 27 January 1999, ETS 173 (entered into force 1 July 2002)

UNTOC – *United Nations Convention against Transnational Organised Crime*, opened for signature 12 December 2000, 2225 UNTS 209 (entered into force 29 September 2003)

CoE Civil Law Convention – *Council of Europe Civil Law Convention on Corruption*, opened for signature 4 November 1999, ETS 174 (entered into force 1 November 2003)

SADC Protocol – *Southern African Development Community Protocol against Corruption*, opened for signature 14 August 2001 (entered into force 6 July 2005)

EU Convention – European Union Convention against Corruption involving Officials, opened for signature 26 May 1997, Official Journal C 195 (entered into force 28 September 2005)

UNCAC – *United Nations Convention against Corruption*, opened for signature 9 December 2003, 2349 UNTS 41 (entered into force 14 December 2005)

AU Convention – *African Union Convention on Preventing and Combating Corruption*, open for signature 11 July 2003, 43 ILM 5 (entered into force 5 August 2006)

Annex B: extracts from UNCAC and the Implementation Review Mechanism

Extracts from UNCAC

Article 15. Bribery of national public officials:

1 Each State Party shall adopt such legislative and other measures as may be necessary to establish as criminal offences, when committed intentionally:

(a) The promise, offering or giving, to a public official, directly or indirectly, of an undue advantage, for the official himself or herself or another person or entity, in order that the official act or refrain from acting in the exercise of his or her official duties;
(b) The solicitation or acceptance by a public official, directly or indirectly, of an undue advantage, for the official himself or herself or another person or entity, in order that the official act or refrain from acting in the exercise of his or her official duties.[1]

Article 16. Bribery of foreign public officials and officials of public international organizations

1 Each State Party shall adopt such legislative and other measures as may be necessary to establish as a criminal offence, when committed intentionally, the promise, offering or giving to a foreign public official or an official of a public international organization, directly or indirectly, of an undue advantage, for the official himself or herself or another person or entity, in order that the official act or refrain from acting in the exercise of his or her official duties, in order to obtain or retain business or other undue advantage in relation to the conduct of international business.

Article 17. Embezzlement, misappropriation or other diversion of property by a public official

1 Each State Party shall adopt such legislative and other measures as may be necessary to establish as criminal offences, when committed intentionally, the embezzlement, misappropriation or other diversion by a public official

for his or her benefit or for the benefit of another person or entity, of any property, public or private funds or securities or any other thing of value entrusted to the public official by virtue of his or her position.

Article 23. Laundering of proceeds of crime

1 Each State Party shall adopt, in accordance with fundamental principles of its domestic law, such legislative and other measures as may be necessary to establish as criminal offences, when committed intentionally:

(a) (i) The conversion or transfer of property, knowing that such property is the proceeds of crime, for the purpose of concealing or disguising the illicit origin of the property or of helping any person who is involved in the commission of the predicate offence to evade the legal consequences of his or her action; (ii) The concealment or disguise of the true nature, source, location, disposition, movement or ownership of or rights with respect to property, knowing that such property is the proceeds of crime;

(b) Subject to the basic concepts of its legal system:

(i) The acquisition, possession or use of property, knowing, at the time of receipt, that such property is the proceeds of crime; (ii) Participation in, association with or conspiracy to commit, attempts to commit and aiding, abetting, facilitating and counselling the commission of any of the offences established in accordance with this article.

Extracts from The Implementation Review Mechanism

Chapter IV. Review process

A Goals

11 Consistent with the Convention, in particular article 63, the purpose of the review process shall be to assist *States parties* in their implementation of the Convention. In this regard, the review process, inter alia, shall:

(a) Promote the purposes of the Convention as set out in its article 1;
(b) Provide the Conference with information on the measures taken by *States parties* in implementing the Convention and the difficulties encountered by them in doing so;
(c) Help *States parties* to identify and substantiate specific needs for technical assistance and to promote and facilitate the provision of technical assistance;
(d) Promote and facilitate international cooperation in the prevention of and the fight against corruption, including in the area of asset recovery;

(e) Provide the Conference with information on successes, good practices and challenges of *States parties* in implementing and using the Convention;

(f) Promote and facilitate the exchange of information, practices and experiences gained in the implementation of the Convention.

Note

1 UNCAC, 2004, Chapter III, Article 15, p17

Annex C: regional overview of domestic anti-corruption law

Country	*Law*	*Year*	*Reference*
Australia	Criminal Code Act		OECD Report
New Zealand	Crimes Act/ Secret Commissions Act	1961/1910	Serious Fraud Office, New Zealand: https://www.sfo.govt.nz/legislation
Niue	Niue Act	1966	Pacific Islands Forum Secretariat Good Leadership Report (2008)
Cook Islands	Crimes Act	1969	OECD Report
Papua New Guinea	Criminal Code	1974	OECD Report
Tonga	Criminal Offences Act	1988	Wickberg, S (2013) Corruption and Anti-Corruption in Tonga
Samoa	Crimes Ordinance	1961	OECD Report
Fiji	Penal code/ Prevention of bribery promulgation/ crimes decree	1970/2007/2009	Wickberg, S (2013) Corruption and Anti-Corruption in Fiji; Matakitoga (2010) presentation at the 2nd National Anti-Money Laundering Conference, Suva
Solomon Islands	Penal Code	1978	Paclii
Vanuatu	Penal Code	1981	OECD Report
Tuvalu	Penal Code	1965	Paclii
Nauru	Criminal Code	1899	Pacific Islands Forum Secretariat Good Leadership Report (2008); Paclii
Federated States of Micronesia	Code of the Federated States of Micronesia	1982/amended 1997	Paclii; World Bank, Code of the Federated States of Micronesia
Palau	Palau National Code Chapter 7	1966	OECD Report

Annex D: domestic anti-corruption law in PNG

Leadership Code

Constitution of the Independent State of Papua New Guinea. 1975. Part III. Division 2

27. Responsibilities of office.

(1) A person to whom this Division applies has a duty to conduct himself in such a way, both in his public or official life and his private life, and in his associations with other persons, as not—

- (a) to place himself in a position in which he has or could have a conflict of interests or might be compromised when discharging his public or official duties; or
- (b) to demean his office or position; or
- (c) to allow his public or official integrity, or his personal integrity, to be called into question; or
- (d) to endanger or diminish respect for and confidence in the integrity of government in Papua New Guinea.

(2) In particular, a person to whom this Division applies shall not use his office for personal gain or enter into any transaction or engage in any enterprise or activity that might be expected to give rise to doubt in the public mind as to whether he is carrying out or has carried out the duty imposed by Subsection (1).

(3) It is the further duty of a person to whom this Division applies—

- (a) to ensure, as far as is within his lawful power, that his spouse and children and any other persons for whom he is responsible (whether morally, legally or by usage), including nominees, trustees and agents, do not conduct themselves in a way that might be expected to give rise to doubt in the public mind as to his complying with his duties under this section; and
- (b) if necessary, to publicly disassociate himself from any activity or enterprise of any of his associates, or of a person referred to in paragraph (a), that might be expected to give rise to such a doubt.

(4) The Ombudsman Commission or other authority prescribed for the purpose under Section 28 (*further provisions*) may, subject to this Division and to any Organic Law made for the purposes of this Division, give directions, either generally or in a particular case, to ensure the attainment of the objects of this section.

(5) A person to whom this Division applies who-

(a) is convicted of an offence in respect of his office or position or in relation to the performance of his functions or duties; or

(b) fails to comply with a direction under Subsection (4) or otherwise fails to carry out the obligations imposed by Subsections (1), (2) and (3), is guilty of misconduct in office.

Organic Law on the Duties and Responsibilities of Leadership (OLDRL)

Organic Law on the Duties and Responsibilities of Leadership 1975. Being an Organic Law to implement Division III 2 (**leadership code*****) of the* Constitution.**

PART II. –RESPONSIBILITIES OF LEADERSHIP.

4 STATEMENT OF INCOME, ETC. (Omitted)

5 **USE OF OFFICE FOR PERSONAL BENEFIT, ETC.**

(1) A person to whom this Law applies who, except as specifically authorized by law, directly or indirectly asks for or accepts, on behalf of himself or an associate, any benefit in relation to any action (past, present or future) in the course of his duties, or in the course of or by reason of his official position, is guilty of misconduct in office.

(2) Subsection (1) extends to the case of a person to whom this Law applies who, except in the course of and for the purpose of his official duties or his official position, uses or allows his name or his official position to be used for the benefit of himself or any other person.

6 PERSONAL INTEREST. (Omitted)

7 COMPANY DIRECTORSHIPS, ETC. (Omitted)

8 SHAREHOLDINGS. (Omitted)

9 ENGAGING IN OTHER PAID EMPLOYMENT. (Omitted)

10 INTERESTS IN CONTRACTS. (Omitted)

11 **ACCEPTANCE, ETC., OF BRIBES.**

A person to whom this Law applies who, or any of whose associates, corruptly asks for, receives or obtains, or agrees or attempts to receive or obtain, any property, benefit or favour of any kind for himself or any other person in consideration of his actions as a public official being influenced in any manner, or on account of his having acted as a public official in any manner (whether generally or in a particular case) is guilty of misconduct in office.

12 ACCEPTANCE, ETC., OF LOANS, ETC. (Omitted)

13 **MISAPPROPRIATION OF FUNDS OF PAPUA NEW GUINEA.**

A person to whom this Law applies who–

(a) intentionally applies any money forming part of any fund under the control of Papua New Guinea to any purpose to which it cannot be lawfully be applied; or

(b) intentionally agrees to any such application of any such moneys, is guilty of misconduct in office.

14 PERSONAL ADVANTAGE NOT TO BE GAINED FROM OFFICIAL INFORMATION.

(1) Subject to Subsection (2), a person to whom this Law applies who–

(*a*) except in the course of his official duty, divulges, directly or indirectly, any confidential or secret information acquired by him in the course of his official duty; or

(*b*) for personal gain or advantage or for the personal gain or advantage of some other person discloses or uses any information acquired by him in the course of his official duty, is guilty of misconduct in office.

(2) The provisions of Subsection (1) do not apply to information which has been officially released by the person or body having power to release it for public information.

15 DISCLOSURE OF INTEREST BEFORE DEBATE OR VOTING. (Omitted)

16 AGENTS, ETC. (Omitted)

Criminal Code Act

Criminal Code Act 1974. Part III. Division 2 (Corruption and Abuse of Office)

87. OFFICIAL CORRUPTION.

(1) A person who–

(a) being–

(i) employed in the Public Service, or the holder of any public office; and

(ii) charged with the performance of any duty by virtue of that employment or office, (not being a duty touching the administration of justice), corruptly asks, receives or obtains, or agrees or attempts to receive or obtain, any property or benefit for himself or any other person on account of any thing done or omitted to be done, or to be done or omitted to be done by him in the discharge of the duties of his office; or

(b) corruptly gives, confers or procures, or promises or offers to give or confer, or to procure or attempt to procure, to, on or for any person, any property or benefit on account of any such act or omission on the part of a person in the Public Service or holding a public office, is guilty of a crime.

Penalty: Imprisonment for a term not exceeding seven years, and a fine at the discretion of the court.

(2) A person shall not be arrested without warrant for an offence against Subsection (1).

88. EXTORTION BY PUBLIC OFFICERS.

A person employed in the Public Service who takes or accepts from any person, for the performance of his duty as an officer of the Public Service any reward beyond his proper pay and emoluments, or any promise of such a reward, is guilty of a misdemeanour.

Penalty: Imprisonment for a term not exceeding three years.

89 PUBLIC OFFICERS INTERESTED IN CONTRACTS. (Omitted)
90 OFFICERS CHARGED WITH ADMINISTRATION OF PROPERTY OF A SPECIAL CHARACTER OR WITH SPECIAL DUTIES. (Omitted)
91 FALSE CLAIMS BY OFFICIALS. (Omitted)

92. ABUSE OF OFFICE.

(1) A person employed in the Public Service who, in abuse of the authority of his office does, or directs to be done, any arbitrary act prejudicial to the rights of another is guilty of a misdemeanour.

Penalty: Subject to Subsection (2), imprisonment for a term not exceeding two years.

(2) If an act prohibited by Subsection (1) is done, or directed to be done, as the case may be, for purposes of gain, the offender is liable to imprisonment for a term not exceeding three years.

93 CORRUPTION OF VALUATOR. (Omitted)
94 FALSE CERTIFICATES BY PUBLIC OFFICERS. (Omitted)
95 ADMINISTERING EXTRA-JUDICIAL OATHS. (Omitted)
96 FALSE ASSUMPTION OF AUTHORITY. (Omitted)
97 PERSONATING PUBLIC OFFICERS. (Omitted)

97A. CORRUPTLY PROCURING WITHDRAWAL OF TENDERS.

A person who–

with intent to obtain a contract from, or provide a service to, a public body, offers a gratification to another person, to induce that person to refrain from making a tender or withdraw or alter a tender; or solicits or accepts a gratification as an inducement or reward for refraining from making a tender or withdrawing or altering a tender made for such contract, is guilty of an offence.

Penalty: A fine at the discretion of the Court or imprisonment for a term not exceeding seven years, or both.

97B. BRIBERY OF MEMBER OF PUBLIC SERVICE.

(1) A person who offers to a person employed in the Public Service, or being a person employed in the Public Service, solicits or accepts a gratification as an inducement or reward for–

- (a) the person employed in the Public Service voting or abstaining from voting at any meeting in favour of or against any measure; or
- (b) the person employed in the Public Service performing or abstaining from performing or aiding in procuring or hindering the performance of an official act; or
- (c) the person employed in the Public Service aiding in procuring or preventing the passing of any vote or granting of any contract in favour of any person; or
- (d) the person employed in the Public Service showing or refraining from showing any favour or disfavour in his capacity as a person employed in the Public Service, is guilty of an offence.

Penalty: A fine at the discretion of the Court or imprisonment for a term not exceeding seven years, or both.

(2) An offence under Subsection (1) is committed notwithstanding that the person employed in the Public Service had no right or opportunity to show or refrain from showing favour or that the inducement was not in relation to the affairs of the public body.

97C. DUTY OF PERSON OFFERED GRATIFICATION.

(1) A person who is corruptly offered or given a gratification shall report the offer or gift at the earliest opportunity to a commissioned police officer.
(2) A person who, without reasonable excuse, fails to comply with the provisions of Subsection (1) is guilty of an offence.

Penalty: A fine not exceeding K1,000.00 or imprisonment for a term not exceeding 12 months, or both.

Annex E: interview participant details

Table of interview participants

Participant Name	*Transcript Number and Details*
Dimitri Vlassis	UNODC Executive [Transcript No. 1]
Charmaine Rodrigues	UNDP Official with experience in PNG working on the National Anti-Corruption Strategy [Transcript No. 2]
Effery Dademo	Act! Now PNG [Transcript No. 3]
Tony Prescott	UNDP South Pacific Democratic Governance Branch [Transcript No. 4]
Anonymity Requested	Member of an Australian Law Enforcement Agency with Experience in PNG [Transcript No. 5]
Sam Koim	Head of Task Force Sweep PNG [Transcript No. 6]
Anonymity Requested	Royal Papua New Guinean Constabulary, Fraud and Anti-Corruption Directorate [Transcript No. 7]
Lawrence Stephens	Chairman of Transparency International Papua New Guinea [Transcript No. 8]
Anonymity Requested	Attorney Generals Department PNG, Legal Policy and Governance Branch [Transcripts No.9]
Christopher Asa	Director of Social Policy and Governance for PNG National Executive Council [Transcript No. 10]
Anonymity Requested	National Executive Council [Transcript No. 11]

Mary Boni	Eco Forestry Forum PNG [Transcript No. 12]
Paul Barker	Executive Director, Institute of National Affairs PNG [Transcript No. 13]
Michael Wilson	Australian Federal Police Transnational Crime Unit PNG [Transcript No. 14]
Anonymity Requested	Office of the Public Prosecutor PNG [Transcript No. 15]
Anonymity Requested	Previously Employed at AusAID working in PNG [Transcript No. 16]
Lorraine Kershaw	Legal Advisor for Pacific Islands Forum Secretariat [Transcript No. 17]

Annex F: interview question structure

Views of self and organisational affiliation

Can you describe your background and current position?

What is your organisation's main role and your role within that organisation?

Views of corruption

How would you define corruption? Example?

Has your understanding of corruption ever changed or developed?

Do you believe corruption to be morally wrong? Expand?

Is corruption ever justifiable? Why/why not?

What you think about attempts to justify corruption? (eg on the basis of culture and tradition, or because of government institutions failing to efficiently or effectively provide necessary goods and services)

What do you think causes corruption? Expand?

What you see as the consequences of corruption? Expand?

Should all countries seek to eliminate corruption? Why/why not?

Role in combatting corruption (experiences, successes, challenges)

What role have you played in combatting corruption?

What were some of the challenges you faced?

How did you overcome these challenges?

What has been your greatest success in combatting corruption?

Have you interacted with other nations or foreign organisations in your anti-corruption efforts? How and to what effect?

Have other organisations or countries achieved successes in combatting corruption which you find to be particularly noteworthy?

If you could change one thing about the context in which you operated, in order to achieve further success in combatting corruption, what would you change?

Views of UNCAC (purpose, value, limitations)

Are you aware of UNCAC?

What do you see as UNCAC's primary purpose?

Whose values and interests do you think UNCAC most accurately reflects?

Is UNCAC relevant to you and your anti-corruption efforts? Expand

Does UNCAC reflect your views of corruption and methods for combatting corruption? Expand

Are there any differences between your view of corruption and anti-corruption methods, and those of UNCAC?

What would you say is UNCAC's greatest strength?

What do you think are some of UNCAC's limitations?

Experiences with UNCAC

Did you or your organisation engage in the negotiation of UNCAC? Why and How/Why not?

Have you engaged with UNCAC in your anti-corruption efforts since its adoption? Expand? (specific example)

Would you say that your engagement with UNCAC has been productive? In what way?

Has UNCAC engagement ever resulted in a change to the way you understand corruption or your approach to combatting corruption? Expand

Has your engagement with UNCAC ever resulted in a change to the way others view or seek to combat corruption? Expand

Improvements to UNCAC

If you could change one thing about UNCAC, what would you change? Why?

If you could change one thing about the way you engage with UNCAC what would you change? Why?

Improvements to overall approach to combatting corruption, beyond UNCAC

What single change do you think would most significantly reduce corruption levels in your sector? Why?

Do you think this change would benefit all sectors seeking to combat corruption? Why?

Do you think this change is possible? How?

Index

Note: Tables are indicated in **bold** and Figures in *italics*.

For Product Safety Concerns and Information please contact our EU representative GPSR@taylorandfrancis.com
Taylor & Francis Verlag GmbH, Kaufingerstraße 24, 80331 München, Germany

www.ingramcontent.com/pod-product-compliance
Ingram Content Group UK Ltd.
Pitfield, Milton Keynes, MK11 3LW, UK
UKHW010959180926
475701UK00004B/462

* 9 7 8 0 3 6 7 5 8 6 8 3 6 *